Pre-Raphaelite Sisters

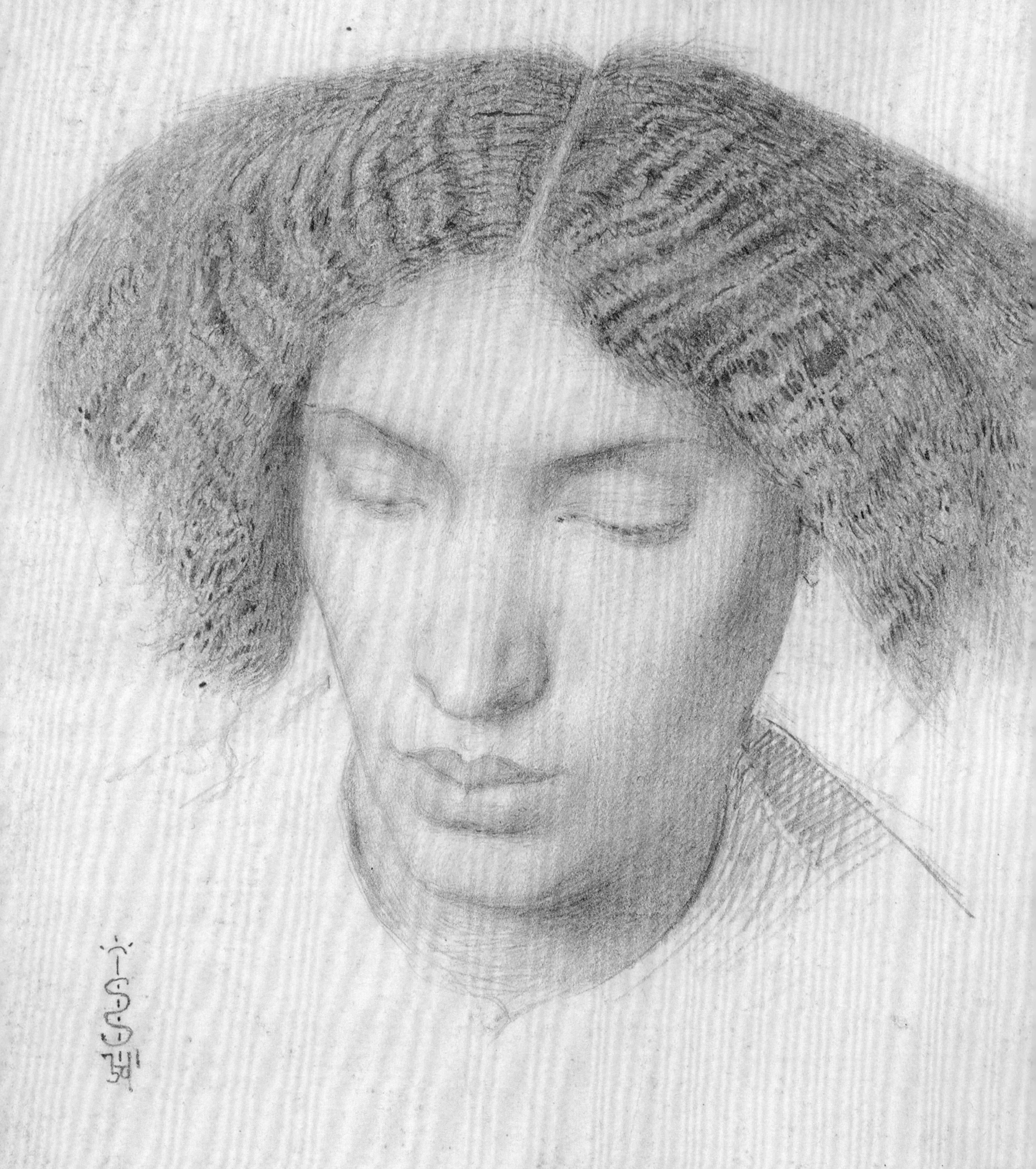

Pre-Raphaelite Sisters

Jan Marsh
With contributions by Peter Funnell, Charlotte Gere,
Pamela Gerrish Nunn and Alison Smith

National Portrait Gallery, London

14
Pre-Raphaelite Models

Jan Marsh

56
Brotherhoods & Artistic Masculinities

Peter Funnell

22
Elizabeth Siddal

64
Annie Miller

34
Christina Rossetti

74
Fanny Cornforth

44
Effie Gray Millais

86
Joanna Boyce Wells

Director's Foreword

For an institution whose foundation, in the mid-nineteenth century, was contemporaneous with that of the original Pre-Raphaelite Brotherhood, it may come as a surprise to many that this is the National Portrait Gallery's first exhibition dedicated to the movement. Even more so perhaps, considering the collection's abundance of treasures by renowned members and associates of the group, including portraits by Dante Gabriel Rossetti and John Everett Millais.

After two centuries, the art and lives of the Pre-Raphaelites retain immense popular appeal and the romantic spirit of their work and subjects offer continuous inspiration for successive generations of artists. A Pre-Raphaelite sensibility can be detected even in some of the Gallery's most recent acquisitions, including Tom Beard's enigmatic portrait of Florence Welch, reproduced in Alison Smith's essay (ill. 143).

This exhibition and accompanying publication look beyond the well-known artists who first formed the Brotherhood and the often-idealised visions of their work, to place the women of Pre-Raphaelitism firmly centre stage. Showcasing a wealth of paintings, works on paper, photographs and ephemera, it proposes an elucidation of the Pre-Raphaelite movement for our current moment, as a thoroughly more open, inclusive and diverse undertaking, whose advancement depended fundamentally on the endeavours of women as models, artists and creative partners.

Female artists of the past have so often been overlooked in the story of the Pre-Raphaelite movement, and so we are delighted to showcase works by previously marginalised figures, including Joanna Boyce Wells, Marie Spartali Stillman and Evelyn De Morgan, whose work can certainly stand alongside that of their more famous counterparts. Hitherto also obscured has been the indispensable role of artists' wives and partners as the hidden lynchpins of art production. The exhibition and publication's foregrounding of Effie Gray Millais, Georgiana Burne-Jones and Jane Morris reveals their vital contributions in managing studios, careers, costumes and clients.

The exhibition offers, too, a significant opportunity to assess the interaction between artist and model in nineteenth-century art, alongside the more familiar discussion of the relationship between artist and portrait sitter, which informs so much of the National Portrait Gallery's collection. As well as inspiring now-iconic works, Pre-Raphaelite models often transformed their own lives through active engagement in art. They transcended the roles of harlot, princess or goddess they performed to become lasting celebrities, on whom much of the enduring popular fascination with the movement centres. In doing so they laid the example for future generations to own the profession of model and change perceptions of it from a disreputable form of employment to one with greater empowerment and agency.

Pre-Raphaelite Sisters is made possible thanks to the hard work of many colleagues. First and foremost, I would like to thank Dr Jan Marsh who has curated the exhibition with such vision and dedication, based on pioneering scholarship about the 'silenced sisterhood'. Peter Funnell, in his role as Head of Research and Senior Curator whilst at the National Portrait Gallery, led on the exhibition's initial development. At the Gallery, I wish to thank Alison Smith, Chief Curator, for her support for the exhibition and contribution to this catalogue along with essays by Peter Funnell, Charlotte Gere and Pamela Gerrish Nunn. Thanks also go to Pim Baxter, Deputy Director, Sarah Tinsley, Executive Director, Programmes and Partnerships, and Rosie Wilson, Head of Exhibitions, collaborating with Andrew Horn, Exhibitions Manager and Claire Floyd, Exhibitions Officer, who have skilfully led the exhibition's production, and to Jude Simmons, Head of Design and Andrea Easey, Interpretation Manager. This catalogue has been overseen by Tom Furness, Editor, Ruth Müller-Wirth, Production Manager, Kara Green, Publishing Manager and Anna Starling, Head of Commercial, with thanks also to Mark Lynch, Picture Research and Rights Clearance Co-ordinator. Other colleagues that I wish to acknowledge are Melanie Aram, Georgia Atienza, Carol Blackett-Ord, Helena Cuss, Sarah Davies, Clare Freestone, Alexandra Gent, Richard Hallas, Karl Lydon and the art handling team, Laura McKechan, Adam Norris, Polly Saltmarsh, Eleanor Shakeshaft, Fiona Smith, Denise Vogelsang and Helen Whiteoak.

Beyond the Gallery, I would like to thank those who have supported Dr Marsh in her research and contributed to the publication: Philip Atwood, Richard Barber, Caroline Bressey,

Ann Bukantas, Jane Cohen, Sarah Colegrave, Colin Cruise, Harriet Drummond, Brian and Mary Eaton, Suzanne Fagence Cooper, Margaretta Frederick, Colin Harrison, Rupert Maas, Fiona MacCarthy, Sarah Miller, Nic Peeters, Christopher Newall, Victoria Osborne, Susan Owens, Terence Pepper, Frank Sharp, the late Virginia Surtees, and Stephen Wildman. I would also like to thank Aaron Jones for his contribution to the exhibition design. For their editorial contributions to the publication I would like to thank Helen Armitage, Anjali Bulley, Hilary Bird and, for their fine design work, Astrid Stavro and Susanna Foppoli.

The exhibition is fortunate to have loans from many institutions. I am grateful to the many lenders, both public and private, who have supported this project, in particular the De Morgan Foundation, Delaware Art Museum, National Museums Liverpool, the National Trust, Tate and the Victoria and Albert Museum. Around one quarter of the works are lent from private collections and we are greatly indebted to them for the opportunity to display seldom-seen pictures, many on view for the first time. We are grateful to all of the lenders, named and anonymous, without whom it would not have been possible to present this exceptional exhibition. The exhibition has been most kindly supported by the Pre-Raphaelite Sisters Exhibition Circle, the Michael Marks Charitable Trust and the Peter Cadbury Charitable Trust and this publication made possible by a generous grant from the Tavolozza Foundation, and we thank them all.

Dr Nicholas Cullinan, Director
National Portrait Gallery, London

Introduction: The Sisters & the Movement

Think of Pre-Raphaelitism. Think of pale-faced women with tumbling locks and loose gowns, gazing soulfully out from the picture frame or depicted in dramatic scenes, painted in glowing colours. The first Pre-Raphaelite works were exhibited in 1849 by the Pre-Raphaelite Brotherhood (known as the PRB), a group of young men who aimed to overturn the stale conventions of Victorian art. As the self-styled 'Young Painters of England', they challenged tradition with startling colours and compositions.

But who were the young women behind the pictures? How did they get involved in Pre-Raphaelite art? What do we know of their lives and their roles in a movement that, in successive phases, stretched over half a century? Some were models, plucked from obscurity to pose for figures in Pre-Raphaelite paintings. Some were family and friends, persuaded to sit for appropriate roles, in portraits or subject pictures. Some were artists themselves, with aspirations to match those of the men, sharing the same artistic and social networks yet constrained by gender to occupy a separate sphere.

Some of the family members involved were sisters, wives and daughters, who lived in and sustained the art world as partners in production, maintaining households and studios for the menfolk, supervising servants and socialising with patrons to ensure the business of art ran smoothly. Some were skilled in the arts of interior decoration, dressmaking, embroidery and jewellery-making, the fine crafts that formed a supportive tier for the 'higher' arts of painting and sculpture. All these women were vitally engaged in creating Pre-Raphaelite art.

For too long the male artists have dominated accounts of Pre-Raphaelitism. Step forward, Pre-Raphaelite Sisters: Elizabeth Siddal, Christina Rossetti, Effie Gray Millais, Annie Miller, Fanny Cornforth, Joanna Boyce Wells, Fanny Eaton, Jane Morris, Georgiana Burne-Jones, Maria Zambaco, Marie Spartali Stillman and Evelyn De Morgan.

Each woman occupies a creative role within the Pre-Raphaelite movement; some held more than one role. They came from diverse backgrounds and had different life experiences. Some died young; others outlived the other members of the movement. In most cases they shared the same artistic and social circles, although they were not all closely acquainted.

They appear in varied guises in the story of Pre-Raphaelite art: models, sitters, makers, partners and poets. The creative endeavours to which they contribute span five decades, from 1850 to 1900. Intertwined with their life stories, a diverse range of contextual themes is considered: the position of female models, the masculine art world of the time, the careers of female artists and the role of wives and partners.

It would be disingenuous to ignore the fact that Pre-Raphaelite art was overwhelmingly made by men in male-dominated studios, or that male artists' reputations, created by male patrons and critics, similarly commanded the historical record. But it is equally mistaken to ignore women's agency and present the female presence as the aesthetic equivalent of the bowl of fruit or flowers.

The subject invites debate. Finally, the reception and interpretation of the Sisters' lives in written histories and popular culture is reviewed. After a severe decline in popularity during the early twentieth century, by the 1980s the Pre-Raphaelites had regained the public and critical favour that endures. Much of contemporary interest in the group centres on the women as icons, role models and as retrospective celebrities. A closer look at the 'sisters' of Pre-Raphaelitism offers us understanding and insight into the continuing appeal of the art.

The story of the Pre-Raphaelite movement can be told in different ways. But it must begin with the formation of the PRB, a group of young British artists, active in the middle of the nineteenth century, who were inspired by Italian art before the time of Raphael and Michelangelo, chiefly by the works of the Florentine painters then known as the 'Italian primitives'. The Brotherhood also aimed to shake British art free of its prevailing post-Renaissance tradition, enshrined in Britain in the lectures of Sir Joshua Reynolds, founder of the Royal Academy of Arts (RA) in London in 1768. The group felt this tradition was moribund. It aimed to return to sincerity of feeling and naïvety of style, with bright colour, flat perspective and realistic rendering of people and places, from 'nature' rather than idealised forms and standardised compositions. It found its subjects in religious and literary texts, its landscapes in the world around it, and its messages in contemporary life.

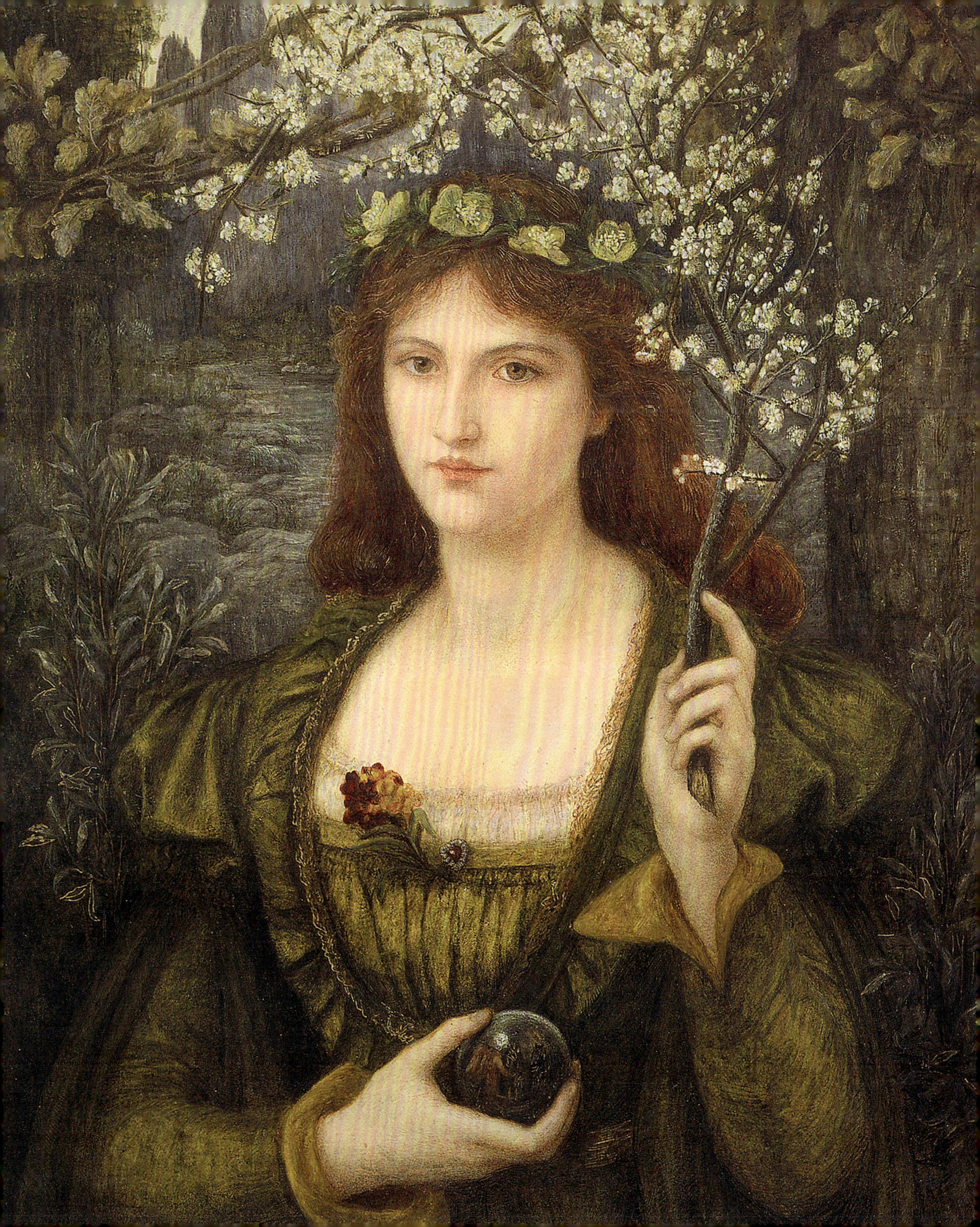

The exact date of the PRB's formation remains obscure. Subsequently, the anniversary of its foundation was set for 'the last day' of every succeeding year, which indicates it was founded on 31 December 1848.[1] Its launch, however, is known and came in spring 1849 with the first paintings in the new mode by Dante Gabriel Rossetti, John Everett Millais and William Holman Hunt, the only Pre-Raphaelite Brothers whose works would prove significant. Signed with the initials 'PRB', these works were notable for their angular figures and clear colours, while the subjects were Romantic and devotional.

By the following year, their art was being critically attacked as uncouth, ugly and foolishly archaic, until defended by cultural critic John Ruskin. If the PRB 'adhere to their principles and paint nature as it is around them…with the earnestness of the men of the thirteenth and fourteenth centuries,' he predicted, 'they will…found a new and noble school in England.'[2]

By January 1853, the group had disbanded, but, according to Rossetti's brother William, 'Preraphaelism' [sic] was 'as real as ever'.[3] Steadily, over a decade it gained acceptance and adherents. Ford Madox Brown, an artist closely linked to the group, supported the emergent movement, while declining to adopt what he regarded as the 'juvenile' aspect of its name.

In 1850 the PRB published four issues of *The Germ*, a magazine with poems, prose, etchings and reviews. Its prime contributors were Dante Gabriel Rossetti and his sister Christina Rossetti, already a published poet. In 1856 it was emulated by a group of university men headed by William Morris and Edward Burne-Jones, who soon joined the Pre-Raphaelite circle, importing distinctly medieval enthusiasms, such as Thomas Malory's tales of the *Knights of the Round Table* (1485). By 1860, there also existed an accomplished number of female Pre-Raphaelites, of whom Joanna Boyce, later Wells, was the most successful.

A number of young men, including John Brett, Frederick Sandys and Simeon Solomon, then nailed their colours to the movement's mast, providing a second wind for evolving Pre-Raphaelitism, as pictorial tastes altered in response to declining religious faith and rising bourgeois prosperity. The linear 'Florentine' manner was eclipsed by 'Venetian' colour, softer forms and sensuous themes, as Pre-Raphaelitism extended its range, with especial growth in richly painted half-length female subjects and scenes of fantasy, which Burne-Jones described as 'a beautiful romantic dream of something that never was, never will be – in a better light than any light that ever shone – in a land that no one can define or remember, only desire – and the forms divinely beautiful.'[4]

This softer edge blossomed in the 1870s into the Aesthetic movement, which has now been popularly subsumed into Pre-Raphaelitism, despite its distinctive quality, which favours visual form over content or storyline and, in the words of art critic Walter Pater, 'aspires to the condition of music.'[5] Indeed, historians claim that, after 1870, Pre-Raphaelitism was itself eclipsed by later trends in art, retaining only the link that tied certain artists to the Aesthetic showcase, London's Grosvenor Gallery (1877–90). Hunt regarded his own the only art that adhered to PRB principles of pictorial clarity and piety.

In the last years of the nineteenth century, the Pre-Raphaelite movement received a new impetus, thanks to retrospective exhibitions of work by Rossetti, Millais and Burne-Jones and its aims chimed with the mystical subjects and often swirling forms of the emerging Symbolist movement. Only in the twentieth century did Pre-Raphaelite art fall from favour, plunging into depths of disregard alongside most manifestations of Victorian culture. The PRB centenary of 1949 went virtually unremarked, but interest revived in the 1970s, building to the major exhibition, *The Pre-Raphaelites*, at the Tate Gallery, London, in 1984, which brought an unexpected renewal of popular acclaim and scholarly attention, which continues.

From the 1984 account, and from most histories, women appear signally absent from Pre-Raphaelitism, except as subjects and models-turned-muses. In fact, however, women were active in all phases of the movement. Their presence has been obscured by structural or contingent causes, which still impede critical analysis of the art production.

One very early female Pre-Raphaelite was Anna Mary Howitt, who projected an 'art sisterhood' on the lines of the PRB, providing mutual support for other women artists, although nothing substantial followed. Howitt's paintings included *Gretchen at the Fountain* (1853) and *The Castaway* (1855), two 'fallen woman' pictures contemporary with Hunt's

The Awakening Conscience (1853), and a heroic head of Boudicca. All were destroyed when Howitt suffered a major breakdown. From the following generation, the female artists invited to exhibit at the Grosvenor Gallery included Marie Spartali Stillman and Evelyn De Morgan, both of whom had sustained outputs but little posthumous recognition.

At first, the revival of Pre-Raphaelite fortunes in the late twentieth century featured the male 'stars'. *The Pre-Raphaelites* at the Tate in 1984, which surveyed the movement up to 1870, included twenty-eight men and – against resistance from feminist art historians – just one woman: Elizabeth Siddal, previously only acknowledged as a model. Since then, a more diverse approach to the movement has been explored and shown in exhibitions.

As the revival coincided with the rise of a new feminist movement, women artists began to receive substantial attention from scholars like Pamela Gerrish Nunn and Deborah Cherry. The year 1989 saw the exhibition *Pre-Raphaelite Women Artists*, featuring work by eighteen women, curated by Gerrish Nunn and myself. This and other studies incorporated female Pre-Raphaelites into the movement, albeit on a parallel track. There were the Pre-Raphaelites, and 'over there' were female emulators.

Its major successor, *Pre-Raphaelites: Victorian Avant-Garde*, at Tate Britain in 2012, contained 175 exhibits, which included nine pictorial works by women: four small watercolours by Siddal, two very small nature studies by Rosa Brett, two photographs by Julia Margaret Cameron and a satirical illustration by Florence Claxton. These were augmented by four textiles designed or worked by May Morris and her aunt Elizabeth Burden, which effectively consigned female artists to the minor, decorative arts.

Given the prominent depiction of women in the art of the Pre-Raphaelite movement, and their well-documented presence in the men's lives and social circles, it is surprising that the strong female aspect in and around the movement has not been more appreciated; that no attention has been devoted to the collective contribution of women to making Pre-Raphaelite art. For women were not only fellow artists in Pre-Raphaelitism; they also and, often simultaneously, were cast as models, acted as inspiration, worked as helpmeets and life partners, stitched costumes, kept accounts, promoted the careers of husbands, brothers, friends, wrote reviews, managed homes and families (so that the men could pursue painting, sculpture, architecture and the fine crafts), all of which active roles demonstrate female engagement and agency, although apparently invisible to history.

What follows is a reflection on the participation in Pre-Raphaelite art by a dozen women over half a century. Some are already well known; others as yet unfamiliar. It shows how they contributed to Pre-Raphaelitism in diverse ways and adds a new dimension to a previously partial picture. Their presence challenges the standard view of Pre-Raphaelitism, as a movement of Romantic male genius and beautiful female models, to show that, like most art movements, it involved individuals of diverse skills in a collaborative enterprise that was embedded in the class, gender and ethnic contexts of its time, although not wholly constrained by them. Received wisdom declared 'women can't paint', that non-Europeans were not beautiful, and the working classes lacked refinement. Pictorially, professionally and personally, the Pre-Raphaelite movement ignored such prescriptions, to its great and unceasing benefit.

Dr Jan Marsh, Curator
National Portrait Gallery, London

Chronology

1837   Accession of Queen Victoria to the throne

1840   Marriage of Victoria and Albert

1848   Marriage of Effie Gray and John Ruskin

1848   Formation of the Pre-Raphaelite Brotherhood by John Everett Millais, William Holman Hunt, Dante Gabriel Rossetti and four others in December

1849   PRB paintings by John Everett Millais, William Holman Hunt and Dante Gabriel Rossetti first exhibited

1850   Publication in January of the first issue of the PRB magazine *The Germ*

1850   *Ecce Ancilla Domini!* by Dante Gabriel Rossetti exhibited at the National Institution

1851   The Great Exhibition held in London during Summer

1852   *Ophelia* by John Everett Millais exhibited at the RA

1853   John Everett Millais's *The Order of Release* exhibited at the RA

1853   Annie Miller first models for William Holman Hunt

1854   Start of the Crimean War

1854   William Holman Hunt's *The Awakening Conscience* exhibited at the RA

1855   Joanna Boyce makes her exhibition debut at the RA

1855   The Exposition Universelle held in Paris

1855   The marriage of Effie Gray and John Everett Millais

1856   National Portrait Gallery founded

1856   John Everett Millais's *Autumn Leaves* exhibited at the RA

1856   Fanny Cornforth first models for Dante Gabriel Rossetti

1857   The *Art Treasures Exhibition* held in Manchester

1857   Elizabeth Siddal's exhibition debut in the Pre-Raphaelite show at Russell Place

1857   Jane Burden first models for Dante Gabriel Rossetti

1857   The marriage of Joanna Boyce and Henry Tanworth Wells

1858   Fanny Cornforth models for Dante Gabriel Rossetti and J.R. Spencer Stanhope

1859   The marriage of Jane Burden and William Morris

1859   Fanny Eaton first models for the Pre-Raphaelite artists

1859   Fanny Cornforth models for Dante Gabriel Rossetti's watershed work, *Bocca Baciata*

1860	The marriage of Elizabeth Siddal and Dante Gabriel Rossetti
1860	The marriage of Georgiana Macdonald and Edward Burne-Jones
1861	William Morris and Pre-Raphaelite colleagues form Morris, Marshall, Faulkner & Co.
1861	Death of Joanna Wells
1861	Death of Prince Albert
1861–5	American Civil War
1862	Death of Elizabeth Siddal
1862	*Goblin Market and Other Poems* by Christina Rossetti published
1863	Annie Miller marries Thomas Ranelagh Thompson
1864	Marie Spartali studies with Ford Madox Brown
1866	Maria Zambaco and Marie Spartali pose for *Cupid and Psyche* by Edward Burne-Jones
1866	*The Prince's Progress and Other Poems* by Christina Rossetti published
1867	Marie Spartali's exhibition debut at the Dudley Gallery
1868	Maria Zambaco studies with Edward Burne-Jones
1868–70	*The Earthly Paradise* by William Morris published
1869	Girton College, Cambridge, founded by Barbara Bodichon and others
1870	*Poems* by Dante Gabriel Rossetti published
1870	Death of Charles Dickens
1870–71	Franco-Prussian War
1871	The marriage of Marie Spartali and William Stillman
1871	Leasing of Kelmscott Manor by Dante Gabriel Rossetti and William Morris
1873	Evelyn Pickering studies at Slade School
1876	Evelyn Pickering's exhibition debut at the Dudley Gallery
1877	The opening of the Grosvenor Gallery, London
1877	Dante Gabriel Rossetti's *Proserpine* exhibited in Manchester
1878	Marie Spartali Stillman living in Florence
1880	London University issues first degrees for women
1880	Maria Zambaco studies at the Slade School under Alphonse Legros
1882	Death of Dante Gabriel Rossetti
1883	Socialist League launched by William Morris, Eleanor Marx and others
1886	Maria Zambaco exhibition debut at the RA
1887	Marriage of Evelyn Pickering and William De Morgan
1887	Arts & Crafts Exhibition Society launched
1887	Marie Spartali Stillman moves to Rome, later exhibiting with In Arte Libertas group
1894	Death of Christina Rossetti
1896	Deaths of John Everett Millais and William Morris
1897	Death of Effie Millais
1898	Death of Edward Burne-Jones
1900	Death of John Ruskin
1901	Death of Queen Victoria
1909	Death of Fanny Cornforth
1914	Death of Jane Morris
1914	Death of Maria Zambaco
1914–18	First World War
1919	Death of Evelyn De Morgan
1920	Death of Georgiana Burne-Jones
1924	Death of Fanny Eaton
1925	Death of Annie Miller
1927	Death of Marie Stillman

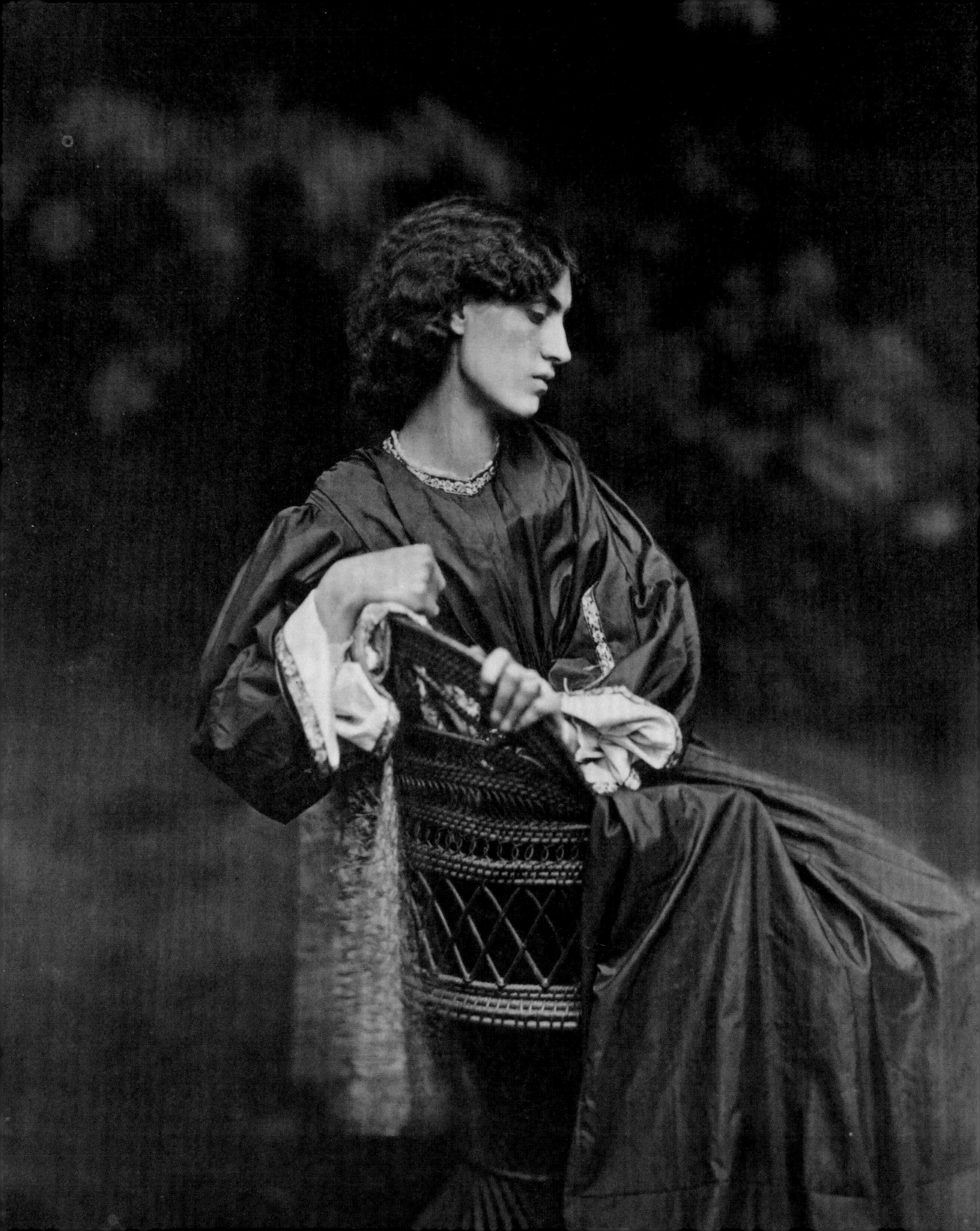

In the past, artists' models were often regarded as little more than animate mannequins, passive accessories who barely contributed to the pictorial result. Now, partly owing to the prestige of fashion models, their active participation in the creation of visual culture is recognised.

Pre-Raphaelite Models

by Jan Marsh

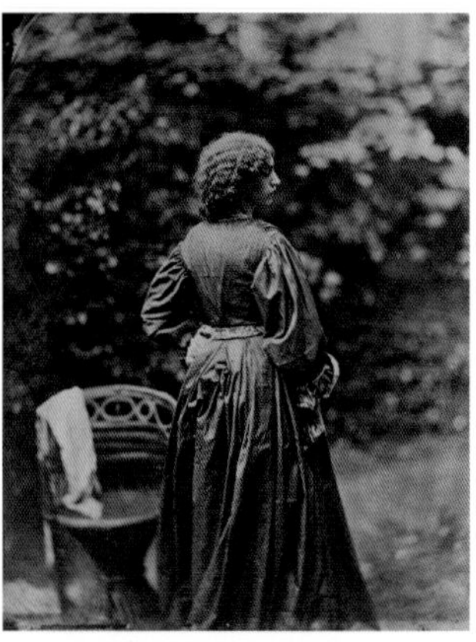
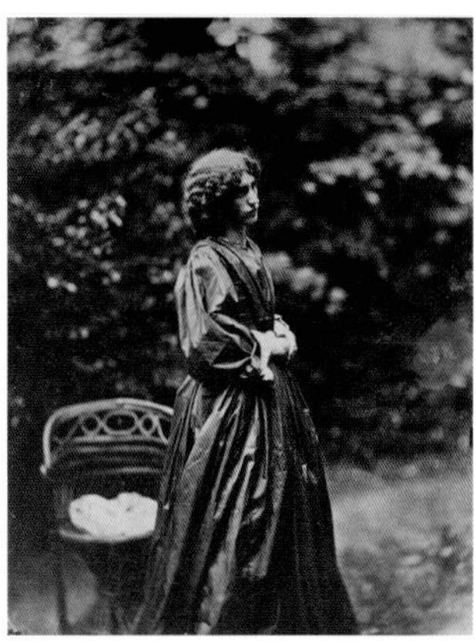
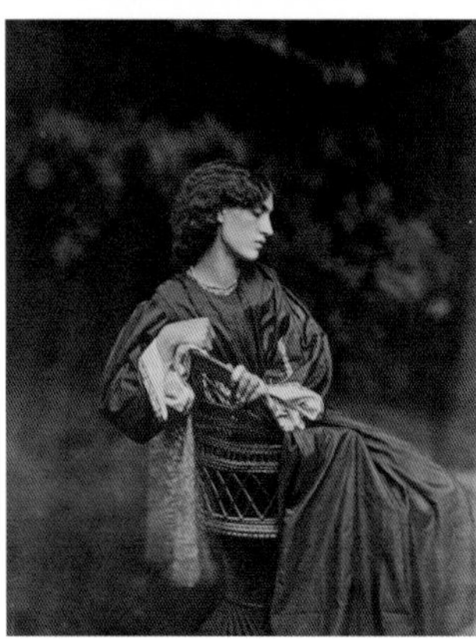
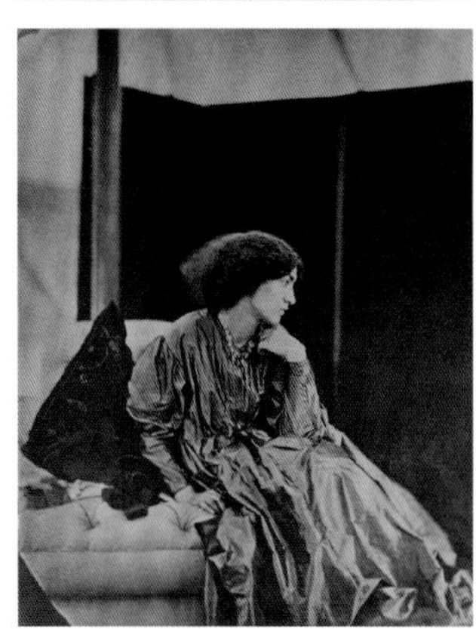

The role of the model is akin to that of the performer or actor in a dramatic collaboration; a partnership that, in the twenty-first century, can lead to the model enjoying greater fame than the artist. To appreciate their shared role in picture-making revises our understanding of past practice.

While many women and men who modelled for Pre-Raphaelite artists have attracted attention, so that their names are known, their active contribution has been overlooked. The women, especially, are viewed at best as artists' romantic, sexual or marital partners; seldom as artistic collaborators. But as this study of twelve women, actively involved in Pre-Raphaelitism, investigates, models played key roles in the making of Pre-Raphaelite art.

Conventions around female modesty and the worthlessness of female opinions combined to render most Victorian models voiceless. Autobiographical records are few, so models' views about their participation must be inferred rather than quoted. Overall, those represented here engaged positively. Effie Ruskin reported with barely concealed delight on sitting for *The Order of Release, 1746* (ill. 28), and not only posed frequently for her second husband John Everett Millais during their fateful summer in Scotland but also volunteered (and maybe chose the subject) to stand in her shift in moonlight for *The Eve of St Agnes* (see ill. 36). When Annie Miller realised William Holman Hunt's offer of marriage was over, she sought other artists, 'determined on sitting again in preference to doing anything else'.[1] Describing one as 'the best ever done', Jane Morris valued the first drawings of herself by Dante Gabriel Rossetti, kept the sequence of camera images taken in 1865 (ill. 1) and in old age willingly adopted the same poses for photographers (ill. 89).[2]

Modelling has become viewed not only as a glamorous occupation – the latest fashions and hairstyles, catwalks, photo shoots in exotic locations, glossy magazines, movie roles – but also as a contribution to the artistic enterprise; as the model Kate Moss has remarked: 'I still turn up for work wanting to get a picture that hasn't been done. I still get excited, and I like being part of the process of creating an image.'[3] Even in the more prosaic circumstances of life drawing, modelling has been described as a silent, static performance art, albeit done on a solo basis, and this is true of the past as well as the present.[4] It is therefore useful to outline its context in the Pre-Raphaelite era, from 1850 to 1900.

In the Victorian period, artists' models were virtually anonymous, hired by the session to don a costume and hold a pose. Their experience was that of working in ill-heated academies and studios, of holding often awkward positions for long minutes in silence and of being paid in pennies. Yet, as those who modelled for Pre-Raphaelite pictures show, it could also mean taking part in the creative process, making it an equivocal, ambiguous occupation.

While much Victorian artists' modelling was done fully clothed, the job was not socially acceptable and ranked alongside domestic service as suitable for young working-class women. As casual labour, it did not provide accommodation, and as it involved working with male strangers in private spaces, and being visually scrutinised, it was regarded as shameful, if not immoral. It could also lead to sexual exploitation. To some observers, the mere fact of working in the studio, as in the theatre, precluded social acceptance. When, in 1854, Rossetti introduced Elizabeth Siddal to artist Barbara Leigh Smith, her position was perceived as doubtful. 'I do not doubt if circumstances were favourable [Rossetti] would marry her,' Leigh Smith told a friend. 'She is of course under a ban having been a model (tho' only to 2 PRBs) ergo do not mention it to anyone.'[5]

Economic circumstances, nonetheless, provided a supply of such labour, which, although irregular and insecure, was less arduous than scrubbing floors, laundering linen or stitching shirts for twelve hours a day. Art schools, such as that run by the Royal Academy (RA), hired a squad of male and female models for morning or evening sessions; established artists employed individuals for specific tasks; amateurs and students paid models for sketching-club sessions. Owing to the higher status of history paintings – think *The Death of Nelson* (1859–64) by Daniel Maclise or *The Derby Day* (1856–8) by William Powell Frith – male models were more in demand than women. But there was also steady custom for sentimental scenes and 'fancy pictures' of pretty girls, ultimately derived from Sir Peter Lely's 'Windsor Beauties' of the Restoration court.

Typically, artists exchanged models' names and addresses, engaging them by the session. Willingness, reliability and the ability to 'look the part' were prized. The Pre-Raphaelite Brothers and friends, at the start of their careers, often planned ambitious subjects, for which models were essential, such as dramatic scenes from history and literature with multiple figures, like Walter Howell Deverell's *Twelfth Night* (ill.6). Typically, they could barely afford the cost of models on top of the expense of paints, brushes and canvas, and lay figures to hold draperies in place. Visual evidence indicates they came together to draw, in studios and classes: studies show Elizabeth Siddal in a difficult kneeling pose, drawn by at least three artists, and images of Fanny Eaton from four or five aspects. Sources record artists taking turns to 'set' a pose or informing their friends of a new model's arrival.

For the PRB an additional aspect was the commitment to paint 'from nature'. In *Modern Painters* (1843–60), John Ruskin famously urged artists to 'go to nature in all singleness of heart, and walk with her laboriously and trustingly… rejoicing always in the truth', arguing that 'from young artists nothing ought to be tolerated but simple bona fide imitation of nature… Their duty is neither to choose, nor compose, nor imagine, nor experimentalize; but to be humble and earnest in following the steps of nature.'[6] This valorisation of the actual over the ideal encouraged artists to choose models who, like actors, conformed to their roles, such as selecting a pious sister to personate a nun or saint, a young married woman to pose as a Jacobite wife, a streetwalker to portray a 'fallen woman' or a dark-skinned model to depict a Hebrew heroine or African sibyl. Like actors, a model could bring added 'natural' verisimilitude.

Where possible, the PRB used friends and family members to pose. Christina Rossetti sat as the Virgin Mary, Georgiana Burne-Jones as Clara von Bork. But these could not be asked too often or chosen for figures whose features would be seen on an immodest or unpleasant character. Household servants could also be used: Joanna Boyce deployed domestic employees in several compositions; Jane Hales was a family nursemaid who became Evelyn De Morgan's most regular model. When first married, Georgiana Burne-Jones recalled 'thinking it quite natural that in the middle of the morning I should ask our only maid – a pretty one – to stand for me that I might try to draw her'.[7]

When acquaintance failed, it could be risky to approach strangers. *The P.R.B. Journal* (William Michael Rossetti's diary of the PRB, 1849–53) records how one day, in search of possible models, Millais, Holman Hunt and Charles Allston Collins went 'parading' along Tottenham Court Road in London, seeking but scared to speak lest the young women they approached proved either prostitutes, who would assume the men were clients, or 'respectable' women, who would allege insult. Nonetheless, several Pre-Raphaelite models were recruited in public places. Annie Miller was reputedly working at The Cross Keys pub in Chelsea when seen by Hunt as a perfect model – in both senses – of a young woman, sexually 'at risk', for his painting *The Awakening Conscience* (ill.43). Fanny Cornforth met Rossetti, Ford Madox Brown and Edward Burne-Jones one evening at one of the London pleasure gardens. Jane Burden was 'discovered' by Burne-Jones and Rossetti at a popular theatre in Oxford.

A cautionary note: many tales about models are uncertain, if not quite fanciful. I do not believe the legend that Elizabeth Siddal was spotted in a bonnet

Jane Morris
John Robert Parsons, 1865
Gelatin silver prints
various dimensions
National Portrait Gallery

2
Kate Moss
Corinne Day, 2006
Gelatin silver print
1510 × 1305mm
National Portrait Gallery

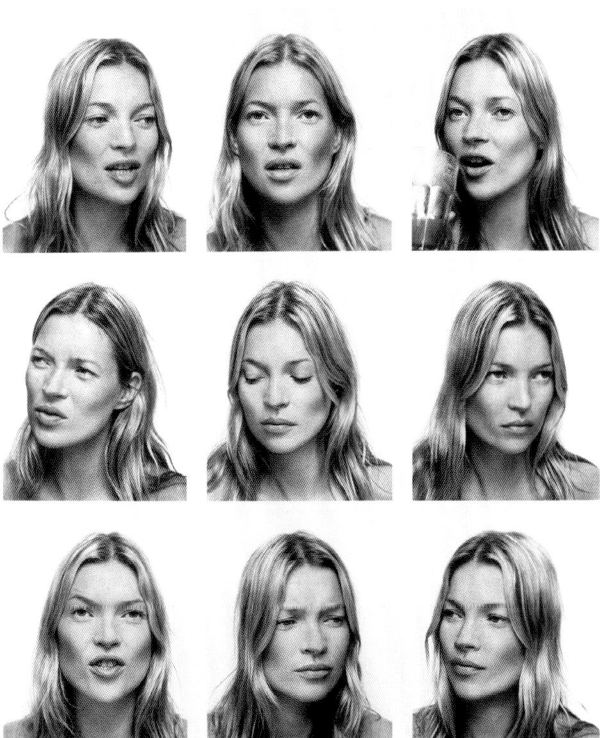

shop; rather that she met Walter Deverell (for whom she then went on to pose) through the Government School of Design, in London, where his father taught and where pattern and copying classes for female students were taught.

Fanny Eaton's relationship with the artists was more professional. Although it is not known when she began modelling, she is listed as a casual employee at the Royal Academy Schools, and probably also worked at Heatherley's school of art in Newman St, central London, where life models were hired for evening-class sessions. Her contact details were later exchanged by Madox Brown and Rossetti and several other artists.

Once engaged, a model was 'cast' in a specific role. Siddal posed as a cross-dressed character from *Twelfth Night* and for Hunt as a British girl in the time of the druids; in both instances a certain plainness of aspect was required. Annie Miller sat both as a bashful lass reading a letter from her sweetheart and as a harlot suddenly struck with remorse. Fanny Cornforth was initially cast in similar fashion as a bedraggled whore and the evil Sidonia, before blossoming as a series of Venetian courtesans. Jane Burden was recruited to stand for Guinevere, caught with Sir Lancelot. Fanny Eaton portrayed Moses' mother, the sorceress Morgan le Fay, an enslaved African and an Indian ayah.

If their appearance provided the first inspiration for the artists, their adoption of each role, and active participation in the picture-making process also, or often, contributed to success. In character and in costume, they presented dramatic gestures and emotions, as Ophelia, Guinevere, Helen of Troy, Proserpine, Lilith or the sorceress Vivien. From the multiple roles in which an individual was cast, it is possible to infer that they enjoyed their share in the creation of visual art. Alexa Wilding, a model not represented here, had aspirations towards a stage career, despite lacking animation – an aspect that made her a good model for Rossetti's allegorical figures. Later, Lillie Langtry established her status as 'Professional Beauty' by both sitting to artists and acting on stage. Documentary evidence that Pre-Raphaelite models chose roles is lacking, but incidental remarks like Madox Brown's descriptions of Annie Miller as 'siren-like' and Elizabeth Siddal as 'looking thinner and more deathlike and more beautiful and more ragged than ever' indicate something of the performative nature of their self-presentations.[8] First cast as Guinevere, Jane (Burden) Morris modelled as Iseult, Mariana, Beatrice, Proserpine, Beatrice, and Pandora, but disliked her presentation as Venus Astarte, a work she described as 'my old abomination'.[9]

Pay rates for models, traditionally, are said to have been a shilling an hour. Typical art-school and atelier sessions ran for around three hours, with poses held for about 50 minutes with a 15-minute rest between each pose.[10] In an economy where a craftsman's wage seldom rose above 20s. (£1) a week and in view of the casual nature of the employment, with the low social class of the young women employed, this rate seems overestimated. Yet, in 1856, Joanna Boyce reported:

> The girl with the golden hair did not come yesterday, but sent a note in the evening to say...that her charge was 2s.6d. I suppose she means that an hour. I have written to her saying that, if she wants 2s.6d. an hour, she need not come; if she wanted that for the sitting, she is to come on Monday; and I have offered to give her more if she stops more than two hours.[11]

When the model arrived, she asked for two shillings an hour and was engaged. Although the 'hair did not fulfil its bonnet promises'; being redder than expected, and 'artificially crimped,' the session went ahead.[12]

Such rates were far higher than the average earnings in casual female employment of around seven pence per day.[13] And even if a model worked only for occasional sessions, weekly earnings of 4 or 5 shillings would be well

regarded in working-class homes. In 1860, lawyer Arthur Munby, with a fetish
for girls in grimy occupations, paid a dustwoman one shilling to pose for
a photograph in her working clothes; he also registered incredulity at
a commercial photographer's claim that women could earn 'five or six pounds
a week' for nude sessions. 'No wonder such a trade is preferred to the hard
and self-accusing life of a prostitute,' Munby noted in his diary.[14]

Although nude modelling, female and male, was the basis of traditional
figure painting, written information on female practitioners is elusive, perhaps
recorded scantily to protect reputations. As it was usual to draw an unclothed
pose before adding costume or drapery, evidence is, however, extensive: studies
and sketches show that, among others, Burne-Jones, Frederic Leighton and Evelyn
De Morgan regularly drew nude figures, while Rossetti's attempts were notably
inept. Photographers produced nude female studies described as artists' aids
but widely purchased by other men as pornography.[15] For professional use,
but clandestinely, cartoonist Linley Sambourne took his own sequences of nude
models, recruited from The Camera Club, where such posing was routine. With
the exception of De Morgan's model Jane Hales, none of the Pre-Raphaelite
models was connected with nude posing but wore costumes or drapery.
At the same time, the perceived immorality of nude images tended to 'infect'
all modelling with salacious suggestion.

Owing to her family situation, and as her list of 'appearances' on canvas
record, of those included here, only Fanny Eaton will have modelled primarily
for money (and never nude). Elizabeth Siddal, Annie Miller and Fanny Cornforth
were equally attracted by studio life and the world of art, free from customary
employer demands. Enjoyable work conditions were ample compensation for
erratic earnings.

An established artist could pay a retainer to a favourite model, to be
available on demand. Rossetti did so with Alexa Wilding, and cartoonist Harry
Furniss recorded his employment of 'Nellie', a young girl 'with a beautiful face,
fair short-cut curly hair, an exquisite neck and shoulders, and well-shaped arms',
who, for most of a decade, worked for him two days a week, often costumed in
black lawyer's gown to represent the business of Parliament. Her other employers
were Albert Moore and Sir James Dromgole Linton, who produced painstaking
costume scenes.[16]

By 1875, painter Louise Jopling's account books show payments to models
ranging from 2s. and 6d. to 10s. and 6d. per sitting, presumably calculated
on both length and pose difficulty.[17] In 1889, the rates were somewhat lower,
according to one report. 'On the whole the English female models are very
naïve, very natural, and very good-humoured,' declared a London magazine that
year, continuing: 'The virtues which the artist values most in them are prettiness
and punctuality. Every sensible model consequently keeps a diary of her
engagements, and dresses neatly.' Hired by half-day or whole day, '[t]he tariff
is a shilling an hour, to which great artists usually add an omnibus fare'.
Generally, a model, was 'a pretty girl, from about twelve to twenty-five years
of age, who knows nothing about art, cares less, and is merely anxious to earn
seven or eight shillings a day without much trouble'.

The author of that this magazine article, presenting himself as a
knowledgeable guide to bohemia, was Oscar Wilde – probably less informed
than he thought, for sessions of seven or eight hours were rare. He continued:

English models rarely look at a picture, and never venture on any aesthetic
theories...they merely desire that the studio shall be warm, and the lunch hot,
for all charming artists give their models lunch...As to what they are asked
to do they are equally indifferent. On Monday they will don the rags of a
beggar-girl for Mr. Pumper, whose pathetic pictures of modern life draw such

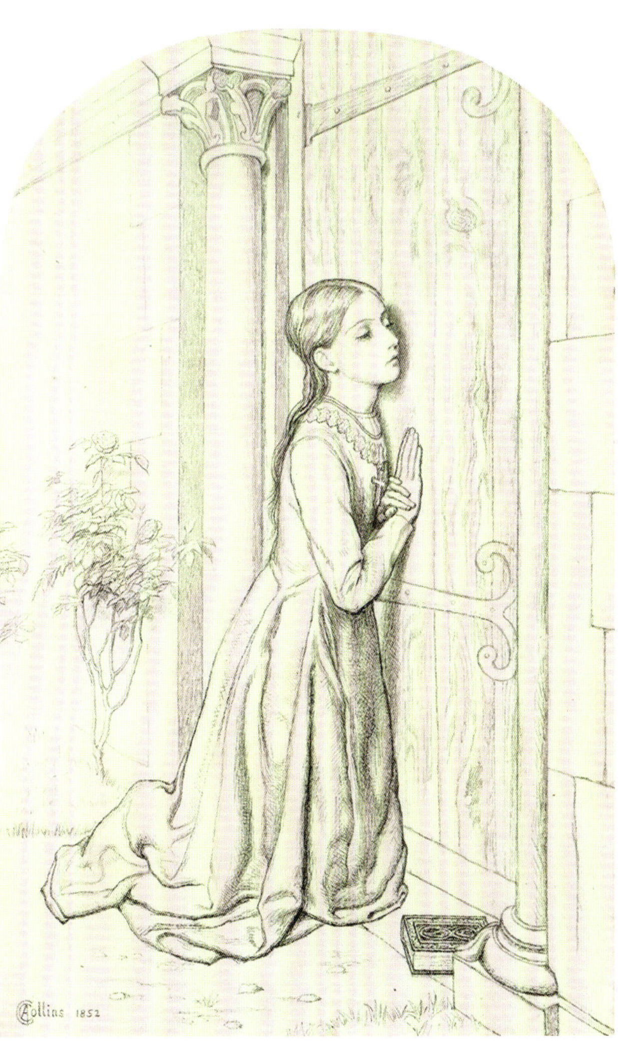

3
**Study for *The Devout
Childhood of St Elizabeth
of Hungary***
Charles Collins, 1852
Graphite and ink on paper
273 × 175mm
Tate, London

tears from the public, and on Tuesday they will pose in a peplum for [neo-classicist] Mr. Phœbus… They career gaily through all centuries and through all costumes, and, like actors, are interesting only when they are not themselves.[18]

Then, Wilde concluded, 'They usually marry well, and sometimes they marry the artist,' in which case the artist 'gets no sittings'. The throwaway line resonates with Pre-Raphaelite experience, however, for the striking aspect of those who modelled for these artists is the fact that several did marry 'well' in this manner: Emma Hill married Madox Brown, Siddal married Rossetti and Matilda Booth married Frederic Shields. While Fanny Cornforth did not marry an artist, she was Rossetti's regular companion in his widowhood, and Mary Emma Jones had ten children with Frederick Sandys. With ambition and the ability to learn social skills and graces, modelling could lead to social mobility, into a different social class. 'Although she is not a lady, her mind is poetic,' wrote Barbara Leigh Smith of Elizabeth Siddal, adding that Rossetti wished her to mix with 'ladies'.[19] Thanks in large part to the education in manners provided by Hunt, social mobility was most notably achieved by Annie Miller in her marriage to Captain Thomas Ranelagh Thomson, a relative of Lord Ranelagh. It was almost equally experienced by Jane Burden, an ostler's daughter, who became the wife of wealthy William Morris. Even some from middle-class backgrounds rose up the scale. Effie Gray and Georgiana Macdonald became Lady Millais and Lady Burne-Jones respectively, which may not have pleased the democratically minded latter but did impress a social world where precedence was observed.

Among the cohort represented here, only Fanny Eaton failed to enjoy any social advancement, primarily because she was already married and did not forsake her existing partner for the life of bohemia; when modelling employment ceased, she returned to domestic service. Had marriage to a driver not fixed her social status, however, it is probable that mixed ancestry would have done so.

While their contemporaries, and the women themselves, will have attributed their marriages to luck, in a society that restricted female opportunity, it is also testimony to their own actions and ambitions. Modelling could be an astute route to advancement. Often, the initial encounter with artists has been presented as accidental, but such was standard practice when women were reviled for 'ensnaring' men and were obliged to play Cinderella. It is, moreover, evident that new and rewarding lives opened to some who lacked educational and cultural advantages, and that they quickly seized the opportunity to share in the world of art. Elizabeth Siddal hoped to persuade first Deverell and then Hunt to assist her own aspirations before securing Rossetti's support. Effie Gray cultivated her talents as helpmeet, Jane Burden appealed silently (as it seems) to Morris when the other artists left Oxford, then enthusiastically shared his decorative projects. Fanny Cornforth supported Rossetti through several reverses.

Overall, the anecdotal accounts indicate that modelling was seen as an independent occupation, with uncertain but alluring prospects, and that for women with enterprise, however expressed, it offered entry to an enjoyable and varied life. This was well-expressed by Georgiana Burne-Jones, who responded so eagerly to the new world of visual culture. Much later she wrote of reliving the excitement, when talking with another, unnamed Pre-Raphaelite model about 'the days when we were all young'. Her companion felt the same, she reported. 'Her regard for the young artists she remembered was still fresh and she loved to dwell on their memory. "It was like being in a new world to be with them. I sat to them and was there with them, and they were different to everyone else I ever saw."'[20]

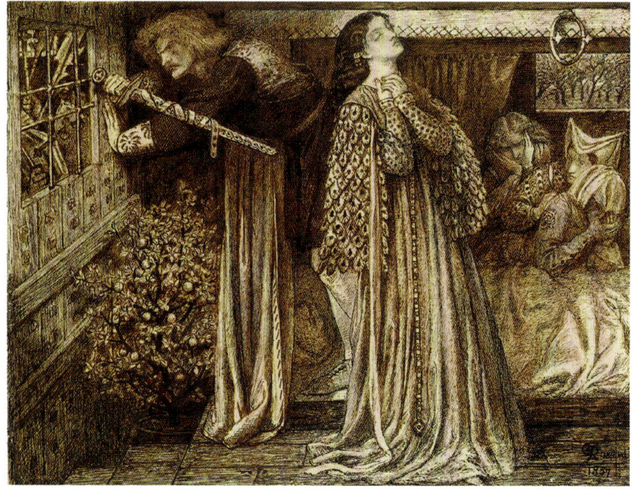

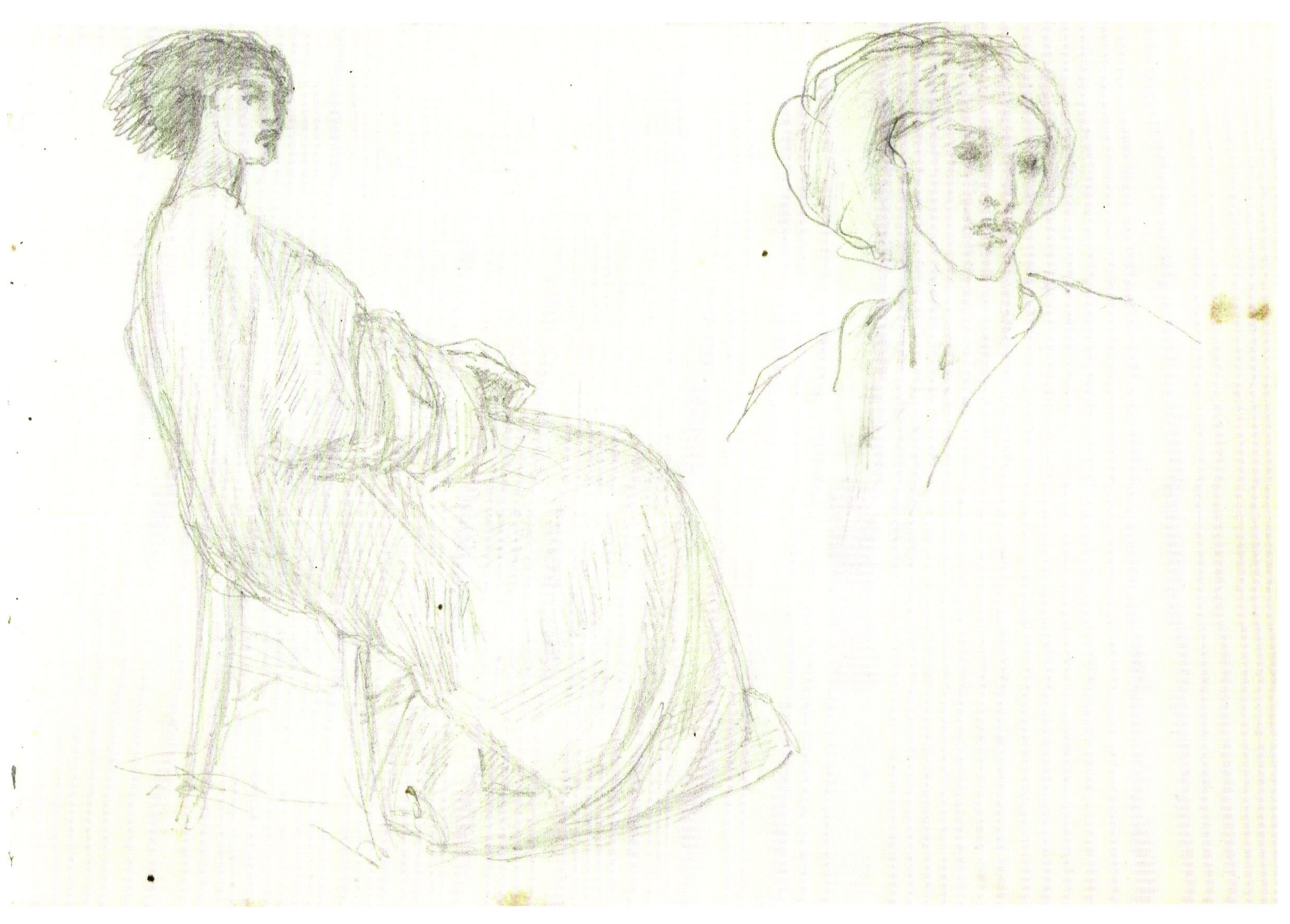

Elizabeth Siddal

1829–1862

The story of an astonishingly beautiful young woman plucked from obscurity is a fairy tale. First told in 1897 by artist Arthur Hughes and elaborated by William Holman Hunt, it relates how the painter Walter Howell Deverell, close friend of the Pre-Raphaelite Brotherhood, accompanied his mother to a milliner's. 'Through an open door he saw a girl working with her needle; he got his mother to ask her to sit to him.'[1] The girl was Elizabeth Siddal, familiarly known as Lizzie. The painting was a scene from *Twelfth Night*.

What is the source of this hearsay? Deverell, his mother and Siddal were long dead, and none of them left their own testimony. Hughes and Hunt had known Deverell, but Hunt's allegedly verbatim account is a dramatised reconstruction: 'By Jove! she's like a queen, magnificently tall, with a lovely figure.'[2]

In fact, artistic ability is the keynote of the earliest version of her story, an obituary published in 1862 by William Ibbitt, a local artist who had met Siddal in Sheffield, her father's birthplace, in 1857. Evidently repeating her own account, he states that, at age 20, she was a dressmaker, who was introduced to the family of an artist – to Deverell's father – to whom she showed some of her own drawings.[3]

Mr Deverell senior was then Secretary of the Government School of Design in London, which provided classes for artisans and was an obvious source of advice for a tradesman's daughter with artistic ambitions. Furthermore, according to Ibbitt, Deverell's son Walter 'formed a strong attachment to Miss Siddall [the common spelling of her name – later altered by her] and proposed a friendship to her that was to last for life'. Sadly, within a couple of years, both Deverells, father and son, had died, leaving 'the amiable young artist a disappointed lover'.[4]

This narrative notably omits all mention of modelling. Yet the visual and anecdotal evidence is clear, revealing Siddal's introduction to the art world.

Born in July 1829, in London, Elizabeth Eleanor was the third of eight children born to the wife of Sheffield cutler Charles Siddall, who by 1845 had a shop on a busy stretch of the Old Kent Road in Southwark, London. During the winter of 1849–50 she went to model as Viola/Cesario for Deverell's

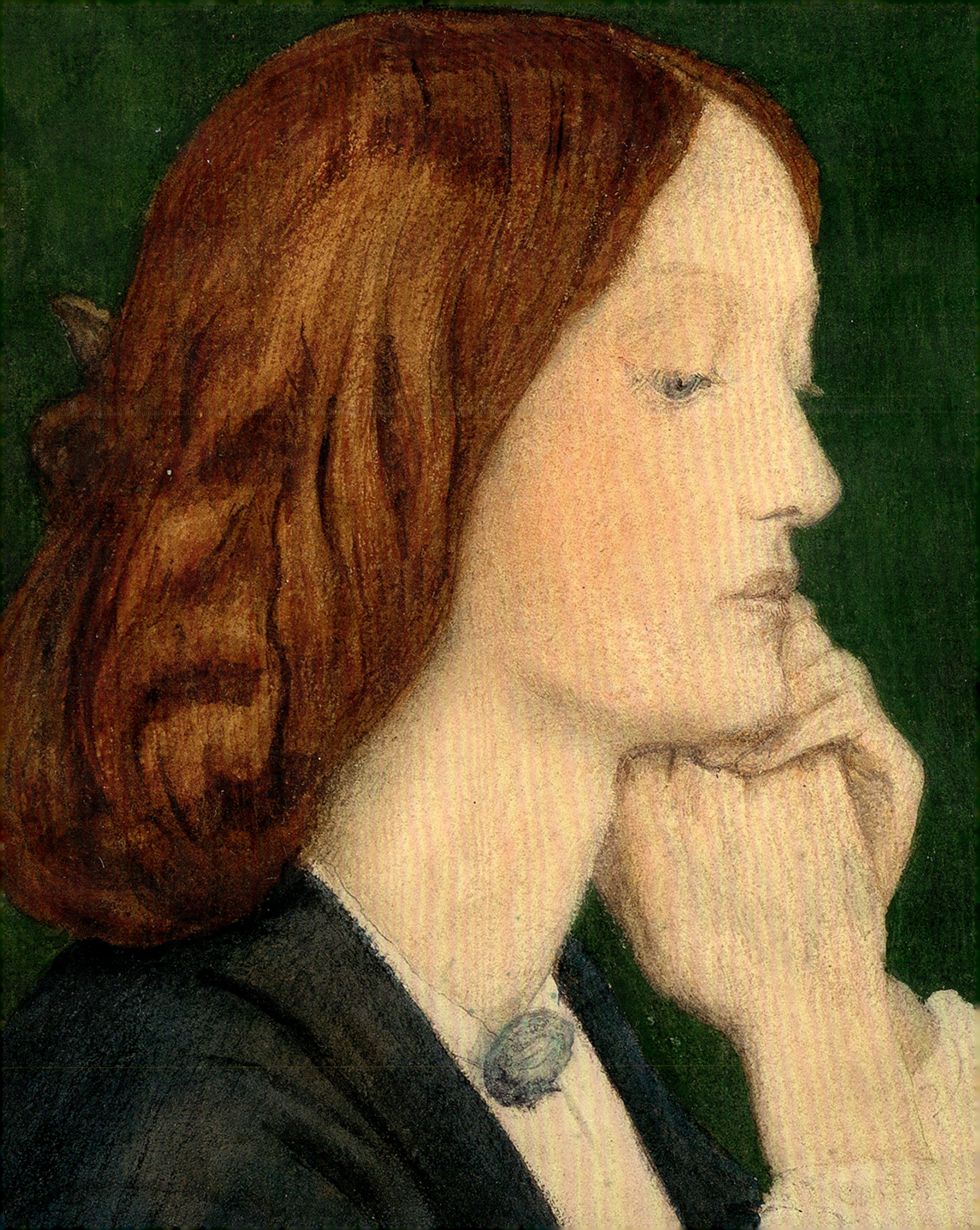

6
Twelfth Night Act II, Scene IV
Walter Howell Deverell, 1850
Oil on canvas, 1016 × 1321mm
Private Collection

7
Viola and Olivia
Walter Howell Deverell, 1850
Etching in *The Germ: Thoughts
towards Nature in Poetry,
Literature and Art*, illustrating
John L. Tupper's poem of the
same name, 224 × 145mm
The British Library, London

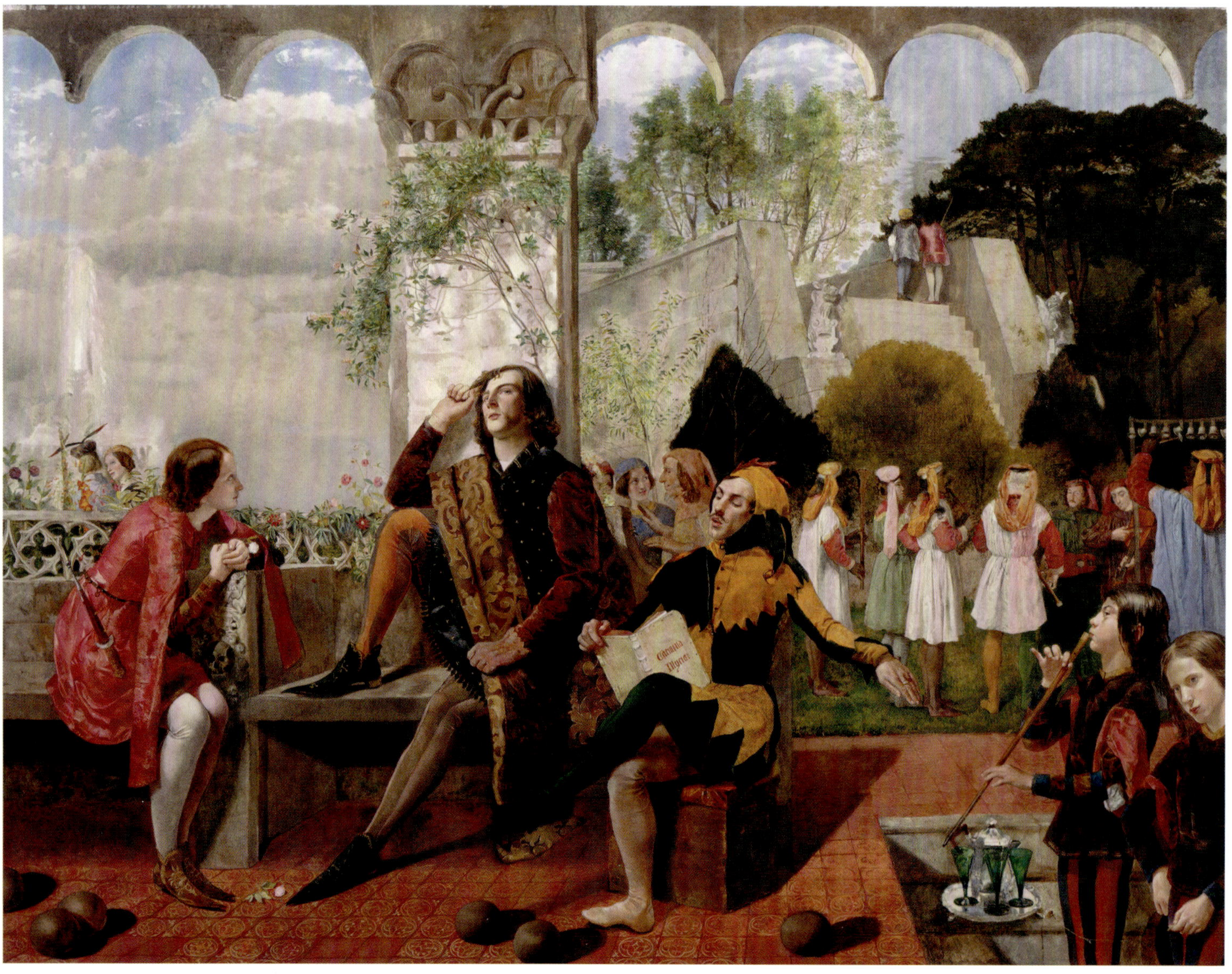

painting *Twelfth Night* (ill. 6). She must have volunteered, because, although the Siddalls were not rich, they were respectable, and modelling was not.

She must also have been bold, because the drawings show Viola/Cesario wearing male theatrical attire of tunic and tights. Or, one can only guess, she was enchanted by the art world, the School of Design, the studio in the Deverell home. She had artistic ambitions and liked poetry, and no doubt she would have seen the PRB magazine, *The Germ*, in which Deverell's etching of her as Viola/Cesario appeared (ill. 7). Moreover, Deverell was handsome and lively, with a promising career ahead.

Well before Deverell's death in 1854, Siddal agreed to model for his friend Hunt, who was having familiar 'bothers with models'.[5] He adapted the figure of an elderly woman to cast her as a British girl in the time of the druids, clad in a hessian sack. Then the roles multiplied: dubbed 'Miss Sid' or 'the Sid', in emulation of French practice, she was a most obliging model and often in Hunt's studio. In August 1850 she was involved in a curious 'hoax' when he and Frederic George Stephens tricked another friend into believing she was Hunt's wife.

Charles Allston Collins painted her as St Elizabeth of Hungary, kneeling at a convent door.[6] Rossetti composed three kneeling women, all drawn from her.[7] Rossetti later dated their meeting to 1851, so this marks their first collaboration as model and artist.[8] The next was a scene of Delia awaiting her lover's return, begun in November. Originally featuring Emma Madox Brown, sitting stiffly in her day-dress, this was transformed when Siddal took over, wearing a shift, with her hair loose, to dramatically convey Delia's yearning through pose and expression.

There is no record of payment for these sessions, and no guessing how Siddal explained to her parents these visits to the artists' studios. On meeting her, Rossetti's brother William noted 'a decided inclination to order her mode of life according to her own liking, whether conformable or not to the views of the British matron'.[9]

In the following year, 1852, having completed the riverbank background of *Ophelia* (ill. 8), John Everett Millais engaged Siddal to pose for the figure – another difficult pose, lying full-length in a tin bath, with water up to her ears. Owing to the death of her eldest brother, Charles, the

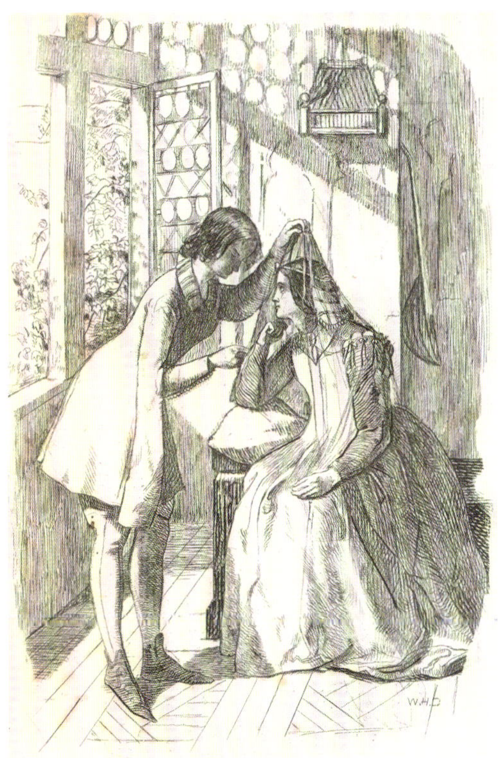

'Her life has been hard and full of trials, her home life unhappy and her whole fate hard'

For Siddal to have taken either a passive or active part in this jape bespeaks unconventional high spirits.

She was not regarded as a beauty, being thin and tall, with red hair and a pronounced overbite. But she was a very willing model, who held difficult poses, including a painful kneeling position in Hunt's next picture, *Two Gentlemen of Verona* (1851). Possibly in shared sittings with Dante Gabriel Rossetti,

sittings were postponed, but by only a fortnight. It would seem that she was as eagerly engaged in the Pre-Raphaelite project as anyone.

By the summer, Rossetti had found a temporary studio in Highgate, north London, that Siddal began to visit regularly, mostly unobserved. Rossetti's lodging there was brief yet significant, for it was in this studio that she persuaded him to support her own

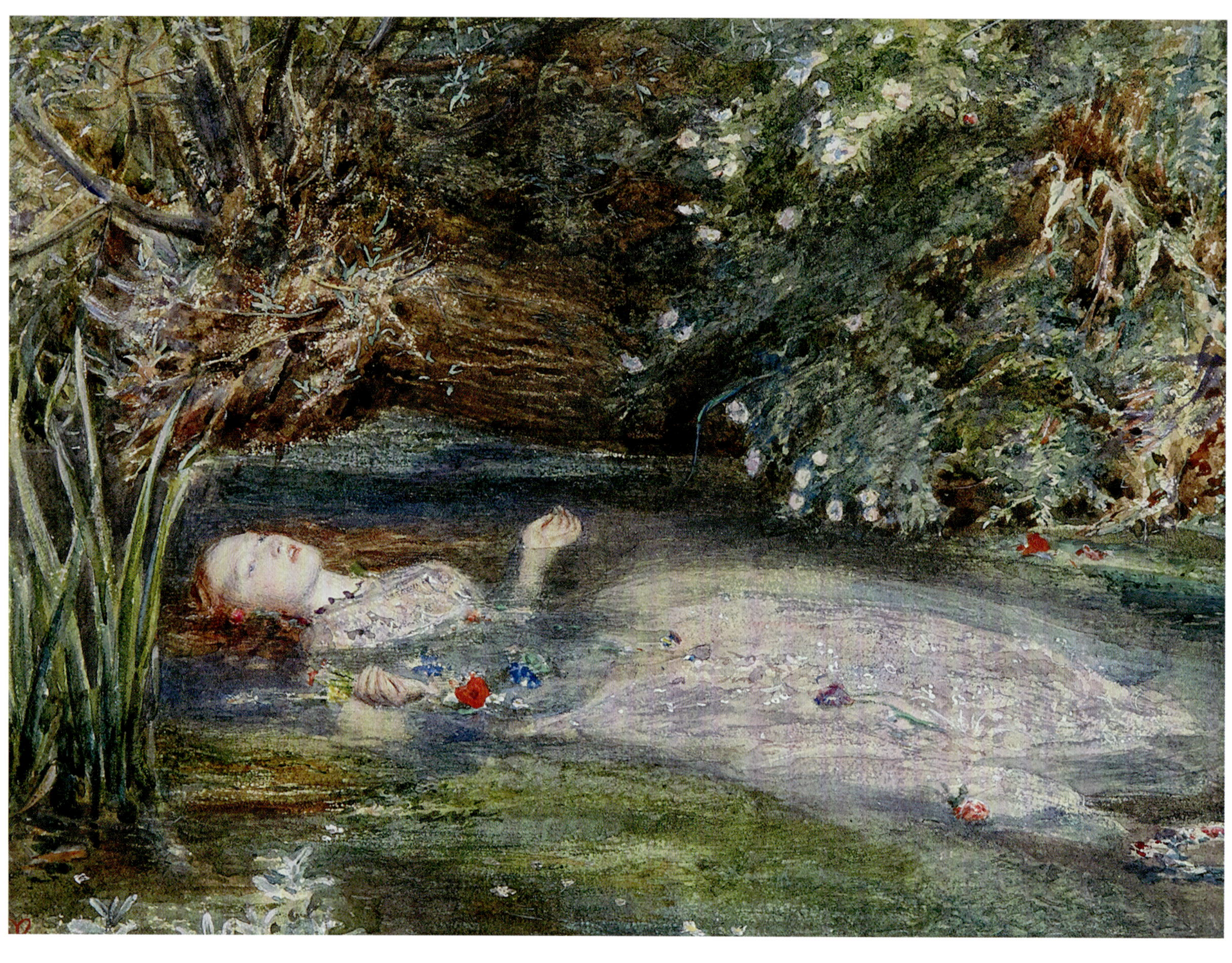

aspirations. To his poet sister Christina, who had also started sketching, Rossetti wrote 'you must take care however not to rival the Sid, but keep within respectful limits'.[10] In November, he moved to an apartment in Blackfriars, within walking distance of the Siddall home. Asking Siddal to sit again, Collins received a 'freezing' response, stating that she had 'other occupation'.[11] By January 1853, she had transitioned from model to student. Madox Brown helped her open an account with the art supplier Charles Roberson and Co.

Siddal had also become Rossetti's sweetheart. Can it be inferred that she appealed to his chivalry? As Rossetti told it: 'her life has been hard and full of trials, her home life unhappy and her whole fate hard.'[12] She must have presented her situation thus, for he amplified the dismal future:

And on her lover's arm she leant,
And round her waist she felt it fold,
And far across the hills they went
In that new world which is the old

A drawing made by Rossetti during the trip (ill.10) shows her standing by a window in their lodgings. Her pose and elusive gaze confirm her characteristic 'attitude of reserve'.[14] Six years and some heartbreak later, they returned to Hastings to marry.

Elizabeth Siddal's first-ever composition had illustrated William Wordsworth's poem 'We Are Seven' (1798), showing a child by the graves of her siblings. The second, more daring, was from Robert Browning's *Pippa Passes* (1841).[15] In William Rossetti's judicious assessment: 'She had much of sweet and chastened invention, and an ingenious romantic turn in it as well, and a graceful purity is stamped upon everything

8
Ophelia
John Everett Millais, 1865–6
Watercolour with gouache
on paper, 178 × 254mm
Private Collection

9
Lovers Listening to Music
Elizabeth Siddal, 1854
Pencil, pen and ink on paper
210 × 240mm
National Trust Collections,
Wightwick Manor and Gardens,
Warwickshire

Artistic ability is the keynote of the earliest version of her story

Perhaps her soul is never to bloom nor her bright hair to fade, but after hardly escaping from degradation and corruption, all she might have been must sink out again unprofitably in that dark house where she was born. How truly she may say 'No man cared for my soul'…how long have I known her and not thought of this till so late – perhaps too late.[13]

In the early summer of 1854 the young couple vacationed in Hastings, where they roamed on the beach and cliffs as pictured, indirectly, in Siddal's drawing *Lovers Listening to Music* (ill.9). The unidentified subject may relate to Alfred, Lord Tennyson's poem 'The Day-Dream' (1842), which both she and Rossetti were illustrating:

she did.'[16] Grace, purity and invention were qualities prized in the early Pre-Raphaelite period. Technical skill in draughtsmanship, as taught in the academies, was thought overvalued in comparison with sincerity and feeling.

Still, it is a pity that she did not enjoy a thorough training, like Joanna Boyce Wells and Evelyn De Morgan, that included anatomy, as her figures were notably boneless. Encouraged by Rossetti, whose own technique was fallible, and by her own 'decided inclination' to independence, she drew from imagination. But she worked hard, as the many compositional sketches show, tackling subjects from John Keats, William Shakespeare, the border ballads and the Bible, and poems by Rossetti, such as 'Sister Helen', as well as Tennyson, for a projected illustrated edition. Some became

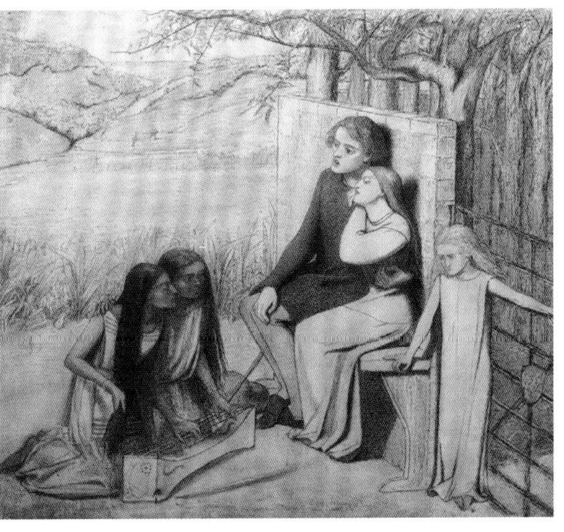

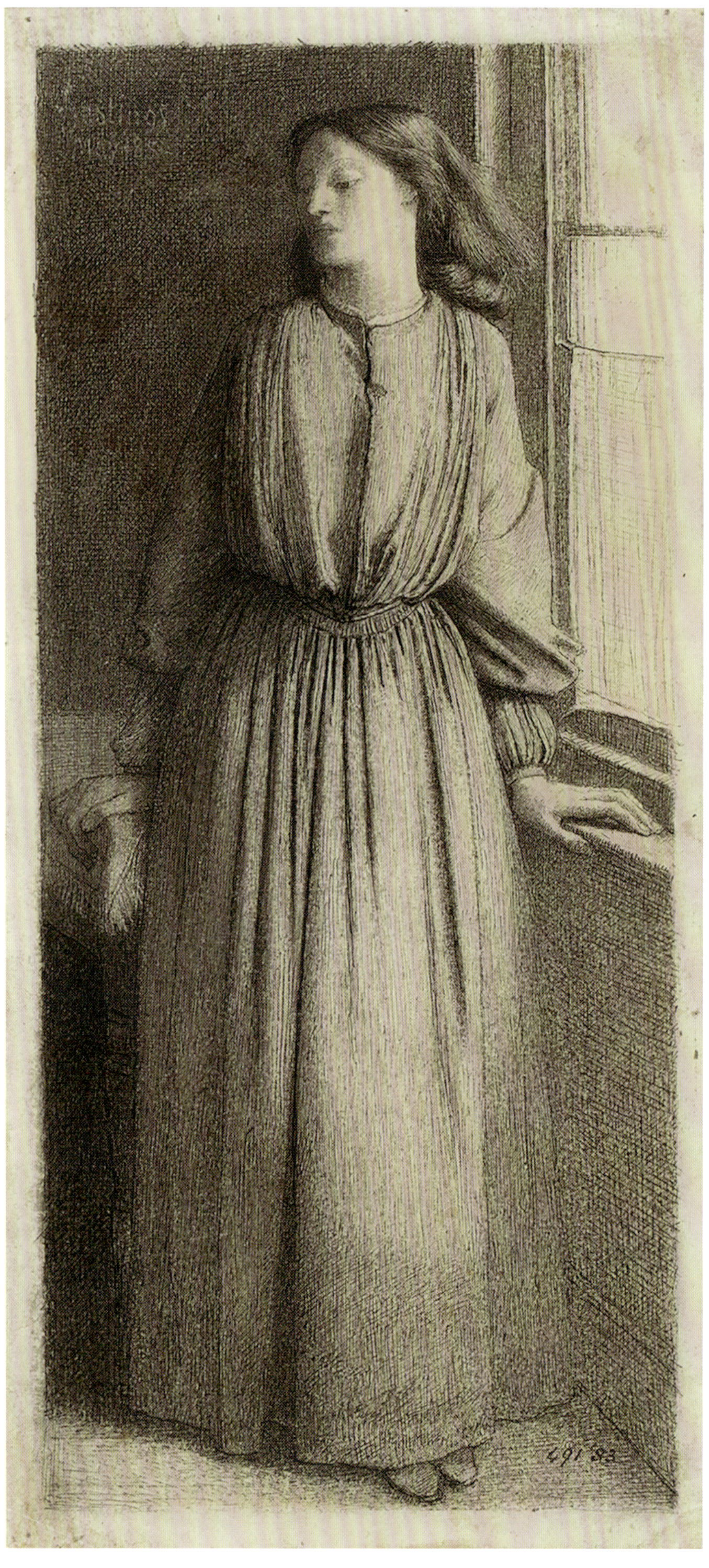

28

finished watercolours; others remained works in progress, and some have been lost. One now unlocated self-portrait was in oil.

Her compositions are notable for their highly charged emotional scenes. *The Macbeths* (ill.11) shows a dramatic moment in Shakespeare's play when Lady Macbeth realises with terror that her husband still holds the murder weapon with which he has slain Duncan, King of Scotland.

Siddal had modelled as several Shakespearean heroines (ills 6 and 8) in paintings by Deverell, Hunt and Millais, but the choice of character for her own work was violently different: unlike Viola and Ophelia, Lady Macbeth is a villain, shown full of murderous resolve. Her husband's fear is expressed through his twisted posture.

The Pre-Raphaelite exhibition of summer 1857 prompted the first critical assessment of her art, from poet Coventry Patmore:

character returning as a ghost to claim his bride, Margaret. Edward Burne-Jones later depicted the same passage in a very similar composition. Siddal's work was bought by American scholar Charles Eliot Norton, who gave it to Rossetti after her death. When later purchased by artist, dealer and collector Charles Fairfax Murray, it was subjected to typical denigration. Shamefully downplaying Siddal's ability, Murray claimed that 'Gabriel Rossetti himself worked on this picture as was customary with him... Much of the merit these works have belongs to him.'[18]

Elizabeth Siddal's life is usually told in terms of her personal relationships, with her professional aspirations minimised. In 1854–5, John Ruskin bought all her sketches, as a form of patronage that would also benefit Rossetti. Siddal resisted

10
Elizabeth Siddal at Hastings
Dante Gabriel Rossetti, 1854
Pen and ink on paper
238 × 112mm
Victoria and Albert Museum, London

11
The Macbeths
Elizabeth Siddal, c.1855–60
Pen and brush, Indian ink with scratching out on paper
214 × 135mm
Ashmolean Museum, Oxford

'Art was the only thing for which she felt seriously'

Her 'Study of a Head' is a very promising attempt, showing great care, considerable technical power, and a high, pure, and independent feeling for that much misunderstood object, the human face divine. 'We are Seven' and 'Pippa Passes', by the same lady, deserve more notice than we can stop to give them.[17]

In the mid-1850s, Siddal began a series of paintings that illustrated traditional ballads from her copy of Walter Scott's *Minstrelsy of the Scottish Border* (1802). In *Sir Patrick Spens* (ill.12) the figures look out to sea, despairing for the ill-fated ship carrying their 'gude Scots lords' to Norway. Despite its small size, the carefully drawn group of women and children includes a standing figure that seems to be a self-portrait.

Another *Minstrelsy* illustration, *Clerk Saunders* (ill.13), shows the eponymous

the arrangement initially, as one considered improper for a wife, as she hoped soon to be. Regarding marriage however, Rossetti was commitment-averse, opposing anything becoming a duty. In late 1857, Siddal went north, visiting relatives in Sheffield, enrolling at the local art school – where a fellow-student recalled her working in the Figure Room and chatting to the director about Pre-Raphaelitism – and joining an excursion to Manchester's *Exhibition of Art Treasures of the United Kingdom*.[19] Rossetti followed her north, and the couple spent several months together in Matlock, Derbyshire, working alongside each other on watercolours and poems.

Her work *Lady Affixing a Pennant to a Knight's Spear* (ill.14), in which a blue-gowned lady helps her knight nail a red banner to his lance, likely dates from this trip. The landscape view suggests

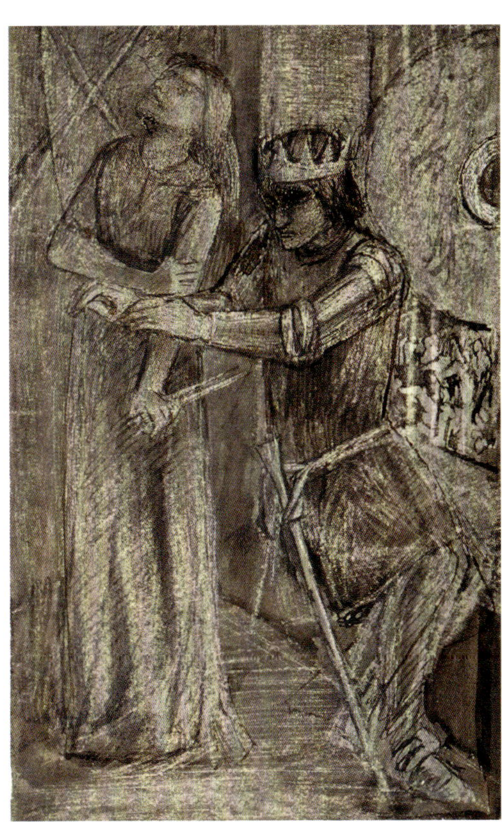

12
Sir Patrick Spens
Elizabeth Siddal, 1856
Watercolour on paper
241 × 229mm
Tate, London

13
Clerk Saunders
Elizabeth Siddal, 1857
Watercolour on paper
284 × 181mm
Fitzwilliam Museum,
Cambridge

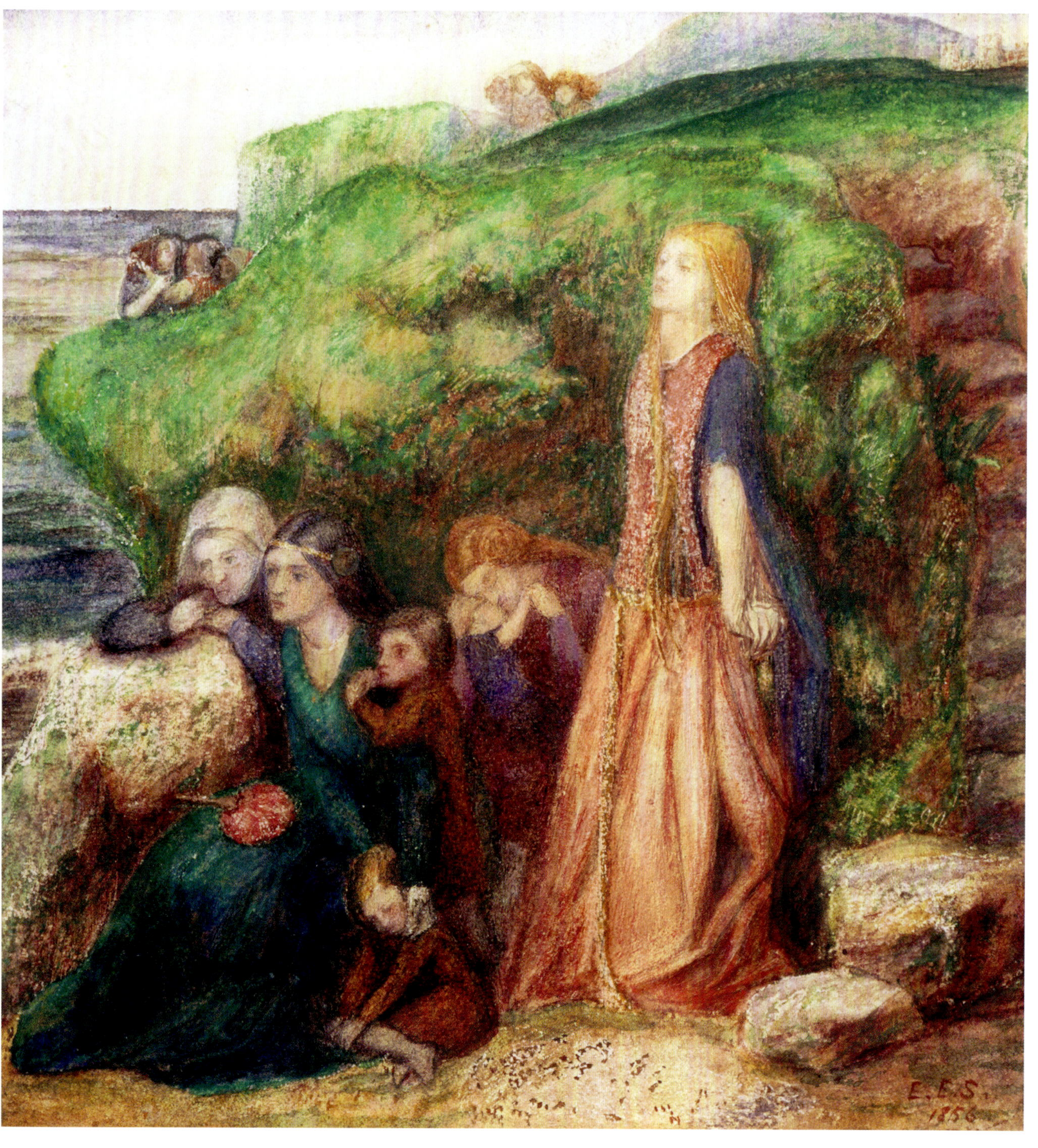

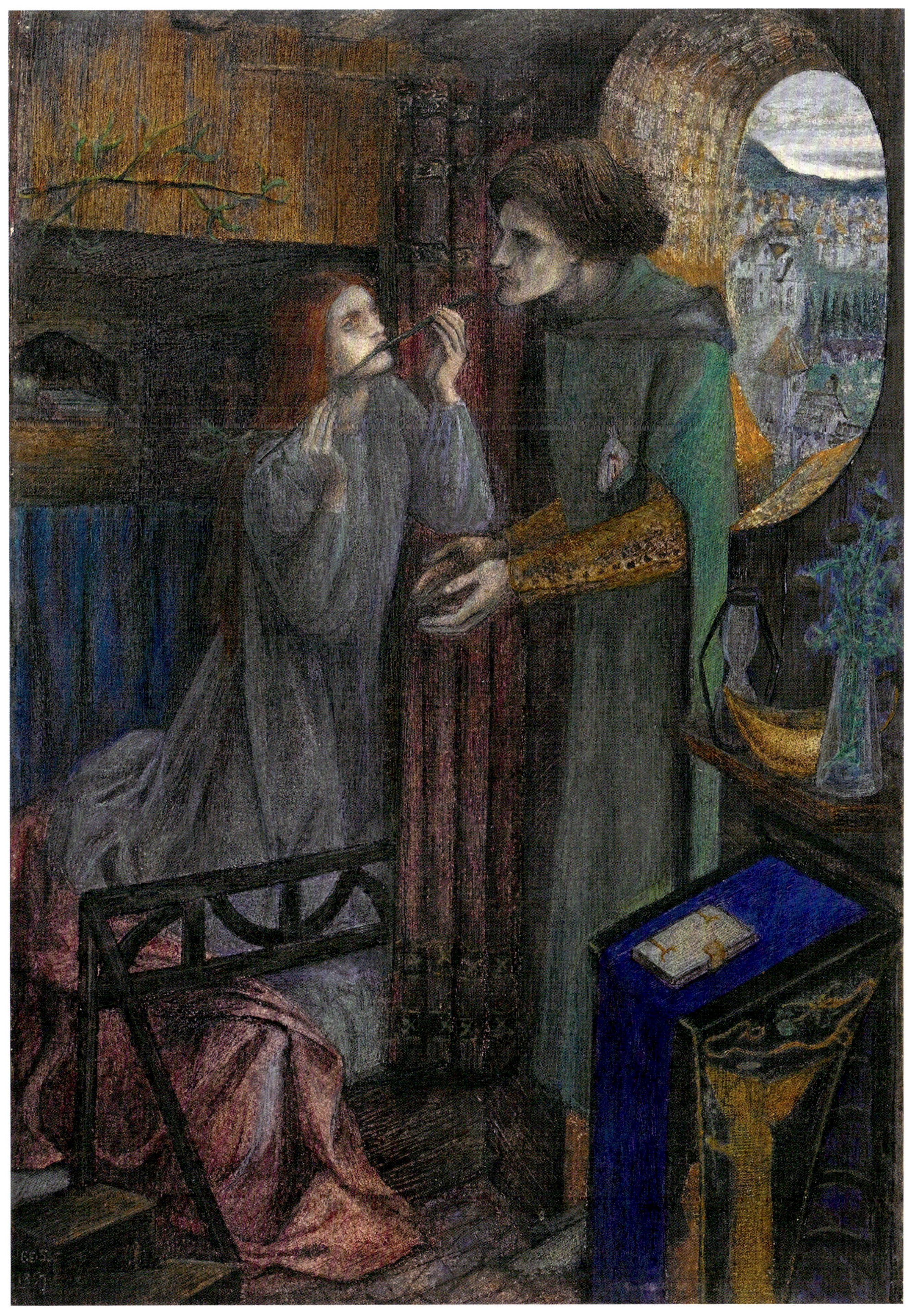

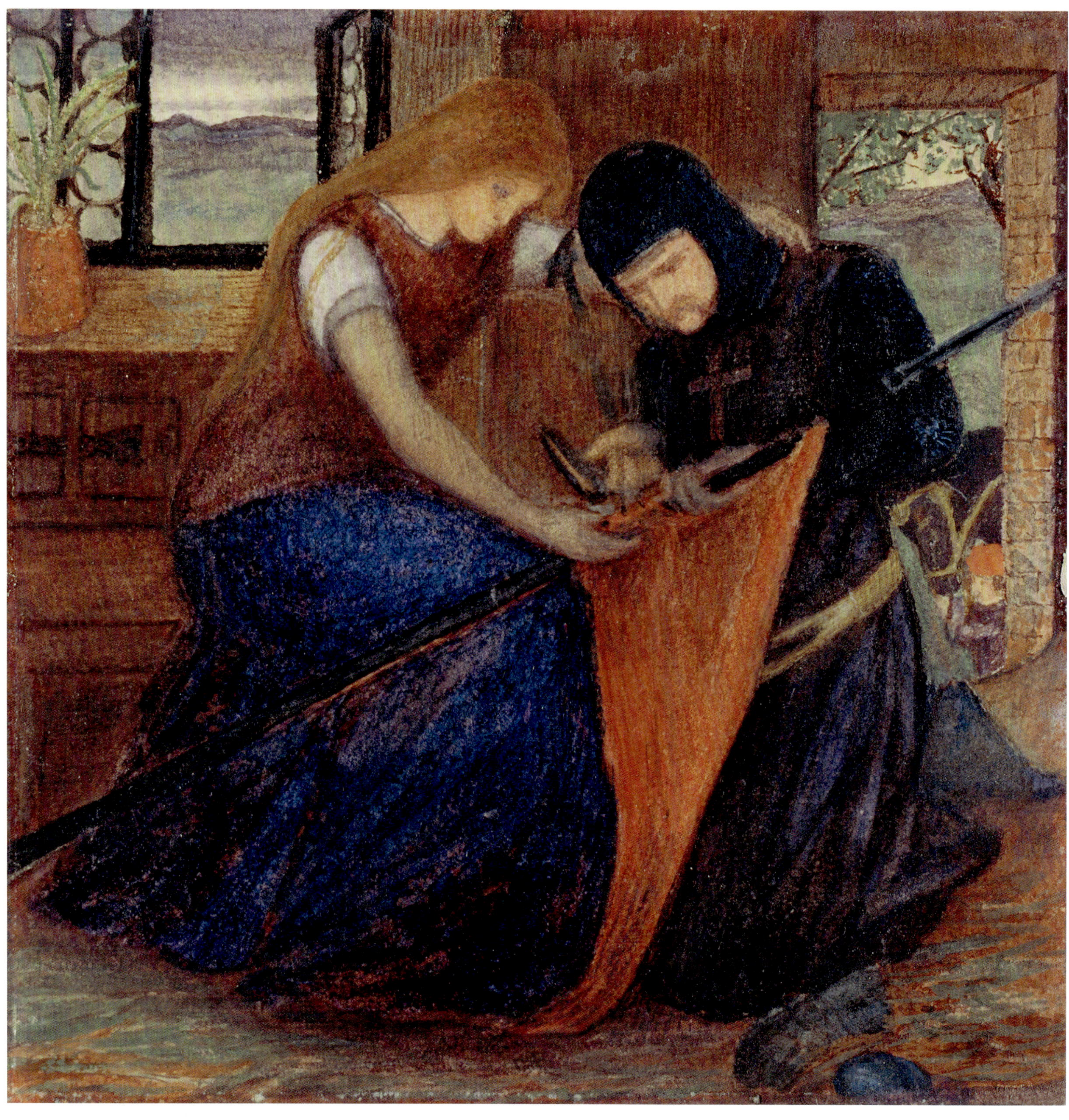

the Peak District, and the scene may have been inspired by a visit to Haddon Hall, with its fourteenth-century great hall.

When Rossetti returned to London, none of his friends, who now included Edward Burne-Jones and William Morris, recorded meeting Siddal. In July 1859, when she was just 30, her father died, which made her unmarried situation awkward. As her great-niece later commented, 'one could hardly imagine that she would have married some perhaps ordinary man and settled down to a humdrum life'.[20]

The following spring, Siddal and Rossetti married in Hastings, and joined a social circle that included the recently married Morrises and Burne-Joneses as well as Joanna and Henry Wells, where spouses shared in art production. Indeed she continued to create new work industriously. As Rossetti told Norton: 'Her last designs would, I am sure, surprise and delight you, and I hope she is going to do better than ever now.'[21] Her latest composition was a complex tournament scene, *The Woeful Victory* (c.1848), with knights, ladies and horses.

Now in rather precarious health, she helped decorate the Morrises' Red House in Kent with a mural figure of Rachel, the remains of which have recently been uncovered. She also planned to collaborate with Georgiana Burne-Jones on a book of tales (see p.129) illustrated with woodcuts. Like the other wives, she soon became pregnant; sadly her daughter was stillborn in May 1861. Distress and depression were treated with the opiate laudanum in increasing quantities. One evening in February 1862, Rossetti returned home to find his wife unconscious from an overdose. Medical intervention failed. She was buried, with his poetic notebook, in the Rossetti grave in Highgate Cemetery, north London. Seven years later, to retrieve the notebook, he had her coffin exhumed, an act that posterity has not forgiven. To their friend the poet Algernon Charles Swinburne, Rossetti wrote:

The truth is, no one so much as herself would have approved of my doing this. Art was the only thing for which she felt seriously. Had it been possible to her, I should have found the book on my pillow that night she was buried; and could she have opened the grave no other hand would have been needed.[22]

Rossetti gathered together all her available drawings, sketches and poems, compiling albums and hoping to publish the verses as a memorial. Artworks and manuscripts were inherited by William Rossetti, who, in 1905, published the first account of Siddal's creative production. One of the scattered poetic drafts, 'At Last', was written in the elegiac style of 'deathbed' lament, a staple of Victorian poetry.

O Mother, open the window wide
And let the daylight in;
The hills grow darker to my sight
And thoughts begin to swim.

And, Mother dear, take my young son,
(Since I was born of thee),
And care for all his little ways
And nurse him on thy knee.

And, Mother, wash my pale, pale hands
And then bind up my feet;
My body may no longer rest
Out of its winding sheet.

And, Mother dear, take a sapling twig
And green grass newly mown,
And lay it on my empty bed
That my sorrow be not known.

And, Mother, find three berries red
And pluck them from the stalk,
And burn them at the first cockcrow
That my spirit may not walk.

And, Mother dear, break a willow wand,
And if the sap be even,
Then save it for my lovers's sake
And he'll know my soul's in heaven.

And Mother, when the big tears fall,
(And fall, God knows, they may),
Tell him I died of my great love
And my dying heart was gay.

And, Mother dear, when the sun has set,
And the pale kirk grass waves,
Then carry me through the dim twilight
And hide me among the graves.

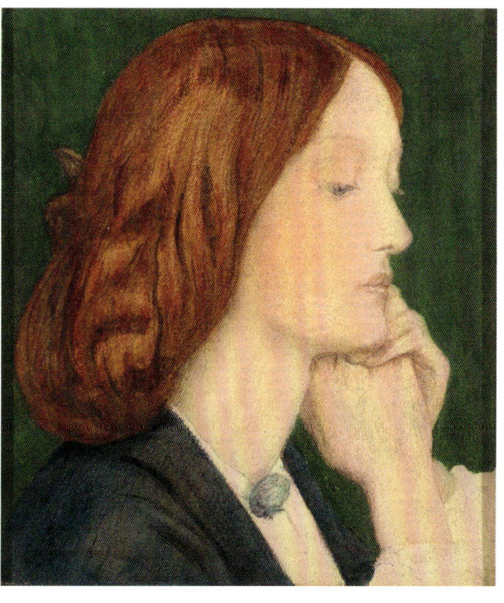

Christina Rossetti

1830–1894

In troubled teenage years marked by episodes of depression and self-harm, Christina Rossetti was swept into Anglo-Catholic religious fervour. 'So you think I once trembled on the convent threshold?' she later wrote, admitting the romantic appeal of prayer and renunciation.[1] With comparable eagerness, she shared the excitement generated by the Pre-Raphaelite Brotherhood. She was, of course, sister to two founding Brothers, Dante Gabriel (known in the family as Gabriel) and critic and writer William Michael, and encountered the other Pre-Raphaelite artists when they gathered in the Rossetti home.

In the role of the Virgin Mary, whose pious obedience was a model for girls like her and her older sister Maria (who later became an Anglican nun), she posed for two paintings, the second being the iconic early Pre-Raphaelite work *Ecce Ancilla Domini!* (ill. 17). Combining Victorian piety with startling pictorial directness, by showing Mary in a nightgown and the Angel as a muscular young man, naked beneath a shift, the painting and subject aptly endorse her lifelong religious commitment and often bold poetic address.

The youngest of four, born in London to an Italian political exile and a mother with 'a passion for intellect', Christina Rossetti composed poetry from the age of 11. A precocious collection appeared in 1847.

An early portrait by Gabriel (ill. 16) records an unexpectedly fashionable coiffure, with chignon and ringlets. Drawn in the home of her lifelong friend Amelia Heimann (the Rossetti siblings studied German with Heimann's husband), it dates from the first phase of her literary renown, when her youthful *Verses* (1847) were printed. Sending a copy to Amelia, she wrote: 'At length it is in my power to lay my famous little book at your feet'.[2]

Late in 1848, she became engaged to Pre-Raphaelite Brother, James Collinson, whom in this intense Pre-Raphaelite period she helped with research for his painting, *The Renunciation of Queen Elizabeth of Hungary* (1850). The monarch-saint featured in her verse, together with lines in which Christ knocks on the door of the soul, an idea given pictorial form by Hunt's *Light of the World* (c.1854).

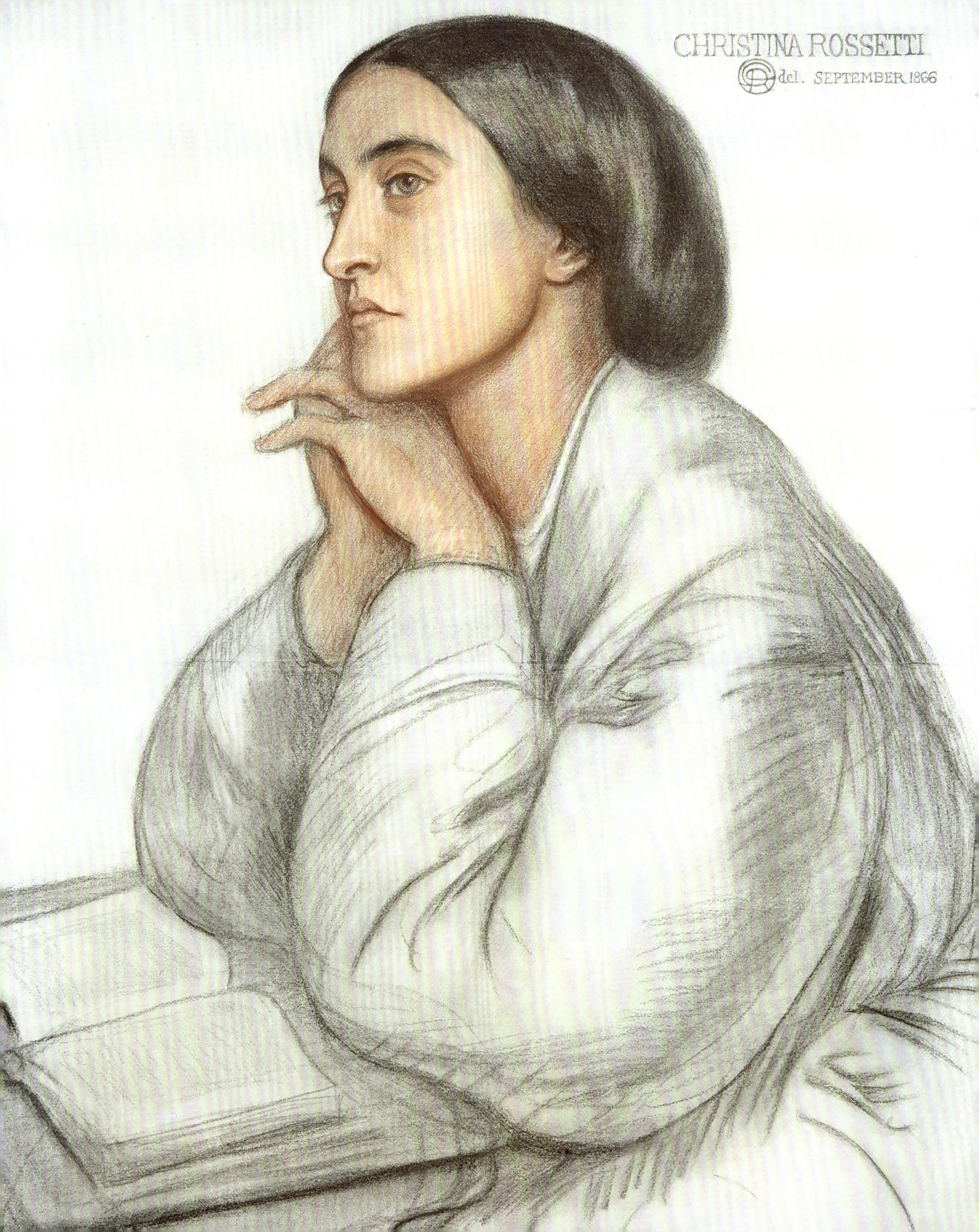

CHRISTINA ROSSETTI
del. SEPTEMBER 1866

16
Christina Rossetti aged 16
Dante Gabriel Rossetti, 1847
Pencil on paper, 110 × 84mm
Victoria and Albert Museum,
London

17
Ecce Ancilla Domini!
(The Annunciation)
Dante Gabriel Rossetti, 1849–50
Oil on canvas, 724 × 419mm
Tate, London

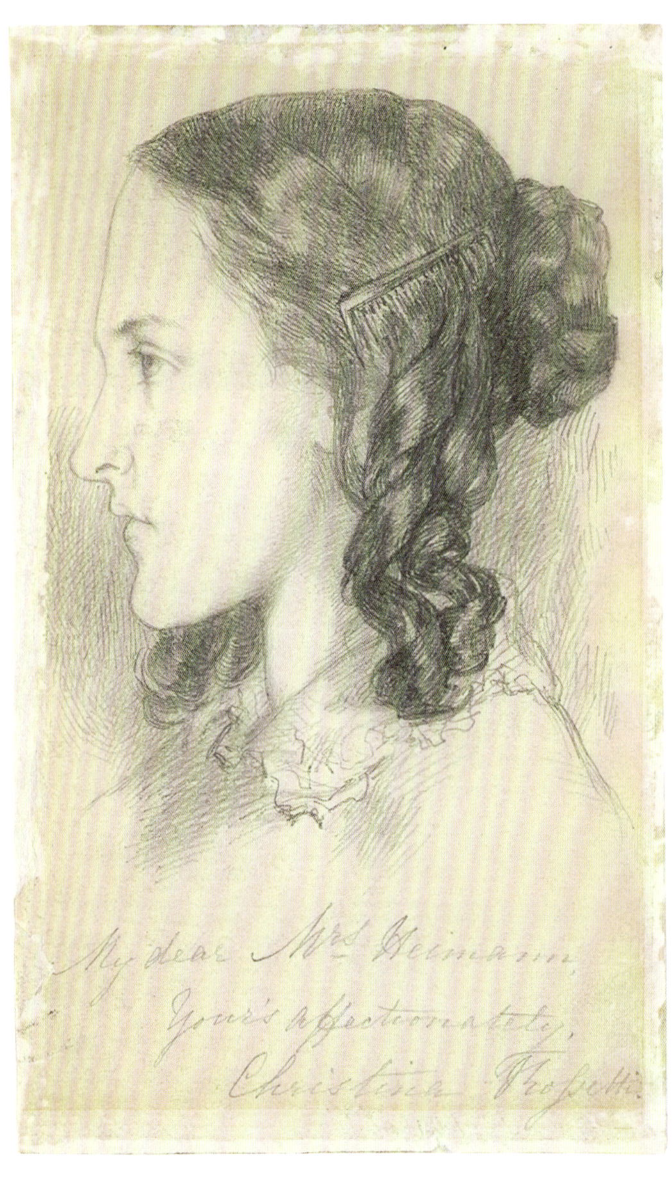

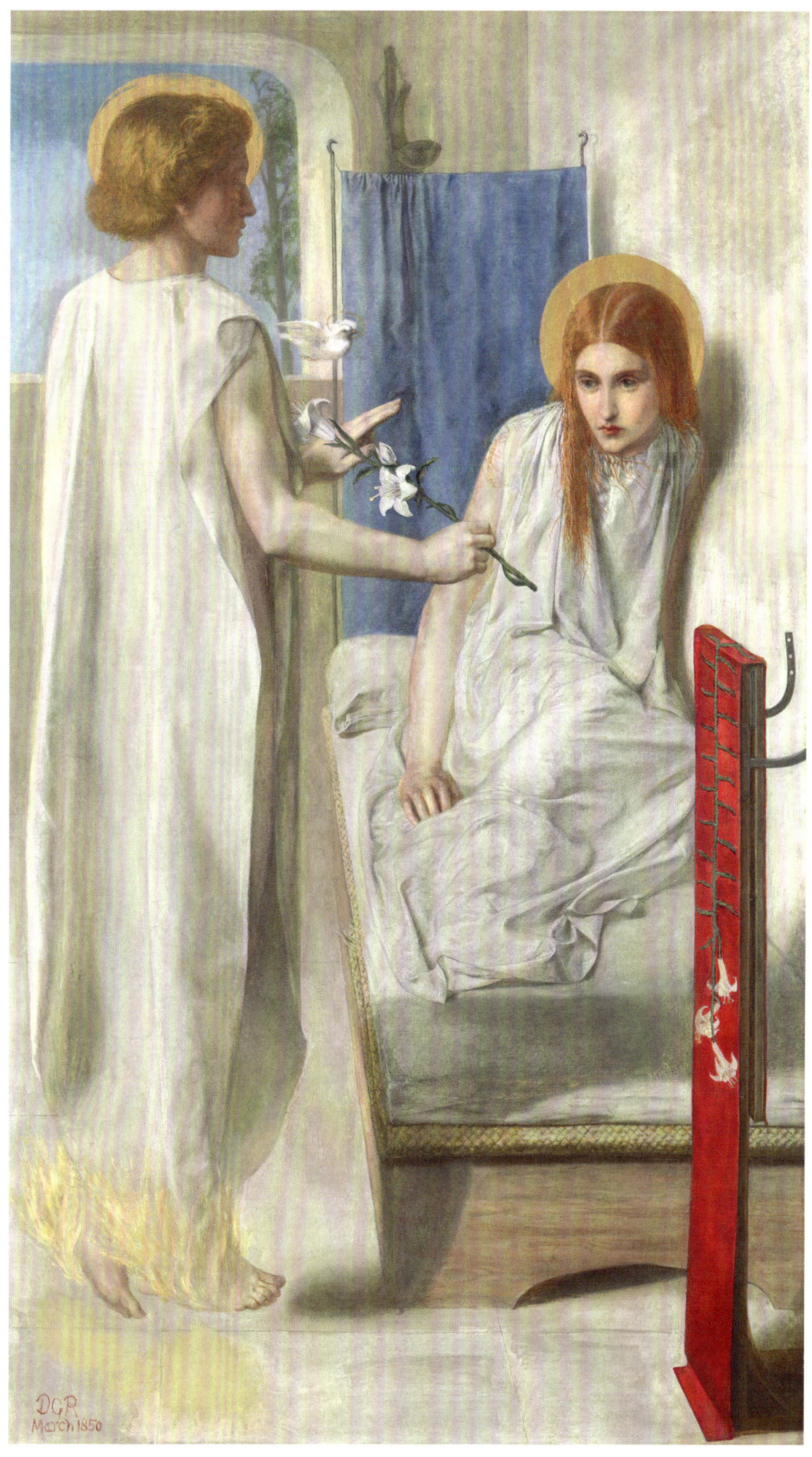

18 (below left)
William Michael Rossetti
Christina Rossetti, c.1853
Pencil on paper, 181 × 127mm
Cleveland Museum of Art

19 (below right)
Mrs Frances Rossetti
Christina Rossetti, 1853
Pencil on paper, 290 × 200mm
Jane Cohen

20 (opposite)
**Goblin Market and
Other Poems**
Christina Rossetti, 1865
Book (2nd edition)
172 × 115mm
British Museum, London

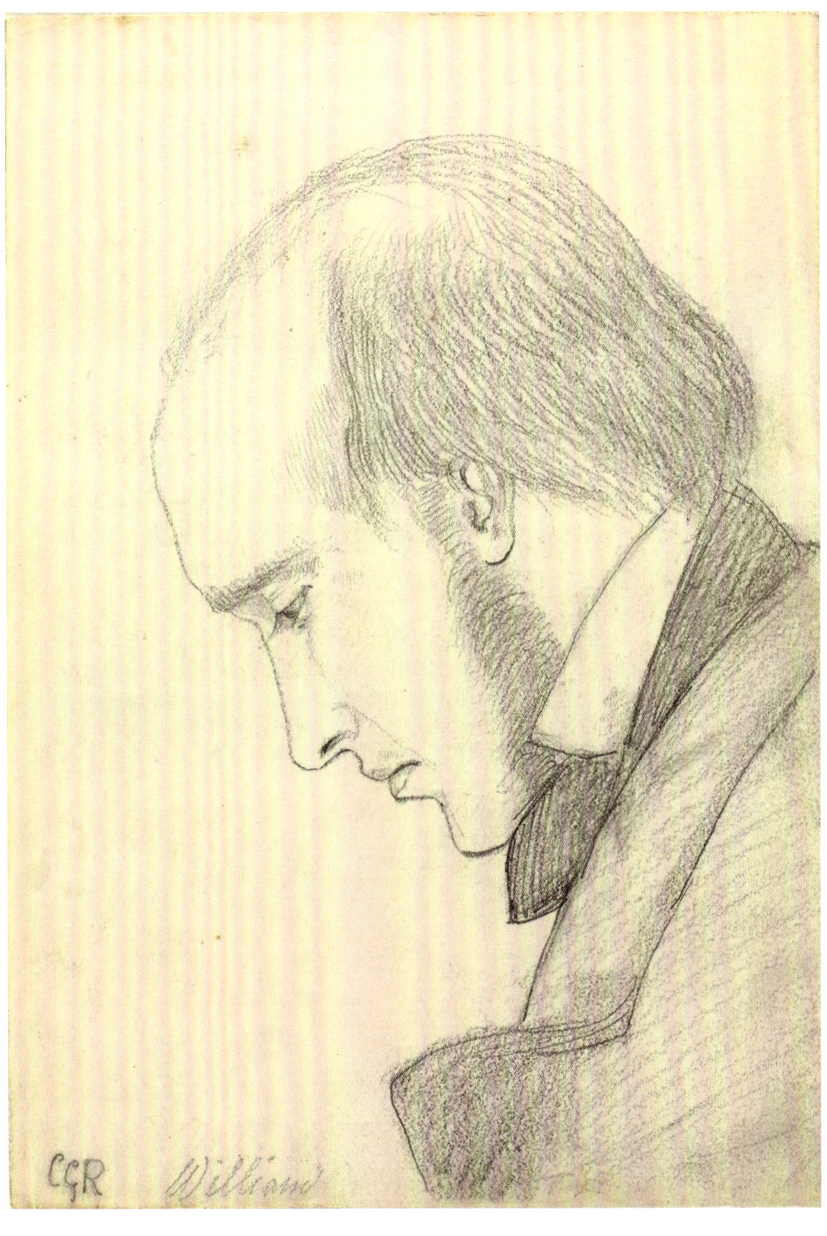

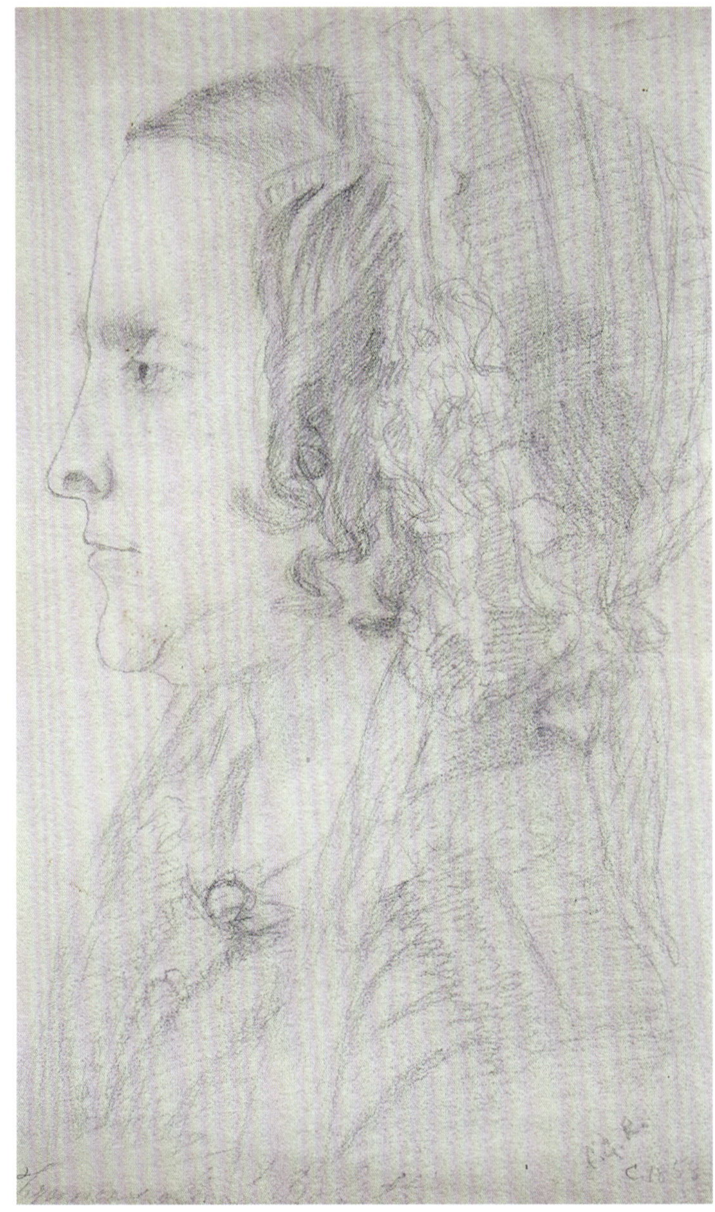

In 1850 Rossetti became a major contributor to the PRB magazine, *The Germ*, which ran from January to April that year. Her early poems, 'Dreamland', 'A Pause of Thought' and 'Repining' as well as 'Song', all written in her late teens, were among the most notable of its contents:

> Oh! roses for the flush of youth,
> And laurel for the perfect prime;
> But pluck an ivy-branch for me,
> Grown old before my time.
>
> Oh! violets for the grave of youth,
> And bay for those dead in their prime;
> Give me the withered leaves I chose
> Before in the old time.

Laurel and bay symbolise the literary achievement to which she aspired. At the same time, young women were instructed in self-denial: 'Not to be first,' began

Then, in 1853, when Hunt departed for the Holy Land, Millais was elected to the RA, and her brother Gabriel failed to exhibit, Christina Rossetti correspondingly lamented the Brotherhood's dissolution in lines that suggest her feelings of keen regret:

> The PRB is in its decadence:
> … So rivers merge in the perpetual sea;
> So luscious fruit must fall when over-ripe,
> And so the consummated PRB.

Much like early Pre-Raphaelite art, her poems range through devotional invocations, heartfelt romance and dramatic fantasy. They offer verbal analogues for the pictorial images and often provided inspiration for later artists and illustrators. Prompted by the PRB commitment to interdisciplinary practice, she joined an art class run by Madox Brown, and drew portraits (ills 18 and 19) and sketches, but she displayed no lasting

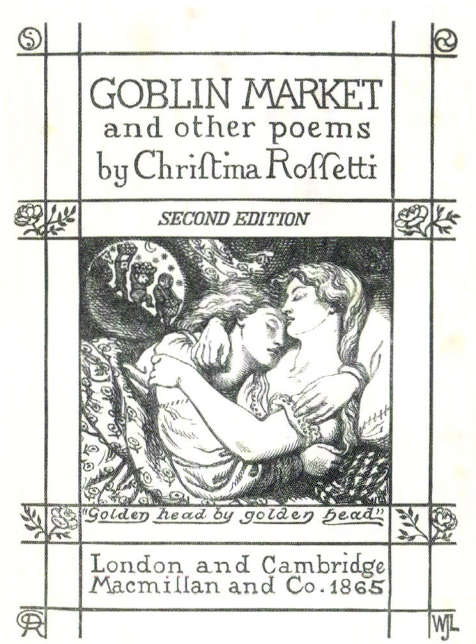

'The faith in the divine flamed out in her with a mild radiance which had in it no earthly warmth'

another poem; 'how hard to learn That lifelong lesson of the past.'

After Collinson had resigned from the Brotherhood to join a Catholic community – also ending their engagement – she hailed the remaining PRBs with doggerel homage:

> The two Rossettis (brothers they)
> And Holman Hunt and John Millais,
> With Stephens chivalrous and bland,
> And Woolner in a distant land,
> In these six men I awestruck see
> Embodied the great P.R.B.
> D.G.Rossetti offered two
> Good pictures to the public view:
> Unnumbered ones great John Millais,
> And Holman more than I can say.

aptitude, later confessing a limited liking for visual art.

From 1842, Rossetti's completed poems were neatly copied into small notebooks, confirming her vocation as 'the poet in the family'. Composed in December 1856, her sonnet 'In an Artist's Studio' records visits to Gabriel's apartment near London's Blackfriars Bridge, with its numerous images of Elizabeth Siddal (ills 10 and 15), 'matchless in beauty', according to Madox Brown.[3] Notable for its cool assessment of the images – 'Not as she is, but as she was when hope shone bright / Not as she is but as she fills his dream' – the sonnet was omitted from her first collection in 1862, no doubt owing to its plainly personal

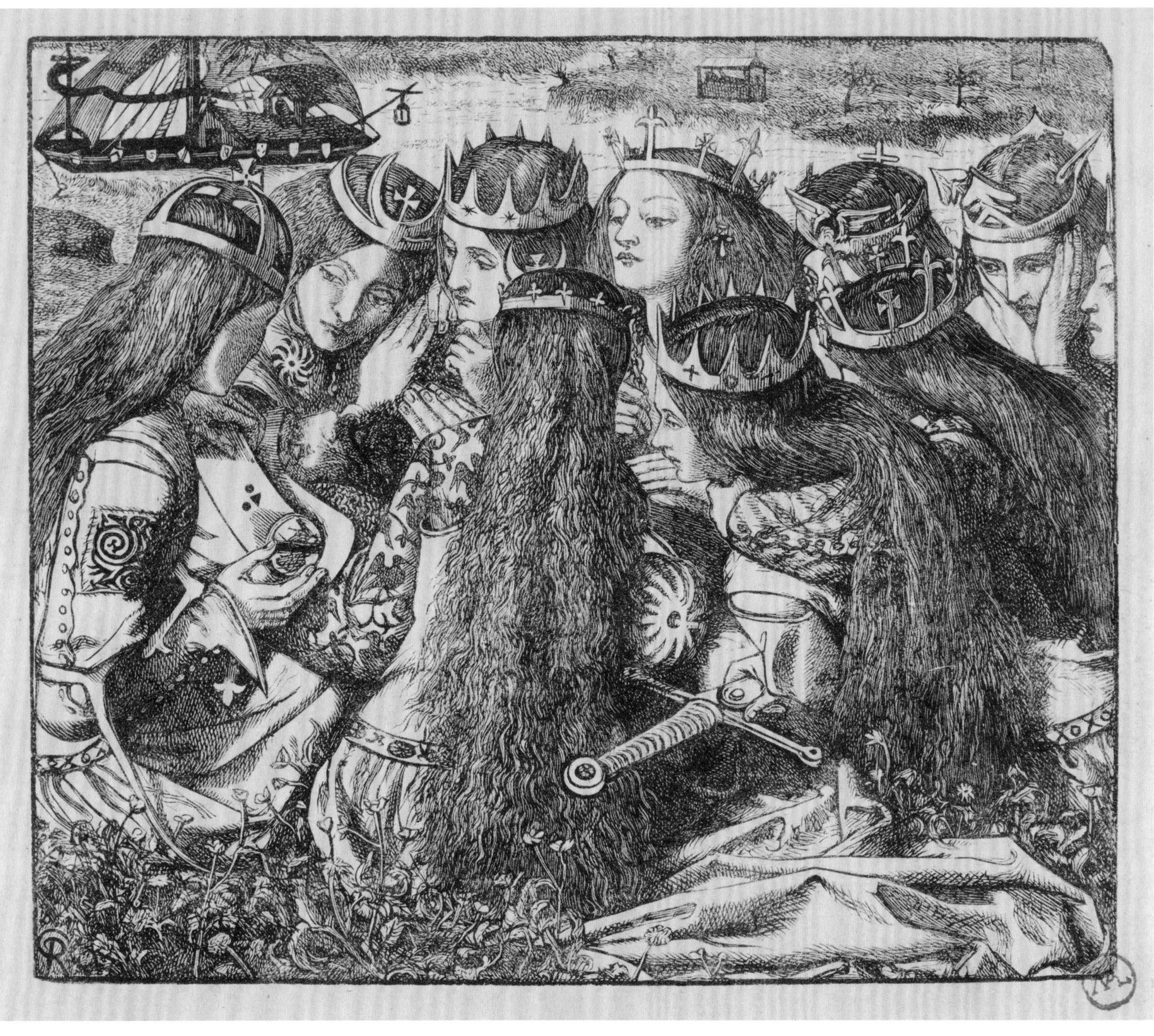

reference, Siddal having recently died. Christina Rosetti had first met Siddal in 1853, and when Gabriel Rossetti contributed illustrations to a new edition of Tennyson's *Poems*, he used them both as models for the bevy of 'weeping queens' shown attending King Arthur to the isle of Avalon (ill.21). Christina is second from left, Siddal fifth.

Lyricism and teasing humour are at play throughout Rossetti's verse, although there is much that is melancholic. Her well-known poems include 'Up-hill', 'A Cristmas Carol' (In the Bleak Midwinter), and 'Remember', which ends:

> Yet if you should forget me for a while
> And afterwards remember, do not grieve
> For if the darkness and corruption leave
> A vestige of the thoughts that once I had,
> Better by far you should forget and smile
> Than that you should remember and be sad.

Rossetti assisted her mother in educating Madox Brown's daughter Lucy and later undertook voluntary work with girls sexually 'at risk'. This prompted her now famous poem 'Goblin Market', about sisters tempted by fair-seeming fruits: 'Taste them and try: / Currants and gooseberries, / Bright-fire-like barberries, / Figs to fill your mouth, / Citrons from the South, / Sweet to tongue and sound to eye; / Come buy, come buy.'

The success of 'Goblin Market' (ill.20) in 1862 compensated for earlier disappointment and secured her reputation as the leading female poet, in succession to Elizabeth Barrett Browning. Its originality responded to the verse of Blake, Keats and Tennyson, and in turn influenced Swinburne, Gerard Manley Hopkins and Emily Dickinson. It was also much admired by Robert Browning and Virginia Woolf.

On 7 October 1863 Charles Lutwidge Dodgson, best known as the author Lewis Carroll and a pioneer photographer, asked the Rossetti family to sit to him. In the garden of Gabriel's house in Chelsea, several poses were arranged, including the unique image that includes her sister Maria (ill.22). 'It was our aim to appear in the full family group of five,' Christina Rossetti recalled; 'but that particular negative was spoiled by a shower [and] we appear as if splashed by ink.'[4] The streaks, in fact, result from mishandling of the photographic chemicals.

Acknowledging the encouraging influence of 'Goblin Market' on his own fantasy fiction, Dodgson would later send her a copy of *Alice in Wonderland*, to receipt of which she responded:

> A thousand and one thanks – surely an appropriate number – for the funny pretty book you have sent. My mother and sister as well as myself have made ourselves quite at home yesterday in Wonderland and (if I am not shamefully old for such an avowal) I confess it would give me sincere pleasure to fall in with that conversational rabbit, that endearing puppy, that very sparkling dormouse.[5]

Several of Rossetti's ballad poems dramatise the 'fallen woman' theme, while others rework familiar tales or invoke complex affections. Many share the playful tone of 'Promises like Pie-crust':

> Promise me no promises,
> So will I not promise you:
> Keep we both our liberties,
> Never false and never true:
> Let us hold the die uncast,
> Free to come as free to go:
> For I cannot know your past,
> And of mine, what can you know?

Elsewhere, the verbal blend of direct address, gossamer texture, elusive meaning and vivid imagery offers a link between Romantic, Aesthetic and Symbolist writing, echoing biblical cadences and foreshadowing modern abstraction. As well as three poetic collections, she published a book of nursery verses, several short fictions and tales for children and continued with religious studies and mystical poems – even as the tide of faith ebbed away from the Victorian world.

A fine, large 'exquisite drawing…by the pencil of a partial brother' (ill.23) shows Rossetti at the age of 35, soon after the issue, in 1866, of her second collection, *The Prince's Progress and Other Poems*.[6] She is seen in contemplative mood, with an open book of verse. The image is distinguished by its compelling sobriety, especially when compared with portraits of Fanny Cornforth (ill.56) and Jane Morris (ill.80). Publication of the collection was delayed by having to

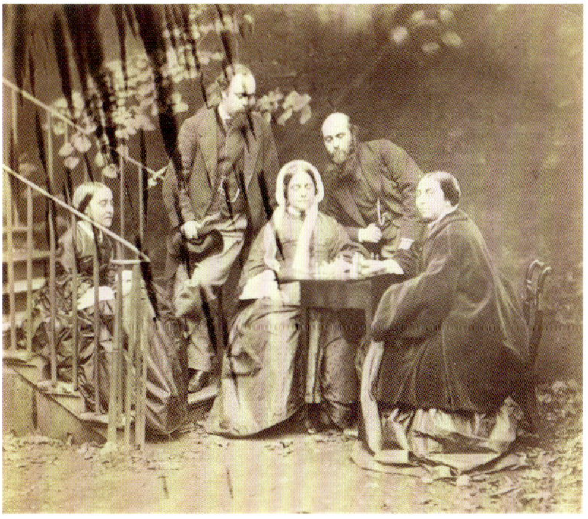

23 (below left and p. 35)
Christina Rossetti
Dante Gabriel Rossetti, 1866
Coloured chalk on paper
790 × 635mm
Private Collection

24 (below right)
**Christina Georgina
Rossetti in a Tantrum**
Dante Gabriel Rossetti, 1862
Pen and wash on paper
220 × 180mm
National Trust Collections,
Wightwick Manor and Gardens,
Warwickshire

25 (opposite)
**Christina Rossetti; Frances
Mary Lavinia Rossetti**
Dante Gabriel Rossetti, 1877
Chalk on paper, 425 × 483mm
National Portrait Gallery

wait for Gabriel's two illustrations, and the book's reception was further affected by association with Swinburne's controversial *Poems and Ballads*. Possibly, the portrait of Rossetti by her brother was drawn to defuse her wrath at his tardiness.

In childhood, Christina Rossetti was notorious for her tempestuous outbursts, struggling to control 'ebullitions' of anger. An earlier affectionate sketch by Gabriel Rossetti (ill. 24) depicts her in a comic rage, in an image signally at odds with her public reputation for emotional restraint. This sketch was prompted by a review stating that her poetry 'could not be mended'.

Increasingly, Rossetti's devotional fervour created distance from the Pre-Raphaelite circle. According to the withering assessment of William Stillman: 'the faith in the divine flamed out in her with a mild radiance which had in it no earthly warmth'.[7] After 1870 her social life was further curtailed by ill health and then by Gabriel's paranoid breakdown, which estranged him from old friends.

Drawn when Rossetti and her mother were caring for Gabriel during a psychotic episode, the gloomy mood of his portrait of 1877 (ill. 25) matches that of both sitters and artist. She described her brother 'in an attitude of dreadful dejection with drooping head'.[8] Her own spirits were low, too; in 'Summer is Ended' she wrote: 'To think that this meaningless thing was ever a rose: Scentless, colourless, this! / Will it ever be thus (who knows?) / Thus with our bliss / If we wait till the close?'

For some years, she had suffered from a thyroid condition that caused persistent fatigue and bulging eyes, as indicated here. This double portrait, in fact, marked a partial recovery for her brother, who, by the year's end, returned to painting and poetry. However, her own last years were spent caring for her aunts and her mother, before she herself succumbed to cancer.

My harvest is done, its promise is ended,
Weak and watery sets the sun,
Day and night in one mist are blended,
My harvest is done...
Was it narrow the way that I wended?
Snares and pits was it mine to shun?
The scythe has fallen, so long suspended,
My harvest is done.

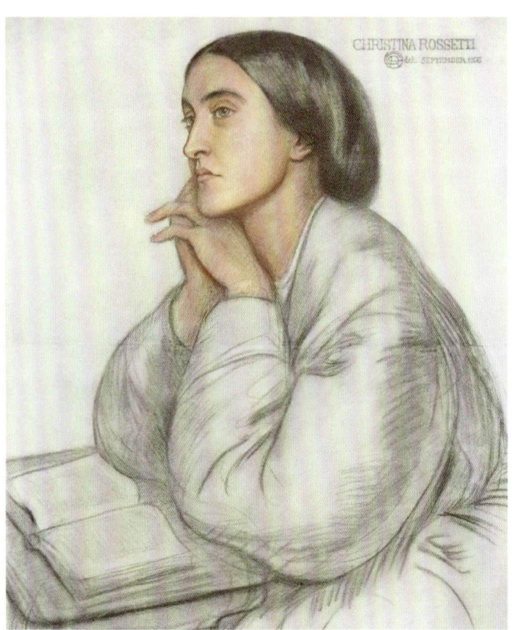

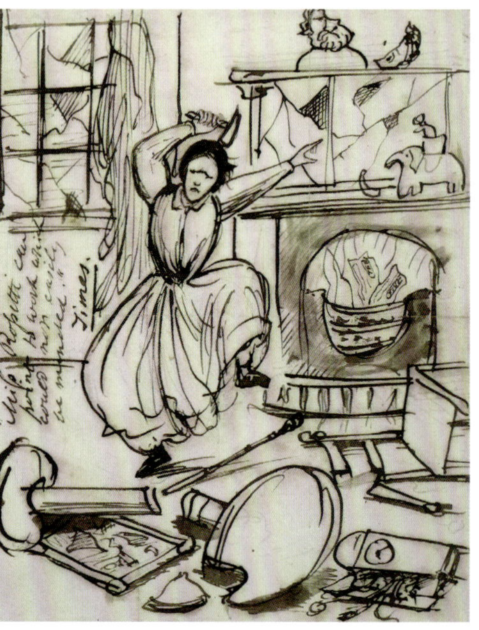

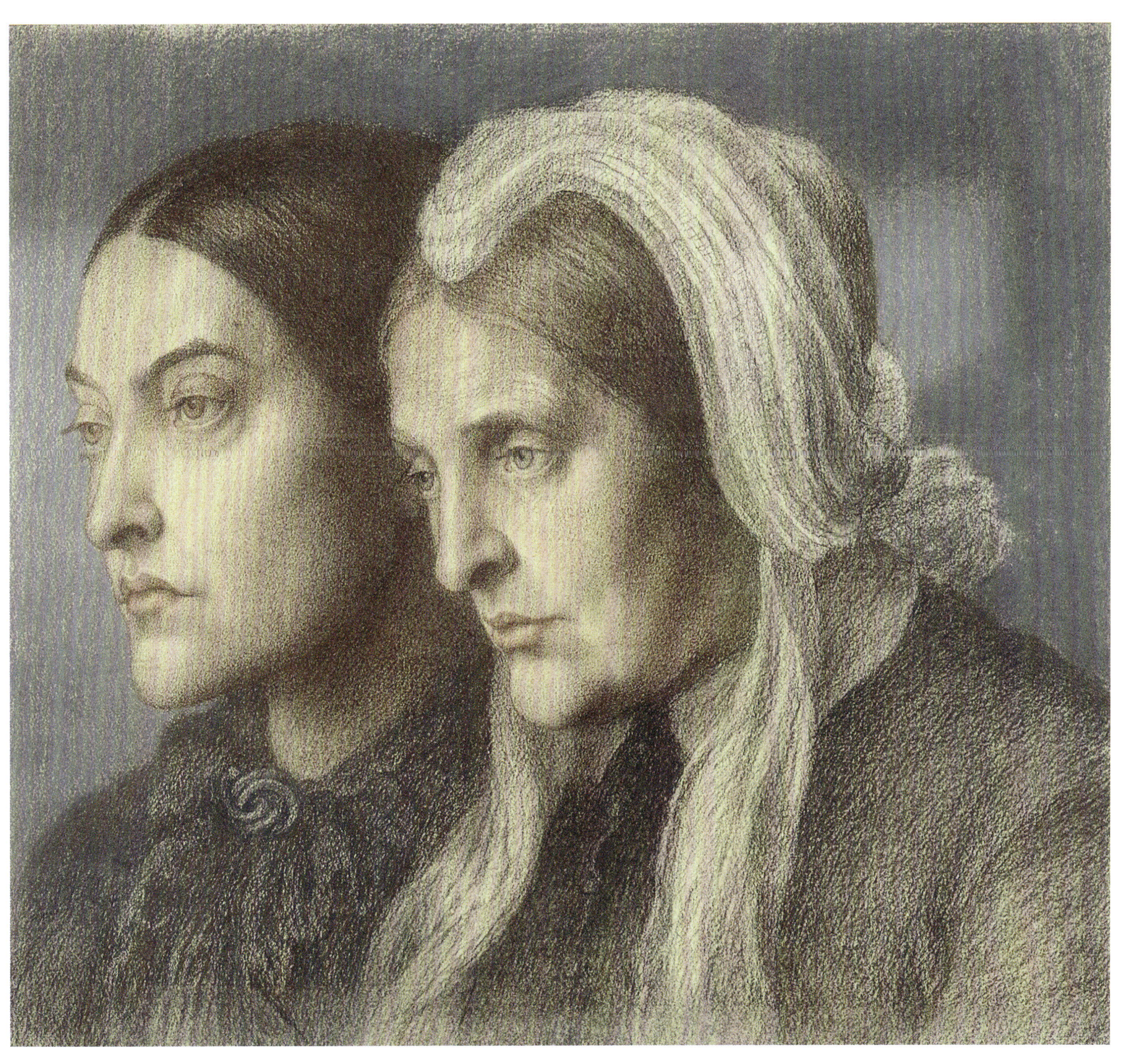

Effie Gray Millais

1828–1897

Euphemia 'Effie' Gray was born in May 1828, in Perth, Scotland, the eldest of eight surviving children. Her introduction to the art world was in London, in 1847, when staying with the family of John Ruskin. Together they visited the Painted Hall at Greenwich, Dulwich Picture Gallery, the new Houses of Parliament and St James's Palace to view Franz Xaver Winterhalter's portrait of the Royal Family. They met J.M.W. Turner, Joseph Severn, Charles Newton, George Richmond 'and other eminent artists who John was so kind to ask that I might meet them'.[1] About Ruskin, to her parents she wrote, 'John is such a queer being, he hates going out and likes painting all day.'[2]

By autumn they were engaged. In letters, Ruskin envisaged his fiancée – an accomplished amateur watercolourist (see ill. 26) – as his architectural researcher who would make:

> unpretending little memoranda of a capital here, an ornament there, a quaint piece of costume, or a graceful line of mosaic…so that in time I should be able to say to you – 'Effie, I want those three capitals, and a bit of that frieze, will you please do them for me while I go up and examine the vaulting?' And that you would do them for me with great pleasure to yourself, and more neatness and accuracy than any architect![3]

They married in 1848. However, on their first 'working tour' in Normandy, where he researched cathedrals for *The Seven Lamps of Architecture* (1849), she was not asked to sketch any capital or frieze but spent her days reading and strolling, while her husband measured and compared.

In London, the pair entered into the London Season, which pleased his ambitious parents. Among other fashionable events, they visited Turner's gallery, 'where we saw such pictures. I would pawn all I had for the "Old Temeraire"', she wrote; 'a Steamer drawing a wreck through calm water and such a sunset as you never see in any pictures but his own'.[4] Taking a town house in London's Mayfair, John wrote while Effie performed the wifely duties of receiving and returning calls, which were necessary to establish her husband's professional

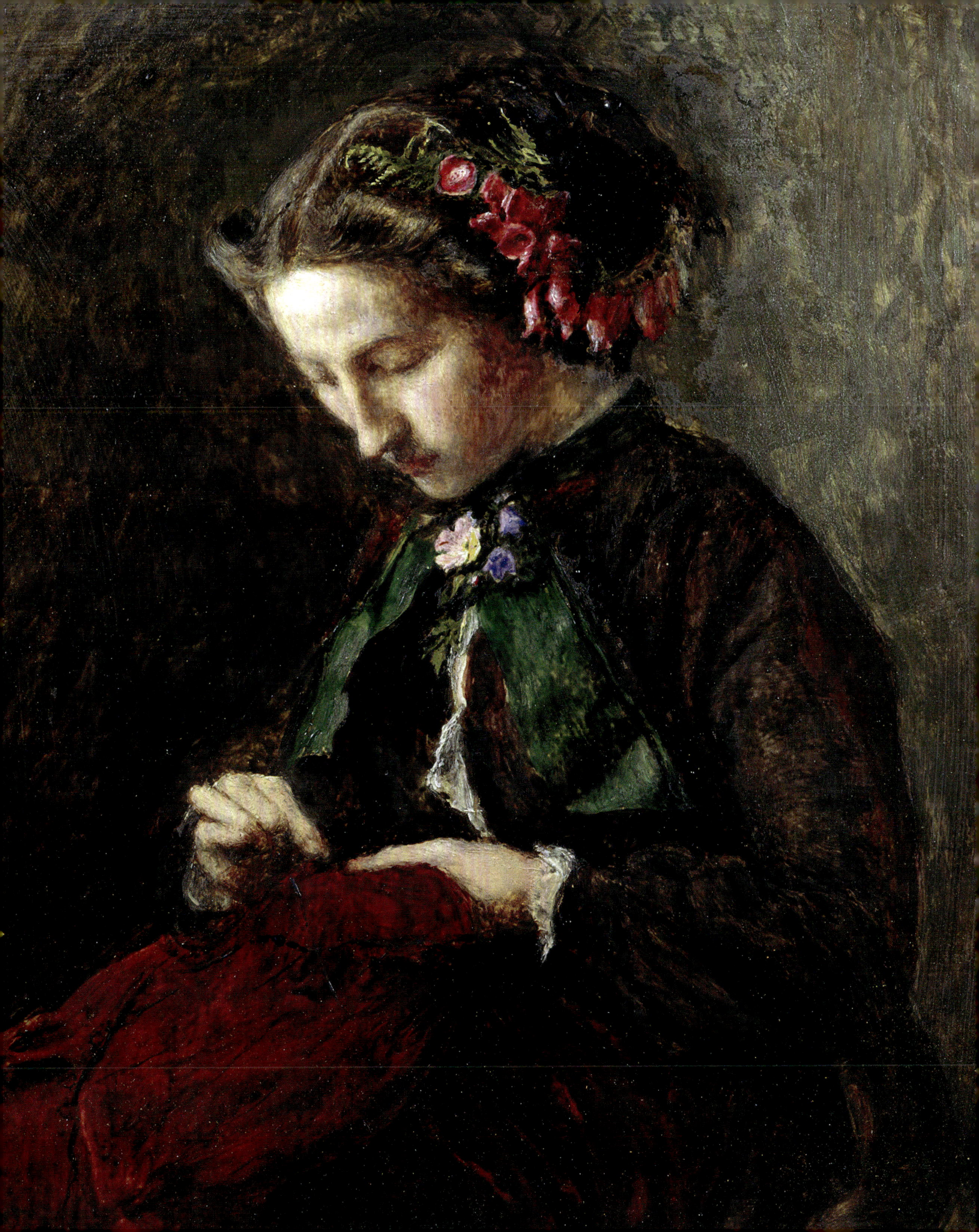

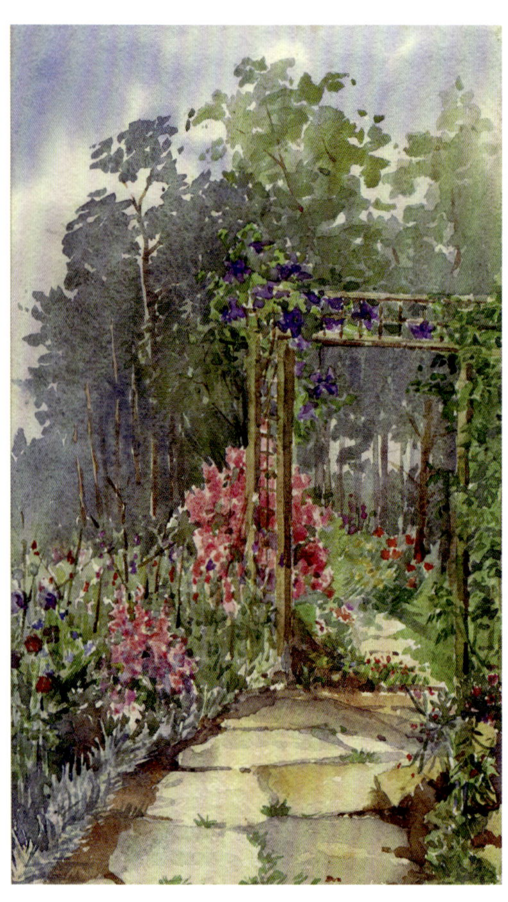

26
**Garden Path
with Rose Arch**
Attrib. Effie Ruskin, undated
Watercolour, 330 × 200mm
The Ruskin,
Lancaster University

27
Effie Ruskin
Thomas Richmond, 1851
Oil on board, 810 × 530mm
National Portrait Gallery

reputation. She cultivated Sir Charles Lock Eastlake, then President of the RA, and sat for her portrait to artists G.F. Watts and Thomas Richmond. Commissioned by her father-in-law, Richmond's painting (ill. 27) portrays Effie Ruskin in conventionally demure mode, standing on a fictive balcony, wearing a velvet paletot jacket over an evening gown. 'It is the most lovely piece of oil painting but much prettier than me,' she told her mother. 'I look like a graceful Doll, but John and his father are delighted with it.'[5] The artist was paid £20 in wine from the Ruskin firm.

As the world came to know, John refused to consummate their marriage, which caused 'tears and depression', interpreted by him as a nervous disorder; this, he explained, prevented his new wife from joining their next European tour. When it suited him, she 'must be prepared to part with me for a month or two' (four in fact).[6] When, in 1849, they went to Venice together, she had a friend as companion, while her husband

[T]hat strange disorder of the mind or the eyes which continues to rage with unabated absurdity among a class of juvenile artists who style themselves 'P.R.B.,'…the authors of these offensive and absurd productions have contrived to combine the puerility or infancy of their art with the uppishness and self-sufficiency of a different period of life. That morbid infatuation which sacrifices truth, beauty, and genuine feeling to mere eccentricity, deserves no quarter at the hands of the public.[9]

As art critic, John Ruskin came to the defence:

The pre-Raphaelites intend to surrender no advantage which the knowledge or inventions of the present time can afford to their art. They intend to return to early days in this one point only – that, as far as in them lies, they will draw either what they see, or what they suppose might have been the actual facts of

'I look like a graceful Doll, but John and his father are delighted with it'

researched his next book, *The Stones of Venice* (1851–3). 'I could hardly see less of him than I do at present', she reported.[7]

In 1850, she met Thackeray, Carlyle, Dickens and Gladstone, and made friends with Elizabeth Eastlake. Faithfully standing in for a husband who loathed social life, she reported that: 'He has given me a general order to refuse all invitations for him and go out everywhere I like which I am very happy to do.'[8]

The following year, that of the Great Exhibition in London's Hyde Park, the works of the Pre-Raphaelite Brotherhood were attacked in the press. 'We cannot censure as amply or as strongly as we desire to do,' declared *The Times*:

the scene they desire to represent, irrespective of any conventional rules of picture making.[10]

He concluded a second letter hoping that

if they do not suffer themselves to be driven by harsh or careless criticism into rejection of the ordinary means of obtaining influence over the minds of others, they may, as they gain experience, lay in our England the foundations of a school of art nobler than the world has seen for 300 years.[11]

Millais and Hunt sent their thanks, which prompted a visit from the Ruskins, who

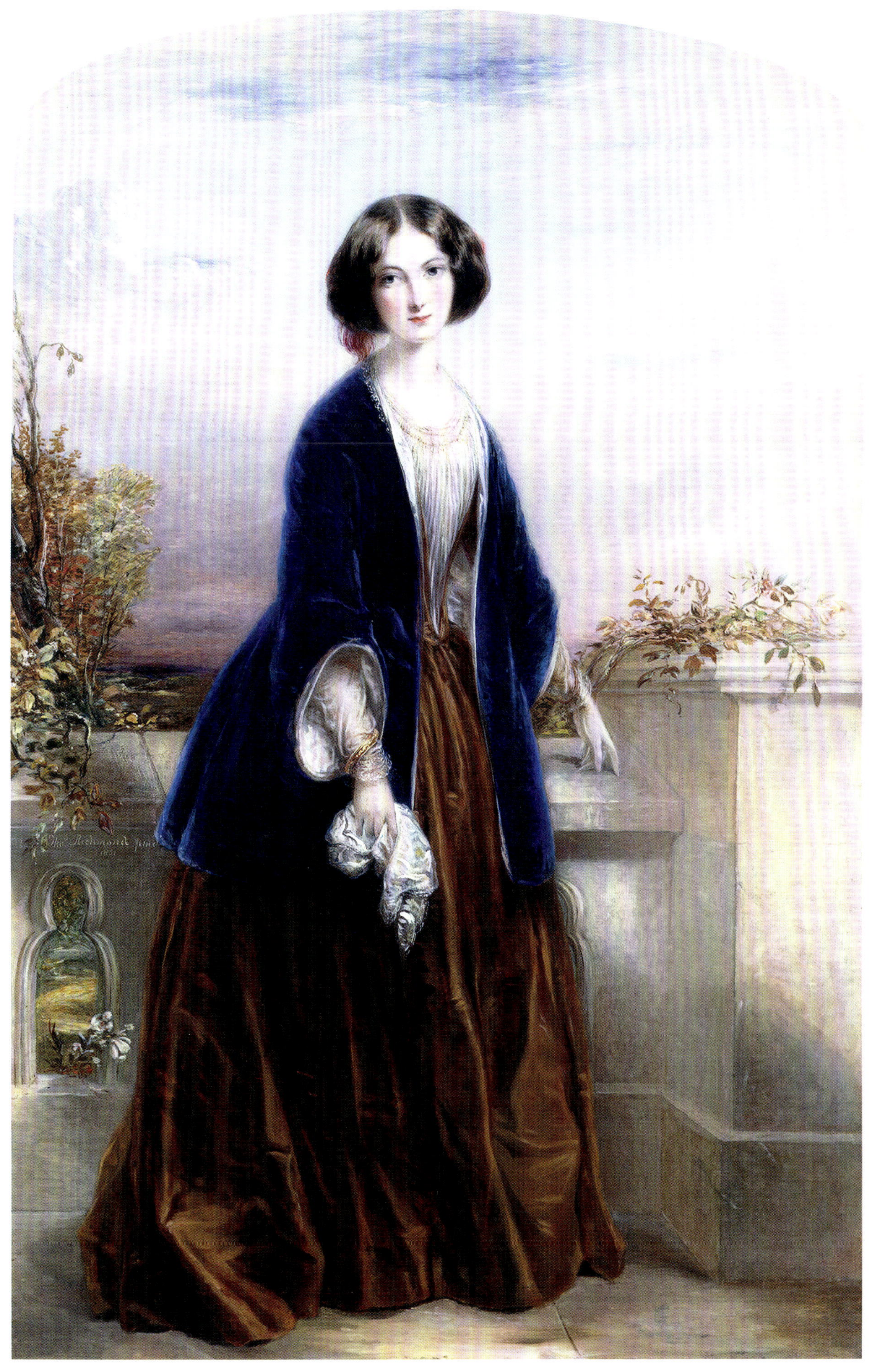

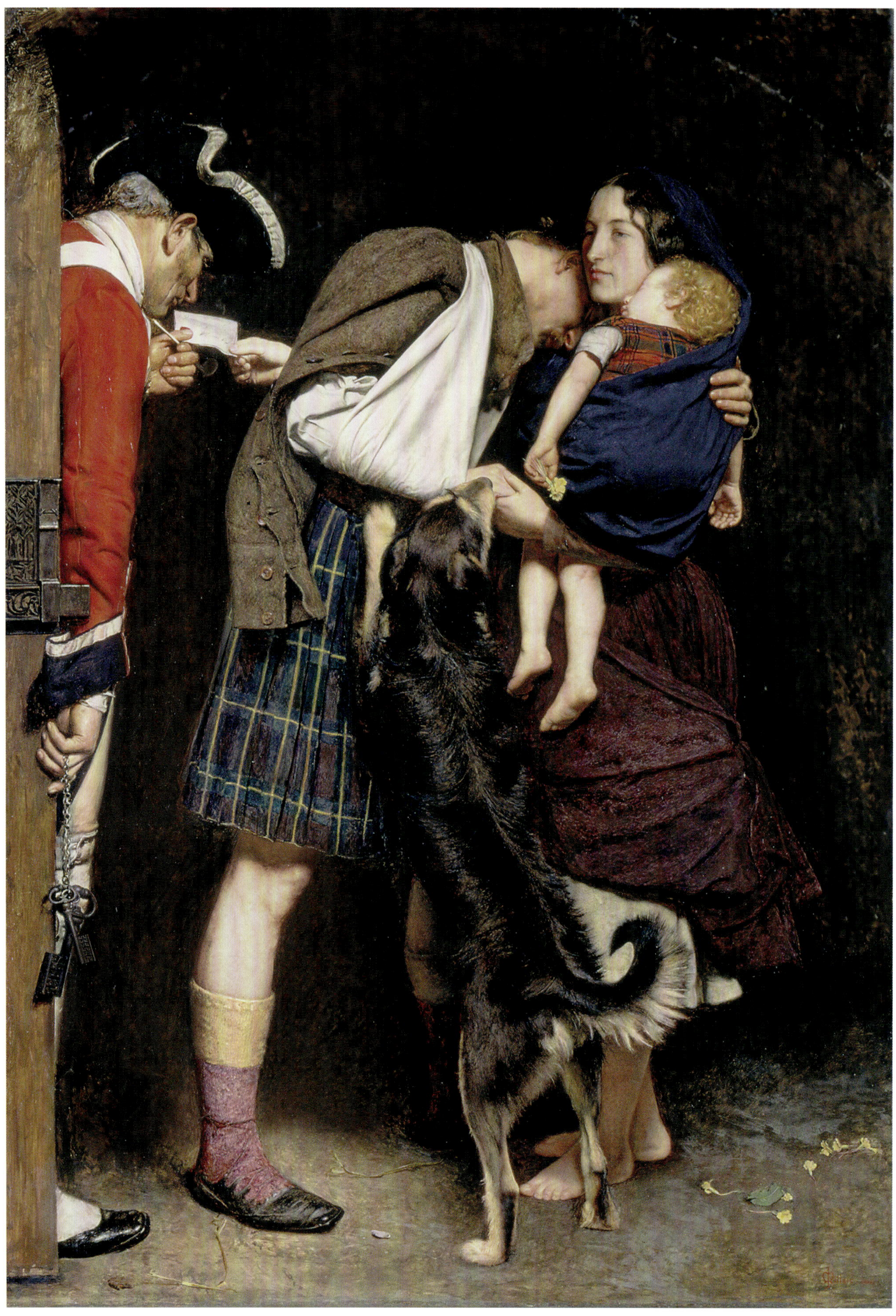

were about to depart again for Venice.
The acquaintance deepened a year later,
when Millais's *Ophelia* and *A Huguenot*
(both 1852) were exhibited, and the
Ruskins commissioned him to paint a worthy
successor. The result was *The Order of
Release, 1746* (ill. 28). The painting's theme
of romantic fidelity echoes that in Millais's
A Huguenot. To please his important
new patrons, Millais proposed that the
highlander's wife be drawn from Effie
Ruskin; the subject was in keeping with her
Jacobite sympathies, and the incident was
perhaps drawn from the tale of a 'common
highlander' from her home town of Perth,
imprisoned after Culloden.[12] Her face was
painted on to the canvas at the Ruskins'
home in March 1853.

This was her first experience of posing
as a model rather than a portrait sitter, and
she conflated the two, writing on 20 March
1853: '[Millais] found my head like everyone
else who has tried it immensely difficult and
he was greatly delighted last night when he
said he had quite got it! He paints so slowly
and finely that no man working as he does
can paint faster.'[13]

The painting provided a new focus of
interest, which mitigated her in-laws' fault-
finding, her husband's increasing coldness
and the extinguished prospect of children.
No doubt she welcomed the plan for Millais
and his artist elder brother William to join
her and her husband in Scotland while
Ruskin prepared lectures and Millais painted
the background for a portrait of him. Rooms
were booked in the village of Brig o'Turk in
Stirlingshire. Effie aimed to make everyone
'as comfortable as I can' and smiled at the
Millais brothers' metropolitan assumption
that all supplies would be locally available,
as she packed 'a great hamper of sherry
and tea and sugar'.[14] She expected the three
men to spend the days outdoors, while she
supervised the domestic scene.

However, after the burnside location
for the portrait was chosen, Ruskin retreated
to his lectures. This left the Millais brothers
to entertain his wife, who enjoyed their
youthful energy in walking, scrambling and
damming streams, and their boyish courtesy
in calling her 'Countess'. Millais painted her
portrait (ill. 30) – intended for, but never
sent to John Ruskin – which she delicately
and skilfully copied (ill. 31) and signed.

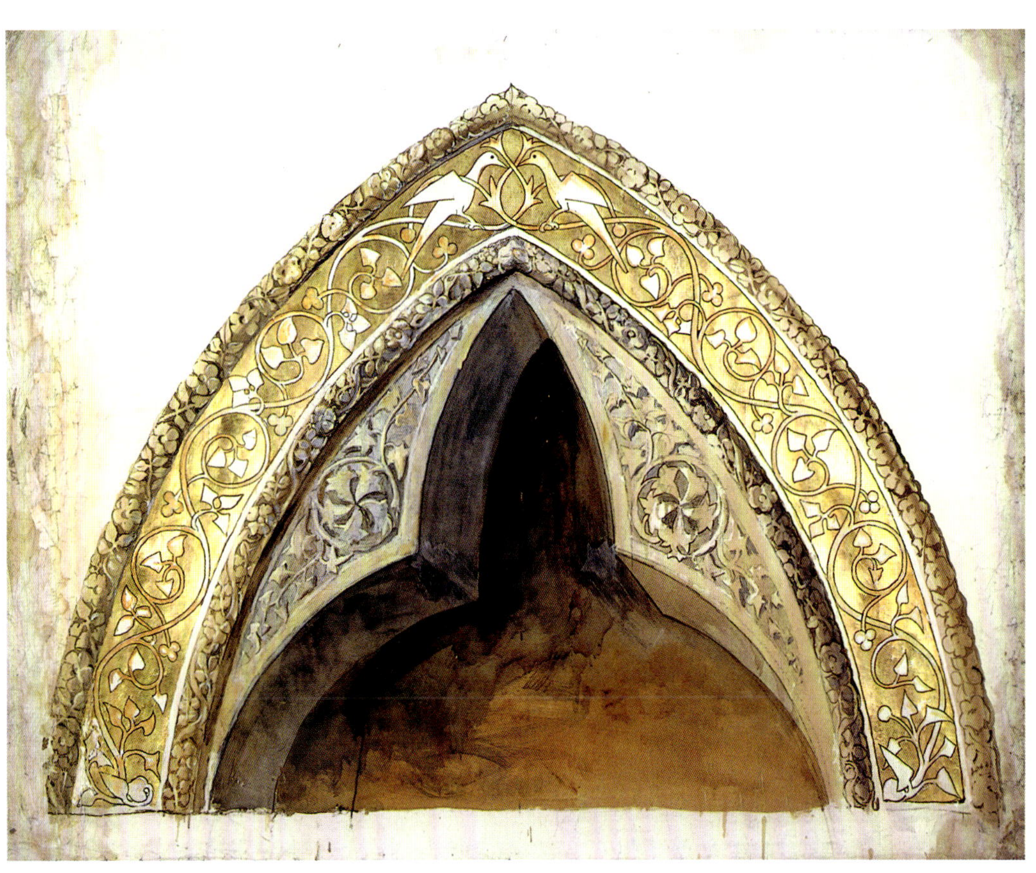

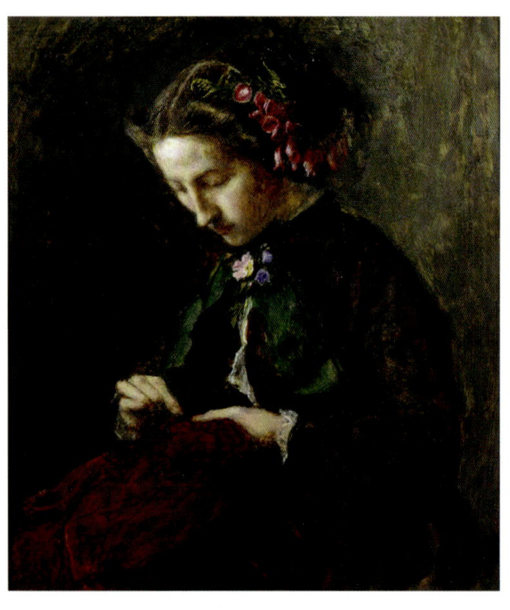

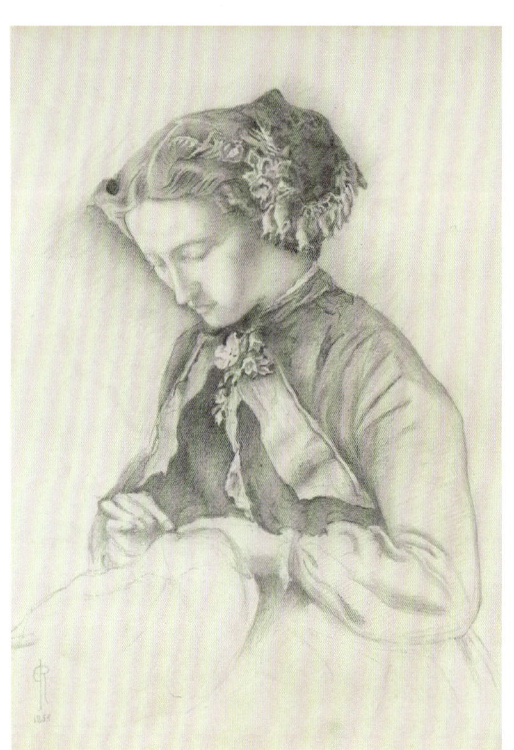

Millais also documented their activities in humorous drawings (ills 32–4), which convey a growing intimacy. In *The Countess as Barber* (ill. 32) she trims his hair while he nurses a bandaged hand, injured building a dam. His later letters express anger at the 'wretchedness' of Effie Ruskin's position, owing to her husband's indifference.[15]

She assisted with her husband's lectures, given in Edinburgh that autumn, tracing and colouring with pigment and gold paint a large drawing of a cusped Gothic window (ill. 29), and greeting the audiences.

Returning to London for New Year 1854, she was warned that her in-laws were scheming to have her declared mentally unfit, so her young sister Sophy became chaperone and witness against their hostility. Sophy Gray (ill. 35), who later posed tending a bonfire for Millais's painting *Autumn Leaves* (1855–6), also acted as a vital line of communication with Millais, who kept away, lest he be accused.

his desire to marry if she were free, despite the inevitable threat to his reputation from scandal and slander. In the event, he also sacrificed some friends, feeling he could not remain on good terms with any who refused to fall out with John Ruskin.

Reverting to her birth name, in July 1855 she became known as Effie Millais, when she married John Everett Millais (whom she always called 'Everett' to distinguish him from Ruskin) and so began her long, unofficial career as assistant and colleague. According to their son, John Guille Millais, she always

took the keenest interest in his work and did all in her power to contribute to his success, taking upon herself not only the care of the household and the management of the family affairs, but the great bulk of his correspondence and saving him an infinity of trouble by personally ascertaining the objects of his callers (an ever-increasing multitude) before admitting them into his presence.[16]

'She took the keenest interest in his work and did all in her power to contribute to his success'

At what stage and how their mutual feeling was manifested is not known, but he sent an illustration of Tennyson's poem 'St Agnes' Eve', which they had read together at Brig o'Turk. When Sophy Gray reported that Ruskin claimed his wife had ensnared Millais and deserved 'harsh treatment,' Effie Ruskin sought Elizabeth Eastlake's advice, and when at last the facts of her marriage were shared, she took the decision to act. With her father's assistance the legal application for annulment was submitted and granted on 15 July.

She and Millais kept their collusion secret, for he must have already declared

Among the first guests were artists Charles Allston Collins, John Leech and Henry Tanworth Wells. As Millais later explained: 'my wife manages all arrangements of visitors, so she appends directions'.[17]

Equally importantly, she had both 'a considerable degree of the artistic sense' and valuable historical knowledge, so when a subject was projected 'she delighted to study anew the circumstance and the characters to be depicted, and to gather for her husband's use all particulars as to the scene and the costumes of the period'.[18] Her education, while typical of the time, was more extensive than her husband's,

30 (opposite above and p. 45)
Effie with Foxgloves in her Hair (The Foxglove)
John Everett Millais, 1853
Oil on millboard, 362 × 356mm
National Trust Collections,
Wightwick Manor and Gardens,
Warwickshire

31 (opposite below)
Copy of *The Foxglove*
Effie Ruskin, 1853
Pencil and grey wash on paper
255 × 205mm
Private Collection

32 (below)
The Countess as Barber
John Everett Millais, 1853
Pen and ink on wove paper
187 × 230mm
The Morgan Library & Museum,
New York

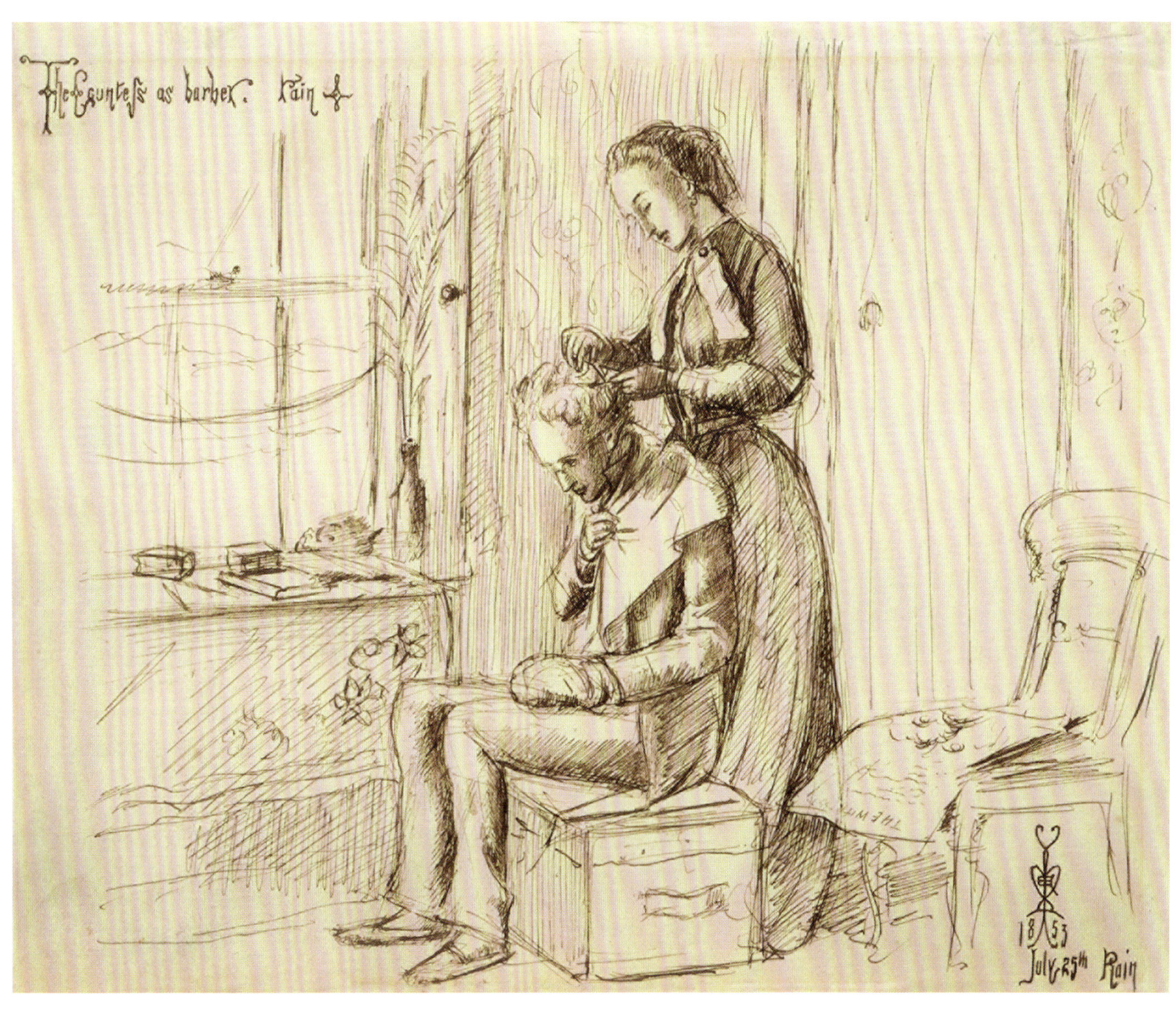

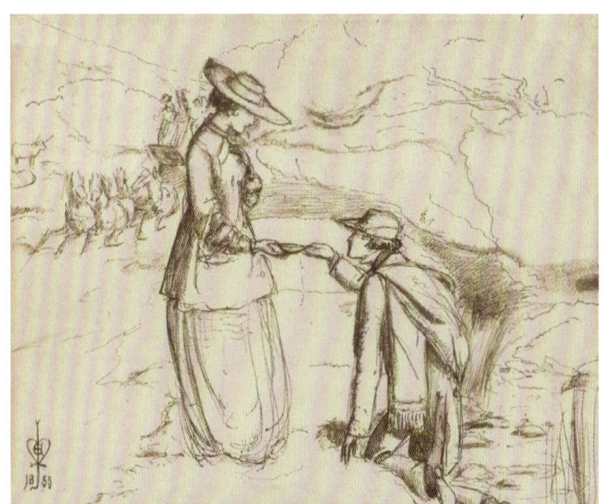

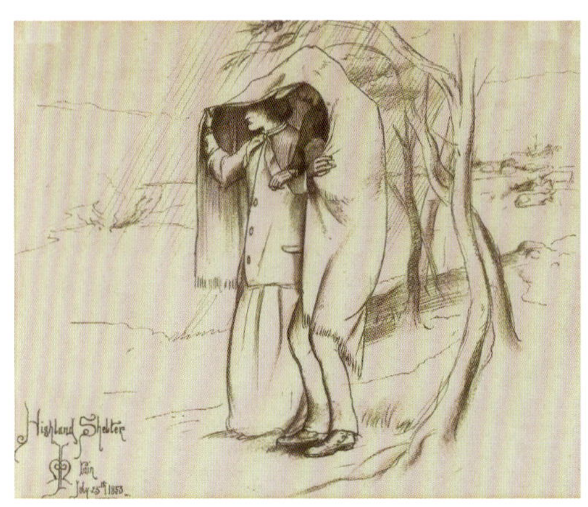

whose studies were all artistic, and it is likely that she often suggested subjects. As she noted, 'we toiled together' on these projects.[19] Her contributions were also practical. For *The Blind Girl* (1854–6), she boldly borrowed a skirt from an old woman in the street because it was the correct colour, and for *The Ransom* (1860–62) she travelled to a nearby castle to sketch details of a tapestry.

From 1855 she kept a notebook with details of each work in progress, listing the pictures of the year in order. Thus she recalled how the idea for *The Vale of Rest* (1858–9) first occurred on their Highland honeymoon, when they passed monastic ruins near Loch Awe and together imagined 'white-robed nuns in boats, singing on the water in the quiet summer evenings and chanting holy songs, inspired by the loveliness of the world around them'.[20]

She also recalled that her husband found the nun digging the grave a difficult figure: 'Every day for seven weeks he painted and repainted her, with the result that the figure was worse than ever and he was almost distracted.' Enlisting her mother's help, the canvas was locked in a cellar, where it stayed for some days – 'Millais furious, the conspirators placid, smiling, but firm' – until he took up another task; 'once calm, he was reunited with the picture and saw at a glance how to solve the problem.'[21]

Effie Millais's management of her husband's working practices has seldom been acknowledged, and her active role in the production of Pre-Raphaelite art has been ignored, but her collaboration was clearly effective, even, on occasion, in a negative sense, as recorded in 1858.

He began a last picture of a Crusader's return and stuck, after five months hard labour. I was much averse to his painting every Sunday, and thought no good would come of it… He made no progress, only getting into a great mess; so when spring came we were thankful to pack up the picture and go to Scotland [where] he occupied himself on his 'Spring' apple blossoms picture… This winter he has achieved an intensity of work, and I attribute his success greatly to his never working on Sunday all this year.[22]

For a while she continued to model for her husband – sitting, for example, for *Peace Concluded* (1856) and *The White Cockade* (1862), another Jacobite subject – but, increasingly, and during her eight pregnancies, professional models were employed. One notable exception was *The Eve of St Agnes* (see ill. 36), depicting John Keats's heroine Madeline disrobing in wintry moonlight, a favourite subject also depicted by Hunt and Arthur Hughes. In authentic Pre-Raphaelite mode, she posed for three nights in succession, enabling her husband to catch 'the spirit of the poet and embod[y] it in his canvas'.[23]

From 1861 the couple lived in London, in fashionable South Kensington, where Effie Millais energetically promoted her husband's career, entertaining and cultivating patrons. To one wealthy banker she suggested a portrait of his daughter, about to marry a marquess; tactfully, she also negotiated a fee of £2,000.[24] She has been blamed for the steady loosening of his style, but, as Pre-Raphaelite modes evolved, this was shared by other artists, eclipsing earlier precision.

Her own last sitting was in 1873 (ill. 37), when the grand mansion that complemented the Millais's rising status was being planned. Here, this portrait hung in the breakfast room, and here her role as business partner flourished, leading in time to her husband's election as President of the RA and her own elevation as Lady Millais. The painting shows her in her matronly mid-forties, some months after the stillbirth of her last child, when, not surprisingly, she looked 'elegant of figure, but worn'.[25] She holds a copy of the *Cornhill* magazine for August 1873, her finger resting on the decorative figure of a man threshing, signifying autumn. To their regret, John Ruskin's existence (albeit with severe dementia) precluded her acceptance at Court, which conventionally remained the pinnacle of social success. Always conscious of and grateful for his wife's share in their joint achievement, Millais arranged for a private audience with Queen Victoria, which was perhaps more gratifying. And their son inherited the baronetcy.

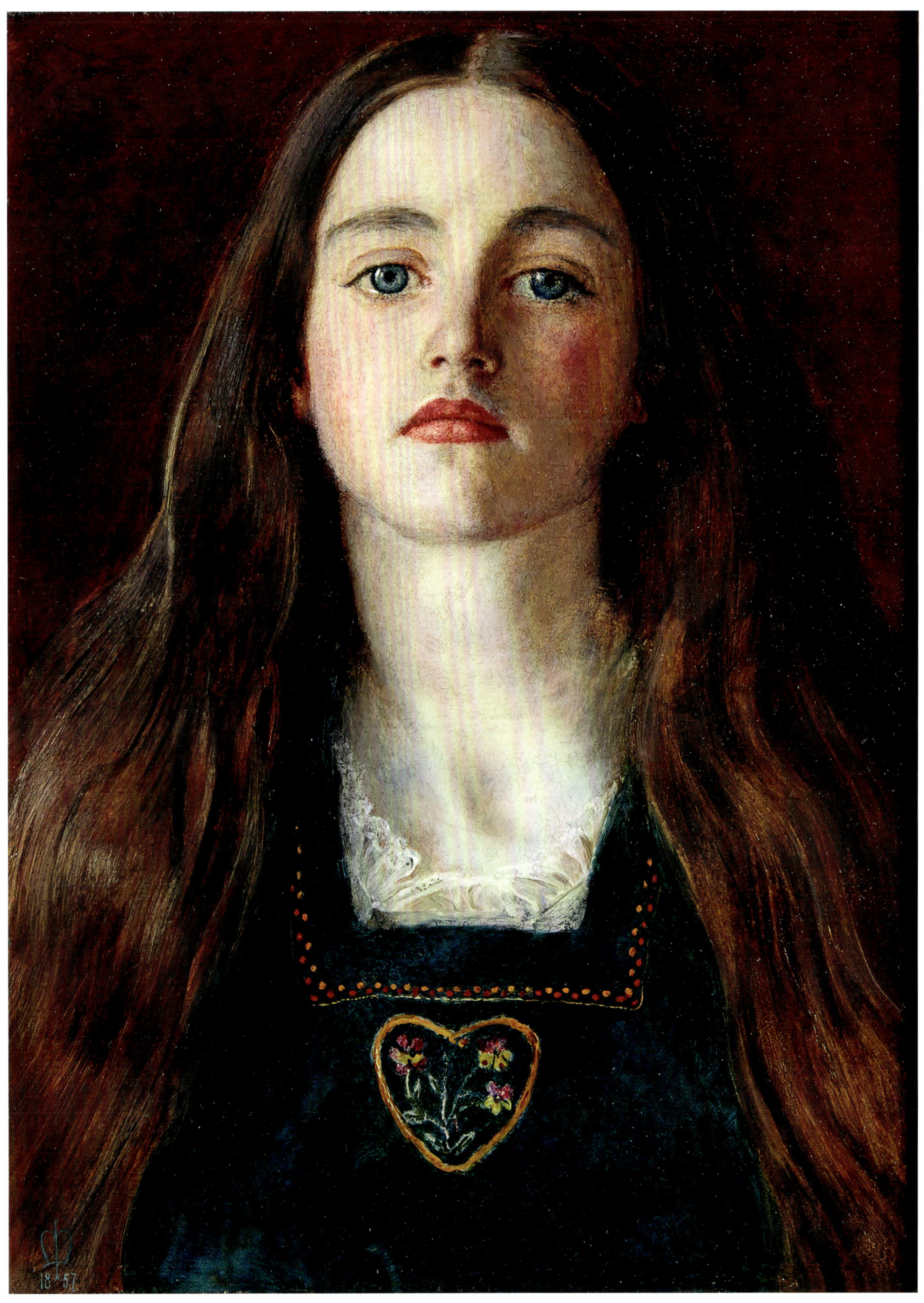

36
**Study for *The Eve
of St Agnes***
John Everett Millais, c.1863
Watercolour on paper
208 × 275mm
Victoria and Albert Museum,
London

37
Effie Millais
John Everett Millais, 1873
Oil on canvas, 990 × 840mm
Perth Museum and Art Gallery

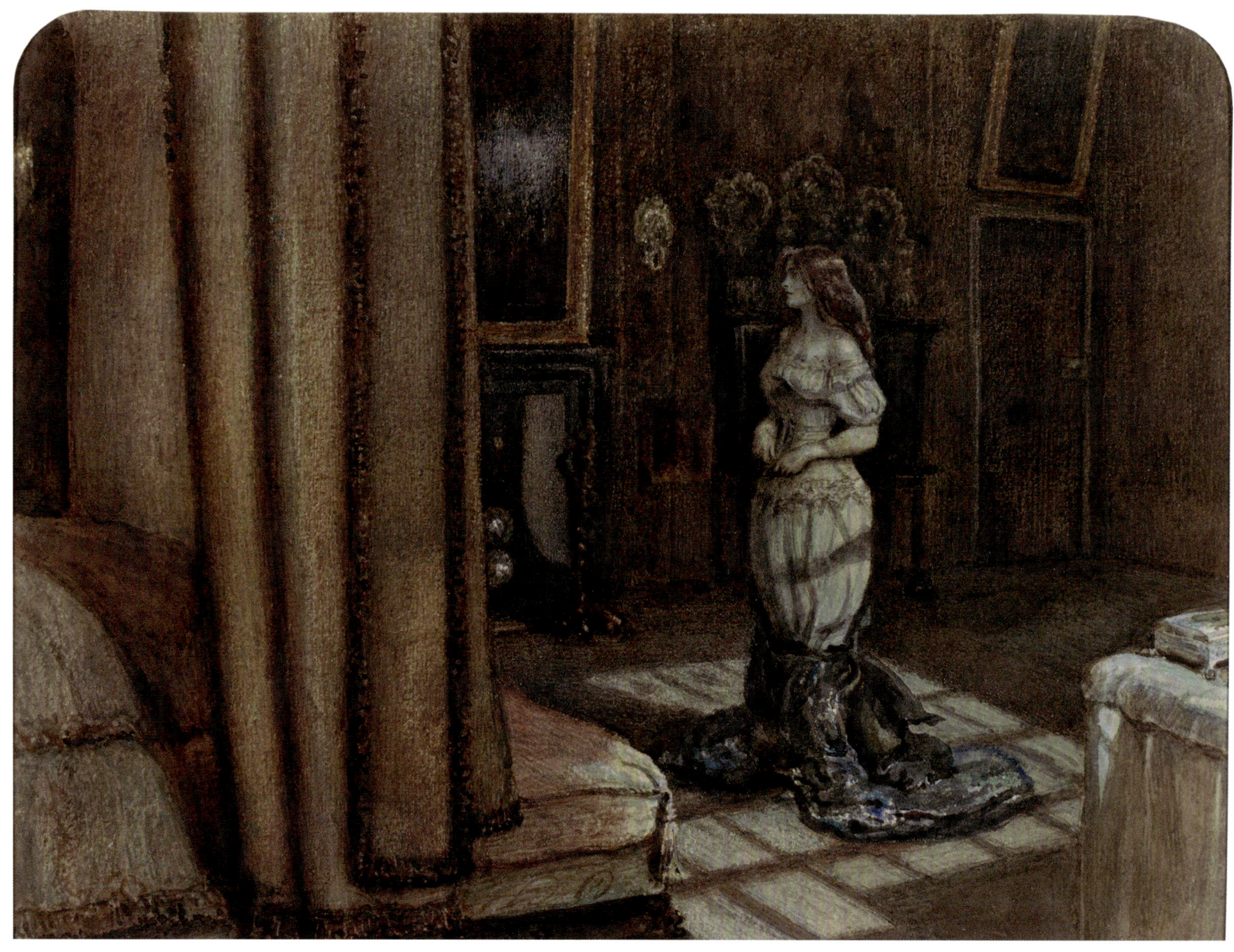

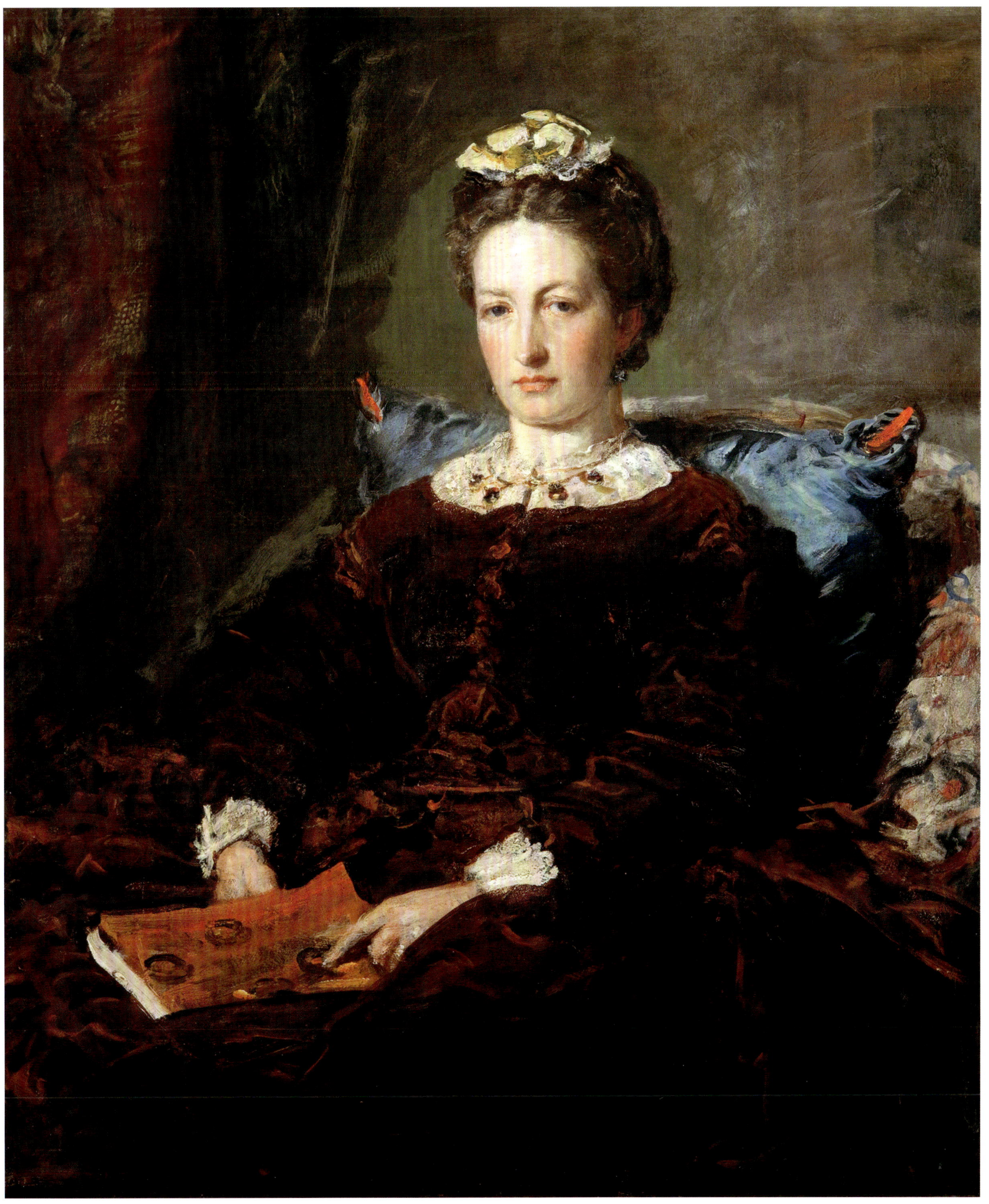

W Holman Hunt to
his PR Brother Tom Woolner April 12th 1853

Pre-Raphaelite women artists operated and struggled for recognition within a staunchly male-oriented art world. The exclusivity and strong bonds formed by artistic brotherhoods throughout the nineteenth century, as well as a critical vocabulary couched in notions of virility, served to preclude women from greater success.

Brotherhoods & Artistic Masculinities

by Peter Funnell

William Michael Rossetti's Pre-Raphaelite journal begins on Tuesday, 15 May 1849:

> At Millais's; Hunt, Stephens, Collinson, Gabriel and myself. Gabriel brought with him his design of 'Dante Drawing the Figure of an Angel' on the first anniversary of Beatrice's death, which he completed in the course of the day and intends for Millais. Millais has done some figures of the populace in his design of the Abbey at Caen since last night, and has also continued painting on the beard of Ferdinand listening to Ariel, being that of Stephens... Having settled to our unanimous satisfaction Compton's identity in appearance with a Llama, we separated.[1]

The roles of women within the Pre-Raphaelite movement cannot be seen in isolation; they must be understood in the context of the male-dominated art world and viewed in the shadow of the now famous Pre-Raphaelite Brotherhood. And the PRB itself has to be considered in the context of the other artistic Brotherhoods that became a phenomenon in European nineteenth-century art. Earlier Brotherhoods ranged from the Barbus or Primitifs, followers of Jacques-Louis David in early nineteenth-century France, through the German Lukasbund (Brotherhood of St Luke), usually known as the Nazarenes, with whom the Pre-Raphaelites are often associated, to the Nabis at the end of the century. As recent scholars have written, 'shared characteristics and elements' of these brotherhoods included the exclusivity and selectivity of the group, their male-oriented and homosocial nature, a collective coding and secrecy, a harking back to medievalism or 'primitive' art and the importance of literary expression of the brotherhoods' creeds.[2]

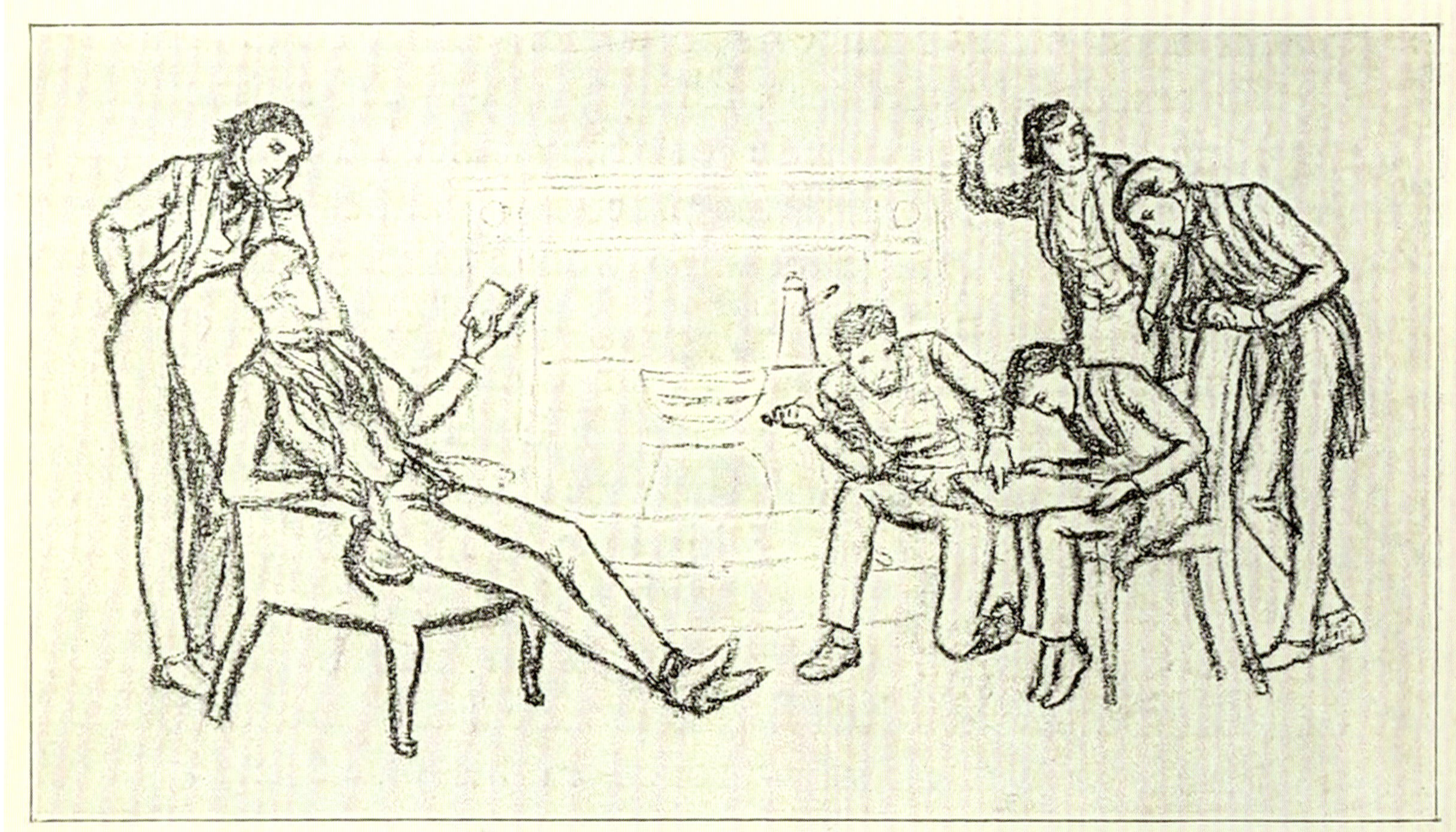

THE PRE-RAPHAELITE MEETING, 1848, BY ARTHUR HUGHES, FROM SKETCH
BY W. H. H.

Above all, of course, the brotherhoods – and many of these traits – are identified with a rejection of the prevailing orthodoxies of contemporary art and those institutions, such as the RA in Britain, that were seen to uphold them. This essay considers how these characteristics manifested themselves in the PRB and the earlier nineteenth-century group, known as the Ancients, and how individual members of each later assumed a more conventional type of masculine self-styling as successful professional artists. A brief coda records how ideas of brotherhood were also central to the next generation associated with Pre-Raphaelitism.

Many of the features just noted were prominent in the formation of the PRB. The tendency towards the cryptic is shown by their use of the initials PRB in the first works they exhibited at the RA Exhibition of 1849, and the literary leanings of the group are evidenced by the publication of *The Germ*, of which William Rossetti became editor. The adherence to medievalism was, of course, a leading trait, both in their subjects and artistic predilections, and as a model for brotherly association. The Brotherhood's homosocial bonding underlies both the rough sketch of a meeting (ill. 38) and *The P.R.B. Journal* entry, combining serious literary and artistic discourse with conviviality (although this should not disguise the intense competition among the group). The unfortunate Compton, not party to the meeting and jokingly likened to a llama, stands for its exclusivity. One of the marked features of *The P.R.B. Journal* is the network of little-remembered figures brought into the group's orbit. As William Rossetti himself stated, his collective record would 'mention only the Members of the Brotherhood, along with some few other persons who came into close relation with them, their purposes, and their work'.[3] But their presence is also a reminder of the size and complexity of the London art and publishing worlds, from which the PRB emerged.

An earlier, very English precedent for the Pre-Raphaelites was the group of artists known as the Ancients, who came under the influence of William Blake and assembled around Samuel Palmer, in the village of Shoreham, Kent, in the 1820s. Like the PRB, the Ancients held radical views on the art exhibited at the RA, showed a predilection for earlier artistic forms as well as a devotion to the natural world and were closely, if briefly, bound by ideas of male association around a common set of beliefs. But, as William Vaughan has pointed out, they did not achieve the Pre-Raphaelites' much wider success and influence on later art, even though the work of each of the three leading PRBs took a very different course.[4] So, indeed, did their public male personas, forged in a later Victorian art world that elevated the celebrity of its participants. The idea of Rossetti as the bohemian shunning societal norms, of Hunt as the prophet or seer and of Millais as the Establishment bourgeois – the clubman as keen on field sports as on artistic pursuits – has shaped the masculine stereotype of the three artists and further served to exclude women from the history of the movement. And so have narratives of rejection of youthful ideals and aspirations, often viewed as amounting to apostasy.

The later careers of two key members of each group – George Richmond and Millais, who were also the most technically accomplished – are instructive in this regard; both exemplified more mainstream versions of the highly successful Victorian artist than they did in their early years. After his engagement with the Ancients in the late 1820s, Richmond turned to more conventional practice. He disparaged their Shoreham work in a letter to Palmer in 1838, although both men remained lifelong friends.[5] Visits to Florence and Rome greatly broadened Richmond's knowledge and understanding of Old Master painting. Back in England, his career flourished as one of the most successful portrait artists of his period, and his income from this line of work increased from £1,000 per annum in 1836 to more than £2,000 in the following decade. Official recognition

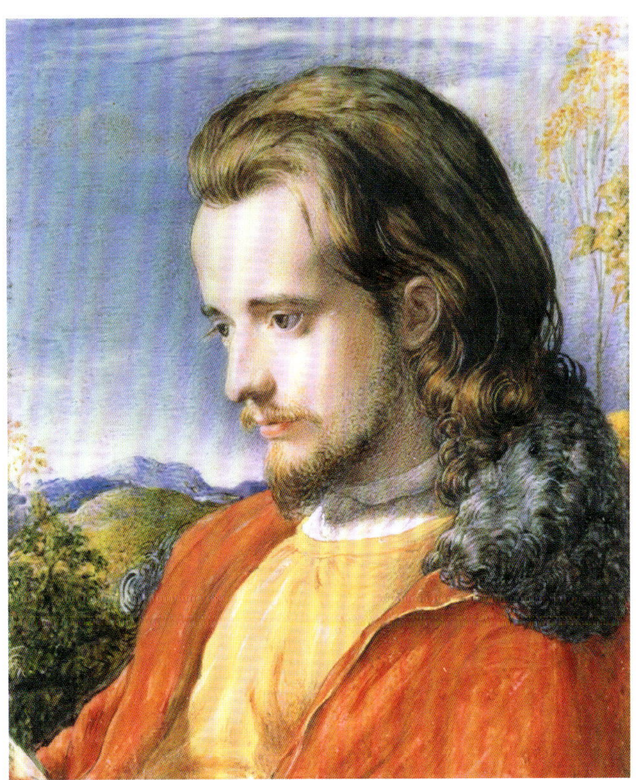

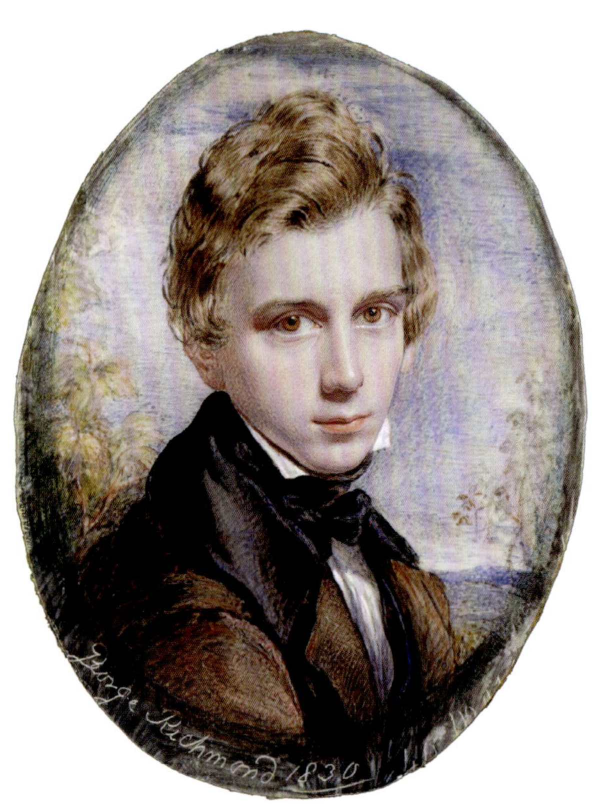

accompanied this. He was appointed to the School of Design council by future Prime Minister William Ewart Gladstone (whom he had met on his first Rome visit); sat on the commission concerning the siting of the National Gallery; enjoyed honorary degrees from both Oxford and Cambridge and became an Associate of the RA in 1857, followed by election to full Academician in 1866.

Famously, it was Millais's appointment as an Associate of the RA in 1853 that, in Rossetti's view, sounded the death knell of the Brotherhood (see also, Christina Rossetti's poem, p.39). He became a full Academician in 1863 and, just before his death in 1896, its President. Among many other honours, he was made a baronet in 1885, also by Gladstone (for long an admirer of the Pre-Raphaelites), whose portrait Millais painted no fewer than four times. Like Richmond, Millais's artistic tastes became far removed from Pre-Raphaelite precepts, notably admiring Frans Hals, Diego Velàzquez and the particular PRB *bête noire*, Sir Joshua Reynolds. Although he continued to paint subject pictures and, from *Chill October* in 1870, a series of remarkable landscapes; as for Richmond, portraiture was a mainstay. He amassed a considerable fortune from it – selling his 1881 portrait of Disraeli, for instance, to The Fine Art Society for no fewer than 1,400 guineas including copyright for, financially, the all-important engraving. His prestige allowed him to be highly selective about whom he painted, and he commanded such high prices that only the most prestigious and wealthy sitters passed through the studio of his palatial house in Palace Gate, Kensington, a household, as noted elsewhere, ably managed by his wife, Effie Millais.

Although not without detractors, the image of Millais's consummate English manliness was frequently evoked in his later years. For his admirers, Millais's qualities, such as his simplicity and straightforwardness, and his plain and unaffected character were linked to traits of rugged geniality and an unerring sociability. And these were further conceived in terms of national and racial virtues. 'Anglo-Saxon from skin to core,' wrote the critic Marion Harry Spielmann in an obituary of Millais in the *Magazine of Art*; continuing to praise him as 'vigorous and full of bluff, full of healthy power of body and mind. I see him true, straightforward, honest.'[6] These same qualities were, of course, registered in the work itself, with Millais emerging, in Andrew Lang's words 'as the strongest, manliest, and most certain in his aims, of all modern English painters'.[7] His portraits of older men, such as Gladstone, were also assessed and much admired for their masculine power and directness.[8]

With reference to the earlier careers of Richmond and Millais, it is notable that the portrayal and celebration of youthful masculinity are significant features of both artists. Richmond's precocious abilities, and his upbringing, as the son and great-grandson of distinguished miniature painters, are shown by two miniature portraits of Palmer and himself, produced during the later years of the Ancients (ills 39 and 40). As William Vaughan notes, the miniature of Palmer records his self-styling of the Shoreham period, with long hair and beard and archaic dress. Richmond, by contrast, presents himself with a neat haircut and the conventional male attire of the period, a foretelling perhaps of the Establishment figure that he was either to become or that was always there beneath the veneer of radical experimentalist.[9]

Portraits of male youths also formed a prominent feature and became a staple of Richmond's art as a professional portraitist. His fine watercolour portraits, of the 1830s and 1840s, of well-born young men deliver an ideal of youthful manhood. A similar celebration of more mature but still relatively young manhood became another characteristic of Richmond's portraiture in the series of no fewer than seventy portrait drawings he made of members of Grillion's Club, commissioned on their election to the club. Members were mainly old Etonians, who had entered public life via Oxford or Cambridge. The portrait of the young Gladstone is typical; as H.C.G. Matthew notes: 'never can a political élite have been made to look more gentle, more high-minded or more élitist (in the best sense of the term)'.[10]

Aside from the rather stiff sketch reproduced at the beginning of this essay (ill.38), the Pre-Raphaelites are not recorded in group or double portraits.[11] What does distinguish them, as makers of mutual portraits, or at least likenesses, is the use of each other as models for their subject pictures. This was partly due to problems securing suitable professional models but also reflects their commitment to truthful representation. A notable example is Millais's *Isabella* of 1848–9 (ill.42), his first painting as a member of the PRB and the only work he submitted to the crucial 1849 RA Exhibition. Members of the Brotherhood, who served as models for the figures lining either side of the table in this remarkable painting, included the two Rossetti brothers and Frederic George Stephens, while fellow painter Walter Howell Deverell posed, as probably did fellow RA student Charles Compton for the figure of the servant – presumably the individual likened by them to a llama.[12] It will also be recalled from *The P.R.B. Journal* entry that Stephens was again posing for Millais for the head of Ferdinand in his *Ferdinand Lured by Ariel* of 1849–50. Although older men, such as Millais's father and the early patron William Hugh Fenn, also modelled for *Isabella*, the meticulous drawings of the Pre-Raphaelites that Millais made as studies are superb renditions of youthful masculinity. As Jason Rosenfeld has observed, many of their early subjects concerned 'inter-male fidelity', frequently featuring young men. Examples include Hunt's *Rienzi*, shown near Millais's *Isabella* at the 1849 RA exhibition and again using Rossetti as the model for its chief figure.[13]

There is, moreover, the set of portrait drawings that they made of each other, on 12 April 1853, to send to PRB founder–sculptor Thomas Woolner, who had emigrated to Australia to seek his fortune in the goldrush (see ill.41).

The idea that this memento of the original Brotherhood should consist of portraits was Rossetti's, who declared: 'I therefore fix that on the 12th of April…we shall each of us, wheresoever we may be, make a sketch of some kind (mutual portraits preferable).'[14] Hunt later recalled that the event duly took place at 83 Gower Street, London:

> We therefore all met one morning at Millais' studio, and set to work to complete a collection of our portraits, in pencil, chalk, or pastel…the drawings all went as they were left that evening, and they were framed together to hang in Woolner's studio at Melbourne.[15]

The drawings are head-and-shoulders studies, showing the members of the Brotherhood in everyday male dress (like Richmond but unlike the Nazarenes or Palmer, for that matter, they never adopted archaising dress). Some are inscribed to Woolner, and some reveal signs of haste as a necessary part of the exercise. And they show men who are still young but four years older than those at the meeting in May 1849, with which this essay began. Indeed as F.G. Stephens, later a leading art critic, remembered, somewhat elegiacally, the event took place as the original PRB was in a state of change and dissolution:

> This meeting was one of the latest 'functions' of the Pre-Raphaelite Brotherhood in its original state. [James] Collinson had seceded, and Woolner emigrated to the 'diggings' in search of the gold he did not find. Up to that time the old affectionate conditions still existed among the Brothers, but their end was near. Millais was shooting on ahead; Mr. Holman Hunt was surely, though slowly, following his path towards fortune; D.G. Rossetti had retired within himself, and made no sign before the world; W.M. Rossetti

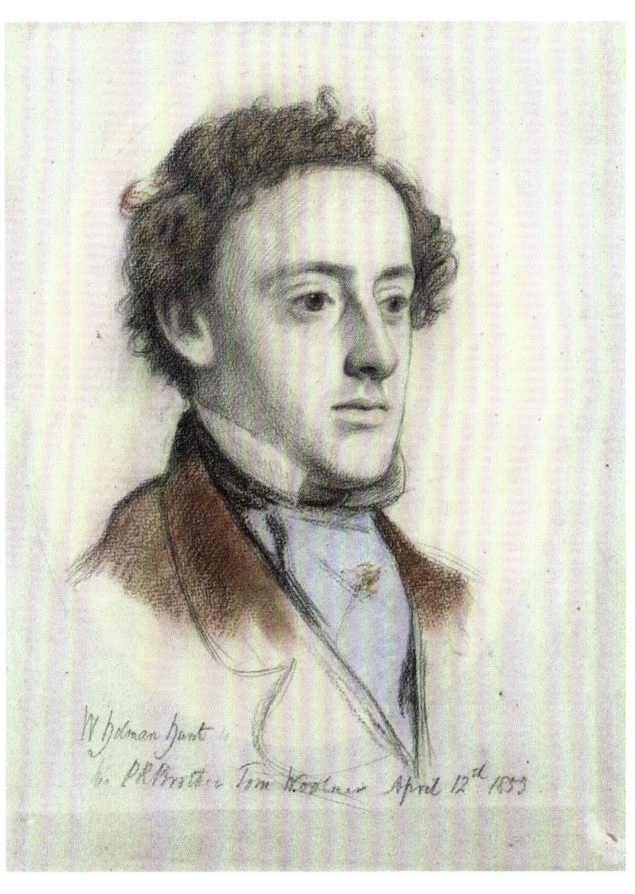

40
Self-portrait
George Richmond, 1830
Gouache on ivory
89 × 68mm
National Portrait Gallery

41 (below and p.56)
John Everett Millais
William Holman Hunt, 1853
Coloured chalk on paper
332 × 288mm
National Portrait Gallery

was rising in Her Majesty's service [in the Inland Revenue]; and I was being continuedly drawn towards that literary work which brought me bread.[16]

In spite of Stephens's comment about Rossetti retiring 'within himself', it was Rossetti who became the pivotal influence for the next group of younger artists – in particular Edward Burne-Jones and William Morris – who formed what became known as the second generation of Pre-Raphaelites. Close male association and a commitment to the ideal of a community of artists were later exemplified by the social and creative innovations of Red House and the establishment of Morris's 'Firm'. But, for Burne-Jones, a deep attachment to spiritual forms of male association extended back to his youth in Birmingham, when he formed an intimate bond with fellow schoolmates. In Fiona MacCarthy's words, 'much of Burne-Jones's life would be a history of brotherhoods,' and his early years saw him drawn both to a chivalric version of masculine behaviour and to Roman Catholic monasticism, as it was being revived in this period.[17] The Birmingham connection continued at Oxford University, where he formed the most critical male friendship of his life with Morris. And in Oxford, in the summer of 1857, after the consolidation in London of the Rossetti, Burne-Jones and Morris circle, at Rossetti's instigation the group and their friends embarked on a project to decorate with murals the newly built Oxford Union building. Although this was a technically failed attempt to revive the art of wall painting, it is the powerful sense of young men engaging closely with each other, again manifested in both serious creative endeavour and a larky joviality and banter, that is relevant here.

The Oxford Union Murals were very much a male concern. While the Red House project can be construed as a joining together of the creative energies of both men and women (the participation of Elizabeth Siddal, Jane Morris and Georgiana Burne-Jones is discussed elsewhere, see, for example, p.33), notions of communal working and living, and of gender equality, have rightly been questioned.[18] Red House was, above all, a project instigated by Morris and led by the male nexus around him: Burne-Jones, Rossetti, Madox Brown and the architect of the house Philip Webb. As has been argued the artistic contributions of women at Red House were respected by their male counterparts, and the women could adopt a freedom of attitude and behaviour that was unusual at the time. But this semblance of artistic equality was at best limited – as Georgiana Burne-Jones later recalled – or, more emphatically, overshadowed by the masculine conventions of the period.

42
Isabella
John Everett Millais, 1849
Oil on canvas
1030 × 1428mm
Walker Art Gallery, Liverpool

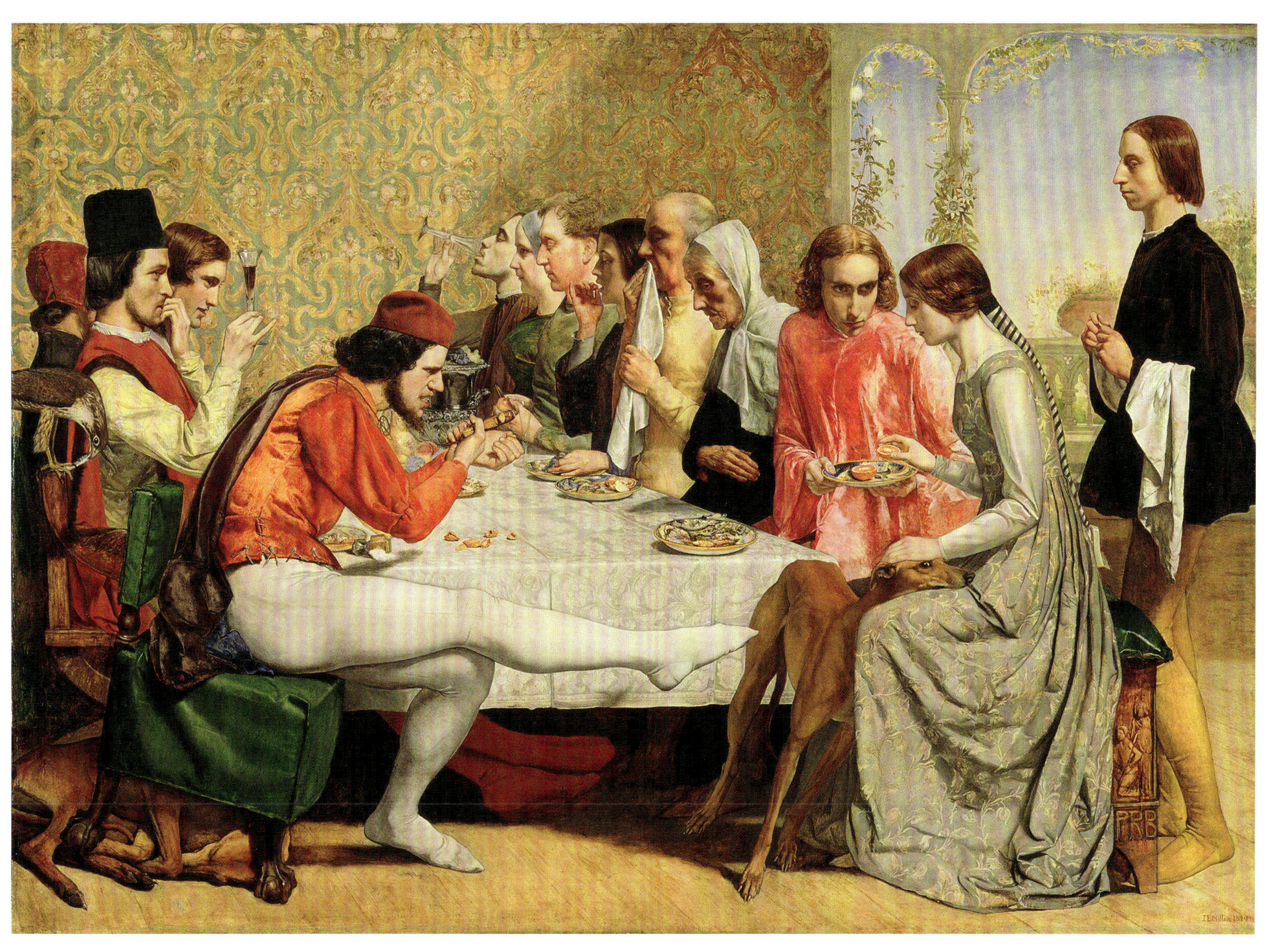

Annie Miller

1835–1925

Annie Miller is one of those in the Pre-Raphaelite circle about whom least is known. She inspired and modelled for *The Awakening Conscience*, Hunt's image of a 'fallen woman' at the moment of remorse – one of the now iconic pictures produced by the PRBs (ill. 43). Plucked from poverty, she also posed for Millais and Rossetti, while being educated as Hunt's prospective wife. When that plan ended, Miller moved away from the world of art, to marry a gentleman and raise a family. Her role in the Pre-Raphaelite movement was then forgotten until the late twentieth century. Like a short-lived star, her role was to burn brightly but briefly.

Born in London in 1835, Annie Miller was the third child of Henry Miller, a former foot soldier, who had served in the Peninsular Campaign in Spain, the battles of Toulouse and Waterloo.[1] Discharged in 1832, her father settled close to the Royal Hospital in Chelsea, London, amid many other veterans. When widowed, he took his daughters Annie and Harriet to live with their aunt and uncle in nearby Cross Keys yard.

Like other working-class children, Annie Miller received little, if any, education. Listed as a servant, aged 16, in the 1851 Census, she reputedly worked as childminder and public-house potgirl. She was evidently poor, but Hunt's later derogatory account of her as unkempt and filthy is unkind and unjust.[2]

From 1850, Hunt had a studio near to the Miller lodgings. In his pursuit of 'fanatical realism', he had employed a girl from Surrey, named Emma, to pose as a flirtatious country lass in *The Hireling Shepherd*.[3] But Emma had a distrustful boyfriend, and so when Hunt decided to paint *The Awakening Conscience*, his choice fell on young Annie Miller, whose family no doubt agreed to her earning a few shillings. Painting took place in autumn 1853, when Annie was 18, although the role in which she was cast is that of a somewhat older woman; moreover, although the shape of the face follows hers, this is not a portrait. Hunt's choice of model was nonetheless apt, for a poor girl with Miller's good looks, luxuriant hair and willing manner was, in modern terms, sexually 'at risk'.

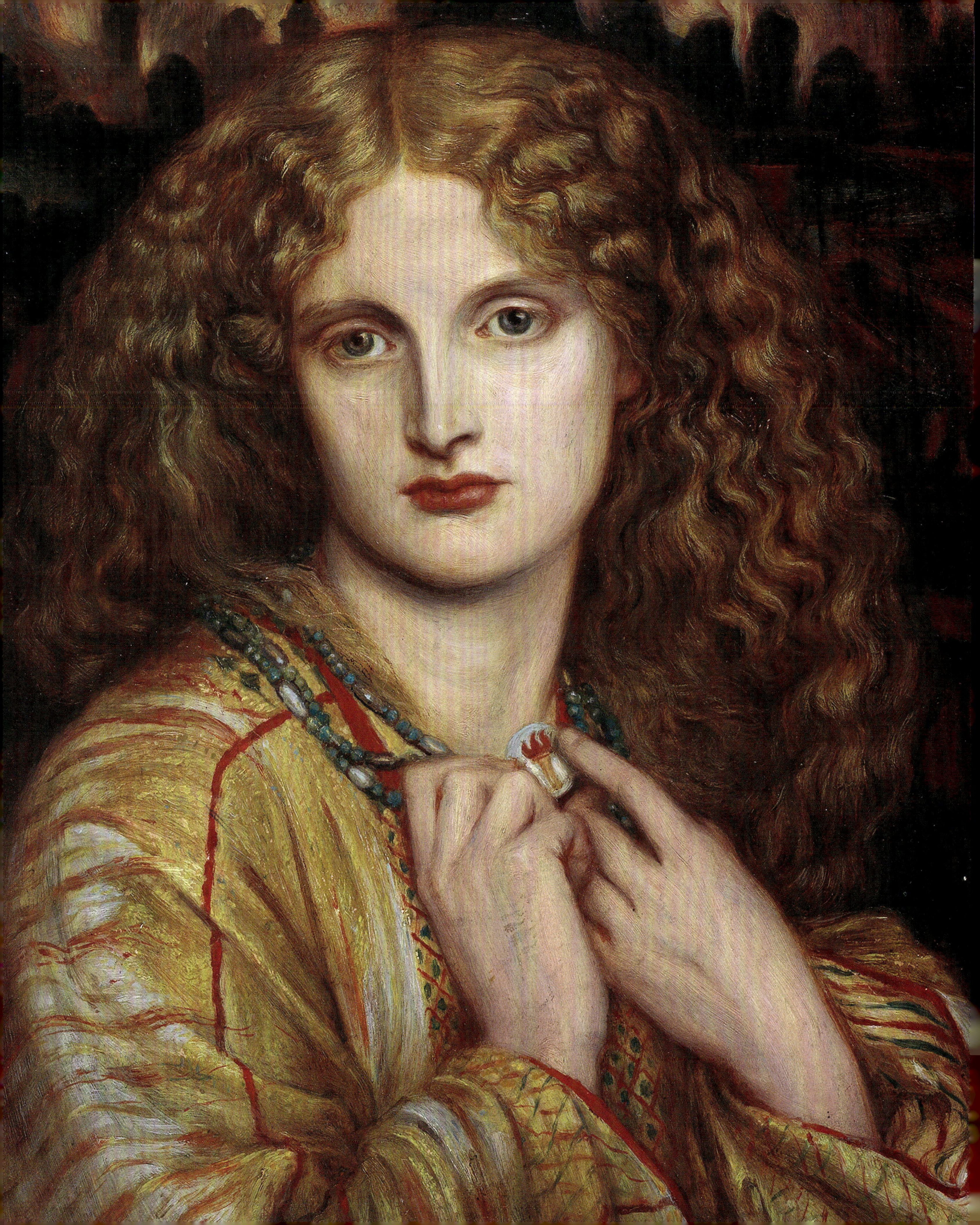

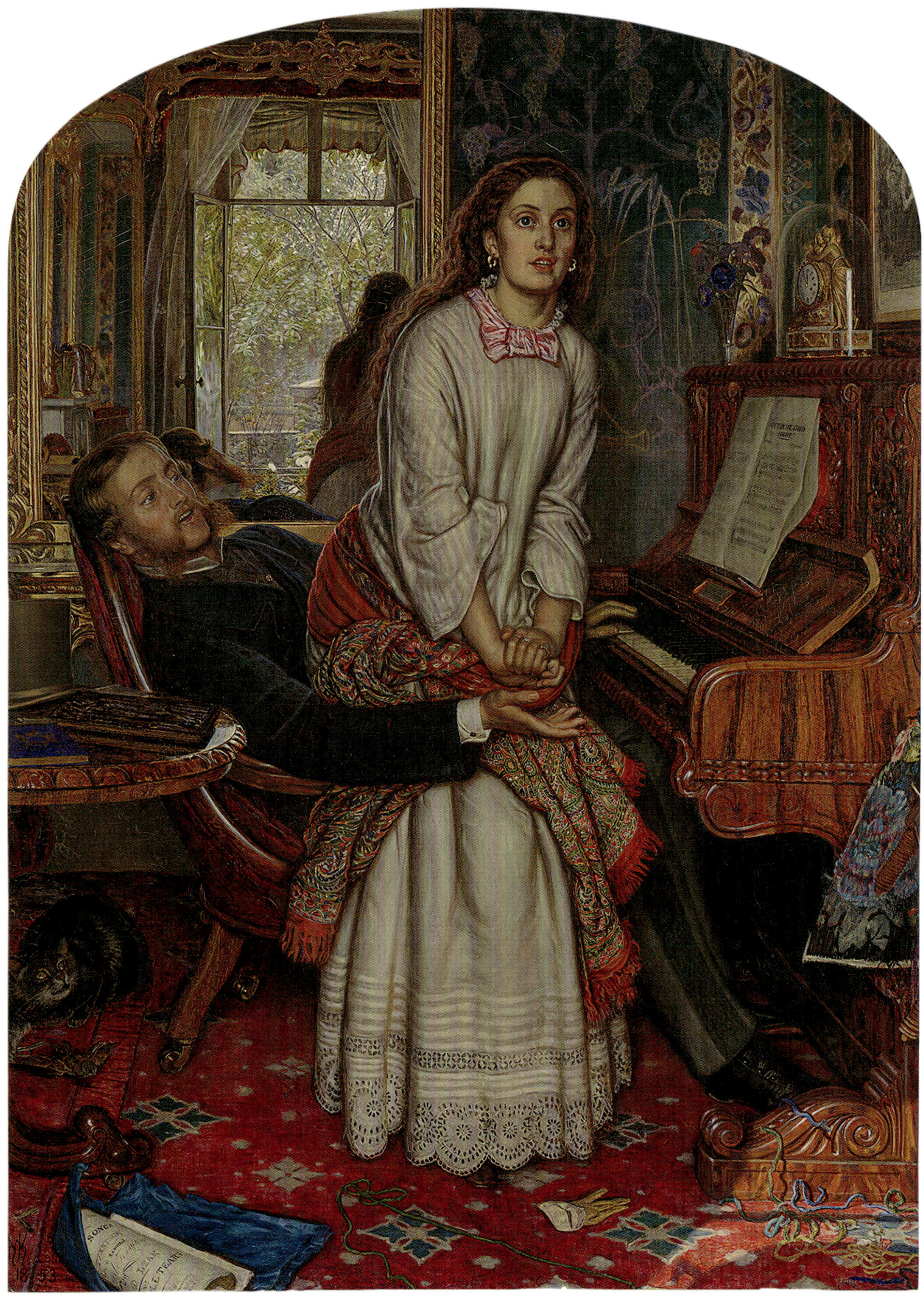

Hunt decided to pay for Miller's education as a suitable bride, as Madox Brown had done for his unlettered model Emma Hill, and as Morris would do for Jane Burden. Accordingly, when, in 1854, he left Britain to travel to Egypt and Palestine in search of authentic biblical settings, Miller was given a programme of schooling in literacy and ladylike manners. Hunt's fellow PRB Frederic Stephens was appointed guardian of her behaviour. Her landlady and instructor was widowed Martha Bramah, who lived in Chelsea's Lindsey Row. To allow some recreational relief and provide pocket money, Miller was permitted to pose for Hunt's friends, notably the soon-to-be married Millais, who, while also working on major subjects, painted her in a couple of 'cabinet' pictures. One of these was *The Violet's Message* (ill. 44), which shows a young woman gently opening an envelope that contains a flower, signifying modesty and faithfulness.[4]

to acquire genteel habits, to speak and dress well, to write a fair hand and to converse politely, perhaps with less restraint than chaperoned girls of the same age. She reported to Hunt that Boyce had always behaved 'most kindly' when he was drawing her, which suggests that she enjoyed the sittings.

Hunt proposed marriage by letter in autumn 1855, and after his return to London in February 1856 he moved to Pimlico, just east of Chelsea. But he apparently took no further action, prompting Miller to arouse his jealousy by going out with others to popular places like Cremorne Gardens; even the decorous William Rossetti escorted her on a river excursion. In July, Hunt confided to Madox Brown about 'Annie Miller's love for him & his liking for her' and his 'perplexities' regarding her pleasure-seeking. As Madox Brown commented, 'they all seem mad about Annie Mill[e]r & poor Hunt has had a fever about it.'[7] She was now 21, and her

'A hopeless, proud, improvident girl, who does not know the value of money because she has never worked for it'

Millais wrote to tell Hunt on 10 April 1854 that 'Annie Miller has been sitting to me and I have been painting a little head from her. She is a good girl, and behaves herself very properly.'[5] George Price Boyce drew a pencil profile, in which she also presents a meek aspect, nervously self-conscious, hair fastened at the nape of her neck. Others to whom she sat included Rossetti, Stephens, Hughes, Augustus Leopold Egg, Collins, Michael Frederick Halliday – all Hunt's friends.[6] No personal accounts survive, so Miller's subjective experience can only be inferred from her actions and others' contemporary reports. These show she evidently seized the educational opportunity

expectation may be figured in Halliday's (untraced) picture of a courting couple, *The Measure for a Wedding Ring*, completed that year.[8]

Hunt's allusion to these events was an indirect quotation in his later autobiography: 'It is said that jealousy is love [but] though jealousy be procured by love…yet jealousy extinguishes love.'[9] Miller's frustrations were expressed in her stony response to Hunt's next suggestion that she attend a young ladies' academy, in order to curb her 'indolence'.[10] An approach to her aunt proved more effective, since the threat to financial support had implications for the Miller family.

44
The Violet's Message
John Everett Millais, 1854
Oil on panel, 254 × 197 mm
Private Collection

45
Il Dolce far niente
William Holman Hunt, 1866
Oil on canvas, 1010 × 812 mm
Private Collection

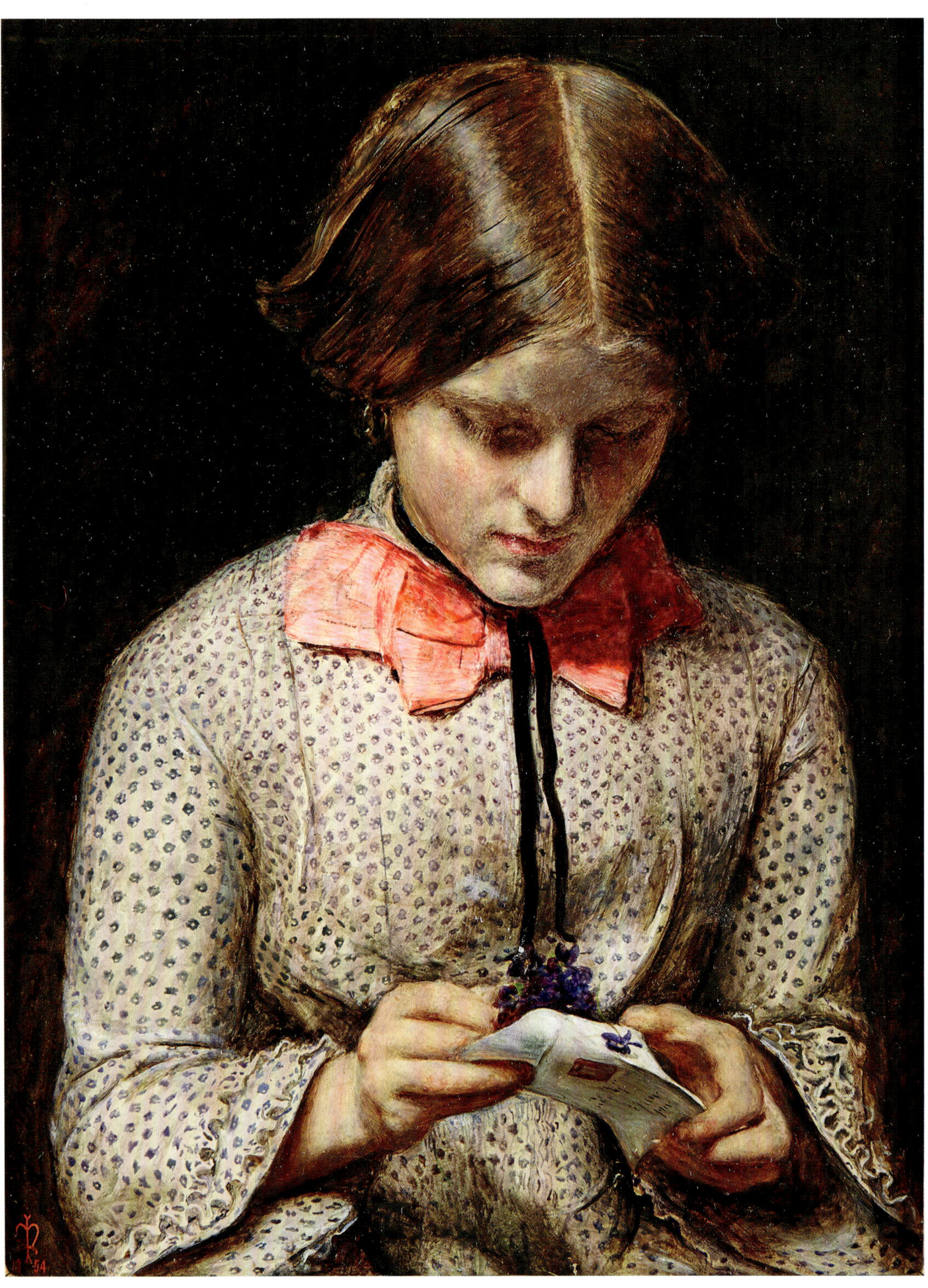

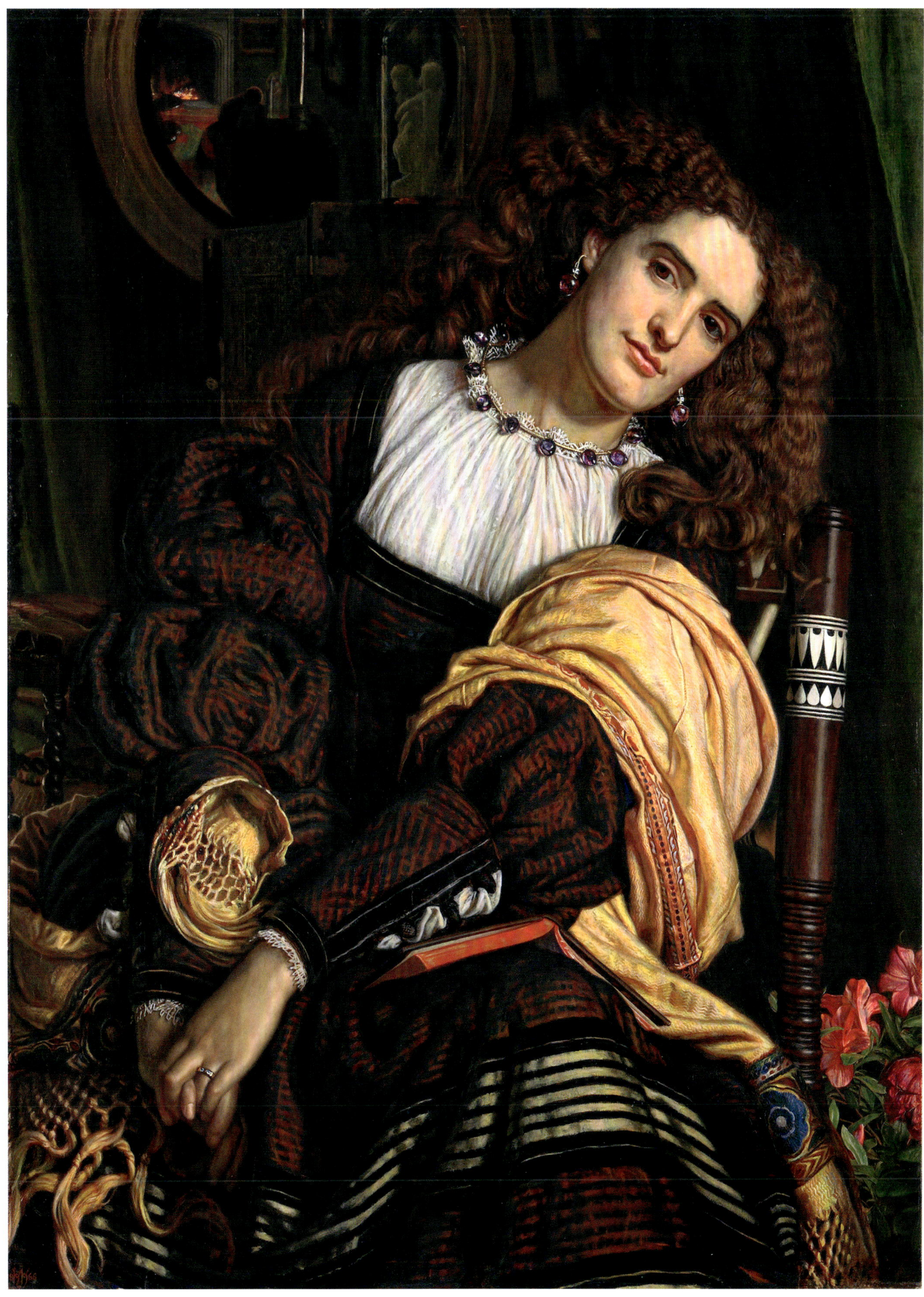

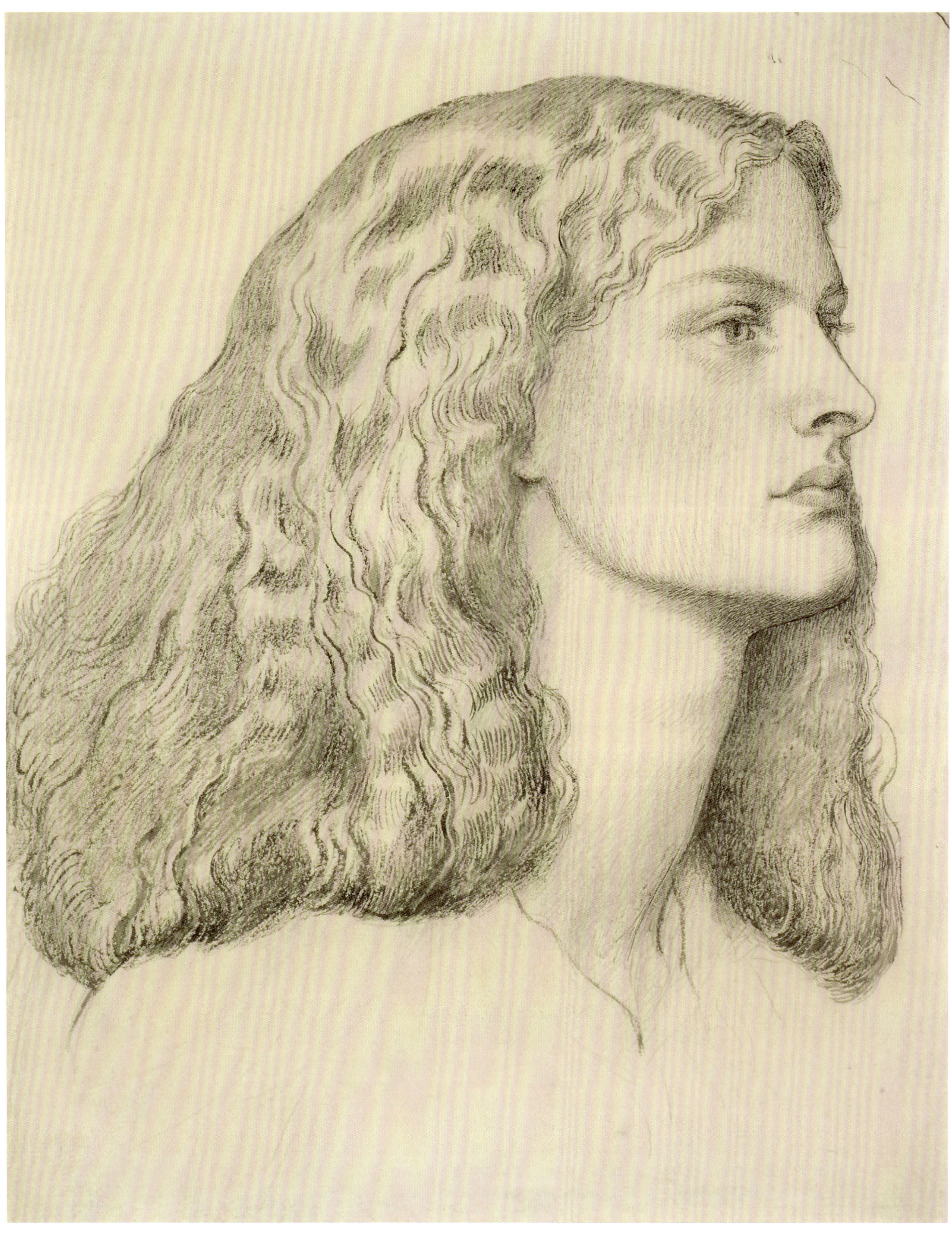

By 1857 Hunt was wholly engaged on major paintings with biblical settings, with which he aimed to secure his reputation. Miller posed regularly for figure studies in the large compositions, and marriage was seemingly postponed. In January 1858 it was back on the agenda, as George Boyce recorded:

> After desultory chat and looking at drawings, etc, Hunt introduced the subject which principally brought him. Having in prospect to marry Annie Miller, after that her education both of mind and manners shall have been completed, he wished to destroy as far as was possible all traces of her former occupation, viz, that of sitting to certain artists...and as mine was the only direct study of her head, as it was, he would hold it a favour if I would give it him... At first I resisted stoutly, but finding that it was a serious point with him and that my refusing would be in some degree an obstacle in the carrying out of his wishes with regard to her (which it would be both selfish and unkind and foolish in the remotest degree to thwart) I at last reluctantly assented.[11]

Hunt continued to upbraid Miller for her frivolity and liking for leisure (which, in her eyes, marriage to a gentleman would secure), and posed her as the image of laziness in *Il Dolce far niente* (ill. 45), in which a young woman basks before a warm fire. She has Miller's features and wealth of hair, and wears a wedding ring.

But obstacles remained, as Hunt demanded Miller relinquish what he unkindly described as 'old objectionable habits'.[12] In the battle of wills, she had little power. But she had anger, represented as wilfulness and 'false pride' by Hunt, on one occasion declaring that 'she did not care about painting and never did' and, on another, accusing him of wishing 'to be rid of her'.[13] Indirectly, one can hear her voice, realising the prospect of marriage was fading. He sent her *Mary Barton*, Elizabeth Gaskell's 1848 cautionary tale of a poor weaver's daughter, and he now suspected her of seeing other men, including Viscount Ranelagh, yet feared that, if abandoned, she would 'fall to the lowest' in poverty and squalor, and therefore 'ought to be helped' to save herself 'by honest industry'.[14] But, finally, as told by Boyce, '[f]inding he could not get her to do what he wanted to make her a desirable wife for him...he had broken off the engagement.'[15] Although apparently mutual, the decision was financially costly to Miller, who rejected his further attempts to find 'honest' employment for her. Having effectively been 'cast off' as a discarded love – the fate emblematised in *The Awakening Conscience* – she turned instead to the other painters. In October she called on Rossetti and then, in December, on Boyce, in a distressed state, asking him to recommend 'someone to sit to' as she was 'determined on sitting again in preference to doing anything else'. Boyce promptly employed her, noting that she 'looks more beautiful than ever'. While he was working, Rossetti arrived and began sketching her too.[16]

In the first months of 1860, she posed for both artists (see ill. 46). In his diary Boyce now called her 'Miss Miller', which must indicate the level of refinement in mind and manners she had achieved. The drawings certainly present a confident aspect that almost advertises her attractions. Both artists began works in oil, Rossetti's using the frontal head-and-shoulders format that had now come into vogue. It is presumed Miller was paid for sittings, although she may have requested payment in kind, as she received from Boyce a Welsh landscape sunset.[17] Perhaps she hoped his attentions were hints of romance, which, if realised, would have made Joanna Boyce her sister-in-law. If so, she was disappointed.

By the end of the year she had quite run out of credit and reapproached Hunt, whose success with *The Finding of the Saviour in the Temple* (1854–60) was well publicised. He replied that she had ignored his instruction against sitting to Rossetti and Boyce, was 'a hopeless, proud, improvident girl – who does not know the value of money because she has never worked for it' and should instead apply for assisted emigration to Australia.[18] She fought back with threats to sue for breach of promise, before eventually giving up. She may or may not have cared about art, but regularly turned to artists as sources of sympathy and assistance. Now she was obliged to look elsewhere.

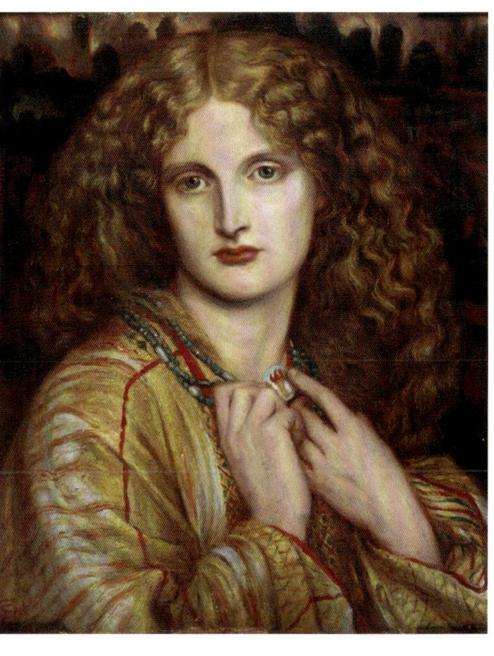

46
Annie Miller
Dante Gabriel Rossetti, c.1860
Pen and ink on paper
287 × 230mm
Nationalmuseum, Stockholm

47 (below and p. 65)
The Flaming Heart
Attrib. Charles Fairfax
Murray after Dante
Gabriel Rossetti, c.1863
Oil on panel, 330 × 279mm
Fitzwilliam Museum, Cambridge

The next sighting of Miller is when Boyce and Henry Tanworth Wells bumped into her at the 1862 International Exhibition in London (where she would have seen design work displayed by Morris & Co.). 'Looking as handsome as ever', she was escorted by a young gentleman, 'rather a swell', who must have been Captain Thomas Ranelagh Thomson, a keen member of the Volunteer Reserves forces.[19] Then, at the beginning of 1863, she again approached Rossetti, who was now widowed and living in Cheyne Walk. He drew the fine pastel *Woman in Yellow* (ill. 48) and also resumed the oil painting that, following a similar *Joan of Arc* (1864), was repurposed as *Helen of Troy* (1863) with 'ships burning in the background', as Boyce noted.[20] An exact autograph copy, retitled *The Flaming Heart* (ill. 47), was possibly presented to Miller on her marriage, for it reappeared around the time of her death.[21] She also called on Millais, to whom she introduced

And thus a striking example of a young woman who had not fallen but risen. Six months earlier, Captain Thomson had been among the 1,700 men invited to the first Court levee held on Queen Victoria's behalf by the Prince of Wales.[23] By this date Thomson regularly attended royal events, which indicates that, following her marriage, Miller was presented at Court, perhaps sponsored by her mother-in-law.

Their daughter Annie Helen was born in 1866 and son Thomas James the following year. One source states that they moved to the house of Thomson's mother, in Richmond-on-Thames. Near here, Hunt encountered her 'driving in a carriage with several children', when they chatted civilly, and he learnt that 'she had married happily'. This account, shared with his male friends years later, included the claim that he had forgiven her 'offence'; indeed, on reflection it had 'in fact worked me good rather than harm'.[24]

'Annie was determined on sitting again in preference to doing anything else'

Captain Thomson. The artists respectively described him as a 'decent' and 'very good gentlemanly fellow'.[22]

Thomson was a cousin of Viscount Ranelagh, his mother's nephew. At the age of 28, Miller married him, on 23 July 1863, and thus joined Elizabeth Siddal and Jane Burden in the ranks of those uneducated young women who rose from poverty to prosperity thanks to posing for Pre-Raphaelite pictures, and were socially transformed into middle-class matrons through participation in art. Contrary to Hunt's expectations, Miller did not become the remorseful plaything of a heartless gent, as in *The Awakening Conscience*, but a very respectable wife to a man somewhat higher in the social scale than Hunt.

Miller's sadly unrecorded reflection on her own experience might have partly concurred, since the invitation to pose for *The Awakening Conscience* had proved a first step towards a comfortable and fashionable life, achieved through her own efforts. Captain (later Major) Thomson remained active in the Volunteers through the 1860s and 1870s, and, by 1885, the family had moved to Bognor Regis on the Sussex coast, where he and, presumably, his wife were active in the Conservative party's organisation, the Primrose League. In 1925 Annie Miller died, aged 90, at Shoreham-on-Sea, Sussex; by then no one, apparently, knew anything about her earlier life.

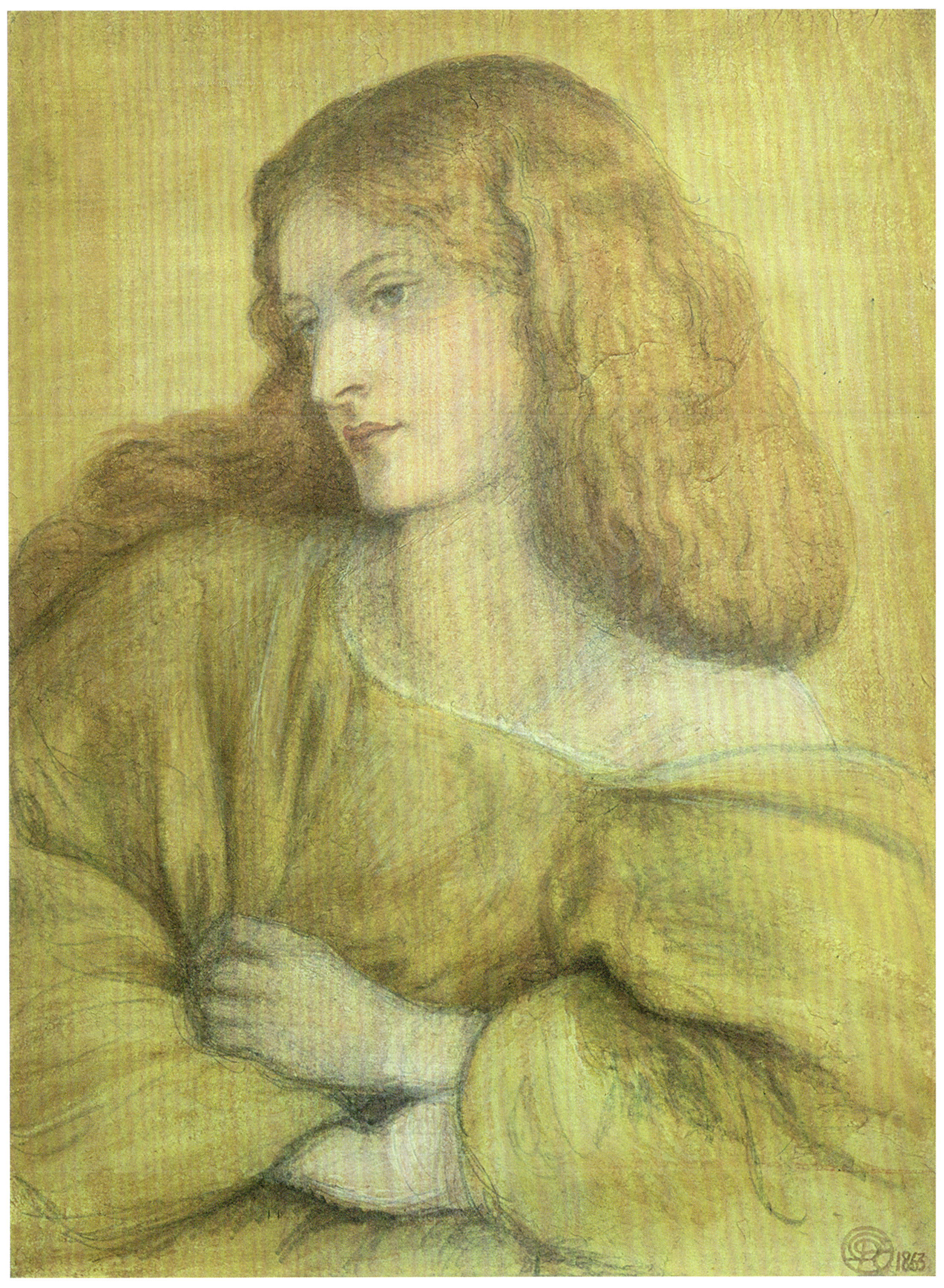

Fanny Cornforth

1835–1909

Myths surround the figure of Fanny Cornforth in the Pre-Raphaelite story, largely because, until recently, facts were few. There is her name, to start with, the name she used soon after meeting the artists. She had been born Sarah Cox, into a blacksmith's family in Sussex, then worked as a servant in Brighton before visiting a relative in London. Fanny was the name of her youngest sister, who died in infancy; Cornforth was the surname used by Timothy Hughes, the man she would marry. On their 1860 marriage certificate, he was Hughes and she was Cox; by the 1861 Census they had become Timothy and Sarah Cornforth. In the artists' circle, she was usually just called Fanny; there would be no confusion with Fanny Eaton, who was always 'Mrs Eaton'.

According to her recollection, one evening

we went over to the Old Surrey Gardens to see the fire-works and were having supper in one of the arbors, when four men came in. There was old Brown, Gabriel, poor Ned Jones and Crom Price. After a while they came by us, and one [Rossetti], coming be'ind me gave my [h]air a flick with his finger as if it were an accident, and it all tumbled down my back. My cousin said 'what a cheek' and began to scold… Then he made all sorts of apologies, and nothing would do but that I should go to his studio and sit to him…so my old cousin took me the next morning to the old studio at Blackfriars Bridge, and he put my head against the wall and drew it for the head of the girl in the calf picture [*Found*].[1]

With *Found* (ill. 49), Fanny Cornforth entered the art world, cast as a 'fallen woman' discovered by her village sweetheart taking his livestock to market, who seeks to rescue her from ruin. Conceived originally alongside Hunt's *The Awakening Conscience* (ill. 43), work on *Found* resumed five years later in 1858 after her chance encounter with Rossetti. The picture dramatises the common belief that country girls were seduced and then abandoned to prostitution in London. In the 1850s the double standard of sexual morality was an urgent social question. But the painting was again abandoned, as the issue faded and perhaps as Fanny's fate did not confirm her expected 'ruin'.

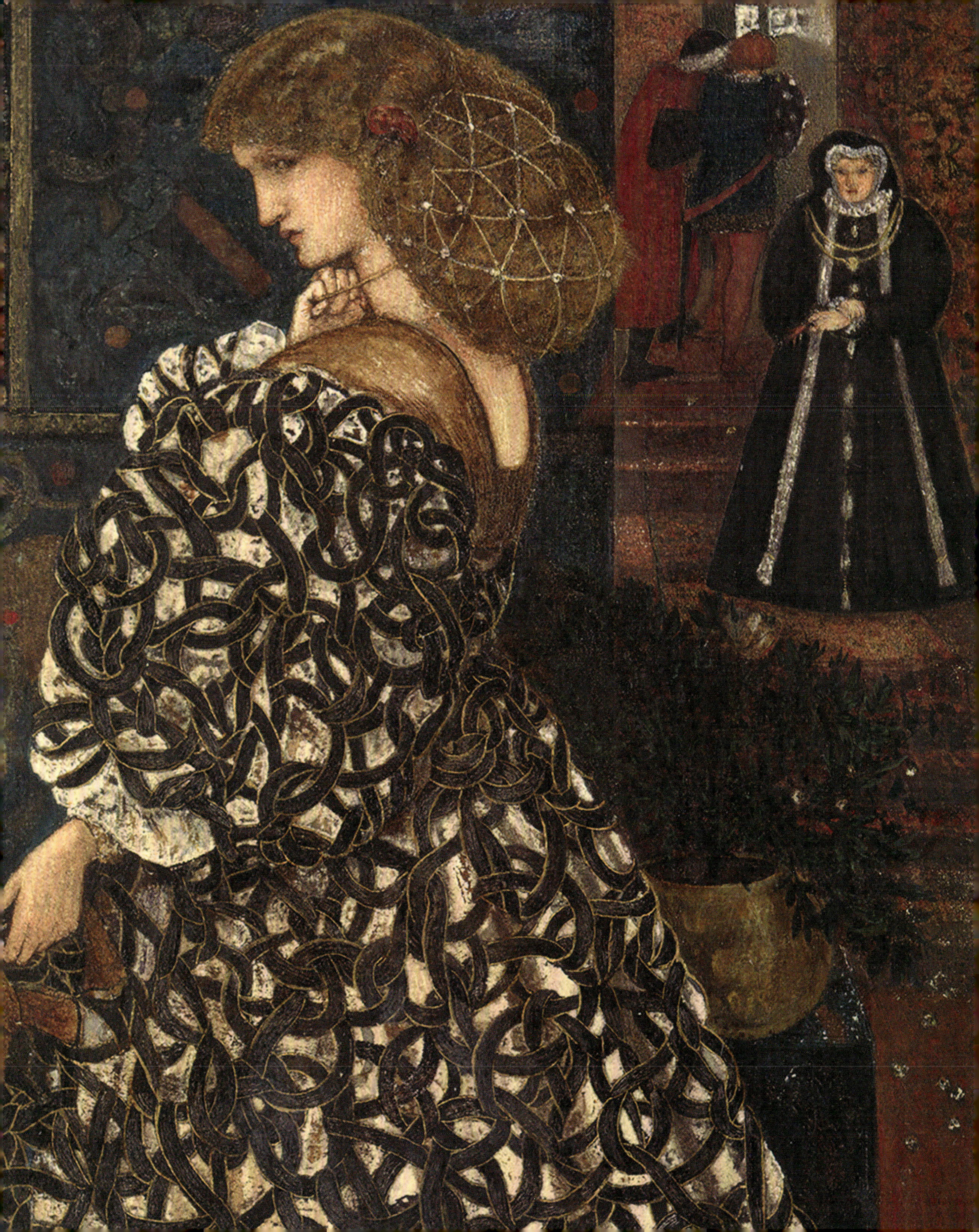

Found
Dante Gabriel Rossetti, 1859
Unfinished, oil on canvas
921 × 811mm
Delaware Art Museum

Thoughts of the Past
John Roddam Spencer
Stanhope, c.1859
Oil on canvas, 864 × 508mm
Tate, London

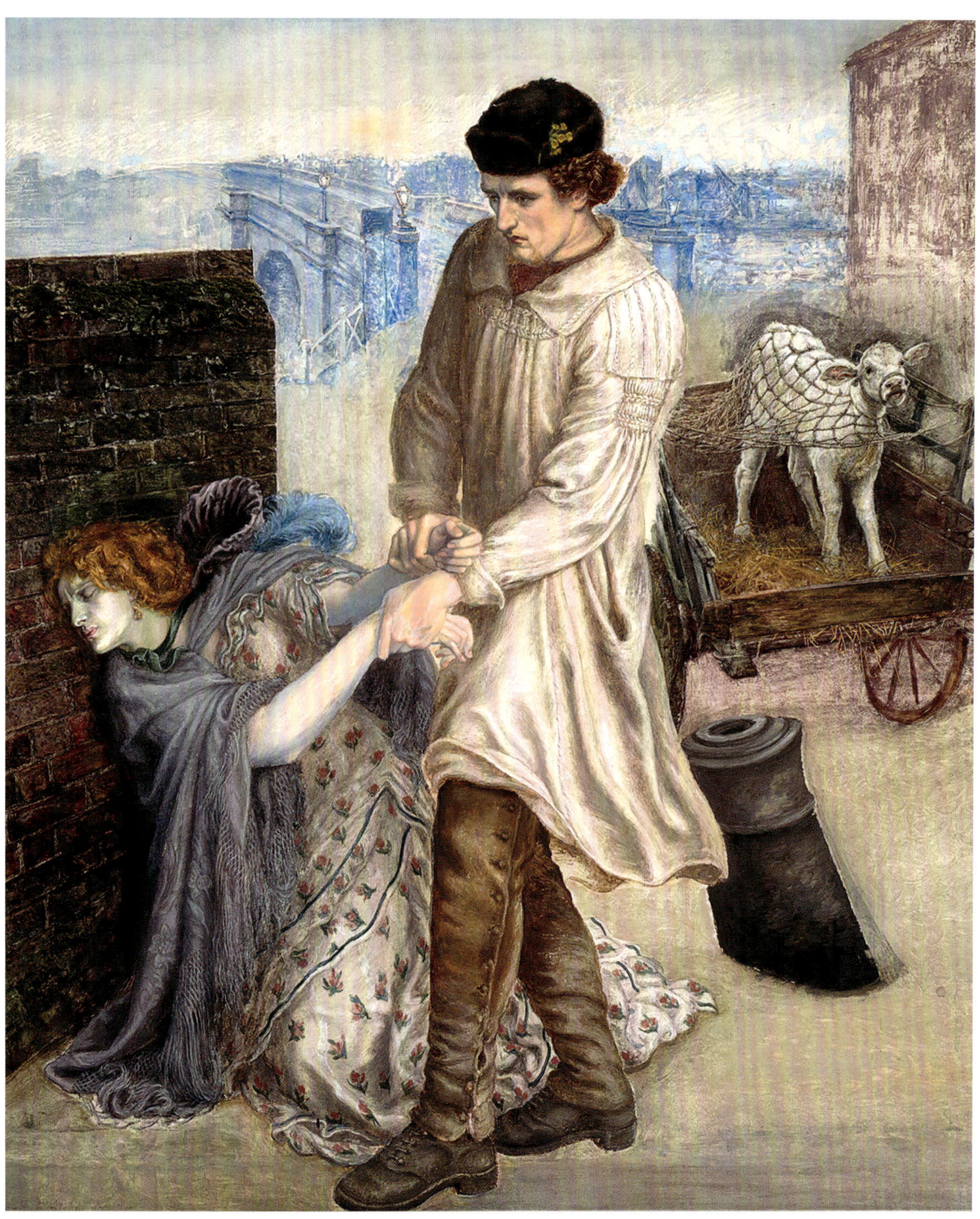

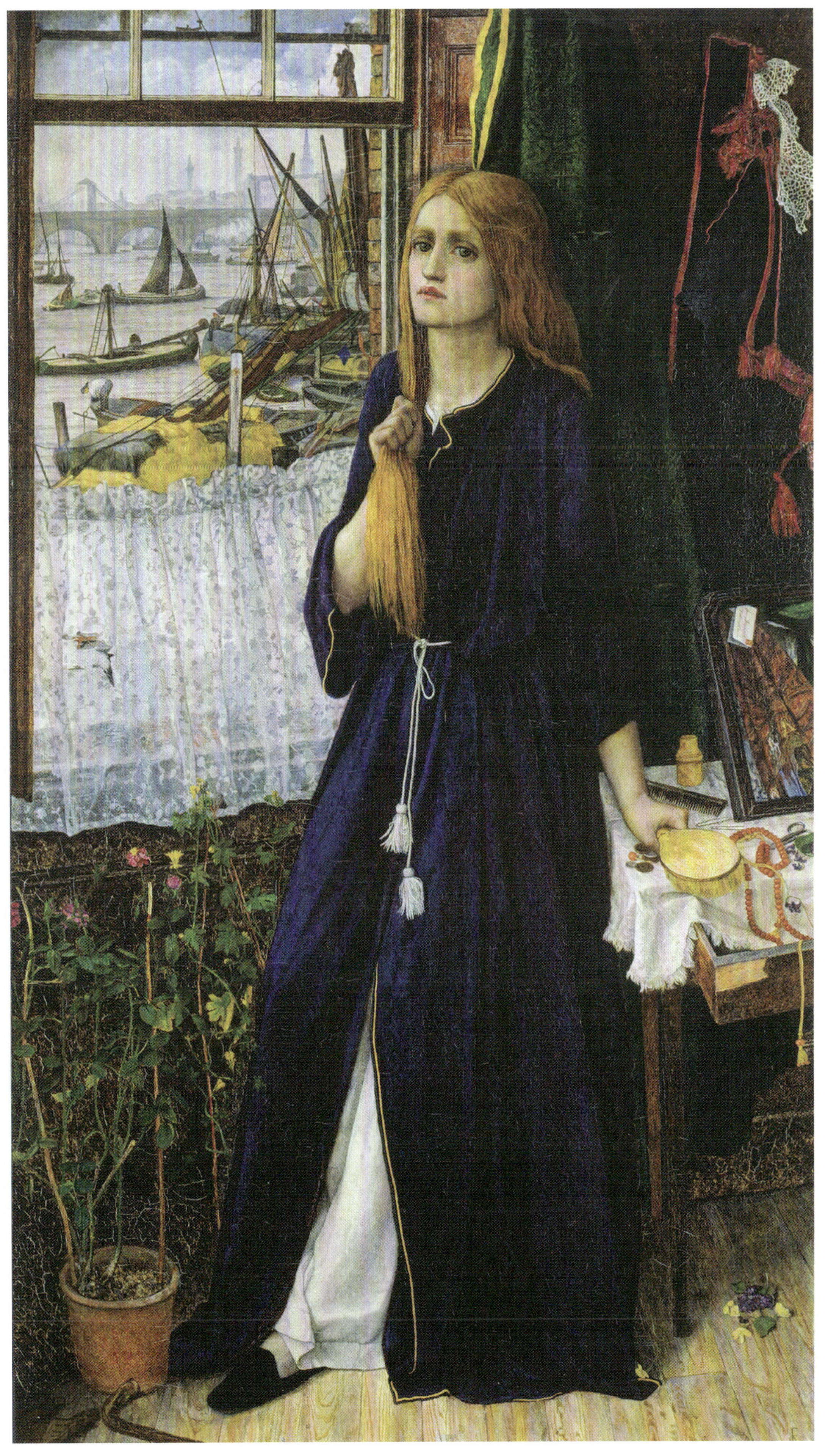

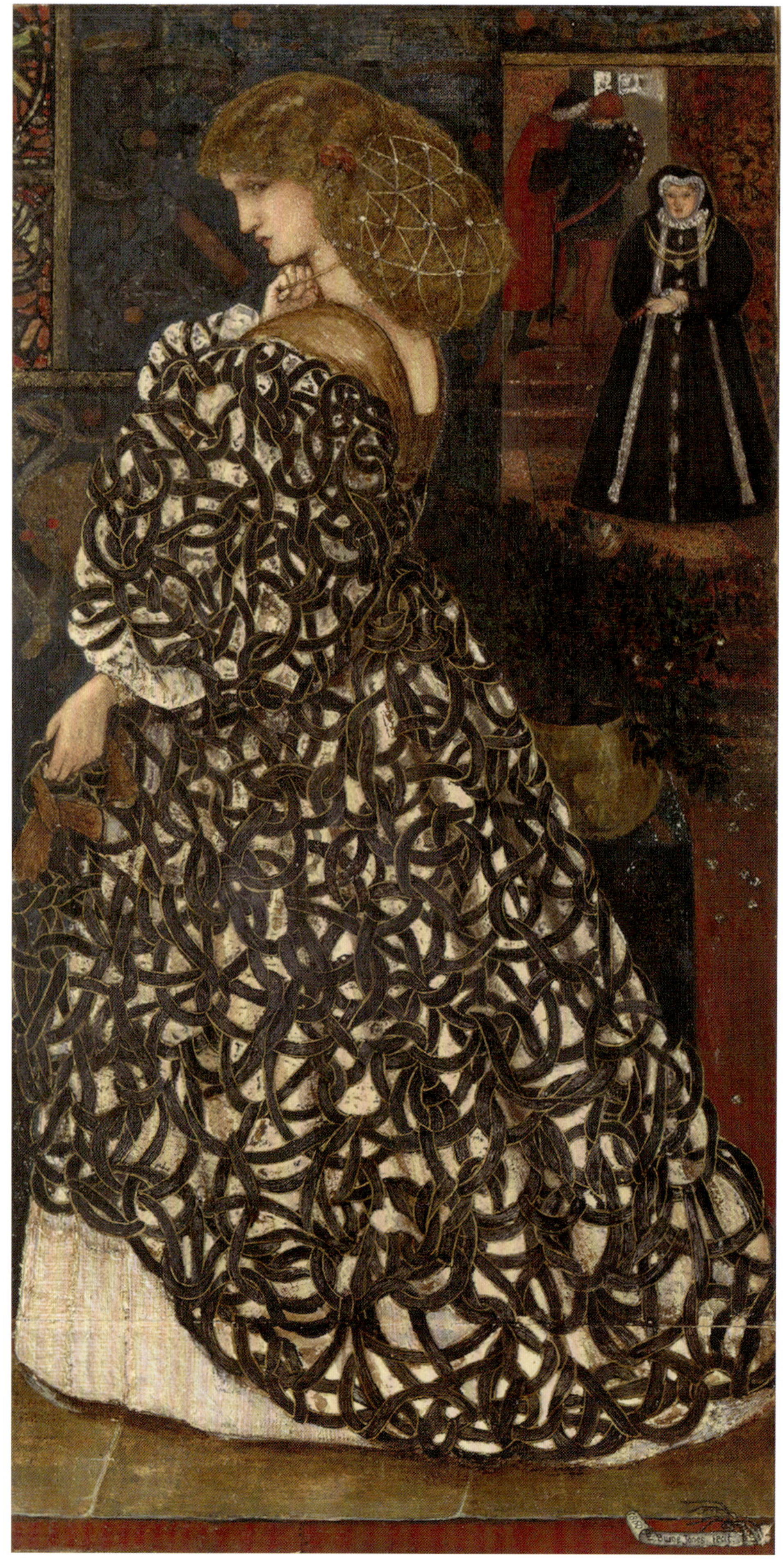

John Roddam Spencer Stanhope, an associate of the Pre-Raphaelites, whose studio was in the same building as Rossetti's, cast her as another 'gay woman [a.k.a prostitute] in her room by side of Thames' (ill. 50).[2] The man's gloves and stick on the floor indicate a departing client, while the shabby room and woman's nightwear convey her moral degradation. As with *The Awakening Conscience*, the theme invokes earlier innocence. Here, the woman's face is not her exact likeness but its haggard look is in keeping with the fate commonly ascribed to a fallen woman. An artist could not ask a friend or relative to pose for such a subject.

In December 1858, Cornforth met George Price Boyce, who noted her '[i]nteresting face and jolly hair and engaging disposition.'[3] In Stanhope's studio the following day

of 'breeding, education, or intellect'.[7] So she was ignorant and vulgar, but physically attractive, uninhibited, fun. Rossetti's poems from 1859 strongly indicate the start of their sexual relationship (his first). They include the dramatic monologue 'Jenny':

Lazy laughing languid Jenny
Fond of a kiss and fond of a guinea,
Whose head upon my knee to-night
Rests for a while, as if grown light
With all our dances.

She clearly liked the artists' world, and lost her heart to Rossetti. Although never introduced to any of his family or 'respectable' female acquaintances, she no doubt optimistically foresaw marriage. The equally uneducated Jane Burden had lately married Rossetti's new

Arrayed in silks and satins from the costume box, she looked the part. Gazing from balcony and boudoir, she was the part

they met again, so she had swiftly become established in the artists' circle, with Boyce an especial admirer.[4] A month later they met once more at the Argyle Rooms, a dancing and drinking venue, and in April, Boyce's diary recorded a visit to 'F.C.' (Cornforth or Cox?) at her new lodging in Waterloo.[5] He then commissioned her to sit to Rossetti, for the painting that became the notorious oil *Bocca Baciata* – 'more stunning than can be decently expressed', in Swinburne's view.[6] It signalled a major shift in Pre-Raphaelite art, from the chaste 'Florentine' mode to the sensuous 'Venetian' style. Fanny embodied this pictorial move from saints to courtesans. Cornforth was now aged 23. She had 'a mass of the most lovely blonde hair', with 'regular and sweet features', according to William Rossetti, which offset her total lack

friend William Morris; Annie Miller would soon be Captain Thomson's wife. So she was more than dismayed when, in spring 1860, Rossetti married Elizabeth Siddal, whose name was perhaps new to her. Her distress prompted a visit from Boyce, who found her ill in bed. 'She frets constantly about R., who is with his wife in Paris,' Boyce noted, adding that she was 'in a very nervous, critical state'.[8]

Several paintings featuring Cornforth – by Rossetti, Stanhope and Edward Burne-Jones – were completed in 1860. Burne-Jones depicted her in *Sidonia von Bork 1560* (ill. 51) as the evil sorceress or Amber Witch from a popular Gothic novel, and a companion picture to *Clara von Bork 1560* (ill. 95). She posed for the figure, her luxuriant blonde hair caught

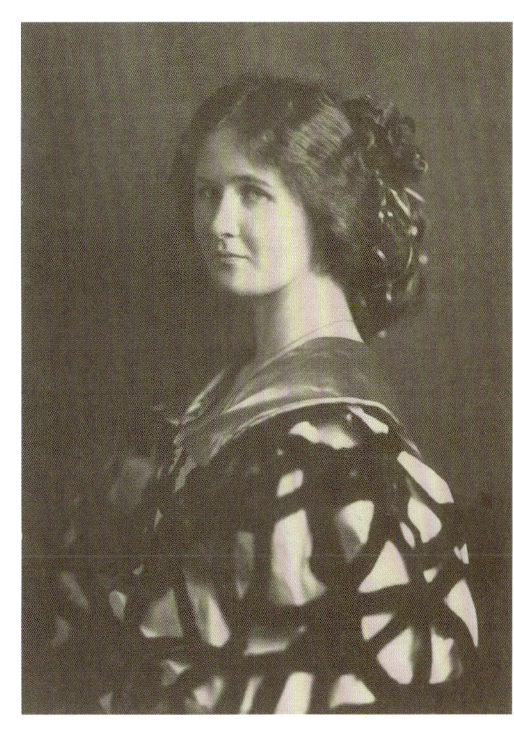

51 (opposite and p.75)
Sidonia von Bork 1560
Edward Burne-Jones, 1860
Watercolour and gouache
on paper, 333 × 171mm
Tate, London

52
Angela Thirkell
John Copperfield, 1910s
Platinum print, 198 × 141mm
National Portrait Gallery

53
Woman's Head
Dante Gabriel Rossetti, 1867
Coloured chalk on paper
420 × 370mm
National Trust Collections, Standen
House and Garden, West Sussex

54
Lady Lilith
After Dante Gabriel Rossetti,
published 1908
Chromolithograph
662 × 482mm
National Portrait Gallery

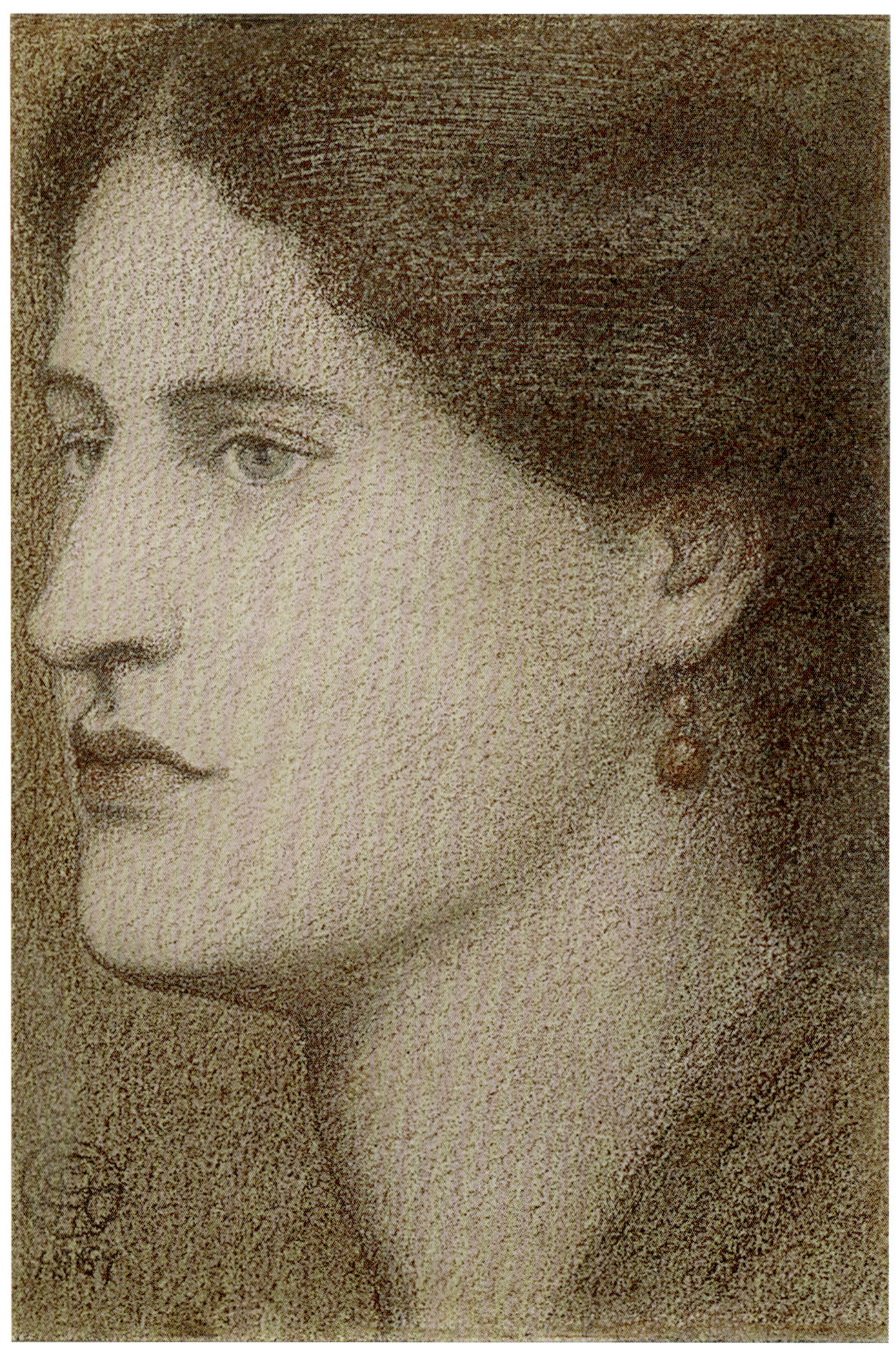

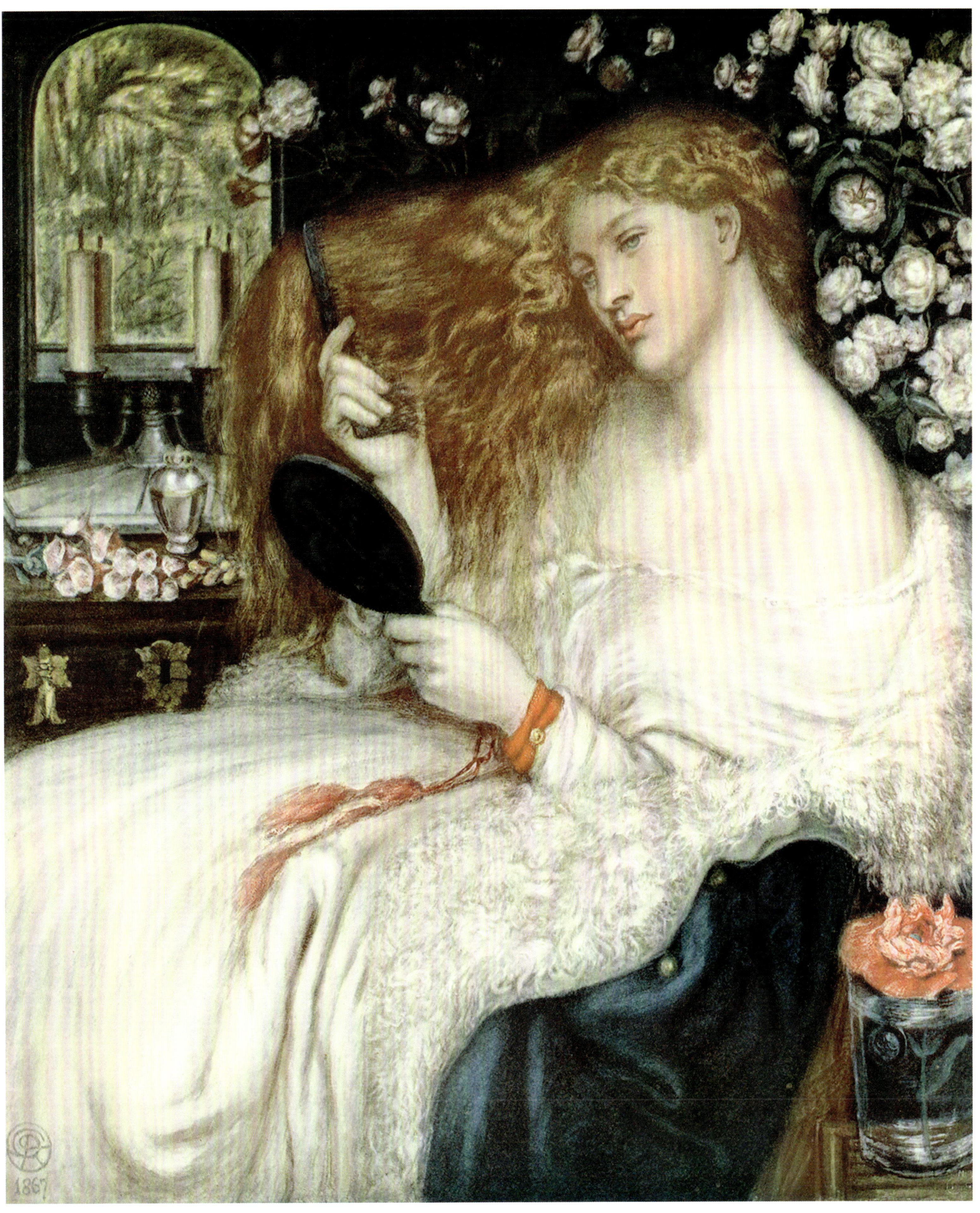

in a net, the links of which are magnified in the interlacing knot-bands or *fantasie dei vinci* on the dress. Pattern and enclosed space symbolise the future ensnarement of Clara, standing in the background. The composition and costume are indebted to a portrait from 1531 by Giulio Romano, which hangs at Hampton Court Palace. A version of the dress was later worn by the Burne-Joneses' granddaughter Angela (ill.52).

On 11 August 1860 Cornforth married Timothy Hughes, a mechanic in a local engineering works. And that might have been the end of her role as Pre-Raphaelite model. But almost as soon as Siddal was buried in early 1862, she reappeared in Rossetti's lodgings, which naturally prompted rumours that their affair had continued – even that Rossetti had been with her on the night of his wife's overdose. When George Boyce returned to London in the autumn and called on Rossetti at Tudor House, Chelsea, he '[f]ound Fanny there'.[9]

Il Dolce far niente. As well as Rossetti's *Bocca Baciata*, which was, incidentally seen as revoltingly sensual by Hunt.[11] Arrayed in silks and satins from the costume box, she looked the part. Gazing from balcony and boudoir, she was the part: concubine, mistress, courtesan in *Fair Rosamund*, *Aurelia (Fazio's Mistress)*, *Woman Combing her Hair*, *The Blue Bower*, *Lady Lilith* (ill.54). In time Rossetti learnt to use others' features for these close-up fantasies, but Cornforth's face, figure and open demeanour created the luxuriant role.

In *The Blue Bower* (ill.55), she gazes boldly at the viewer while fingering a musical instrument based on a Japanese koto, while oriental tiles reinforce the exotic theme. She wears a pale, downy undergarment, and foreground cornflowers evoke her assumed name. Rossetti described it as 'an oil picture all blue', as cobalt and ultramarine are offset by the sumptuous green gown and sensuous flesh tones, making this a triumphant exercise in the emerging Aesthetic mode.[12]

'Ignorant and vulgar, but physically attractive, uninhibited and fun'

On his next visit, Boyce '[f]ound him and Fanny at home. Stayed and dined. He gave me a pencil sketch of her as she lay on a couch, hair outspread, and her right hand under her head.'[10] Burne-Jones made a comparable sketch, a study for *Laus Veneris* (1873–5). And it was over the next few years that she had the greatest impact on Rossetti's art and that of the movement as a whole.

The sad, shame-stricken whores of *Found* and *Thoughts of the Past* were steadily displaced in Pre-Raphaelite art by resplendent beauties with 'jolly hair' and alluring looks, proudly meeting the male gaze. They include Frederic Leighton's Roman *La Nanna* (1859), and Hunt's

From 1863 to 1867, Cornforth was Rossetti's permanent companion, in a more or less unruly house and garden; when Boyce or poet William Allingham called, she was there, alone with Rossetti, sometimes with James McNeill Whistler and his then model Jo Heffernan or Frederick Sandys and Kiomi, 'his gipsy girl'. She sat less frequently, and she and Rossetti grew fat together. He rented a house for her in Royal Avenue, Chelsea, and coined affectionate nicknames – Lumpses, Chump-wump and Elephant (from 'Fan'). He made regular gifts to what he vulgarly called 'the Elephant's hole', depicting it as a money jar buried in the ground. Allingham recorded one June morning at Cheyne Walk:

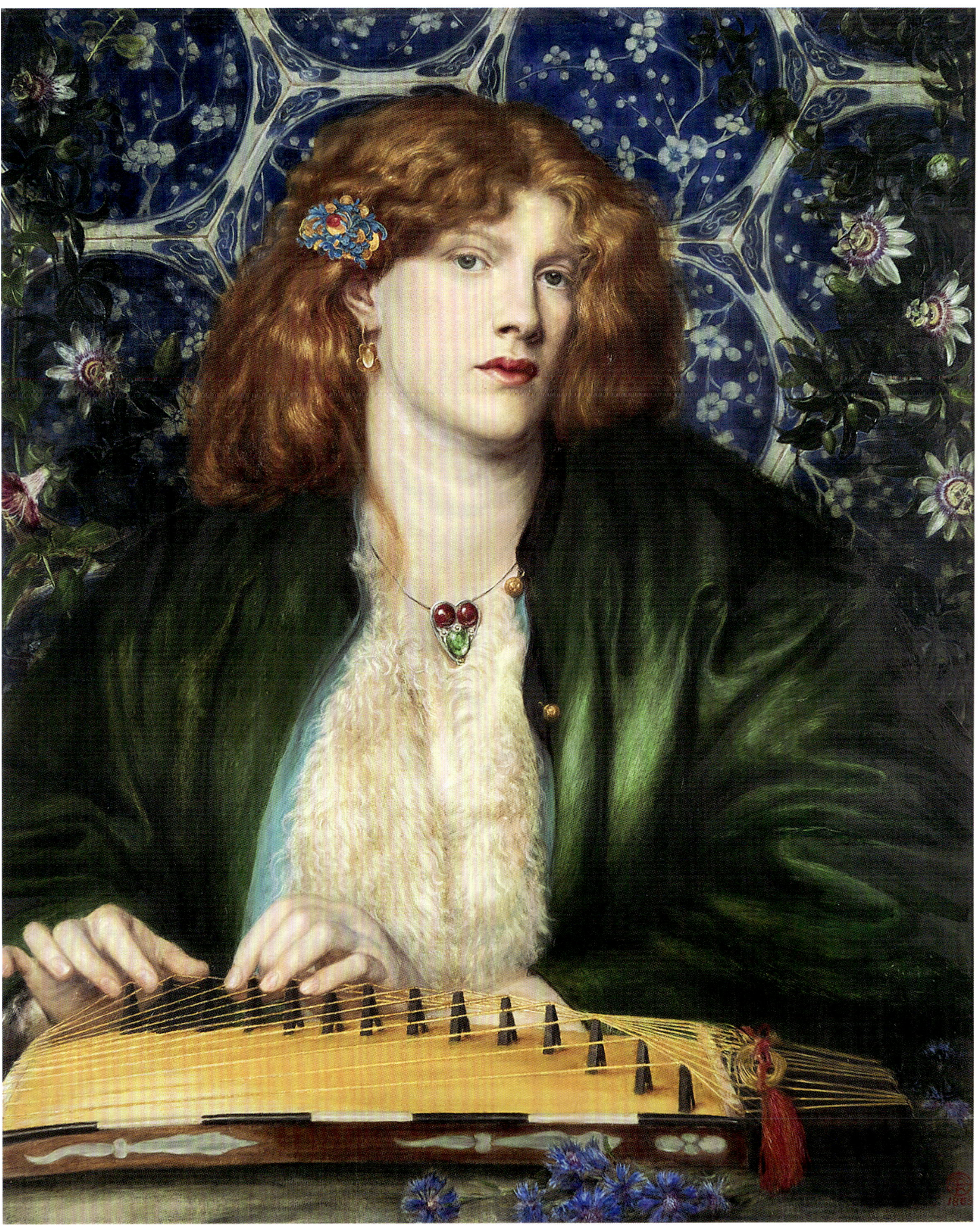

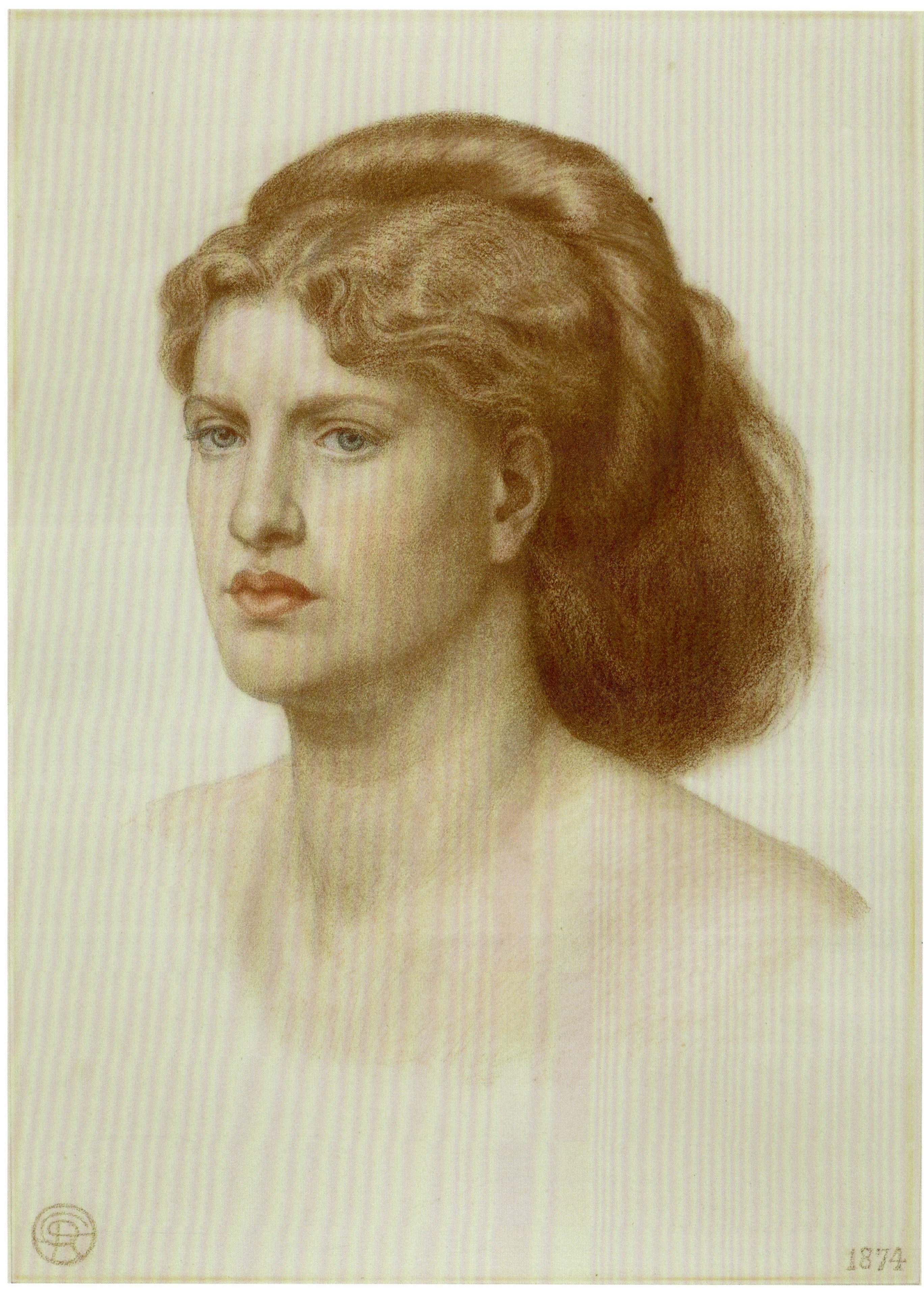

1874
1874

Breakfasted in a small lofty room on the first floor with window looking on the garden. Fanny in white. Then we went into the garden and lay on the grass, eating strawberries and looking at the peacock. F. went to look at the 'chicking', her plural of chicken. Then Swinburne came in, and soon began to recite…and after this Whistler, who talked about his own pictures.[13]

When the men laughed at her working-class accent, she protested: 'Well, I know I don't say it right.' But she also pursued education, taking lessons in 'correct' handwriting.

From 1868 she was less present, as Rossetti's pictorial attention focused on Jane Morris; then on his perceived persecution by critics following publication of his Poems. In 1872 he suffered a major paranoid

when not wanted the keys taken from me and that was the way I was treated for taking your part. I hope I shall see you again and be with you as before but I never wish to meet any of your friends after the cruel way I which I have been treated.[15]

Timothy Hughes having died in 1872, she remarried in 1879, to former bandsman John Bernard Schott, with whom she used her savings to lease a tavern in London's West End. In late 1881 she accompanied Rossetti on a trip to the Lake District. Persuaded to climb a small hill, Rossetti descended on his bottom, 'while Fanny lay down and almost burst with laughter'; she was, he said, 'wonderfully active, climbs and takes leaps and looks wonderfully well'.[16]

Fanny's face, figure and open demeanour created the luxuriant role

breakdown and was taken away from London by Madox Brown and other friends. A glamorised Rossetti pastel portrait from this period (ill. 56) shows her in her maturity, as 'a pre-eminently fine woman'.[14] It was probably intended as a gift and potentially saleable asset. In old age artworks represented her only wealth.

After Rossetti's return in 1874, she came when summoned to lift his despondent spirits, until a relapse in 1877 caused him to write, to declare that he could no longer support her. Her response was eloquent:

My dear R, You surely cannot be angry with me for doing what I have done after receiving such a letter from you telling me I must forget you and get my own living… You shall never say that I forsook you although I felt it very much when another woman was put in my place

On returning to London she was banished from his life, not informed of his final illness and not allowed to attend the funeral in April 1882. After Schott died, she gradually sold artworks and memorabilia, to artist and dealer Charles Fairfax Murray as well as to the Pre-Raphaelite collector, American industrialist Samuel Bancroft Jr, to whom, in 1899, she narrated the account of her meeting with Rossetti in the Royal Surrey Gardens half a century earlier.

When she developed dementia, Schott's sister sent her to West Sussex, where she entered the County Asylum, the equivalent of a care home. The portrait photo (ill. 57) taken on admission in 1907, aged 71, depicts a still handsome woman, albeit one described in the record as confused and agitated.[17] She died on 24 February 1909 and was buried in Chichester district cemetery.

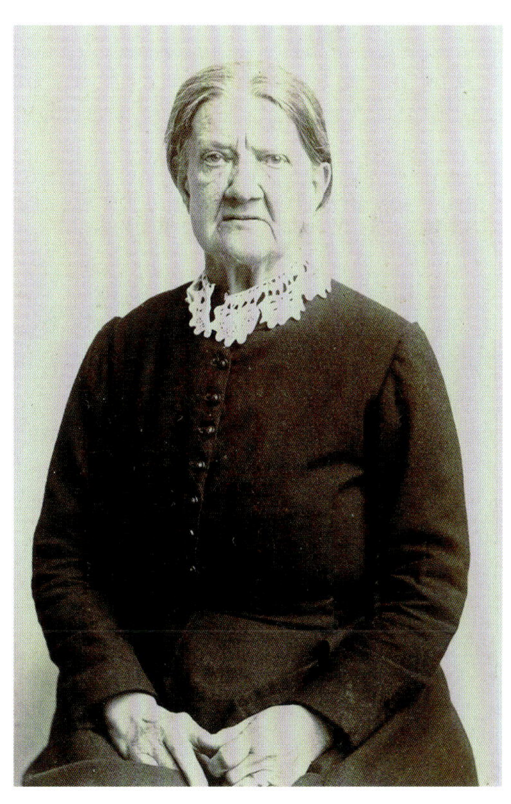

Joanna Boyce Wells

1832–1862

Belonging to the same generation as the PRB, Joanna Mary Boyce (later Wells) shared their ideals of fidelity to nature, honest feeling and fine colour, as well as John Ruskin's endorsement of 'sublimity, imagination and repose' as the hallmarks of excellence. She also shared the contemporary gender ideals of modesty, piety and service that often conflicted with personal aspiration.

She was supported by her businessman father and brothers – fellow artist George and lawyer Matthias – who urged her to prioritise art practice over social duty. 'I should if I so much more enjoyed painting, as you do, than almost anything else,' Matthias wrote.[1] But while her artist brother was able to devote months to study in London and summers to sketching in Wales and Italy, she enjoyed only intermittent courses at Cary's and Leigh's art academies (both in London), and occasional trips away. She was also notoriously self-critical. 'The fact is that what I do is so far inferior to what I admire,' she wrote, 'that I cannot help showing it when I hear my drawings unduly praised, as they so often are.'[2]

She was often obliged to persuade servants and neighbourhood children to pose for small rewards. She sought advice, frequently thanking fellow artist Henry Wells for 'criticising my drawing and pointing the way for improvement' as well as for opportunities to see artworks.[3] In 1852, for example, the pair attended an event where 'exquisite' engravings after Giotto and Fra Angelico were shown. That year also saw a short visit to Paris with her father, where she admired work by Ary Scheffer and Paul Delaroche but deemed other French painting 'in merit below our third-rate artists; disgusting in colour, false in feeling, theatric in attitude and studied and out-dried classicism in drawing of figures and draperies'.[4]

Back in London, she produced a highly accomplished and meticulously painted self-portrait (ill.59), showing the influence of the PRB in its rendering of detail and that of Scheffer in the cool tones and luminous background. She saw Millais's 'exquisite' *A Huguenot* at the RA, and his 'wonderful' *Mariana* (1851), later declaring that 'Millais if he lives must be one of our very first artists'.[5] On a rainy sketching trip in October, again with her father (who, sadly, died some

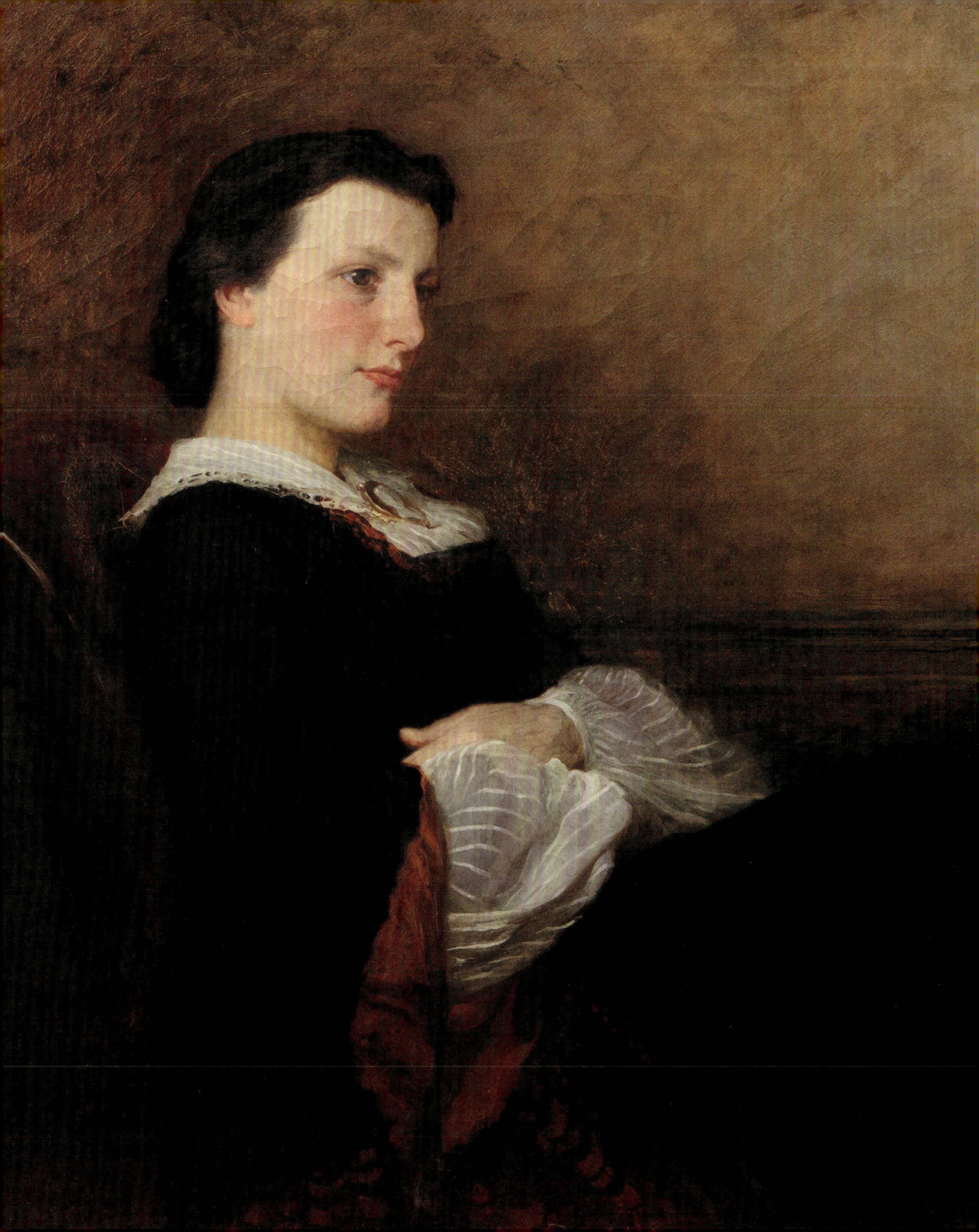

58
**Portable Sketching
Paintbox**
Owned by Joanna Boyce Wells,
1861–5
200 × 150 × 30mm
Private Collection

59
Self-portrait
Joanna Boyce Wells, 1852
Oil on canvas, 410 × 350mm
Private Collection

weeks later), she 'had recourse to a child in the village, a sturdy little chap who stands very still'; whom she depicted as *Little Welsh Boy* and which was noticed admiringly.[6]

The following winter saw the completion of several pictures, including the much-praised *Elgiva* (ill. 60). Using a family friend as model, the painting depicts an Anglo-Saxon queen who was persecuted, forcibly divorced, disfigured to destroy her beauty and finally murdered. Elgiva is shown here just before her face is branded. The 'slight arch of the lip seems to begin to quiver and the eyes fill with ineffable sadness', according to John Ruskin.[7] Both the early English subject and the luminous simplicity of the handling endow *Elgiva* with quintessential Pre-Raphaelite qualities. Joanna Boyce resisted pressure to exhibit:

A subsequent trip to the Netherlands introduced her to the 'wonderfully simple and grand' works by Memling in Bruges and the 'magnificent' altarpiece by van Eyck in Ghent.[12] Antwerp with 'many splendid Rubens' was followed by Breda, Rotterdam, The Hague, Amsterdam, Hanover, Cologne, Brussels and the obligatory Waterloo. And it seems that this tour and Howitt's book strengthened her ambition, for the winter saw several works completed, and the possibility of studying in Paris.

So, in spring 1855, both *Elgiva* and a portrait of Lilly Ridley, Matthias Boyce's bride-to-be, were sent to the RA summer show. Both were disappointingly hung in a corner, but as she was told, 'Never mind where you are now placed – resolve to struggle for your own position'.[13]

'I have talents or a talent and with it the constant impulse to employ it…for the love of it and the longing to work'

'I would give a great deal not to send it [to Exhibition] so soon after dear Pa's death. I cannot bear the idea but George and Wells urge it too and I fear I must yield.'[8] In the event, the picture was not submitted.[9]

She possibly regretted her decision when she saw works by Anna Mary Howitt, which were 'not at all marvellous'; although 'very good in feeling', the actual painting was 'bad in colour and surface'.[10] After reading Howitt's account of study in Munich, she felt 'confident were I placed as she has been and blessed with sound health and God's blessing, I could do greater things in the painting way than she has'. But, Boyce added piously, it was her 'plain duty to give up all hope of improvement in painting rather than in any way neglect Mamma. I have a difficult path to steer, but God will lead me.'[11]

Henry Wells insistently proposed marriage. Boyce wished to develop her career, and her mother was opposed to the match, but eventually agreed to a long engagement. When her works at the RA attracted critical praise, Wells was jubilant: Ruskin's notice was 'certainly the most trumping criticism that ever was awarded to the first exhibited work of an artist'.[14] She was urged to attend the RA exhibitors' party, where 'There will be few painters who this year have not heard of Miss J.M. Boyce.'[15] She confessed that 'for years' she had wanted to attend the soirée, 'that I might see many men whose works I admire… I will not lose this opportunity – it is my first and may be my last.'[16] Nonetheless, she stayed away, lest she be deemed immodest.

After a trip to the great Exposition Universelle, her planned study in Paris was in

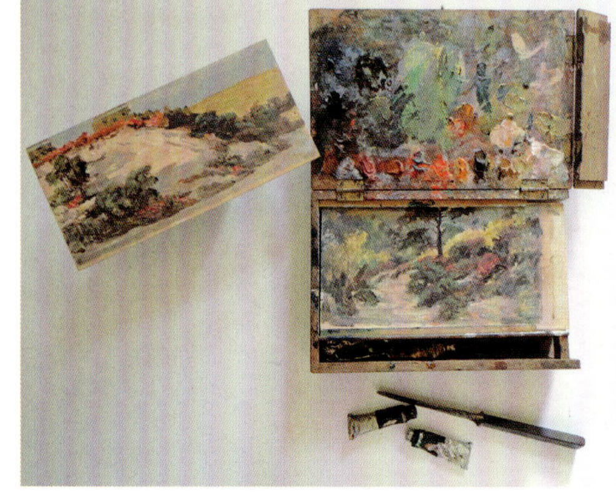

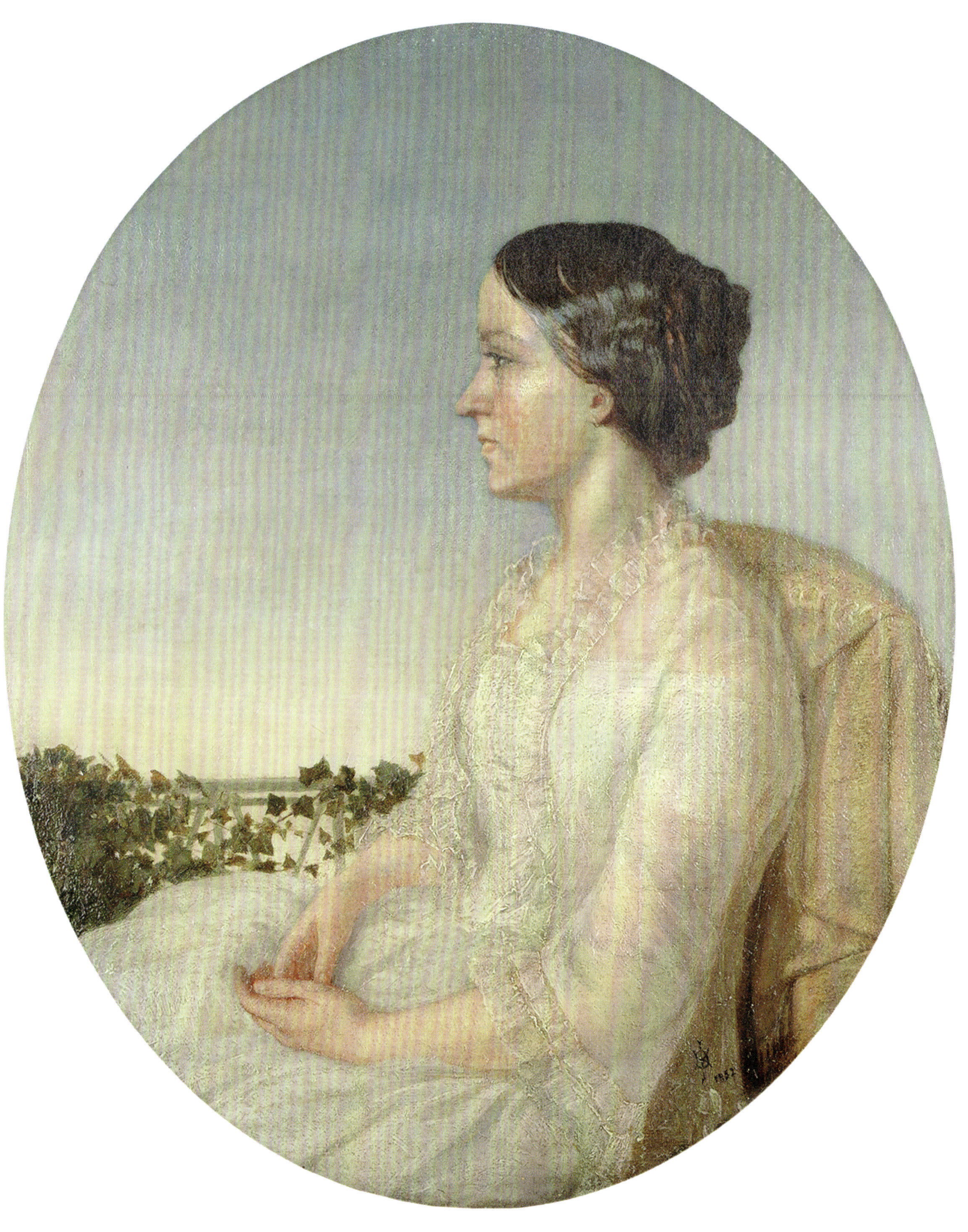

prospect. By mid-November in 1855 she was lodging with Madame Hereau, 'a severe and imperious dame', and attending a ladies' class at the atelier of Thomas Couture, acclaimed artist of *Les Romains de la décadence* (1847).[17] Couture's teaching concentrated on têtes d'expression, to convey emotion, drawn from live models. She wrote:

> I enjoyed my morning's work exceedingly (drawing from the nude). So far from shrinking from it at first, as I expected, I had no sooner taken one glance at the model and put my charcoal to paper, than all reluctance vanished and I am convinced that any girl may draw as I have been drawing yesterday and this morning, as free from harm or any danger of it, as though they studied a bunch of flowers or a landscape.[18]

The daily schedule was work in the studio from 9am to 2pm, with three short breaks, followed by 'reading, writing, practising' in the afternoon.[19] This was valuable experience of sustained art practice without domestic duties, and the goal was a picture for the 1856 RA show. But Couture's technique did not please Boyce, who described it as 'slap-dashism'.[20] In place of the meticulous practice favoured by the PRB, he advocated loose, expressive studies and vigorous, well-loaded brushstrokes. She lamented: 'I am disgusted with what I do… I am certain if I sent a head this year to the Academy folks would think someone had painted *Elgiva* for me'.[21]

Nonetheless, her oil portrait of Mme Hereau was praised by fellow students and brother George for its surprising 'breadth and vigour', a 'general pleasing effect' and 'many "precious passages" of colour'.[22]

Being in Paris brought the additional occupation of art reviewing, which was good training in critical assessment. Notices of the Exposition Universelle, commissioned by the *Saturday Review*, resulted in trenchant opinions, including a severe judgement on Ingres, then one of France's most celebrated painters but who was, in Boyce's view: '[a]n execrable draftsman, a bad colorist, a man with no intensity of feeling or power of imagination, how has he attracted such a crowd of worshippers?

By painting blue satin or ecstatic saints?'[23] She preferred atmospheric views of rural life and Delacroix's *Massacre at Chios* (1824), which exemplified 'the one great secret of picture-making – the power of seeing and working out the moment par excellence which interprets all in itself – that moment which seems to grasp its own past and future, which is at once the casket containing precious things, and the key which unlocks it.'[24] These forthright remarks revealed her as an authoritative and disinterested critic, committed to quality and content.

Bringing several unfinished canvasses and a cast of Charles Cordier's *Vénus africaine* (1852), she returned to London with renewed artistic seriousness and self-criticism, sending her portrait of Mme Hereau to the RA, despite seeing its faults.[25] At the RA Exhibition she liked Millais's *Autumn Leaves* (1855–6) but was baffled by Hunt's *The Scapegoat* (1854–6), seeking from her brother George 'any clue to any hidden meaning there may be'.[26]

Writing on the lesser London exhibitions, she admitted that

> wading through these collections is rather weary work; for the very few pieces that are deserving of notice, are but cases in a desert of upwards of two thousand canvasses. Still, these exhibitions have their uses and advantages, both for artists and for the public, and we may fairly hope that each year will bring us good pictures in increasing proportion, as a new energy is clearly discernible in a large body of our younger artists.[27]

She spent the next months in London and Brighton, painting, freeing herself from her quarrelsome mother, resisting Henry Wells and planning a visit to Italy. She earmarked *Rowena*, a second Saxon heroine in 1856, and *Our Housemaid* (1856–7), a head study painted from a 'fat Welsh' girl named May, for the RA. She also finally determined to marry, on certain conditions. When Henry Wells had declared that for women love came before intellect, Boyce fiercely defended her artistic vocation and independence. What had love to do with the intellect of Catherine the Great, Sarah Siddons, Mary Somerville, George Sand,

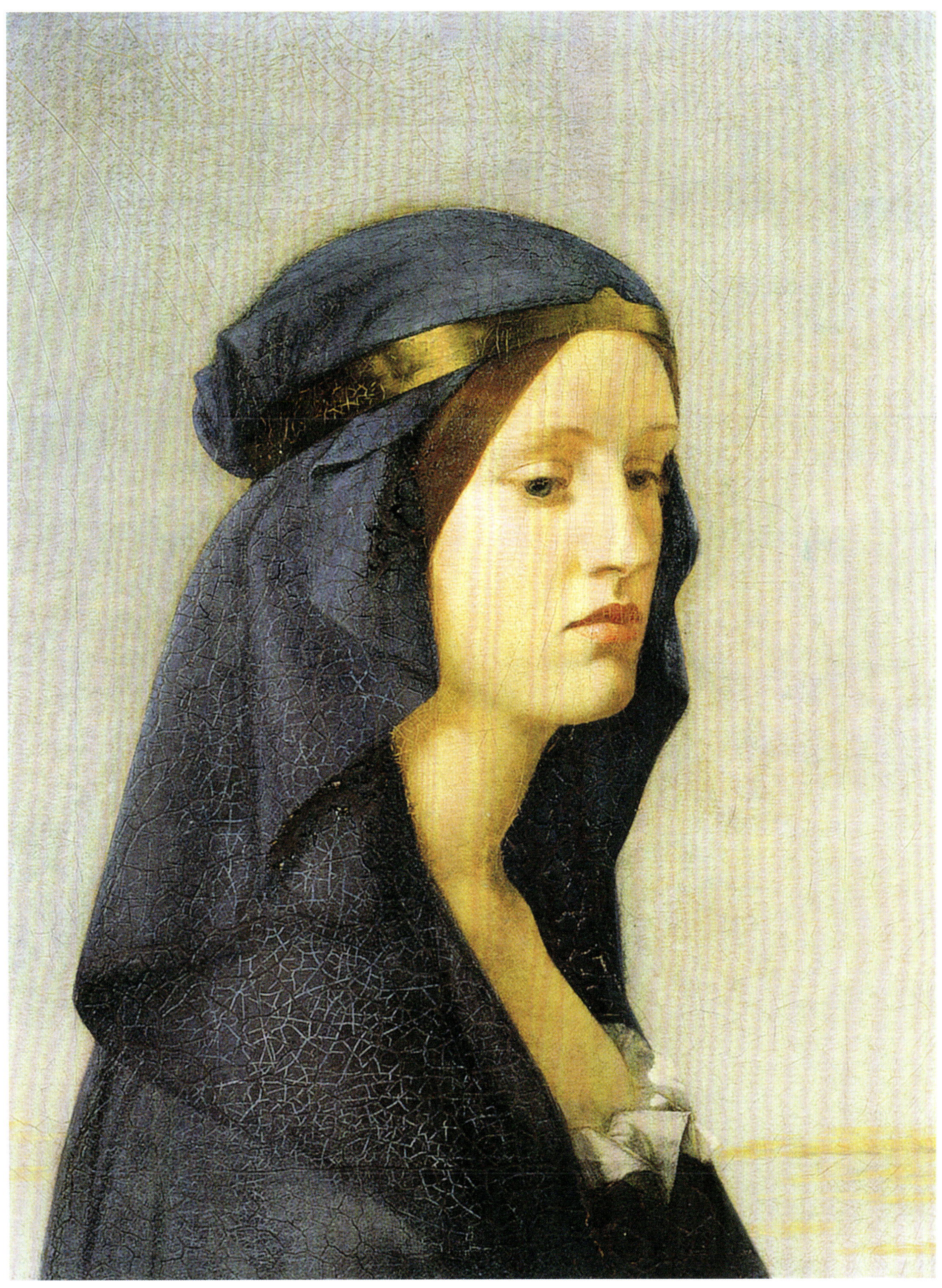

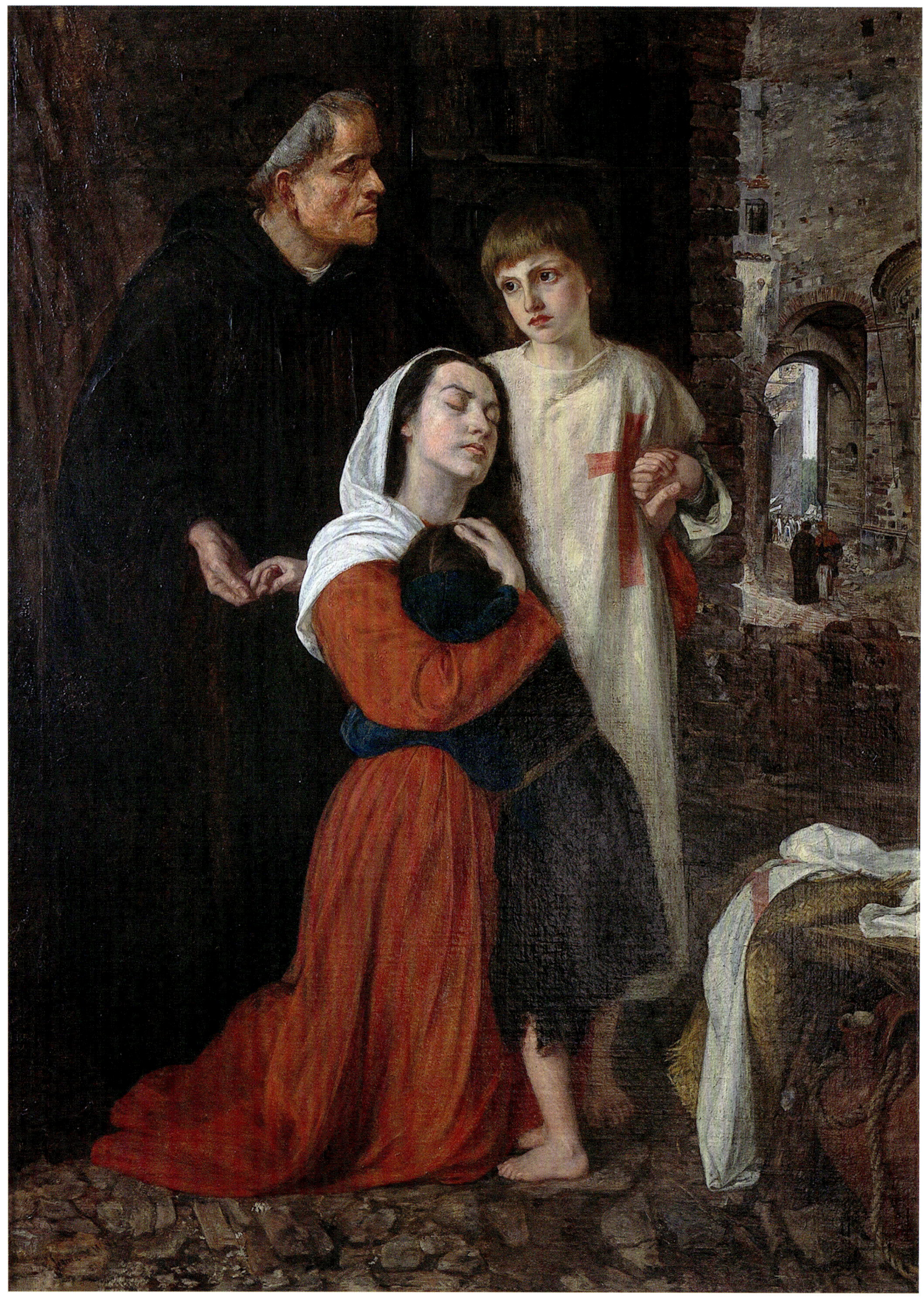

Elizabeth Barrett Browning? Quoting *Aurora Leigh*, she told Wells he thought 'like a man, who sees a woman as the complement of his sex merely':

If Mrs B[arrett]. B[rowning]. had been your wife, you would have said "It is not your duty to engage in the strife of the world for public fame instead of ministering at your own home, sew on my buttons, darn my socks, make my puddings and write no books." Yes, but Mrs B. says, "I have a mind, which wants food and exercise". Answer "Converse with me, soothe me with thy lighter fancies, touch me with thy finer thought"'.[28]

Whereas, Boyce continued, 'Where God gives powers, He gives responsibilities to man or woman; and if men take upon themselves to prevent as much as possible women from improving and making use of the talents committed to them, the responsibility is chiefly at their door.'

Rome, in the company of an art-student friend who had married an Italian. Using opera glasses, she lay on the floor of the Sistine Chapel, studying the fresco figures. Then they moved to the Apennine town of Todi, where she felt 'wonderfully industrious', despite complaining bitterly about mosquitoes and fleas, and set to work on *The Departure* (ill.61), using local models and streetscapes.[30]

The painting depicts an imagined incident from the apocryphal 'children's crusade' of 1212, as a mother bids farewell to boys leaving on a doomed enterprise. Conveying both emotional tension and Pre-Raphaelite piety – the composition echoes that of the traditional Holy Family – it belongs conceptually to the early phase of the movement. The choice of subject may have been prompted by the European location, as well as by Millais's plan to paint a family witnessing British crusaders' departure.

In October Boyce and Henry Wells met in Florence, travelled via Perugia, Assisi and Spoleto to Rome, and married there before continuing to Naples, where they were only

The Departure: An Episode of the Child's Crusade, 12th Century
Joanna Boyce Wells, 1857–61
Oil on canvas, 785 × 590mm
Dr Dennis T. Lanigan Collection

Sidney Wells
Joanna Boyce Wells, 1859
Oil on canvas, 276 × 251mm
Tate, London

'A great artist sacrificed to bringing more kids into the world'

She concluded,
But I have talents or a talent and with it the constant impulse to employ it, – not for notoriety or fame, but for the love of it and the longing to work. In fact the impulse to work constantly in one direction is a God-given proof of a certain degree of power, and no man has a right to say that that warning is to be unheeded.[29]

In May 1857, her *Housemaid* was exhibited at the RA, and *Rowena* was rejected. She and Wells visited *The Art Treasures* exhibition in Manchester, and then she departed for

slightly discommoded by an earthquake and cheerfully climbed to the crater of Vesuvius. They then returned to Rome, where he had portrait commissions and she hired a painting room in a Borghese palazzetto. Further delayed by an early miscarriage, the couple were back in London by April 1858, she bringing several studies and many new ideas.

One task was to complete *The Departure*. When dining with the Wellses, Millais suggested some unrecorded amendments to the work. On exhibition it was 'shamefully and unjustly hung' but praised for its 'forcible and natural'

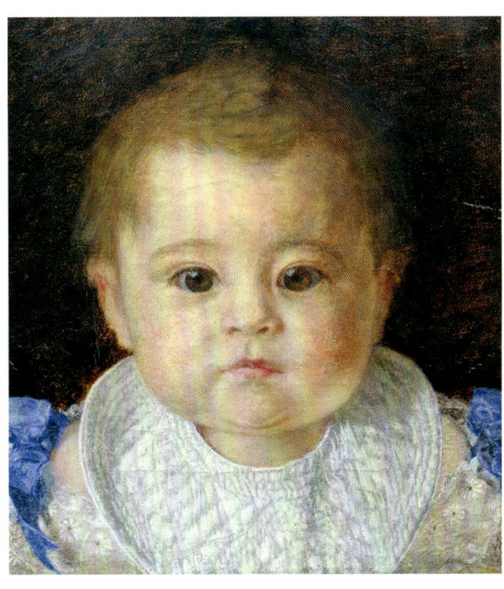

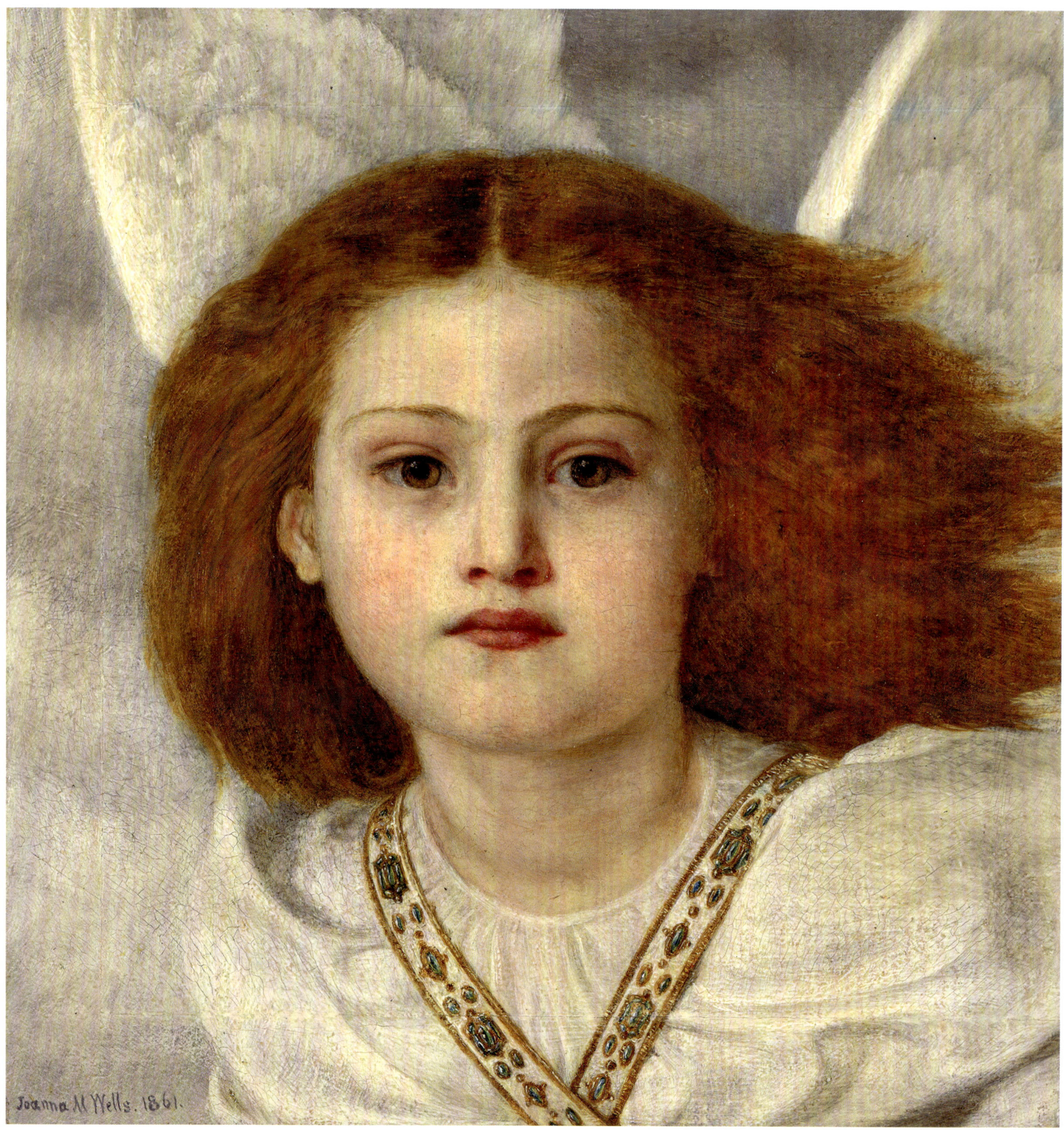
Joanna M Wells. 1861.

expressiveness and original subject –
'a refreshing change from the usual scenes
from Shakespeare'.[31]

Aiming for an industrious artistic
partnership, her life was equally occupied
with childbearing and painting. Henry,
who had no pictorial imagination, pursued
portraiture, while marvelling at Joanna's
capacity to find subjects everywhere:

> She simply sits down at the side of
> one of the country roads and faces
> an angle…where a broad sheep track
> works up the steep incline, the high
> and irregular embankment is surmounted
> with a most magnificent group of gorse,
> which waves about in the wind like
> giant hearse plumes…[and] paints it
> late in the evening, with a stormy sky
> and howling wind [as] up the steep
> bank a poor haggard woman and
> tired child are toiling. I think this is
> real poetry.'[32]

Exhibiting now as Mrs Joanna Wells, she
sent three works to the Liverpool Autumn
Exhibition. A view of 'an old homestead
on the Surrey hills' was hung at the RA,
while a stormy landscape shown elsewhere
was praised by *The Spectator* as 'a painted
thought, and very simply painted'.[33] It sold
to the Pre-Raphaelite patron Thomas Plint.

During the summer of 1859 *Do I Like
Butter?* and *Peep-bo!* were commenced,
followed by a tender, unsentimental
portrait of her son Sidney (ill. 62), born on
19 January that year. She was delighted
by 'his large eyes, dear round little face,
his briskness and his intelligence'.[34] All
qualities are effectively captured in paint
and enhanced by the delicate depiction of
quilted bib and blue bows. Sadly, Sidney
would not live into adulthood. On 4 January
1860 her daughter Alice was born, five
months before *The Departure* was ill hung at
the RA, and *Sidney* was rejected.

Joanna's confidence in her work
nonetheless prevailed. Hearing that Rebecca
Solomon's picture of Peg Woffington was
priced at 250 guineas, she asked her
husband to raise that of *The Departure*
(despite adding, 'I think 150 is more than it
is worth') and declared her pride in fellow
artists' support.[35]

The following year she had more
success: *The Heather-Gatherer* and
La Veneziana, a half-length courtesan
in 'Venetian' mode, were sold before
exhibition, followed by *Peep-bo!*. She was
pregnant for the third time but still working
hard, producing both a head study of Fanny
Eaton and *Thou Bird of God* (ill. 63), inspired
by Robert Browning's poem 'The Guardian-
Angel'. She perhaps felt in need of angelic
safeguarding while working on this small
simple, exquisite painting.

After the birth of a second daughter, she
succumbed to obstetric fever, caused by lack
of hygiene. According to the maternity nurse,
she had asked for a mirror so she might
study the view of a sick room. 'She was
evidently thinking of turning it to account in
her painting,' commented Henry sadly, listing
a score of 'commencements of paintings and
sketches of lovely ideas for future works now
doomed not to be executed'. These included
a study of Faust's Gretchen, two subjects
featuring Fanny Eaton as a Sibyl and Queen
Zenobia, as well as a version of King
Cophetua and the Beggar-maid.[36]

Joanna Wells died at midday on 15 July
1861. At her husband's request, Rossetti was
asked to undertake a study, made the same
afternoon (ill. 64). According to William
James Stillman, Rossetti lamented her death
as that of 'A great artist sacrificed to bringing
more kids into the world, as if there were not
other women just fit for that'.[37]

Henry Wells grieved deeply, striving
to create memorials for their children,
commissioning a death mask and a marble
bust, and endeavouring to complete a
portrait of her.

The portrait (ill. 65) conveys a
confident, thoughtful personality. 'She was
probably conscious of power, but quite free
from self-applause,' wrote William Rossetti;
'looking upon what she had done as
a mere imperfect earnest of what she
might aim at doing.'[38] To Elizabeth
Siddal, she 'must have been the head of
the firm' (that is, the Wellses' marriage
partnership), while to Rossetti 'this
wonderfully gifted woman' reached heights
in art, 'and in private life her greatness
of goodness was no less rare'.[39] As it was,
her role in the evolving Pre-Raphaelite
movement was largely forgotten until
rediscovered by feminist historians in the
late twentieth century.

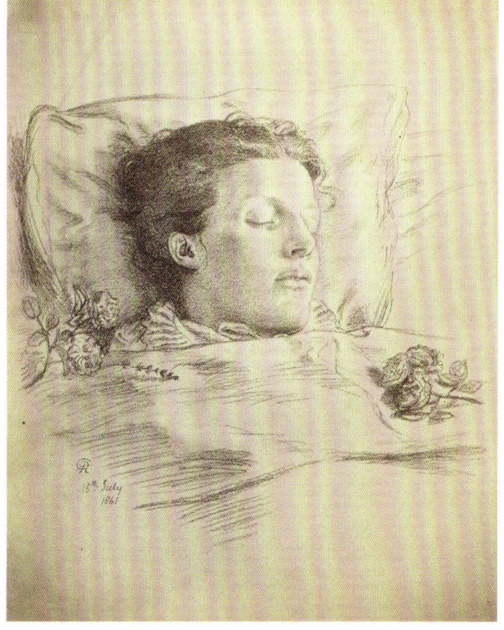

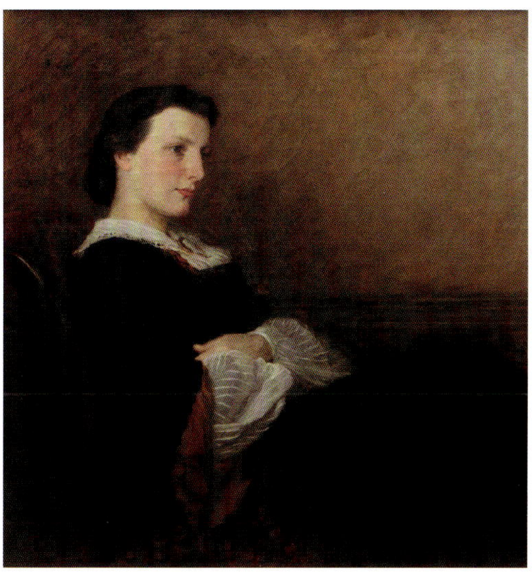

63 (opposite)
Thou Bird of God
Joanna Boyce Wells, 1861
Oil on card, 210 × 205mm
Private Collection

64 (below)
**Joanna Wells
on her Deathbed**
Dante Gabriel Rossetti, 1861
Unmounted cabinet card
181 × 150mm
Private Collection

65 (bottom and p.87)
Joanna Wells
Henry Tanworth Wells, 1850–60
Oil on canvas, 900 × 900mm
Tim and Philip Jackson

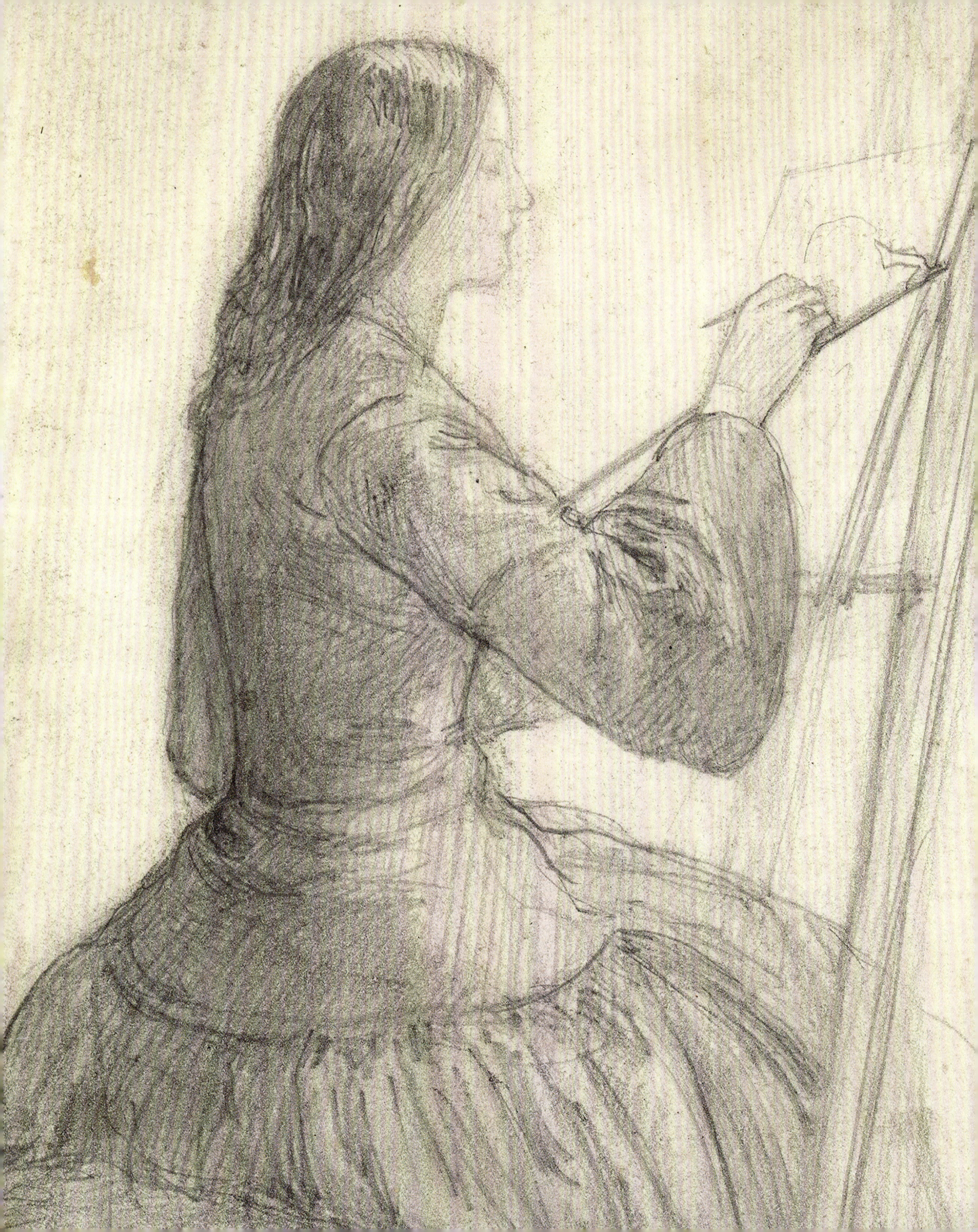

When Pre-Raphaelitism emerged, women's art was seen as a domestic activity rather than a professional practice. But by the end of the century, it was recognised that women were serious contenders for the opportunities that allowed an artist to make their name.

Beyond the Parlour

by Pamela Gerrish Nunn

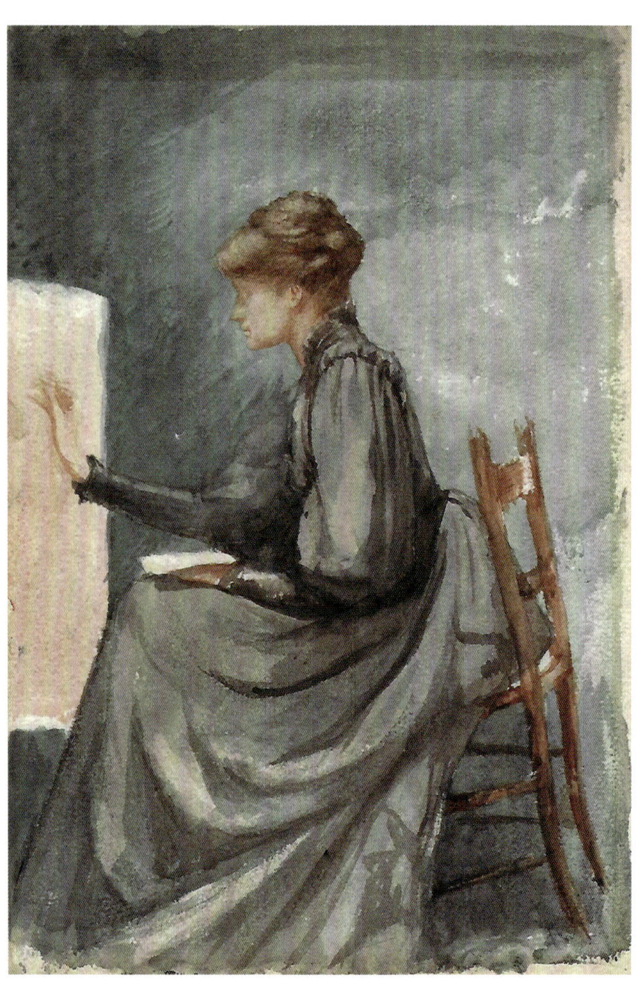

In the first British census, of 1841, a mere 278 women identified themselves as artists – but this career became one of the most visible options available in the climate of change effected by the Women's Rights movement, as it sought greater self-determination for women of all classes from the 1840s. So much so, that artist Anna Mary Howitt, reflecting in 1880 on her Pre-Raphaelite beginnings, wrote: 'The difficulties which the habits of society of that day placed in the way of a young woman seeking an independent career in Art, or, indeed, in any other direction, have now almost wholly passed away.'[1]

The 'woman question', as it was termed, resonated hugely in the cultural world, and the British art scene developed during the second half of the century from being founded on institutionalised male privilege and female marginalisation to accommodating a more diverse and dynamic situation that no longer contained women's artistic interests within domestic confines. Fine-art players such as the RA, the old and the new watercolour societies, the various training outfits that prepared students to be artists, the Government School of Design and the art press came under scrutiny as feminist energy increased in range and force.

Any Victorian artist's concerns had to be how to get a good training, how to put original work before the public, how to attract serious critical attention, and how to secure commissions and sales. Success in this endeavour distinguished the professional from the amateur. Where to begin, then, was a tricky question for the woman wishing to move her creativity beyond the parlour, and to make a profession of what conventional thinking deemed nothing more than a suitable hobby.

The dominant professional body for artists in this period was the RA in London, established around a century earlier in 1768. Its Schools and its annual exhibition enjoyed pre-eminence as taste-making forces, which aided professional advancement through a kind of freemasonry, shaping the face of British art and, until the last quarter of the century, forming public opinion and reputations. Lesser bodies existed, but their assumptions and processes essentially reflected their rivalry with the RA, even when they conducted themselves with less formality and investment in tradition. The trouble for women was that the RA was much like a gentleman's club – tacitly and practically a men-only preserve – a stance imitated by most of the secondary bodies in the field.

Some women, then, like Joanna Boyce, started on the pre-Academic routes to professional proficiency provided by Sass's (later Cary's), Leigh's (later Heatherley's) or the Government School of Design (a system that included a special place for women, the Female School), adding public lectures at various institutions. Sharing the adventurous attitude formed among the Pre-Raphaelites in the crucible of 1848, Howitt went to train in Munich, while Boyce managed six months in a Parisian atelier.[2] Artists' own initiatives to develop their abilities could supplement this formal training; these usually being men-only affairs, Howitt's and Barbara Bodichon's participation in the Pre-Raphaelite circle's Folio Club is notable.[3]

These women were well informed, purposeful, alert to the times and enjoyed some familial encouragement. Many more, such as Elizabeth Siddal and Georgiana Macdonald (Burne-Jones), found themselves drawn by circumstance from amateurism towards the professional practice of their male relatives, involved but untutored.[4] The difference between the untaught amateur – whose art occurred in the home and family – and the trained professional woman – whose art sought remuneration and a public platform – was of great significance: crucially, the former fitted within the status quo, while the latter challenged or even violated it. Feminists and conservatives alike recognised that Victorian society preferred a wife, sweetheart or sister to identify herself as the helpmeet of a male artist, not as his colleague and certainly not as his competitor. Studio assistant or copyist was a recognised job (albeit with low standing and few prospects), but if a woman performed such a part for a man to whom she was related, it would be seen not as a step on the professional ladder but as within her role of wife/daughter/sister. The social constraints that inhibited middle-class women from building a career from their enthusiasm for art are well illustrated by the contrasting experiences of artist siblings John and Rosa Brett, George and Joanna Boyce, and Frederick and Emma Sandys, all attracted by the potential in Pre-Raphaelitism for a more modern art practice. To be related to a male artist, while often seen as the gateway to a career (Rebecca Solomon is a case in point), could simply leave the woman in her father's/husband's/ brother's shadow – emphatically the case of Emma Sandys.

This thinking kept women domesticated and limited their creative ambition. But it had to be publicly justified when, in 1860, Laura Herford passed the RA Schools' entry test anonymously, and the RA baulked at admitting her. Its obvious reluctance to admit that its discriminatory men-only habit was not in fact prescribed by statute ensured that women artists' professional ambitions remained a talking-point – all the more so as the RA attempted to institute a quota for female students in a bid to retain control of the issue. When the Slade School of Fine Art was set up in London a decade later, its first Professor, Edward Poynter, made its promised equal treatment of female students a claim to modernity. Evelyn Pickering (later De Morgan) proved the point when she became one of the School's earliest prizewinners. Maria Zambaco was another to benefit from the Slade's even-handedness after training with its second Professor, Alphonse Legros, to establish herself in the 1880s as a medallist.

Once trained, an artist sought public appearance in a recognised forum. Some exhibiting bodies permitted only members to exhibit, which was called out as a barrier to women's professionalisation.[5] Howitt attempted to start her exhibition career, as Rossetti had, at the independent, unjuried Free Exhibition (aka National Institution), looking for a more open-minded audience than the public that flocked to the RA exhibitions. But, by 1854, Pre-Raphaelitism's presence in London exhibitions had broadened many minds as to what contemporary art might look like, and significantly more women's works were to be seen in the capital's principal shows thereafter: between 1855 and 1860, not only Howitt, Boyce and Solomon but also Anna Blunden, Rosa Brett, Jane Benham Hay and Emily Osborn came to notice alongside the already established exhibitors Margaret Carpenter and Henrietta Ward.[6] In 1857 the establishment of the Society of Female Artists forced the issue of exhibition further, giving women's work an explicit platform.[7] Also that year, the Pre-Raphaelite group sought its own way through the thicket of exclusiveness, tradition and favouritism by putting on an independent exhibition. Here, among the men by this time recognised as proponents of the new style and 'a few other [artists] who have yet their names to make', Elizabeth Siddal's work could be seen.[8] As 'the one lady contributor, Miss E. E. Siddal, whose name was new to us', she was given by Coventry Patmore in his review the curiosity status that conveniently acknowledged the interloping woman without identifying her as a professional artist.

Exhibition, ideally, led to critical attention and thence to sales and commissions, from a public undergoing the marginalisation of the aristocracy and the rise of the middle classes.[9] The pre-eminent seal of approval in the mid-century still came from royalty, but for Pre-Raphaelitism's developing audience it was rather from John Ruskin that commendation was prized. His public promotion of the leading male Pre-Raphaelites is well known, but in the fine print of his support the activities of Siddal, Blunden and Boyce also attracted

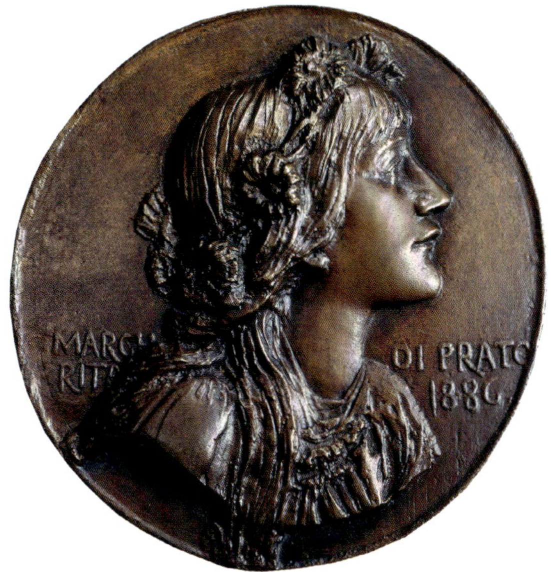

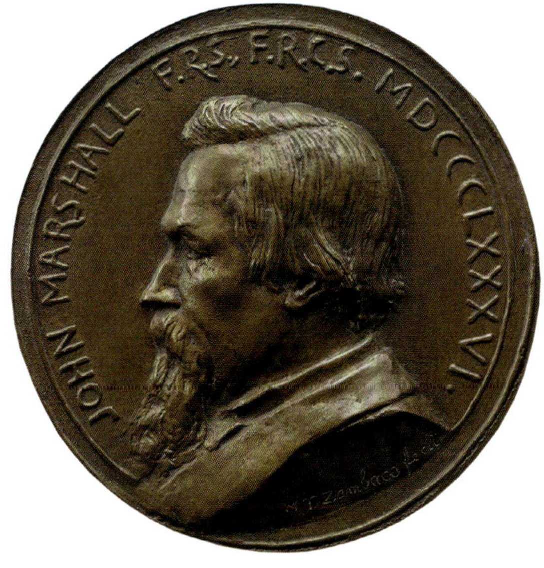

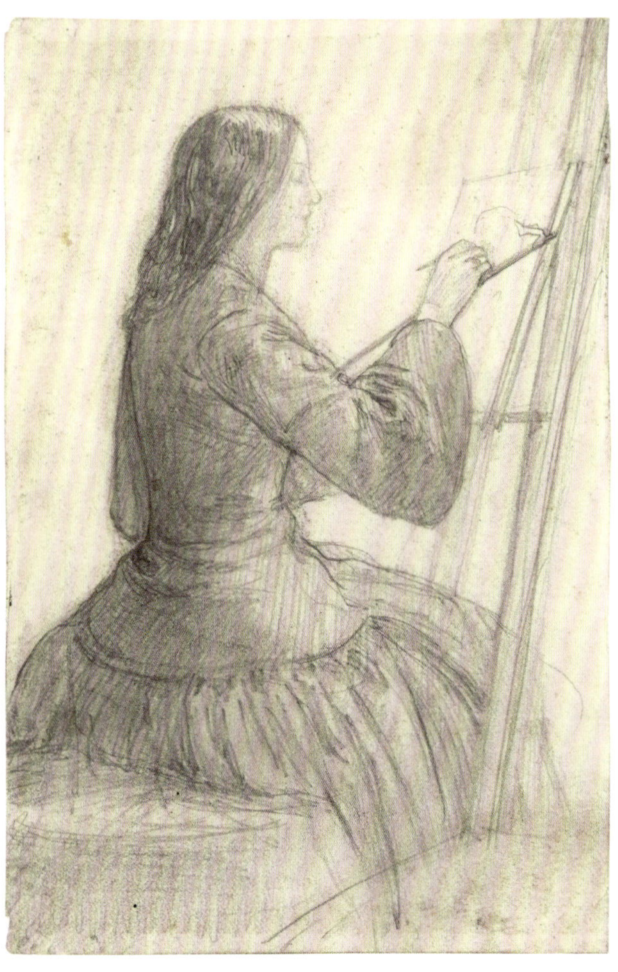

Ruskin's endorsement – despite his now famous assertion, in 1864, that women were incapable of being artists.[10] Siddal, whom he met through Rossetti, elicited the offer of an annual retainer; Blunden, who cleverly secured his attention for herself, was recommended to Ruskin's art-collector friends, such as Ellen Heaton;[11] Boyce, whom he later regretted neglecting, was publicly praised and privately encouraged. Conversely, his disdain of Howitt's work was blamed for triggering her abandonment of an artistic career.[12]

Exhibition was joined explicitly to commercial success by the art dealers who became increasingly influential from the 1860s. The leaders in this sphere were jostling the old school of entrepreneur, such as Agnews and Christie's (Christie, Manson & Woods from 1859), not only in exposing an artist's name to the art-buying public but also in pushing up prices to the ever increasing number of new buyers. But, as Dianne Sachko Macleod's useful study of Victorian art-collecting revealed, women's work had minimal currency in this growing art market.[13] While dealers may not have been, in principle, hostile to the female artist, a woman had to be prepared to spurn conventional norms of behaviour to engage with them (and, of course, they may have refused to endorse Pre-Raphaelitism). Barbara Bodichon, making her own exhibition opportunities, represented a new minority that many found not just disconcerting but also alienating.[14] As she observed to Marian Lewes (the author George Eliot), 'Everybody is astonished at my good fortune in getting my things shown.'[15]

While such self-consciously feminist women as Bodichon and Howitt believed in 'sisters doing it for themselves', the goodwill of individual men could make all the difference in securing patronage, and when Pre-Raphaelite collectors such as Thomas Plint and B.G. Windus purchased women's work it was likely to be because their male colleagues had turned the patrons' attention their way. Although it became a cliché of the public account of women artists that they had a father/brother/husband in the profession, friendship was just as potent an affiliation as family for the women who gravitated towards Pre-Raphaelitism. The men's own awareness of their power to aid a woman's success is particularly conspicuous in the cases of Joanna Boyce, with whom Henry Wells tried vigorously to ingratiate himself through various forms of assistance, and Marie Spartali Stillman, whose work-in-progress Madox Brown and Burne-Jones both clamoured to assist.

Spartali Stillman came before the public at the Grosvenor Gallery, London, which opened in 1877 as the personal project of Sir Coutts and Blanche Lindsay, showcasing the shift from Millaisian Pre-Raphaelitism to the Burne-Jonesian version. Based on a system of invitation rather than selection by committee, the Grosvenor exhibitions overlapped with those of the RA but showed a clear preference for certain trends. While scholars have debated the degree of Lady Lindsay's influence, it is agreed that she had the promotion of female artists on her agenda, and the Grosvenor certainly benefited several women artists markedly (not only Pre-Raphaelite ones).[16] There, Pickering/De Morgan and Spartali Stillman could be appreciated as contributors to a distinctive aesthetic that was purposefully displayed to its advantage, and if this membership of a clique led to conventional underestimation of the female artist's capacity, at least it was as 'the *chief* example of the particular school of which Mr Burne-Jones is the head' [author's italics] that Pickering/De Morgan was recognised in 1881.[17] Her unapologetically large canvases were shown annually from the Grosvenor's first year until 1888.[18] Similarly, Spartali Stillman's work could be seen at every Grosvenor exhibition bar one until 1887. When the New Gallery opened in London in 1888 (the Grosvenor folding in 1890), it likewise provided a forum where ambitious female artists were not feared but often favoured. De Morgan's work was to be seen there until 1909, and Spartali Stillman's throughout its first decade.

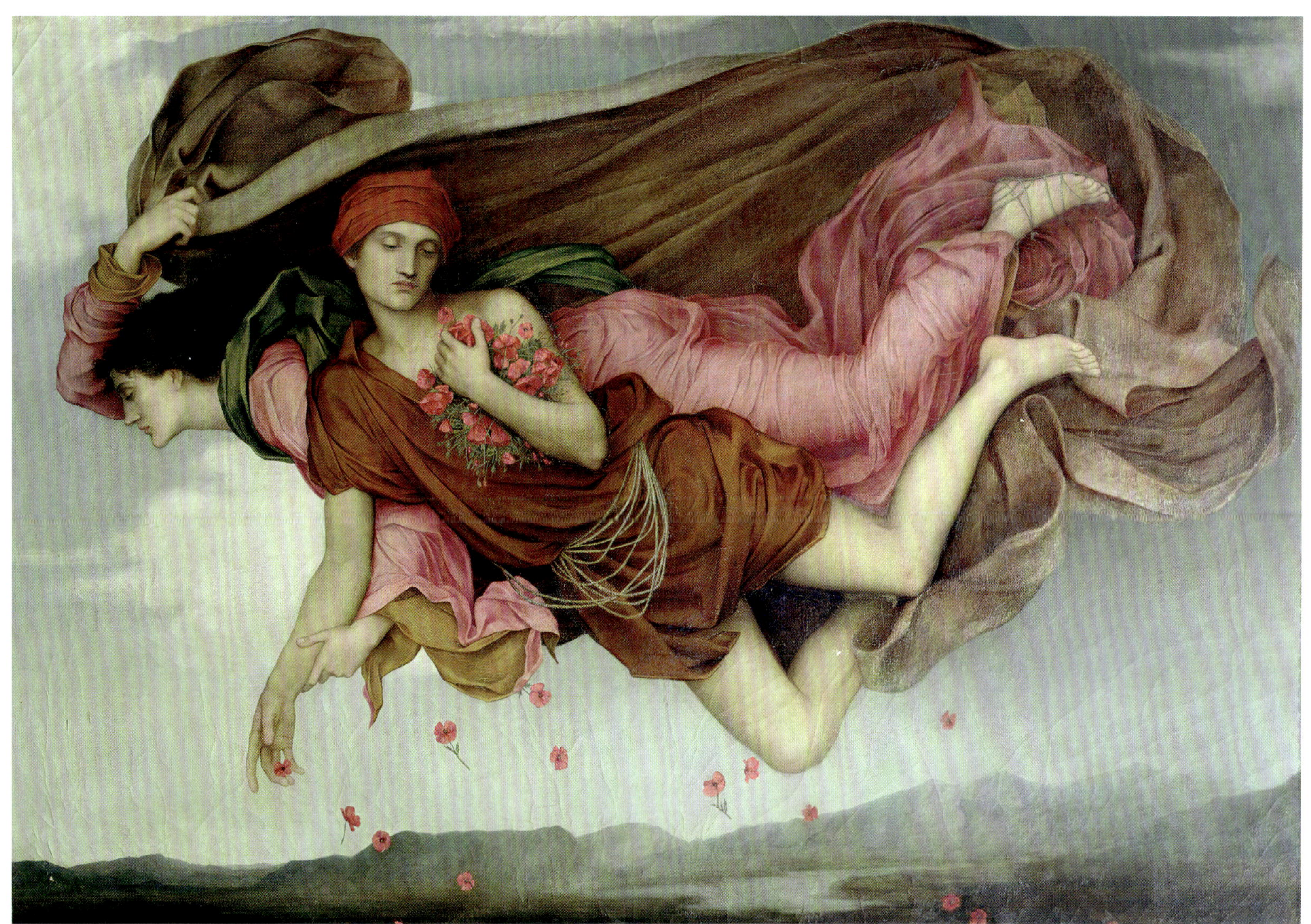

An artistic career became more and more possible for a woman, then, as the century proceeded, and, as Meaghan Clarke writes, 'in spite of socio-economic constraints, women negotiated independent successes and remuneration'.[19] At the same time, entrenched reluctance to admit their cultural value lingered: a review of Ellen Creathorne Clayton's *English Female Artists* (1876) began: 'The first effect produced by this book is to raise in our minds the question, What constitutes an artist?'.[20] Although by the final decade of the century, artists as diverse as Annie Swynnerton, Helen Allingham and Louise Jopling expected to be treated as professionals, the National Gallery of British Art (as it was ambitiously termed), formed in the final years of the century from the collection of sugar tycoon Henry Tate, had only two works by women among sixty-five.[21] It is an indication of the progressive effect of Pre-Raphaelitism that, by contrast, in London's great rival, Liverpool was a city that had taken enthusiastically to Pre-Raphaelitism and by the end of the century its municipal Walker Art Gallery, owned thirteen works by living women artists.[22] It was in this light that the third wave of Pre-Raphaelitism developed at the turn of the century, shaping the art of Eleanor Fortescue-Brickdale, Jessie M. King and others. They continued the style at a time when a range of modern painters, including Laura Knight, Vanessa Bell and Gwen John, made very different choices. The professional female artist had by then a range of opportunity only dreamt of in 1848.

Fanny Eaton

1835–1924

Fanny Eaton is the most recent 'recruit' to the history of the Pre-Raphaelite movement, although, pictorially, she had been 'hiding in plain sight' as a model for biblical and African and near-Eastern figures in many mid-Victorian pictures. First identified by Pamela Gerrish Nunn in 1988, her modelling history is reconstructed visually, while her life story is told through ancestry research by Brian Eaton, her great-grandson, who writes:

When I was young, my father would often talk about 'red-Indian' blood in our family, using the then common name for Native Americans. However, apart from that intriguing remark he would not talk about his family very much, so it was left to me and my wife to find the real story. My wife Mary looked into the many visits of 'wild west' shows to London but couldn't find any links to my family. Then in the late 1980s we were able to search the 1881 census, in the Leeds Library Family History Section, to discover the Eaton family living in Kensington, London and Fanny Matilda listed as born in Jamaica! She was a widow aged just 46, my great grandfather, James having died that February leaving her with ten children, of whom my grandfather, Frank, was the youngest.

That discovery naturally prompted further research. The Archives in Jamaica demanded more information than we had at that stage, but on advice from Caribbean research expert Stephen Porter we visited the Church of the Latter Day Saints Centre in Kensington where copies of the Jamaican records were stored, with his warning that we'd have to search all 22 parishes for Fanny. We spent three solid days there in 2008, eventually finding Fanny's birth in June 1835. Her mother was named as Matilda Foster. Fanny was 'privately baptised' as Fanny Matilda Antwistle in November 1835, but no father was named. We could not find any other people in Jamaica with the surname of Antwistle (or Entwistle) except a soldier who died aged 20 in 1835 and was buried in a military cemetery in Spanish Town.

This period was one of upheaval following the abolition of slavery and its aftermath. Perhaps the spur that

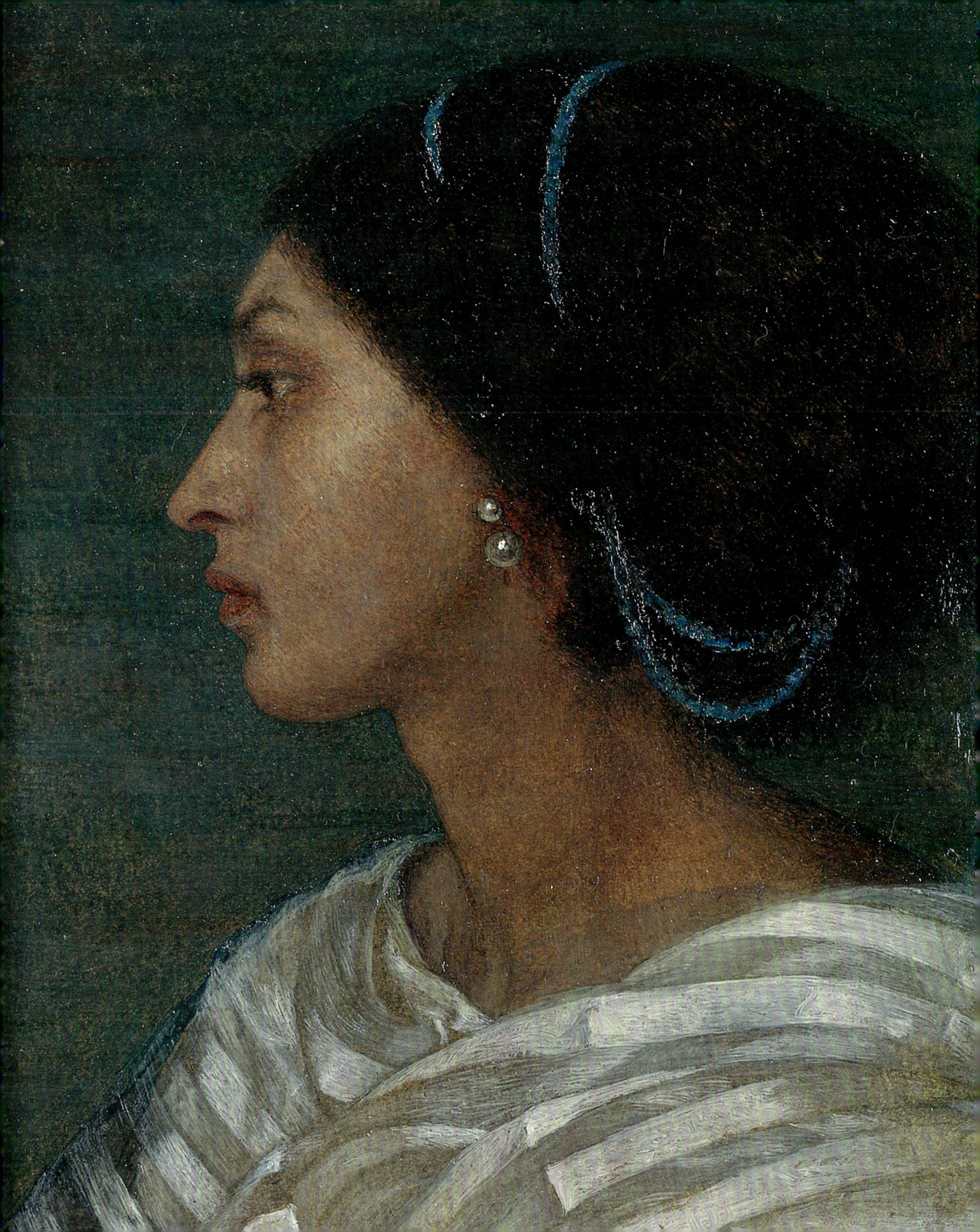

led Matilda and her child to come to England. We tried to find more information regarding Matilda's days as a slave but the records are not that precise and, of course, the enslaved only acquired surnames when freed. Matilda Foster suggests a link to one of the many Foster plantations in Jamaica.

Fanny Eaton and her mother moved to Britain during the 1840s. By 1851, they were living in London, where she, like most working-class girls, was in domestic service. In 1857 she met James Eaton, a driver and cab proprietor, who was born in Shoreditch, London in 1838.

Brian Eaton continues:

We then followed the story of Fanny and James and their 10 children in London over the years from the census returns of 1841 to 1911 as each was released by the National Archives. In 2012 my wife's relative Ann Tong told us that there was now information on the internet describing Fanny as a model for the Pre-Raphaelite artists, which had come to light through the exhibition *Black Victorians* in 2005–6, curated by Jan

who said that someone had suggested that Fanny might have posed for the Life Classes at the Royal Academy. From the Academy archivist we learnt that she had indeed been a model for their Life Classes, and were given her payment records from July 1860 to January 1879. The archivist also told us that some RA instructors recorded that to find models they would walk the surrounding streets looking for likely candidates. Could this be how Fanny was discovered as she went about her work as a charwoman in that area?

The pictorial record indicates that Eaton sat to several young artists around 1860. As well as the RA Schools, this was possibly at a life-drawing class run at Heatherley's art school in Newman Street, in central London. Studies by Albert Moore, Walter Fryer Stocks and Frederick Sandys suggest collective rather than individual sessions, and that they found Eaton's appearance ideal for biblical, Egyptian and near-Eastern subjects. Moore cast her as the unnamed mother in the Hebrew Bible (ill. 73), who vainly watched for the return of her warrior son: 'The mother of Sisera looked out at a

To date, none of Eaton's own words or thoughts are known

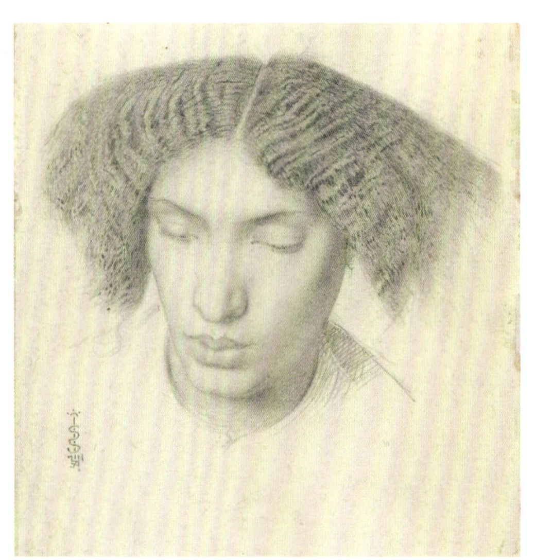

Marsh. Since then we have searched everywhere for paintings and drawings of Fanny – even looking at one on a visit to Melbourne, Australia, after Pamela Gerrish Nunn told us about it. We went to America to look at more paintings, and also visited Jamaica to understand where Fanny and Matilda came from and to try to research more local information. In 2013 we visited the Maas Gallery in London to see a newly discovered drawing by Walter Fryer Stocks (later sold to Princeton University), where we met art dealer Ellis Kelleher,

window, and cried through the lattice, Why is his chariot so long in coming? why tarry the wheels of his chariots?' (Judges 5:28). Described in a review as a 'clever and singularly characteristic study of the head of an Arab woman', the depiction reflects the Victorian recognition that the familiar Bible stories took place historically in Palestine and Egypt.[1]

The earliest dated drawing of Eaton is in a group of studies by Simeon Solomon from November 1859 (ill. 72). Solomon's careful drawing seems a preparatory study for his painting *The Mother of Moses*

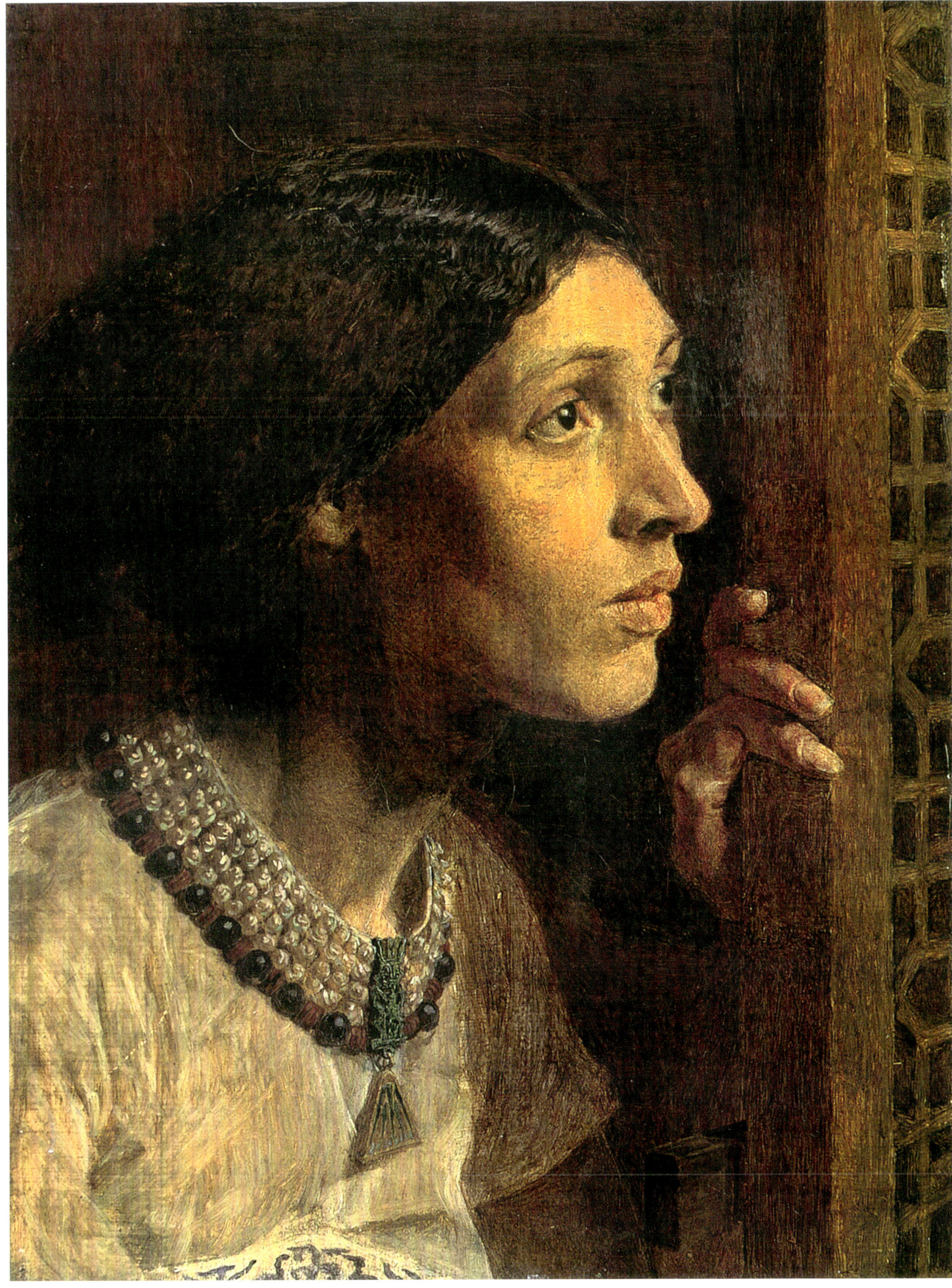

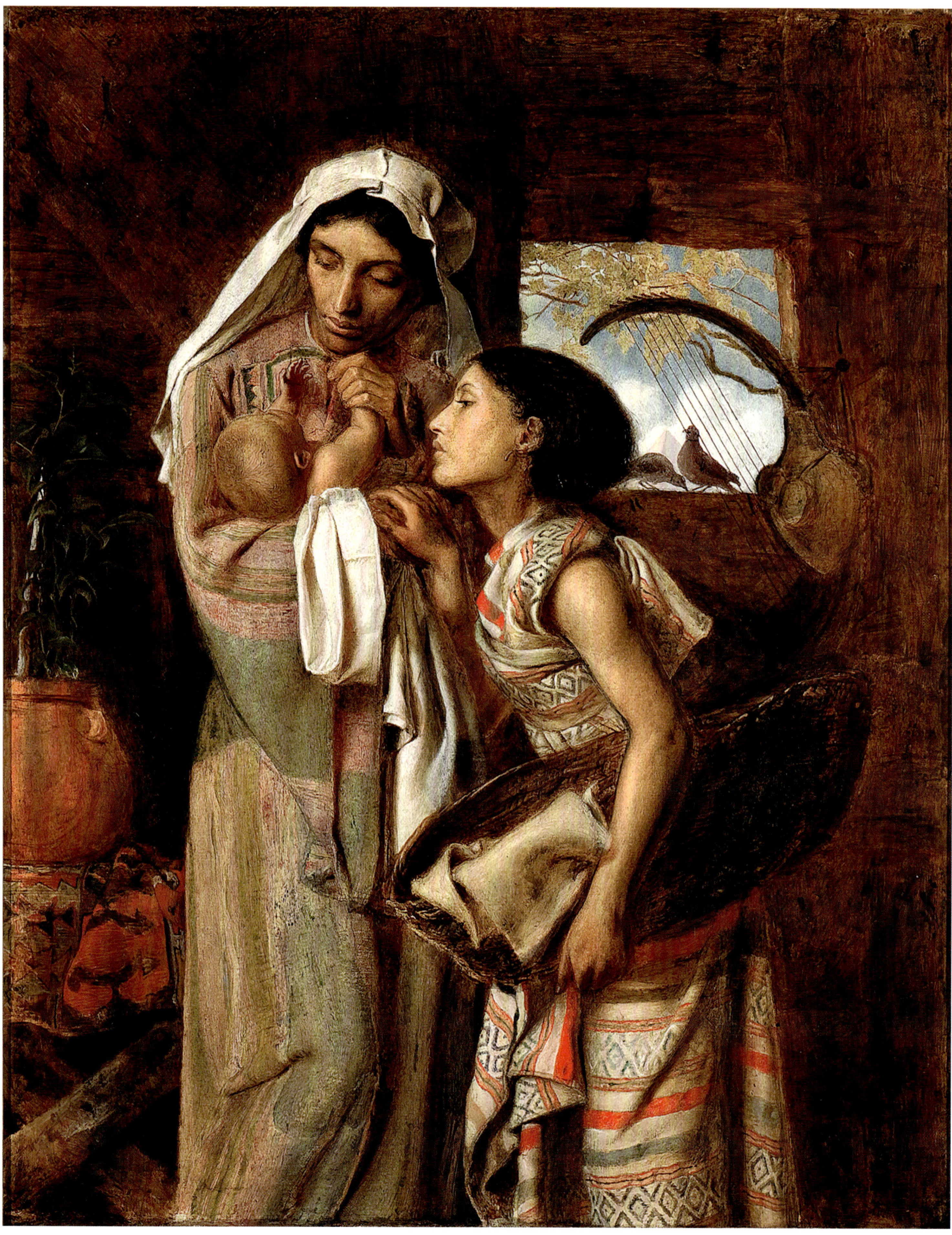

(ill.74), where the figure shares a similar downcast gaze.

In the painting, as Jochabed, she is the centre of the biblical drama as she prepares to entrust the newborn Moses to the Nile, laid in the wicker basket held by his sister Miriam. Set during the Jewish captivity in Egypt, a pyramid is dimly glimpsed through the window. 'A more touching, a more impressive domestic group it would almost be impossible to imagine,' wrote a contemporary, adding that the technique was of 'the highest order…the relief of the figures, the flesh-modelling, the colour, the textural surfaces in every part, all excellent'.[2]

The range of ethnicities for which Eaton's appearance was considered apt is demonstrated by the fact that, at much the same time, Rebecca Solomon, Simeon's sister, cast her in the role of an *ayah* or nanny caring for two British children (ill.75) who is herself learning to read. Seated at a writing table in a middle-class home Eaton is dressed here in a flounced gown, possibly her own, wrapped in a voluminous shawl. Exhibited in November 1861, the picture was noted by several reviewers, and the following year it was priced at 80 guineas.

When Millais was designing his sequence of the 'Parables of Our Lord' for the Dalziel Brothers engraving firm, he also employed Eaton, drawing her as a servant, who holds the donkey of a merchant buying a rare pearl from a fisherman, in *The Pearl of Great Price* (ill.76). First published in 1863, the rhythmically disposed group, with dramatic focus on the entwined arms at the heart of the exchange, demonstrates Millais's visual eloquence.[3] His model is recognised by her features, but the figure may have been drawn from someone else. Later, Millais employed Eaton and one of her daughters for two accessory figures in his painting of *Jephthah* (1867).

Unusual among female models, as a married woman, Eaton's children proved an asset, enabling Solomon to portray her own son James, born early in 1860, as the infant Moses. Madox Brown drew her as the bereaved mother, whose son Elijah resurrects;[4] Sandys cast her as the medieval enchantress in *Morgan-le-Fay* (1862–3), and Rossetti made her one of the diverse group in *The Beloved* (1865). He told Madox

74
The Mother of Moses
Simeon Solomon, 1860
Oil on canvas, 597 × 484mm
Delaware Art Museum

75
The Young Teacher
Rebecca Solomon, 1861
Oil on canvas, 610 × 510mm
Private Collection

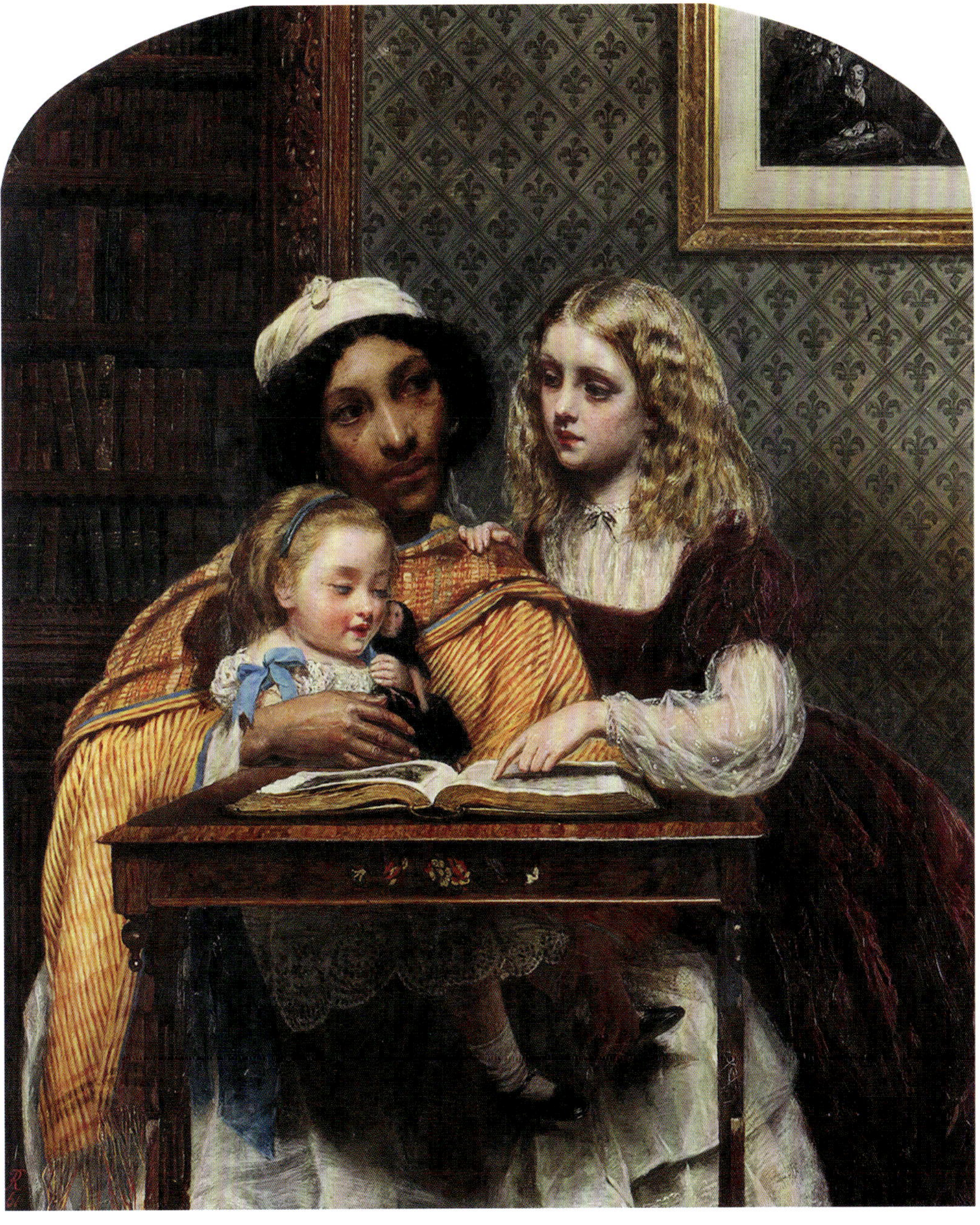

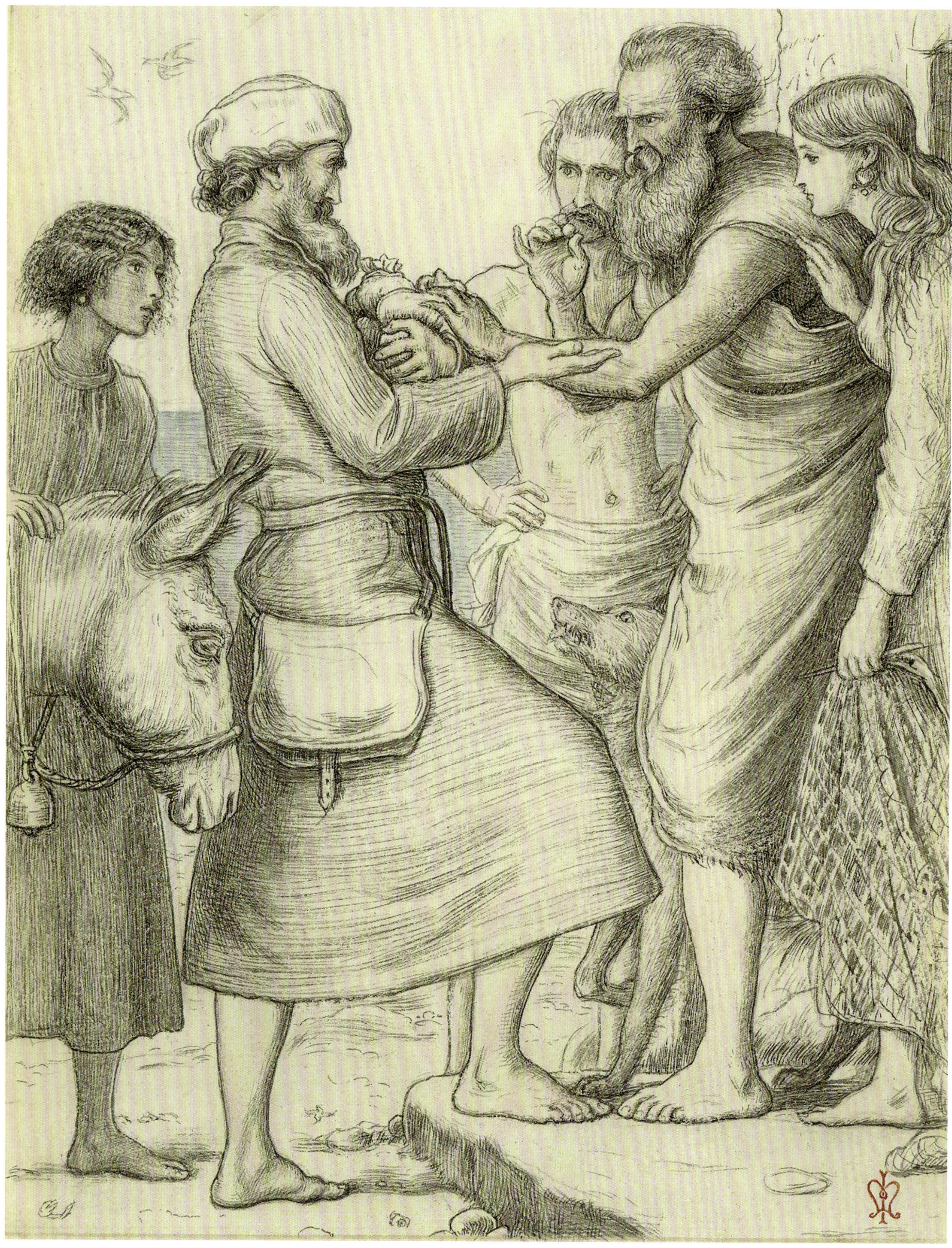

Brown that she was from the Caribbean and to him Eaton's 'very fine head and figure' with their strong features and hair, had 'a good deal' in common with Jane Morris's appearance.[5]

The issue of slavery affected art in the early 1860s, owing to abolition campaigns and the American Civil War. William Blake Richmond thus cast Eaton as a despairing captive, cradling a baby, with a toddler of her personal being. That she modelled for nearly ten years suggests some level of compliance, but as a working-class family, Eaton and her husband were undoubtedly earning money any way they could. Ironically, of course, the one role no one ever painted her in was as a Jamaican, the one role for which she would have been obviously best suited.[8]

More than a score of paintings show figures with her features

at her feet in the 'slave pens' of West Africa.[6] She also modelled as one of the African–American characters in Harriet Beecher Stowe's powerful tale of *Uncle Tom's Cabin* (1852), in a scene painted by Edwin Longsden Long.[7] Altogether, more than a score of paintings show figures with her features, and more may yet be identified. She is seen in numerous works by Joanna Boyce, who in 1860–61 chose her to model for projected paintings of the Libyan Sibyl and Queen Zenobia. Boyce's sketchbook (ill.5) contains several studies of Eaton posing in costume, while an oil sketch (ill.77) depicts her as the classical figure consulting the oracular Sibylline books. According to ancient texts, the Sibyls' wisdom was sought in times of war and pestilence. Some nine or ten Sibyls were said to be located in Persia, Greece, Italy and north Africa, with Eaton's complexion most apt for that legendarily based in Libya. While in Naples, the artist possibly visited the cave of the Cumaen Sibyl, and she recorded herself in the Sistine Chapel in Rome, using opera glasses to study the whole ceiling, which includes Michelangelo's five Sibyls. The absence of Eaton's own voice relating to all the varied depictions is a notable lack. It means that, as Roberto Ferrari observes:

[I]n truth we have no sense how Eaton may have felt about this interpretation

To date, nothing of Eaton's own words or thoughts is known. Widowed in 1881, she later worked as cook–housekeeper in Hammersmith, west London, and on the Isle of Wight. But family research continues. As Brian Eaton writes:

We have also followed the descendants of Fanny's ten children and connected with some of them. Several of the [other] families had also obscured Fanny's West-Indian roots to make up stories of an 'exotic princess' or 'Portuguese lady'– similar to my family story of 'red-indians'.

Another goal was to find where Fanny was buried – she had died in Acton, London, on 4 March 1924 aged 88, after a very hard life. We had previously found James and his father, Henry, in Islington cemetery in unmarked graves, but not Fanny. After many fruitless enquiries we eventually found her in Margravine Road Cemetery in Hammersmith, London, in an unmarked 'non-private' grave with seven other non-related burials. We attended a memorial service there with Jan Marsh in 2017. We intend to mark her grave with some sort of plaque. However, my main aim for Fanny Matilda to gain the recognition that she deserved has I think been achieved, so that our families now have the true and truly remarkable story of our ancestress.

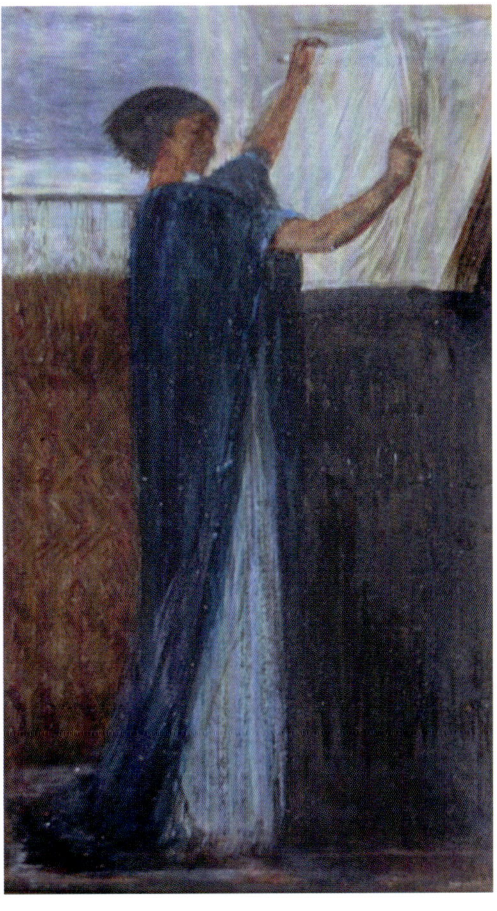

Jane Morris

1839–1914

Late in life, explaining that she had not loved her husband William when they married, Jane Morris added that were she young again, she would do the same. The marriage had not only brought her a life of unimaginable comfort and culture, with the access to music and literature that she valued, but also given her a central role in Pre-Raphaelite art, as model and muse, and a pioneering position in the Arts & Crafts movement through embroidery.

Daughter of a stablehand and a washerwoman, and living in a backyard hovel in Oxford, Jane Burden was spotted in 1857 by the young artists from London who were decorating the University Union debating chamber in the summer vacation. Asked by Rossetti and Burne-Jones to pose for their Arthurian murals, she at first did not understand or respond but, a day or so later, with her mother's permission, she went to pose for Rossetti and so changed her life. This first pose was as Queen Guinevere (ill. 78), a study for the scene where Sir Lancelot is found in her bedchamber (ill. 4). The drawing emphasises her dark hair, lidded eyes, long neck and mobile fingers, the attributes that feature in Rossetti's later images of her.

Rossetti drew her portrait, too, perhaps as a present. Which might have been the end of the story, for very soon the group began to disperse. She had naturally fallen for Rossetti, who praised the beauty of a skinny, shy lass with sallow skin and black hair in an age that favoured 'peaches-and-cream'. Silently, it seems, she appealed to William Morris, who painted her as Iseult (ill. 79), from the same Arthurian tradition and with chivalric zeal proposed.[1] Morris should be content with kissing the feet of his 'perfect stunner', wrote young Algernon Swinburne, voicing a general view; 'The idea of marrying her is insane.'[2]

Before the wedding, Jane Burden was educated to be a gentleman's wife, in all likelihood lodging with Gertrude and Archibald Maclaren, founders of Summerfield school (see p. 124). She seized the opportunity, lost her rustic accent and decisively reinvented herself.

After their wedding in April 1859, the Morrises prepared for life in Red House, designed for them by the architect Philip Webb. Here they began to decorate the

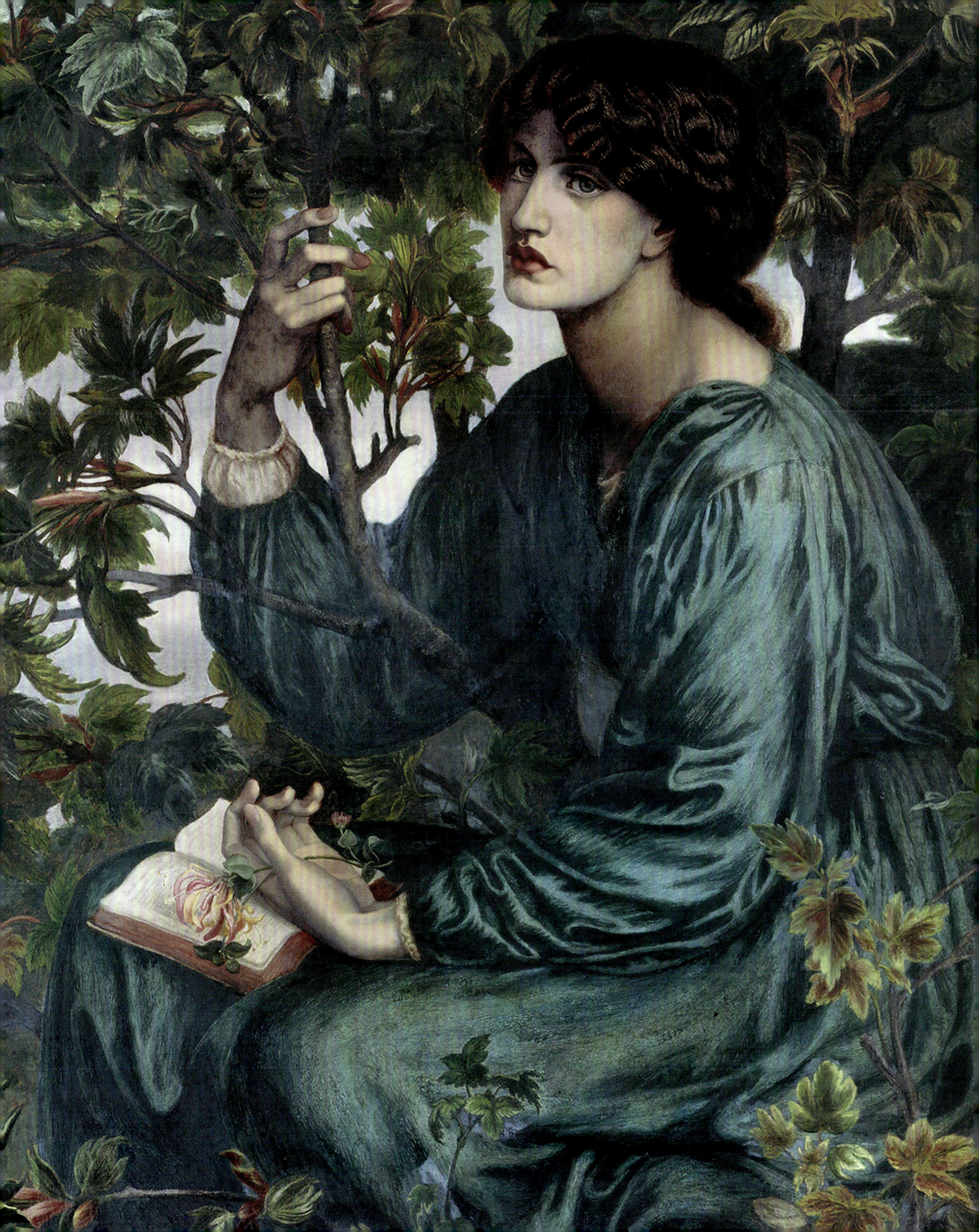

78
Study of Guinevere
for *Sir Launcelot in the*
Queen's Chamber
Dante Gabriel Rossetti, 1857
Pencil and ink on paper
493 × 412mm
Manchester Art Gallery

79
La Belle Iseult
William Morris, 1858
Oil on canvas, 718 × 502mm
Tate, London

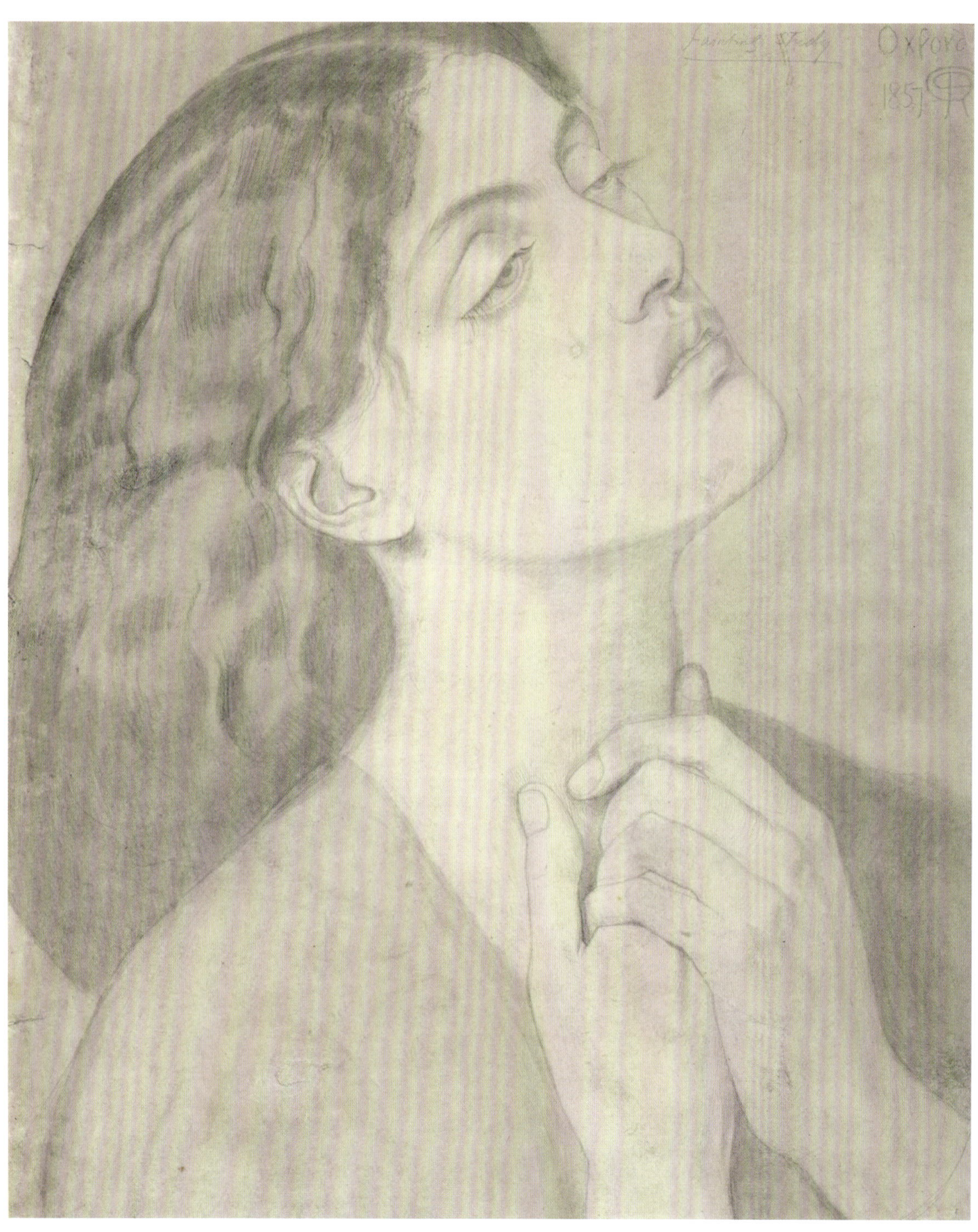

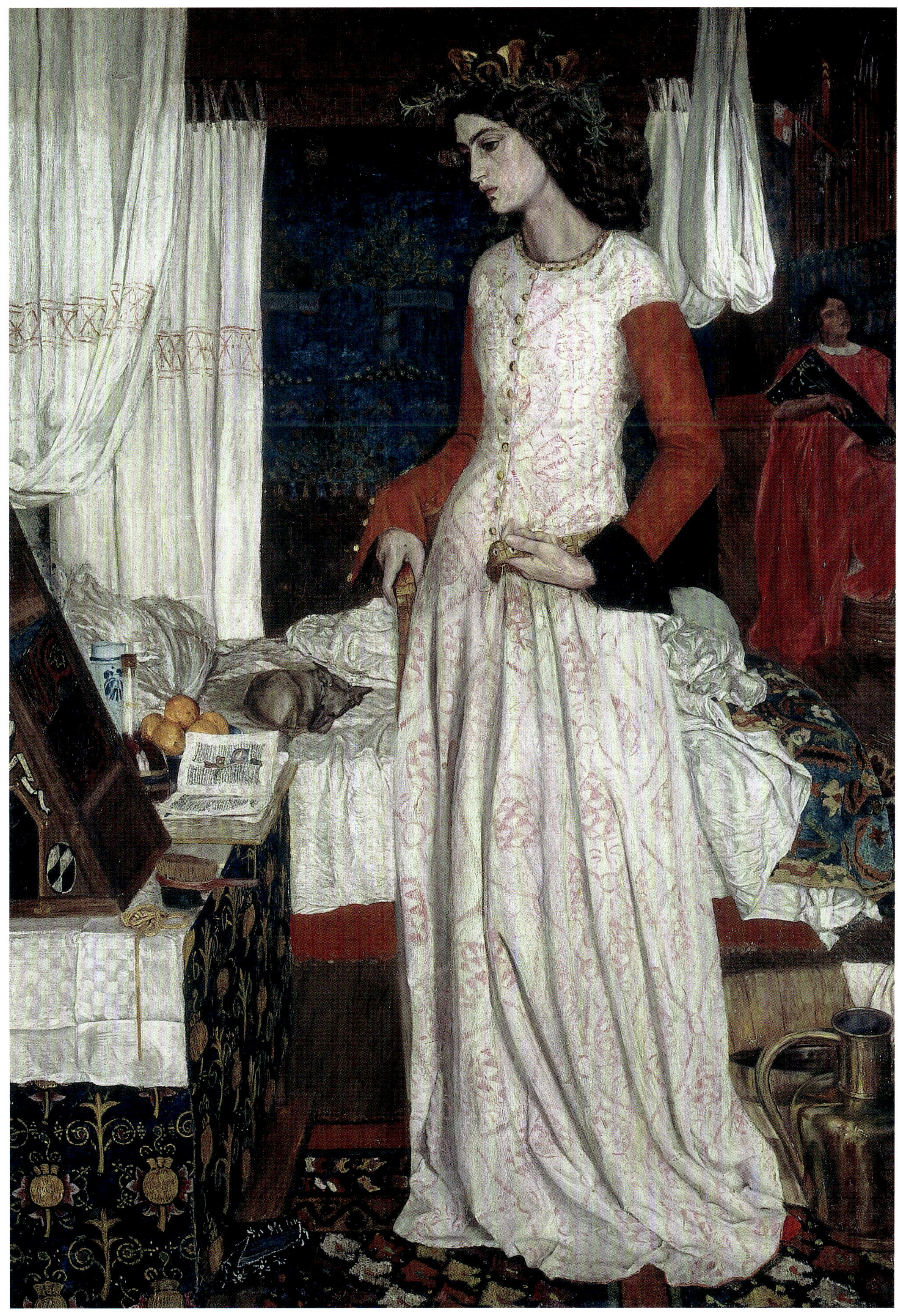

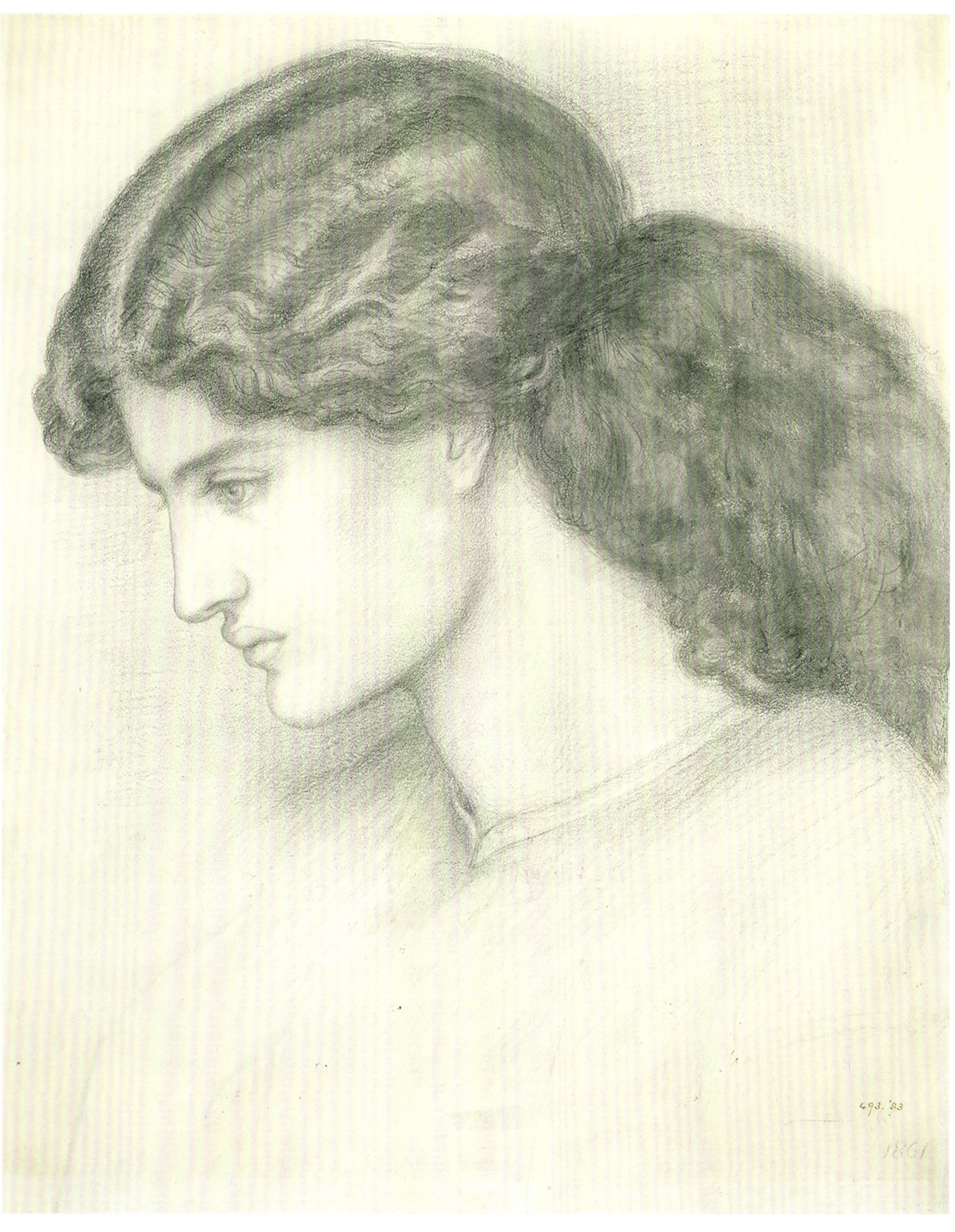
493. '83
1861

interior. A carefully drawn study by William from this period shows Jane as if climbing a ladder to board a ship (ill.81). The Morris & Co. firm, launched at Red House in 1861, produced a stained-glass sequence, depicting the story of Tristram and Iseult, for which this scene may have been projected but not used.

Jane Morris eagerly joined her husband in the needlework revival. 'The first stuff I got to embroider on was a piece of indigo dyed blue serge I found by chance in a London shop,' she told her daughter, explaining how some simple designs were 'worked in bright colours in a simple rough way… The work went quickly and when finished we covered the walls of the bedroom at Red House to our great joy.'[3] The next project was 'twelve large figures with a tree between each two. Flowers at the feet and a pattern all over the background'. Seven were completed. At the same time as 'this gigantic work we were making experiments in silk and gold

sister Elizabeth (Bessie) Burden and other women, including Georgiana Burne-Jones (ill.85). From 1866, following the birth of her two daughters, when family and firm moved to central London, Jane Morris took over management of the needlework commissions, supervising the 'embroidery ladies' stitching altar cloths, vestments, curtains and coverlets on piecework terms. This involved pricking out designs, selecting colours and assessing finished items. She also undertook major items herself, gaining a reputation for outstanding quality, matched only by her friend and colleague Catherine Holiday.

Her naturally sombre expression in repose and her distinctively naïve quality as a model create a key aspect of the 'Pre-Raphaelite' look. A drawing by Rossetti (ill.80), executed around Christmas-time 1861, when the Morrises, Rossettis, Burne-Joneses and other friends gathered at Red House, shows her with characteristic downcast gaze. The study was drawn for

A skinny, shy lass with sallow skin and black hair in an age that favoured 'peaches-and-cream'

wools afterwards to bloom into altar cloths etc.' Later, when gold thread, which would not tarnish, was sought, 'we adopted the plan of lacquering it afterwards which gave it a beautiful rich tone'.[4] Jane Morris's enthusiastic recollection conveys the pleasure of active participation in the overall decorative scheme, which included patterns and paintings on walls, ceilings and doors, plus a mural by Burne-Jones, showing a medieval wedding feast with the Morrises as the presiding couple.

With her husband as instructor, Morris developed the elegant technique and fine colour sense that marked her embroidery skills. The stitching was done by her, her

Rossetti's altarpiece for Llandaff Cathedral, in which she was cast as the Virgin Mary.

Posing in 1865 rekindled her feelings for the now-widowed Rossetti, for his art and for his poetry, itself further inspired by their mutual attraction:

> For then at last we spoke
> What eyes so oft had told to eyes
> Through that long-lingering silence
>   whose half-sighs
> Alone the buried secret broke.[5]

Thus, from the mid-1860s, Rossetti claimed Morris as his principal model, inaugurating a long and prolific partnership. Also largely

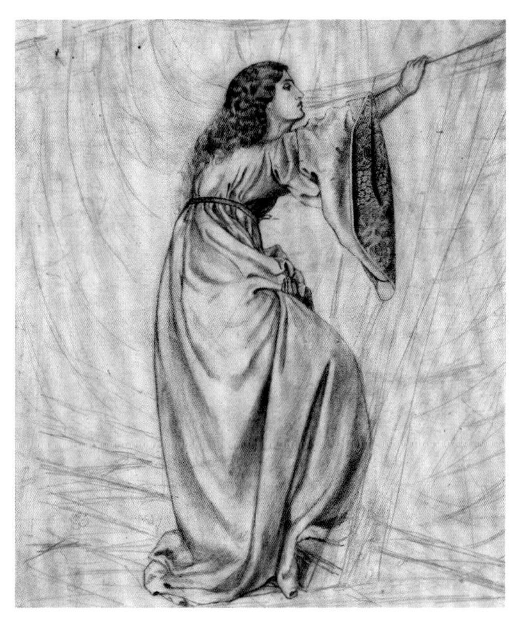

**Rossetti Carrying Cushions
for Jane Morris**
Edward Burne-Jones, c.1868
Pencil on paper, 178 × 115mm
University of Delaware Library

83
Proserpine
Dante Gabriel Rossetti, 1877
Oil on canvas, 775 × 375mm
Private Collection

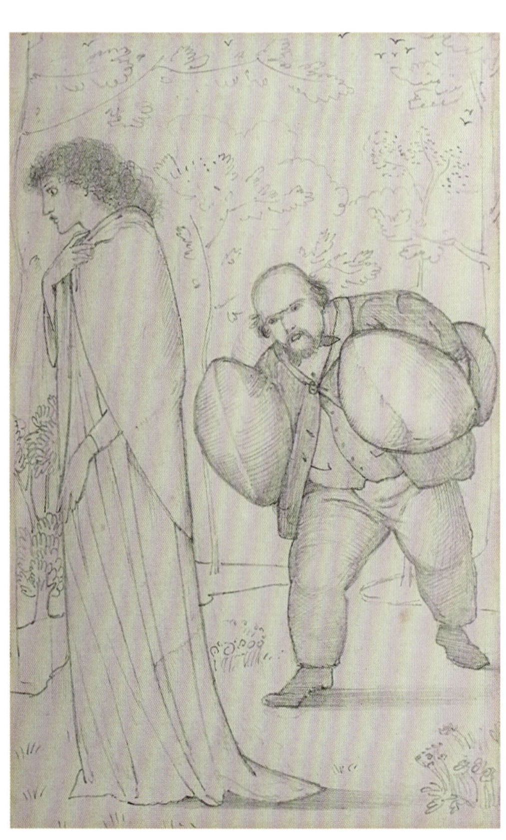

inspired by her, Rossetti's first volume of poetry was published in 1870. By this date their mutual desire was fully acknowledged. Divorce being unavailable Morris sought ways to be with Rossetti without causing scandal.[6] The solution was found in 1871 when the secluded Kelmscott Manor, beyond Oxford, was jointly leased as a summer residence. Here the pair shared an idyllic summer (with her daughters and several servants), while William Morris visited Iceland. She undertook renovation and decoration, demolishing walls, ordering tiles, stitching cushions, finding furniture.

William Morris was devastated but stoical, while friends joked affectionately about the affair. A caricature (ill. 82), drawn by Burne-Jones to charm his muse Maria Zambaco, pokes fun at both Rossetti's gallantry, ensuring his lover's comfort, and the physical contrast between rotund admirer and willowy beloved.

Henceforth, Jane Morris divided her life between her roles as Rossetti's model and muse, and her family responsibilities as mother to daughters Jenny and May and housekeeper and embroidery manager. This division was personified when Rossetti cast her as Proserpine (ill. 83).

This most famous image of Jane Morris depicts her as the mythical figure known as Persephone in the Greek tradition, whose return to Upper Earth from the Underworld symbolises the coming of Spring. She is shown in wintry captivity, holding the pomegranate that sealed her fate when she nibbled a few forbidden seeds. Inspired by the arrangement that Jane spend winters in London and summers in the country, Proserpine's mournful gaze towards the sunlight expresses her sorrow. Several replicas of this masterpiece were painted; this version was once owned by the artist L.S. Lowry.

For a decade Morris featured repeatedly in Rossetti's art, as Mariana, as Beatrice, as Astarte, as La Pia de' Tolomei, frequently representing doomed or unattainable love, and heralding the emergence of the femme fatale in *fin de siècle* painting and literature. Much to her sorrow, in 1872, Rossetti succumbed to a major breakdown into paranoia. Triggered by hostile reviews attacking the immorality of his poems, which many realised were addressed to her, this

effectively ended their affair; Christina Rossetti anticipated this outcome in a poem:

Two gaz'd into a pool, he gaz'd and she,
Not hand in hand, but heart in heart, I think,
Pale and reluctant on the water's brink
As on the brink of parting which must be.[7]

This emotional blow of Rossetti's collapse was compounded in 1876 when her elder daughter Jenny developed untreatable epilepsy, which caused violent seizures and brain damage. Social life was curtailed, and Morris's own health suffered. Music was one solace; she learnt to play both piano and mandolin, and also practised illumination and book-binding.

Rosalind and George Howard (Countess and Earl of Carlisle) offered valued friendship during this difficult period, inviting Morris and her daughters to spend the winter at Oneglia in Italy. Meeting her in Italy, Henry James described Morris as 'strange pale gaunt livid, yet in a manner graceful and picturesque'; adding 'she has wonderful aesthetic hair.'[8]

An illuminated keepsake (ill. 86), created for Rosalind Howard, demonstrates her skill and original handiwork. The dramas of her love life have dominated biographical accounts, but she was also, in the words of her daughters' schoolfriend Helena Sickert, 'a notable housekeeper' and became renowned as a needlewoman, exhibiting with the Arts & Crafts exhibitions.[9]

In hope of recovery she continued to visit and sit to Rossetti, who, until the end of his life, painted obsessional images of her in different roles.

In *The Day Dream* (ill. 87), she is cast as a spirit of Nature, perched amid branches, with a palette of greens. The painting compares with Marie Spartali Stillman's wintry *Madonna Pietra degli Scrovegni* (ill. 122) and Evelyn De Morgan's *The Dryad* (ill. 129).

As enduring homage to his muse, Rossetti composed an accompanying sonnet, also entitled 'The Day-Dream', inspired by their time at Kelmscott Manor and painted on the frame:

The thronged boughs of the shadowy sycamore / Still bear young leaflets half the summer through; / From when

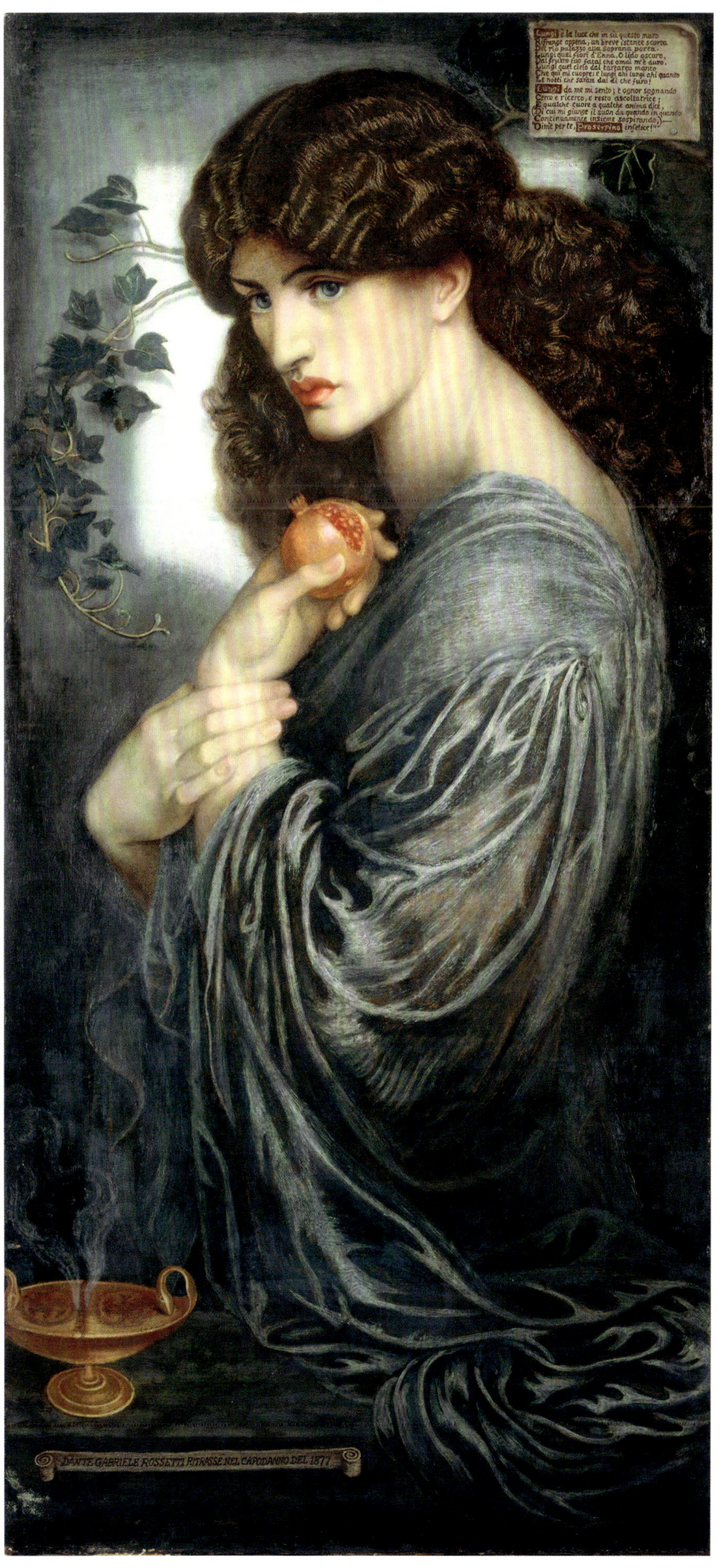

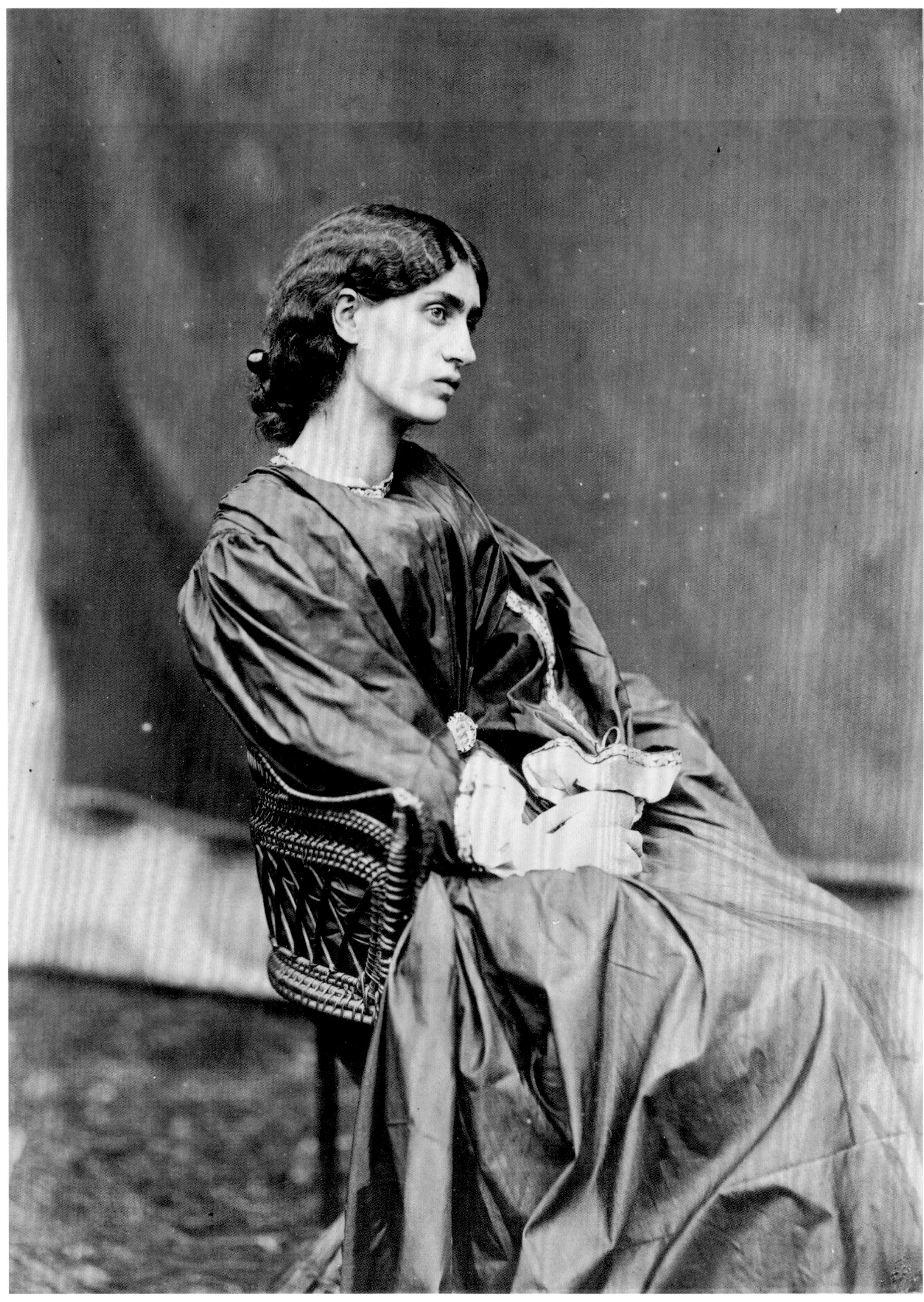

84 (opposite)
Jane Morris at Tudor House
John Robert Parsons, 1865
Albumen print from wet
collodion-on-glass negative
222 × 161mm
Victoria and Albert Museum,
London

85 (below left)
Evening Bag
Stitched by Jane Morris, c.1878
Embroidered coloured silks,
metal mount
220 × 245 × 45mm
Victoria and Albert Museum,
London

86 (below right)
Illuminated Poem
Calligraphy by
Jane Morris, 1878
Watercolour on paper
134 × 91mm
Castle Howard Collection, York

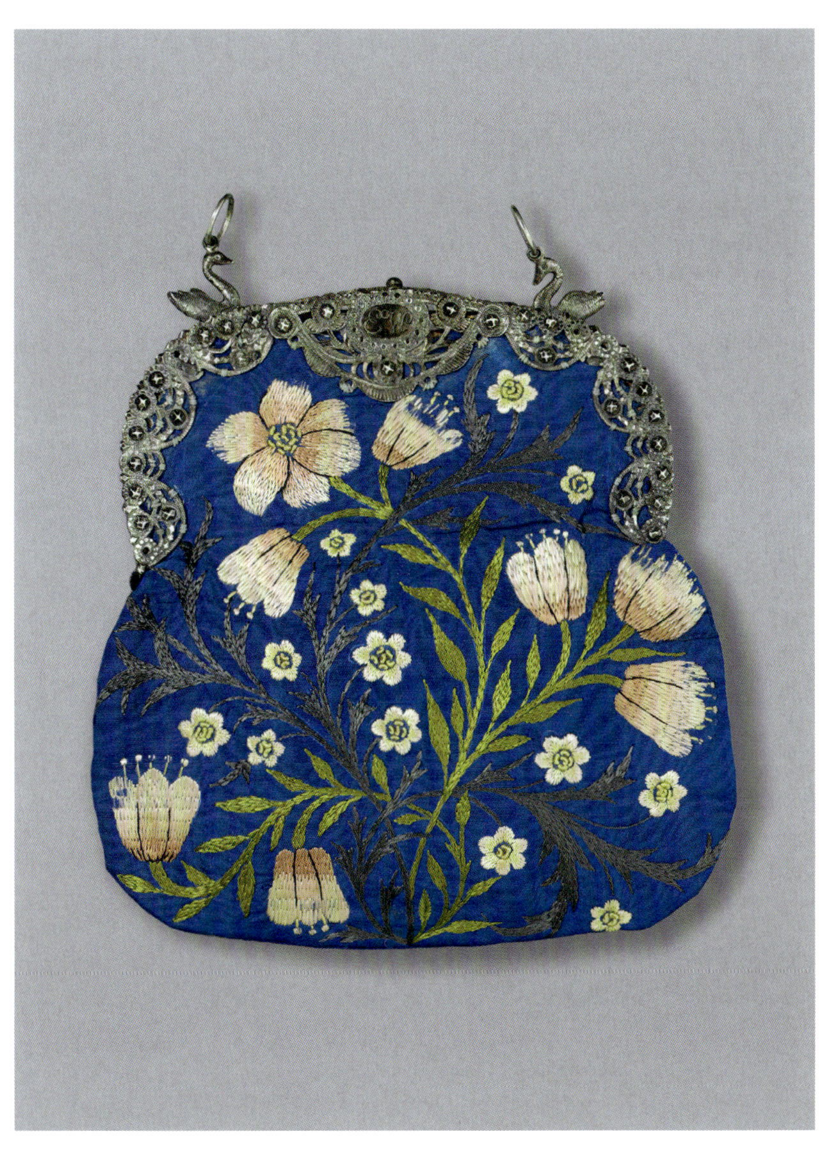

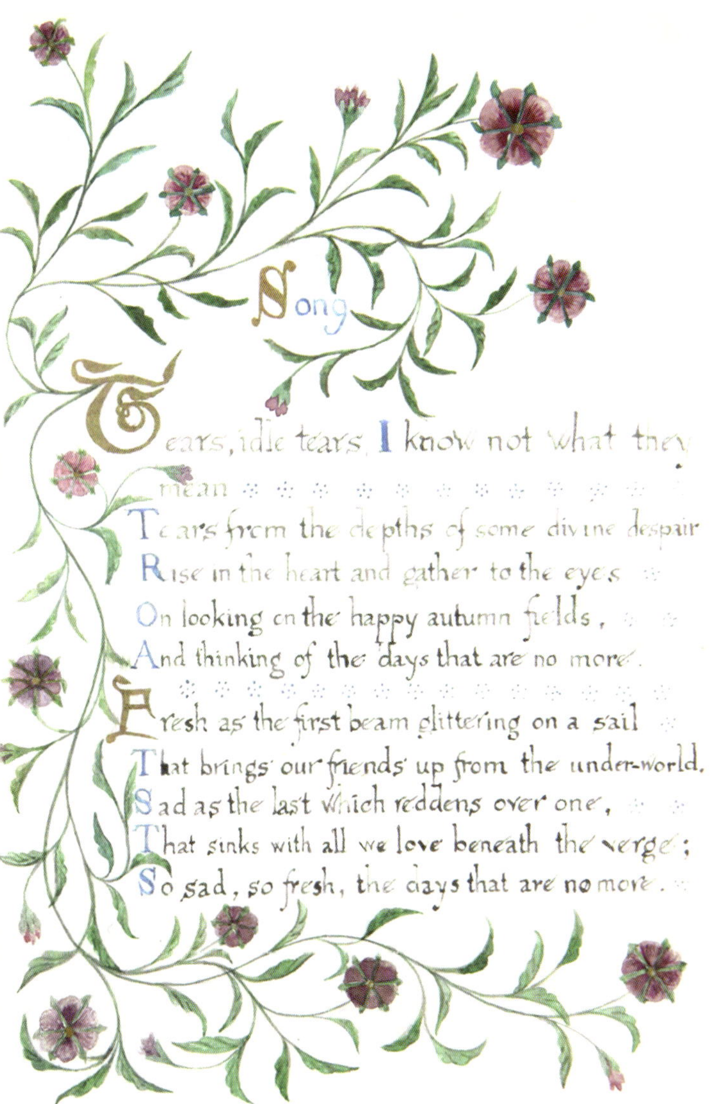

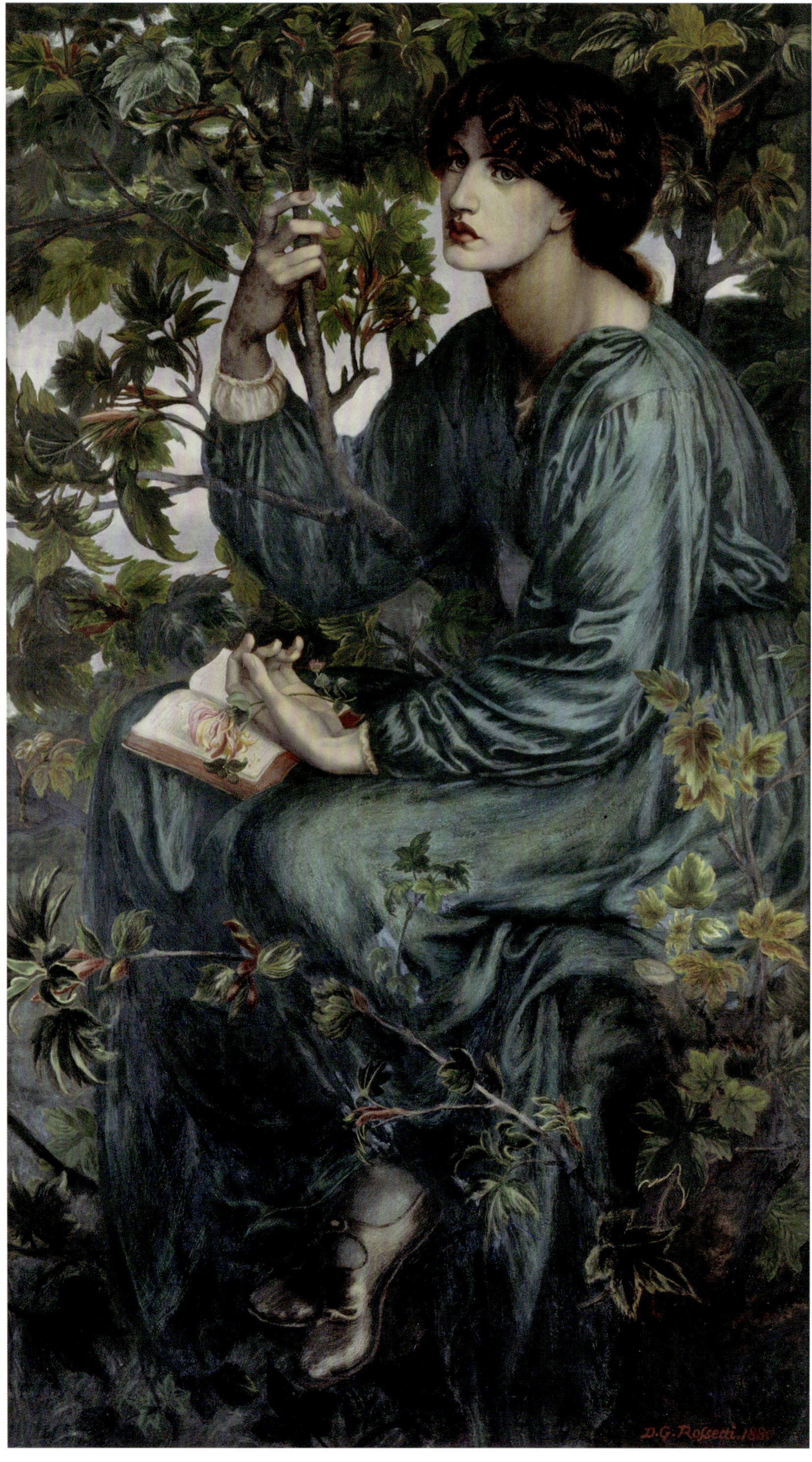

D.G. Rossetti 1880

the robin 'gainst the unhidden blue /
Perched dark, till now, deep in the leafy
core, / The embowered throstle's urgent
wood-notes soar / Through summer
silence. Still the leaves come new; /
Yet never rosy-sheathed as those which
drew / Their spiral tongues from spring-
buds heretofore. / Within the branching
shade of Reverie / Dreams even may
spring till autumn; yet none be / Like
woman's budding day-dream spirit-
fann'd. / Lo! tow'rd deep skies, not
deeper than her look, / She dreams; till
now on her forgotten book / Drops the
forgotten blossom from her hand.

Friendships with Georgiana Burne-Jones,
Spartali Stillman, Jane and Anne 'Annie'
Cobden (ill. 88) and with the De Morgans
(Evelyn and William and his sister Mary)
were valued. Caring for Jenny helped
repair the Morris marriage, despite Jane's
subsequent affair with Wilfrid Scawen Blunt,
who cast himself as Rossetti's successor. Her
husband threw himself into revolutionary
agitation while Jane remained a Liberal.

After her husband's death in 1896,
Morris devoted herself to his memory
and Jenny's care. She built two cottages
in Kelmscott village and assisted May
Morris's work on the edition of her father's
Collected Works. She took a continuing
interest in political affairs, declaring her
dislike of the 'noisy' Suffragettes: 'I want
both sexes to have equal rights when the
women are better educated companions
and housekeepers,' she wrote in 1907.[10]
She grew closer to Spartali Stillman when
both were widowed, and often invited
her to Kelmscott.

Jane Morris declined to write her
own memoirs but acquiesced when new
generations of artists insisted on seeing
her as a Pre-Raphaelite icon, even when
white-haired. Her final role as model was
as Age (ill. 90) in Evelyn De Morgan's
allegorical *The Hour Glass*. Drawn in
De Morgan's studio, it shows her head
against a cushion, her abstracted gaze
seemingly lost in reverie. '[T]hese windings
up of life are not very cheerful,' she wrote;
'if one could just drop off quietly like
Autumn leaves, it would be so pleasant
for everybody.'[11] She died in Bath in
January 1914.

87 (opposite and p.111)
The Day Dream
Dante Gabriel Rossetti, 1880
Oil on canvas, 1587 × 927mm
Victoria and Albert Museum,
London

88
**'The Pilgrims of Siena',
From left: Thomas James
Cobden-Sanderson;
Anne Cobden-Sanderson;
Jane Morris; Jane
Catherine Cobden Unwin**
Paulo Lombardi, 1881
Albumen cabinet card
136 × 95mm
National Portrait Gallery

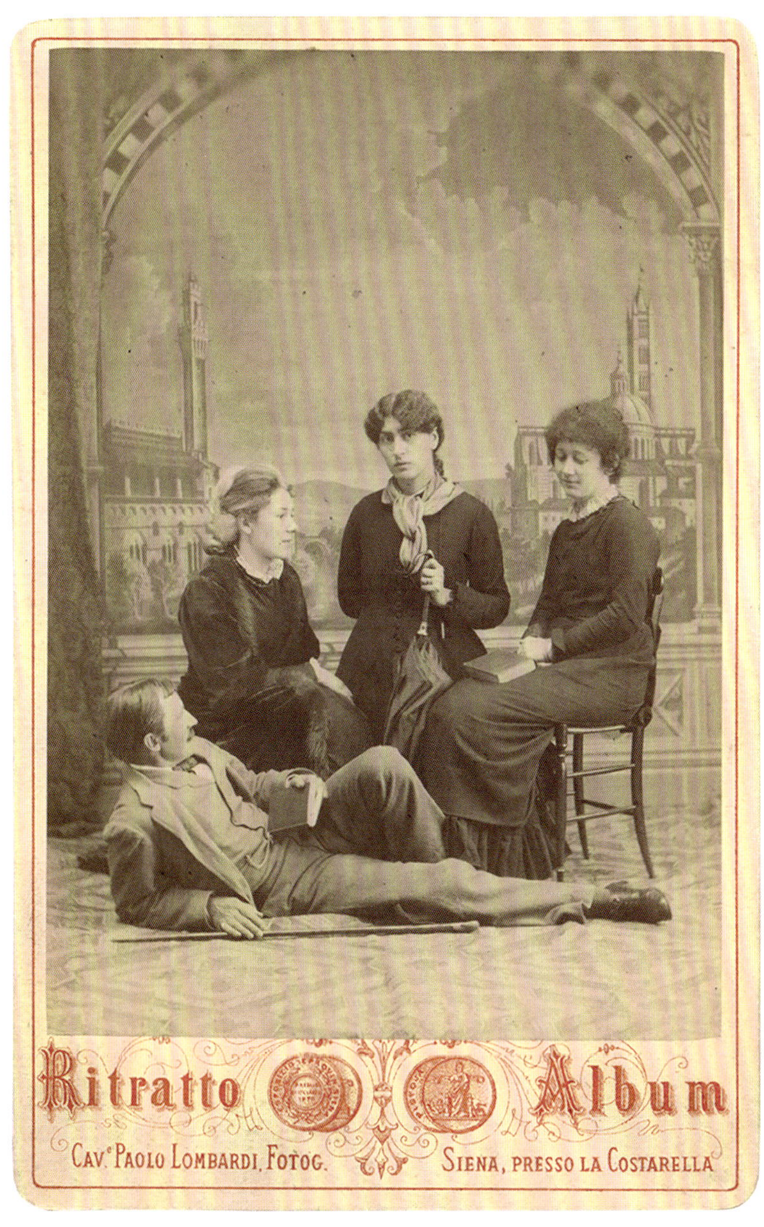

89
Jane Morris
Harry Phillips, c.1900
Platinum print on card mount
140 × 100mm
National Portrait Gallery

90
Study for *The Hour Glass*
Evelyn De Morgan, 1904
Pastel on paper, 460 × 358mm
The De Morgan Foundation

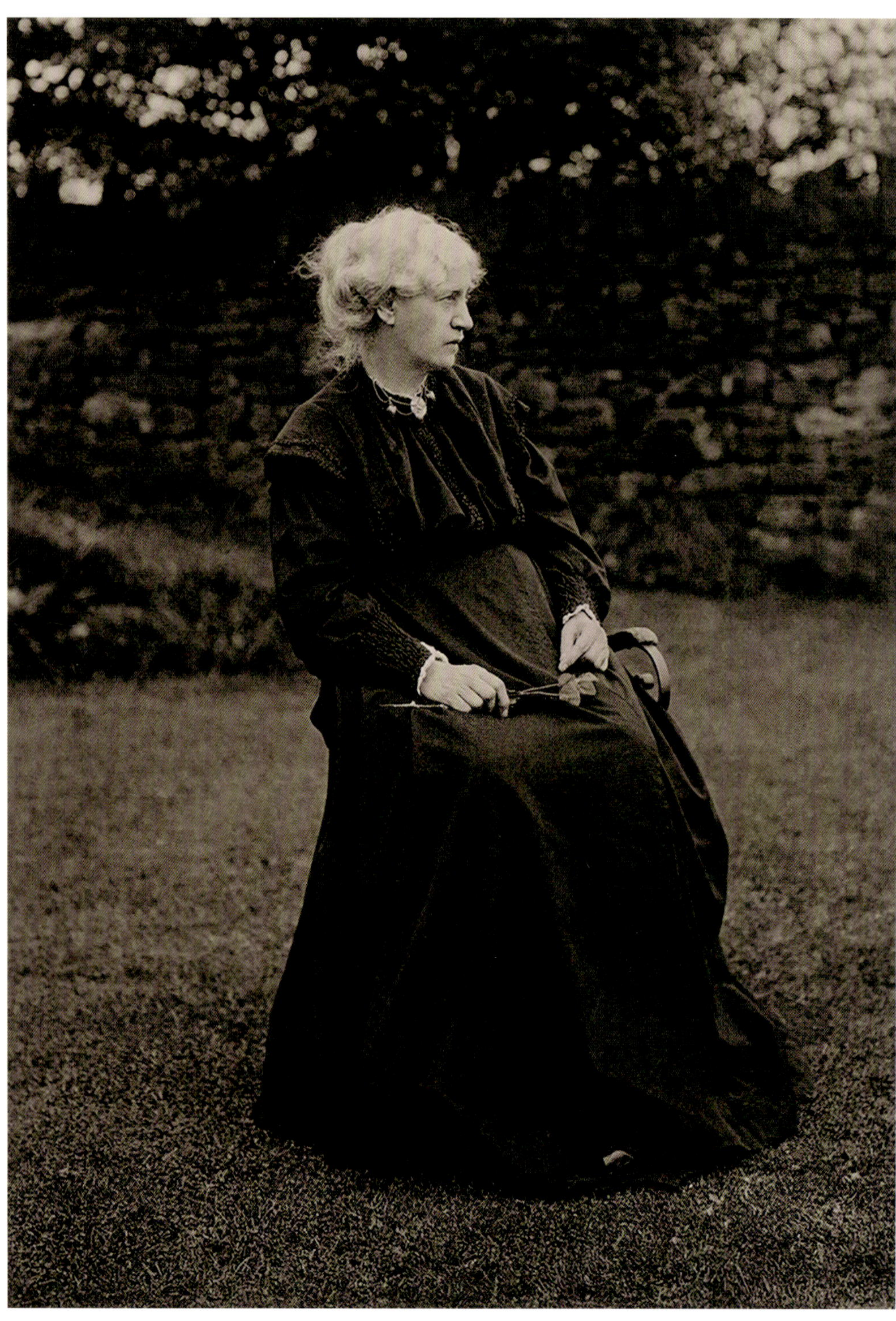

Jane Morris
Harry Phillips, c.1900
Platinum print on card mount
140 × 100mm
National Portrait Gallery

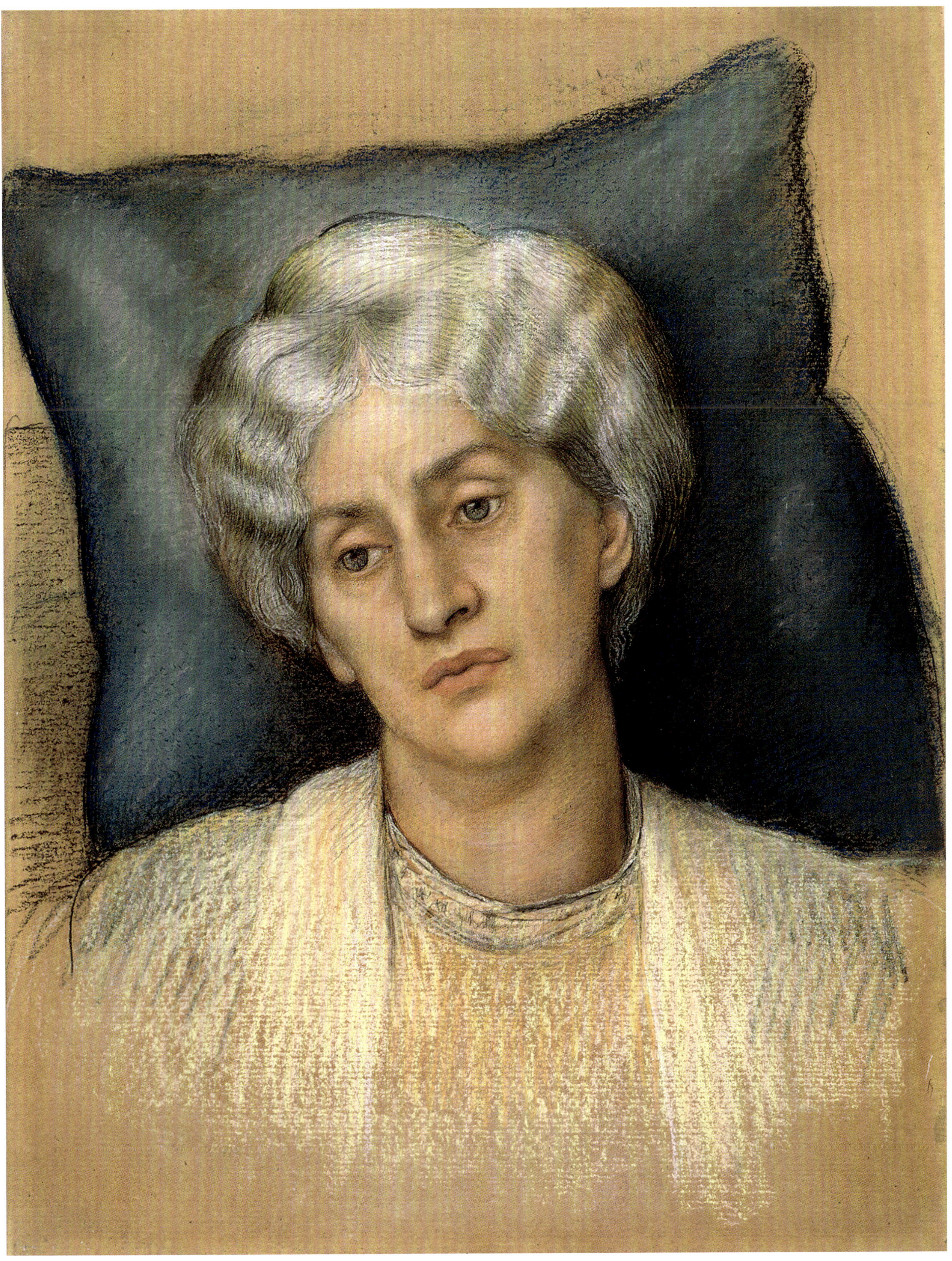

Georgiana Burne-Jones

1840–1920

Aspiring artist, faithful helpmeet, major Pre-Raphaelite biographer, Georgiana Macdonald was one of five sisters in the family of a Methodist minister, raised to become loving wives and mothers. Familiarly known as Georgie, she was introduced to the world of art by Edward Burne-Jones and William Morris, her brother's university friends, and when her family moved to London, at age 15 she took classes at the Government School of Design.[1]

In summer 1856, Burne-Jones proposed, offering a long engagement as he strove to establish himself, while she continued her studies. She met Pre-Raphaelite artists including Millais and Hunt, visited the 1857 Russell Place Pre-Raphaelite exhibition, where Elizabeth Siddal's work was on view, and was introduced to John Ruskin in 1858. She wrote later that the serious pursuit of painting impressed 'a young girl whose experience so far had been quite remote from art' like that of 'a new religion'.[2]

Her earliest surviving work is a naïve Valentine in the form of a strip cartoon with verses (ill. 91). Sent in 1859 to the daughter of Archibald Maclaren, in Oxford, it contains thumbnail images of herself as well as young Mabel Maclaren.

The same year, she joined a class run by Madox Brown, where students were encouraged to 'handle a paintbrush' and to draw from life. A life-size study of a stuffed South American finch (ill. 92), was probably created at this informal 'academy'. The technique conforms to Ruskin's instructions to students: 'lay your colours deliberately, like a mosaic-worker, preparing each carefully and laying it as if it were a piece of coloured cloth'.[3] Madox Brown judged her 'designs in pen & ink' as showing 'real intellect.[4]

One newly discovered example is *The Bridge of Sighs* (ill. 93), a detailed depiction of a group, including top-hatted gentlemen and assorted urchins, around the body of a young woman recovered from the river Thames by a waterman (with the unevenly brimmed hat). Set under Waterloo Bridge, with posters for the London Necropolis and about the ascent of Mont Blanc, it illustrates Thomas Hood's poem about a homeless woman's suicide, 'The Bridge of Sighs' (1844). Although the dead woman's body is out of proportion, the urban setting and crowded composition reflect those of

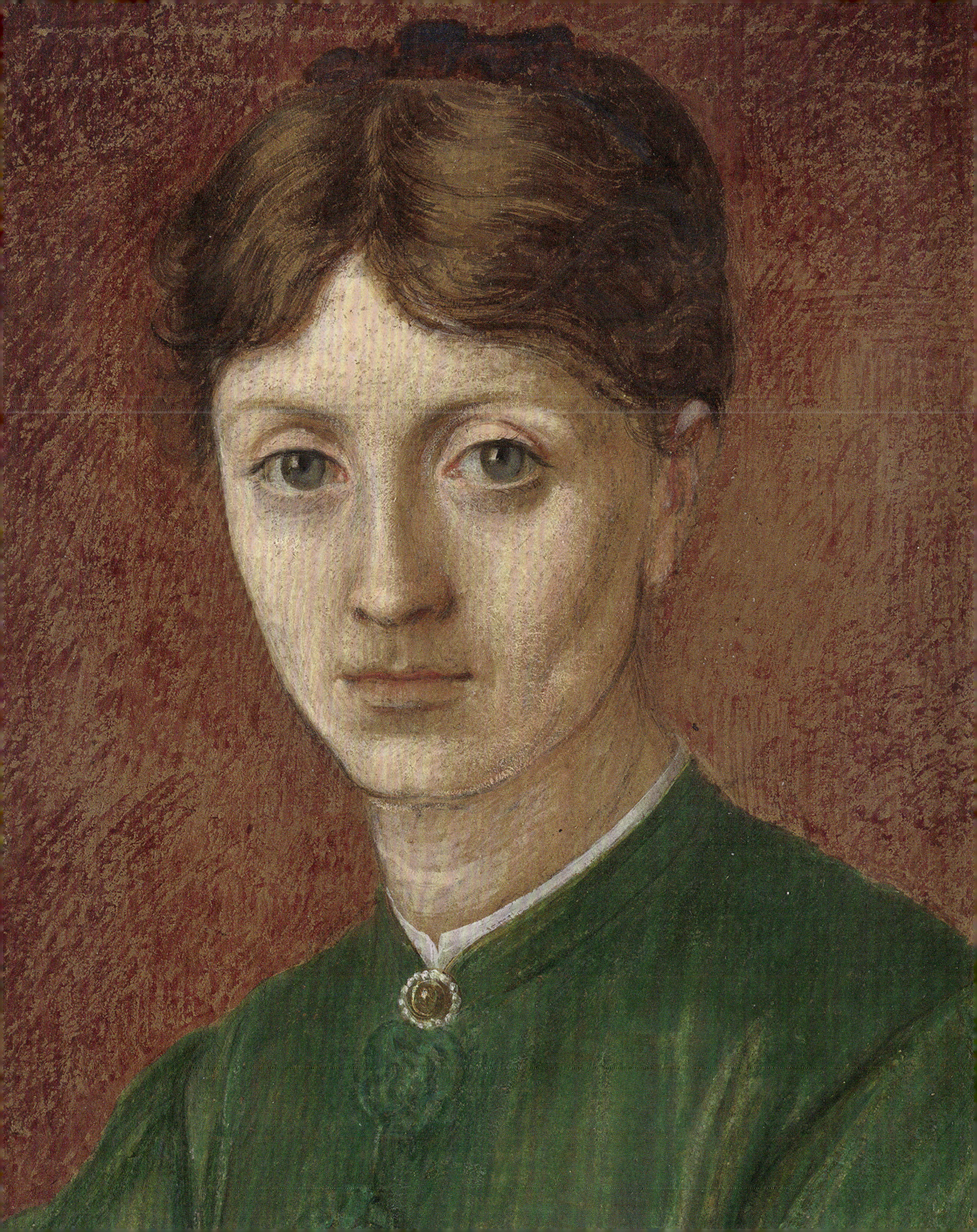

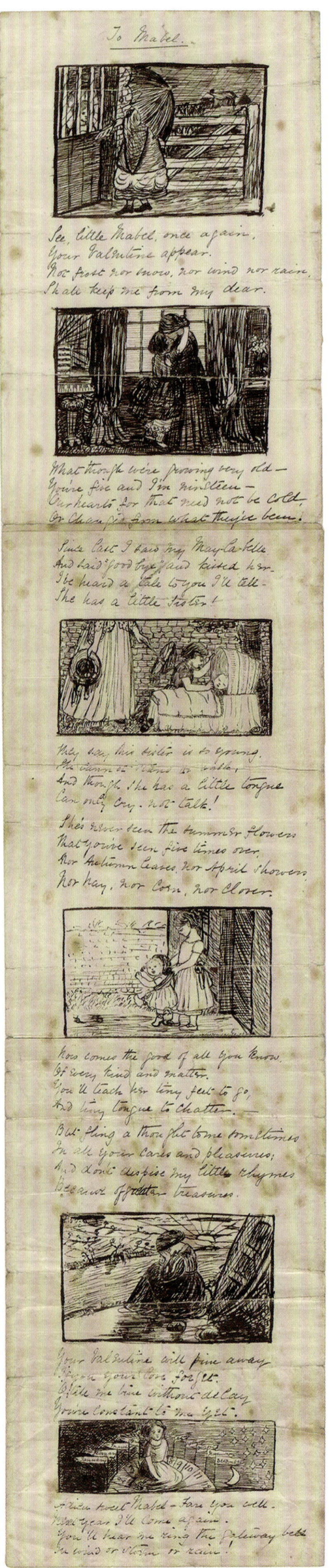

Madox Brown. It is signed with Georgiana Macdonald's initials and was later presented to her grand-daughter Clare Mackail.

With the encouragement of Madox Brown and his wife, Georgie and Ned (as he was now known) married in June 1860, soon after the wedding of Rossetti and Elizabeth Siddal, and just before Jane and William Morris moved to Red House. Georgiana Burne-Jones recalled her personal possessions on marriage as comprising her engraving tools and a small work table (a very welcome wedding present was a sewing machine).[5] Henceforth the three young couples collaborated on decorative schemes – mural painting, stencilling, embroidery: 'Oh, how happy we were, Janey and I, busy in the morning with needlework or wood-engraving,' she recalled.[6] All three women were also soon pregnant.

Although unrecorded, Georgiana Burne-Jones also stitched costumes for use in subject pictures, while her musical talents were a major contribution to Pre-Raphaelite gatherings (see ill.105). Notably, she composed a song from Rossetti's most sensuous poem 'The Song of the Bower' (1860).[8] Rossetti's candlelit portrait of her (ill.94), intended as a wedding gift but never delivered, was probably drawn at the Rossettis' apartment.[9] 'My dear little Georgie I hope you intend coming over with Ned tomorrow evening like a sweetmeat,' wrote Elizabeth Siddal, closing with 'a willow-pattern dish full of love to you and Ned'.[10]

She continued to study and practise after the birth of her son Philip in autumn 1861, later recalling her habit of asking their young maidservant to cease housework 'that I might try to draw her'.[11] Caricaturist George du

'She darts at a little indistinct thing hung away somewhere… and it generally ends in being a Bellini or Bonifacio'

By posing for Ned – in her words, in response to casual requests to 'please take such and such an action for a minute' – Burne-Jones and her sisters regularly shared in the process of art production.[7] In the weeks preceding her wedding, she had modelled for the figure of Clara von Bork (ill.95), the virtuous foil and victim to the evil Sidonia depicted in the companion piece (ill.51). Described as 'intelligent, courageous, and faithful, with a quiet, amiable disposition, and most pious demeanour', Clara is clad in a golden gown, shown cradling baby doves against a predatory cat, in a castle-like interior with whispering maidservants. The date '1560' in the title invokes the tale's late-medieval atmosphere, fancifully anchoring it to history.

Maurier knew her as 'an amateur engraver', willing to teach woodblock skills to his own wife, while Rossetti recommended her as copyist for a book on William Blake, writing that she was 'very diffident, but I believe in her capacities fully, as she really draws heads with feeling'.[12]

A scrapbook contains the surviving designs for a projected collection of tales written and illustrated by Georgiana Burne-Jones and Elizabeth Siddal (see ill.96). The works demonstrate her command of dramatic composition within a small compass. Subject and style here accord with early Pre-Raphaelite practice, and the female figures in two images invite comparison with William Morris's drawings and paintings of his wife in comparable costume and pose as well

91 (opposite)
**Illustrated Poem
with Six Sketches**
Georgiana Macdonald, 1859
Pen and ink on paper
360 × 114mm
British Museum, London

92 (below)
Finch (Dead Bird)
Georgiana Macdonald, 1859
Watercolour on paper
99 × 178mm
Tate, London

93 (bottom)
The Bridge of Sighs
Georgiana Macdonald, 1859–60
Pencil on paper, 200 × 240mm
Dr Dennis T. Lanigan Collection

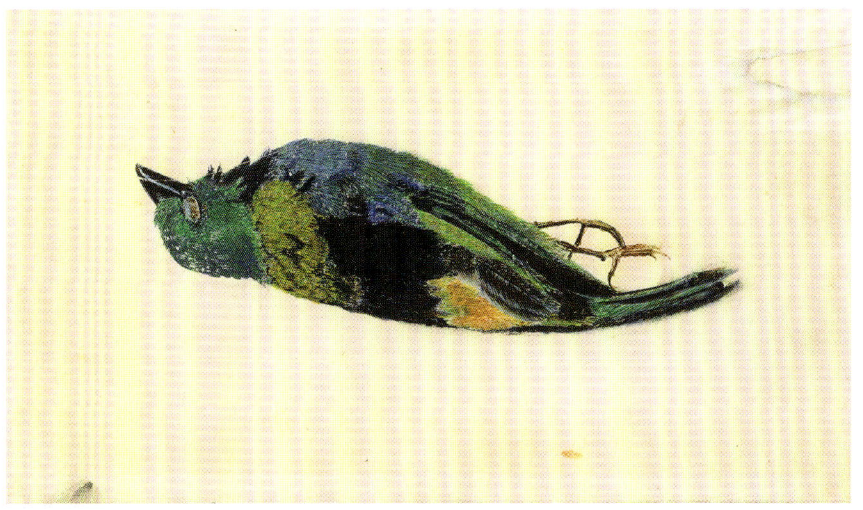

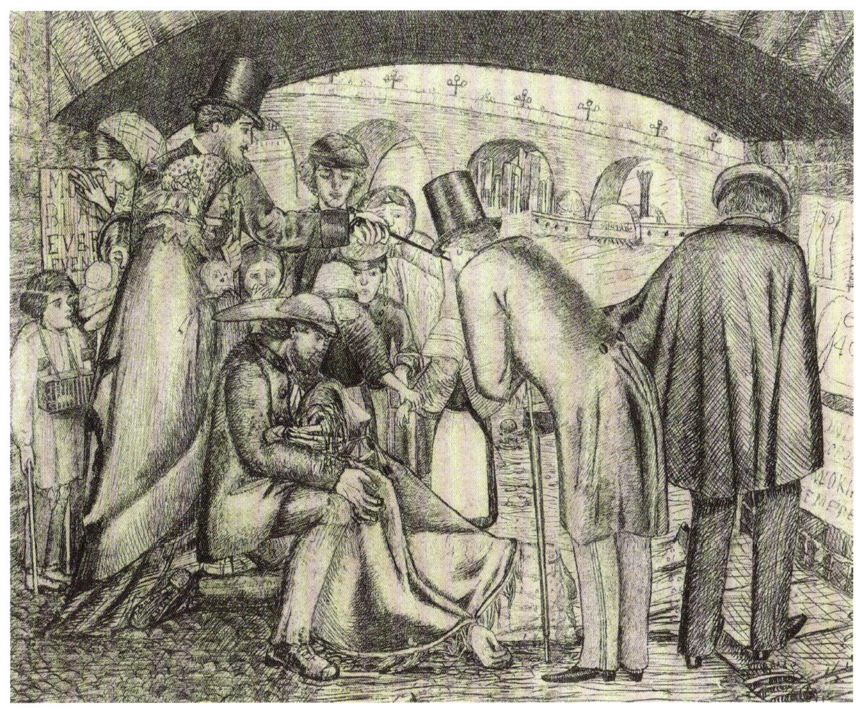

94
Georgiana Burne-Jones
Dante Gabriel Rossetti, 1860
Pencil on paper, 267 × 330mm
Private Collection

95
Clara von Bork 1560
Edward Burne-Jones, 1860
Watercolour and gouache
on paper, 342 × 179mm
Tate, London

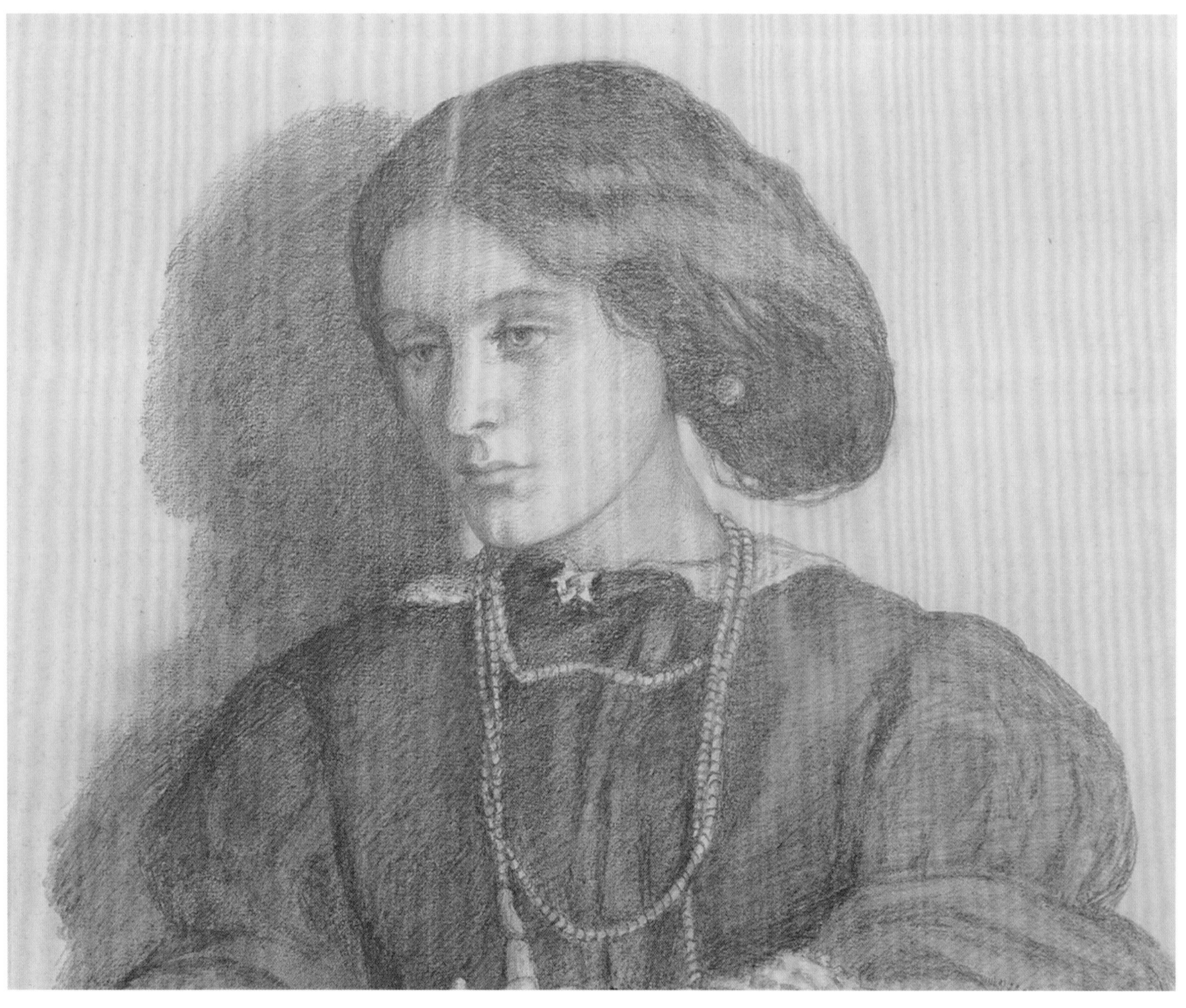

as with early designs for tiles produced
by Morris & Co.

She herself continued to pose, as for
example in her husband's stylised portrait
of 1863 (ill.97), recalling those of the Tudor
era. Inscribed with the initials for Georgiana
Macdonald Jones, it conveys both reserve
and determination. In summer 1862, John
Ruskin took the Burne-Joneses on a tour via
Paris, Milan, Verona, Padua and Venice,
which offered an introduction to Italian art.
'Georgie is growing an eye for a picture,'
her husband reported; 'she darts at a little
indistinct thing hung away somewhere and
says timidly "Isn't that a very nice picture?"
and it generally ends in being a Bellini or
Bonifacio.'[13] Ruskin was conventionally
ambivalent towards her aspirations, saying
that wood-engraving would not interfere with
maternal duties, being 'far more useful and
noble work than any other of which feminine
fingers are capable', and adding:

> I can't imagine anything prettier or more
> wifely than cutting one's husband's
> drawings on the woodblock: there is
> just the proper quantity of echo in it,
> and you may put the spirit and affection
> and fidelity into it which no other person
> could. Only never work hard at it. Keep
> your rooms tidy and baby happy – and
> then after that as much woodwork as
> you've time and liking for.[14]

Burne-Jones had spirit and affection and
fidelity, but her art was impeded by her
husband who firmly excluded her from his
studio. 'I remember the feeling of exile with
which I now heard through its closed doors
the well-known voices of friends together,'
she wrote, 'while I sat with my little son on my
knee and dropped selfish tears upon him.'[15]

Sadly, the planned children's book
inspired by Grimm and Perrault was
abandoned. Later, she recalled the 'several
illustrations that Mrs Rossetti and I were to
make for Fairy Tales written by ourselves.
I made one and Lizzie began another.' But,
she added, 'nothing came of it.'[16] Examples
by both artists show comparable levels of
invention and her own greater knowledge
of the female figure.

Burne-Jones was also involved in the
early work of Morris & Co, in which her
husband was a partner, and probably

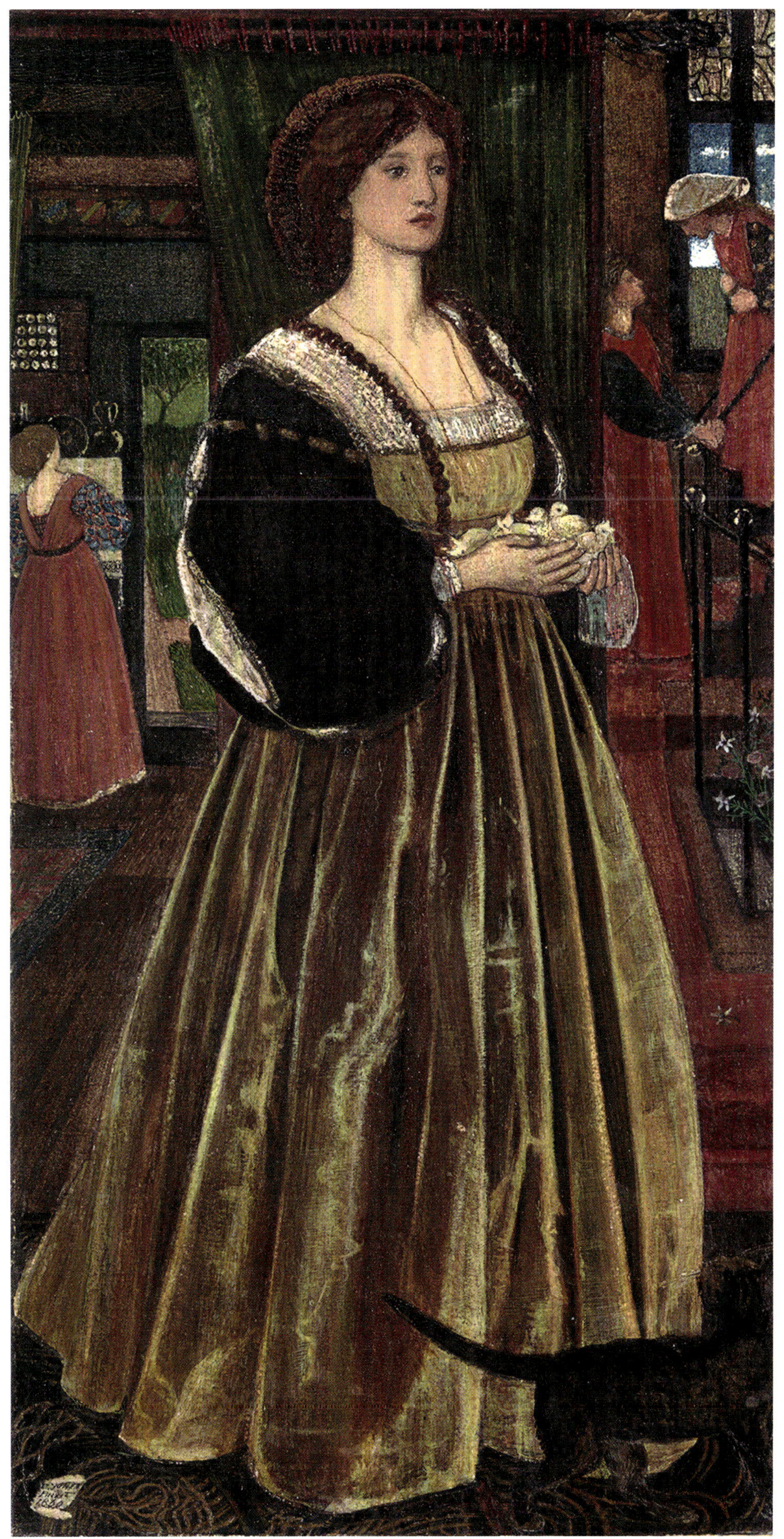

96
Death and the Lady
Georgiana Burne-Jones, 1861
Pen and ink on paper
Private Collection

97
Georgiana Burne-Jones
Edward Burne-Jones, 1863
Gouache on paper
354 × 265mm
Birmingham Museums
and Art Gallery

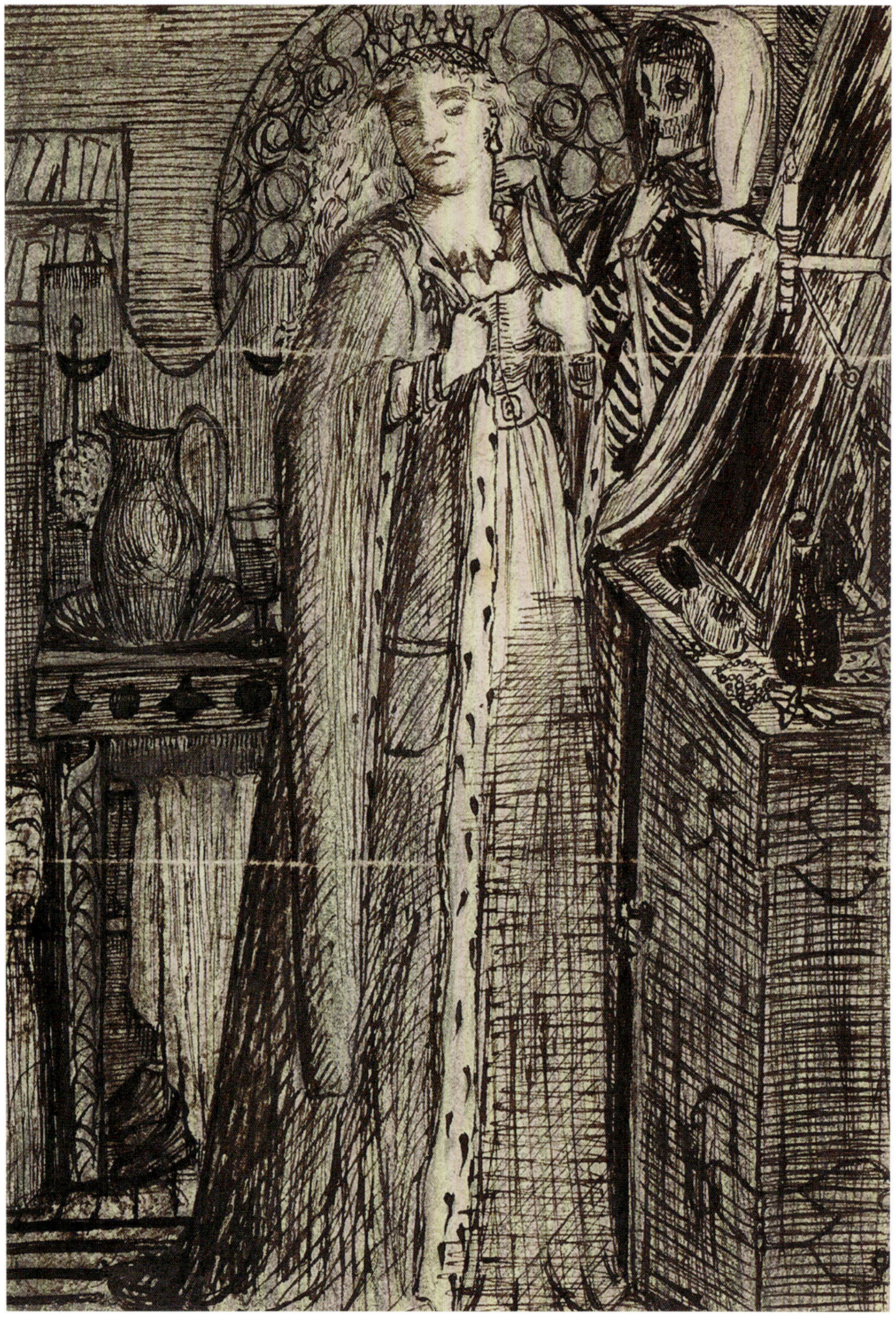

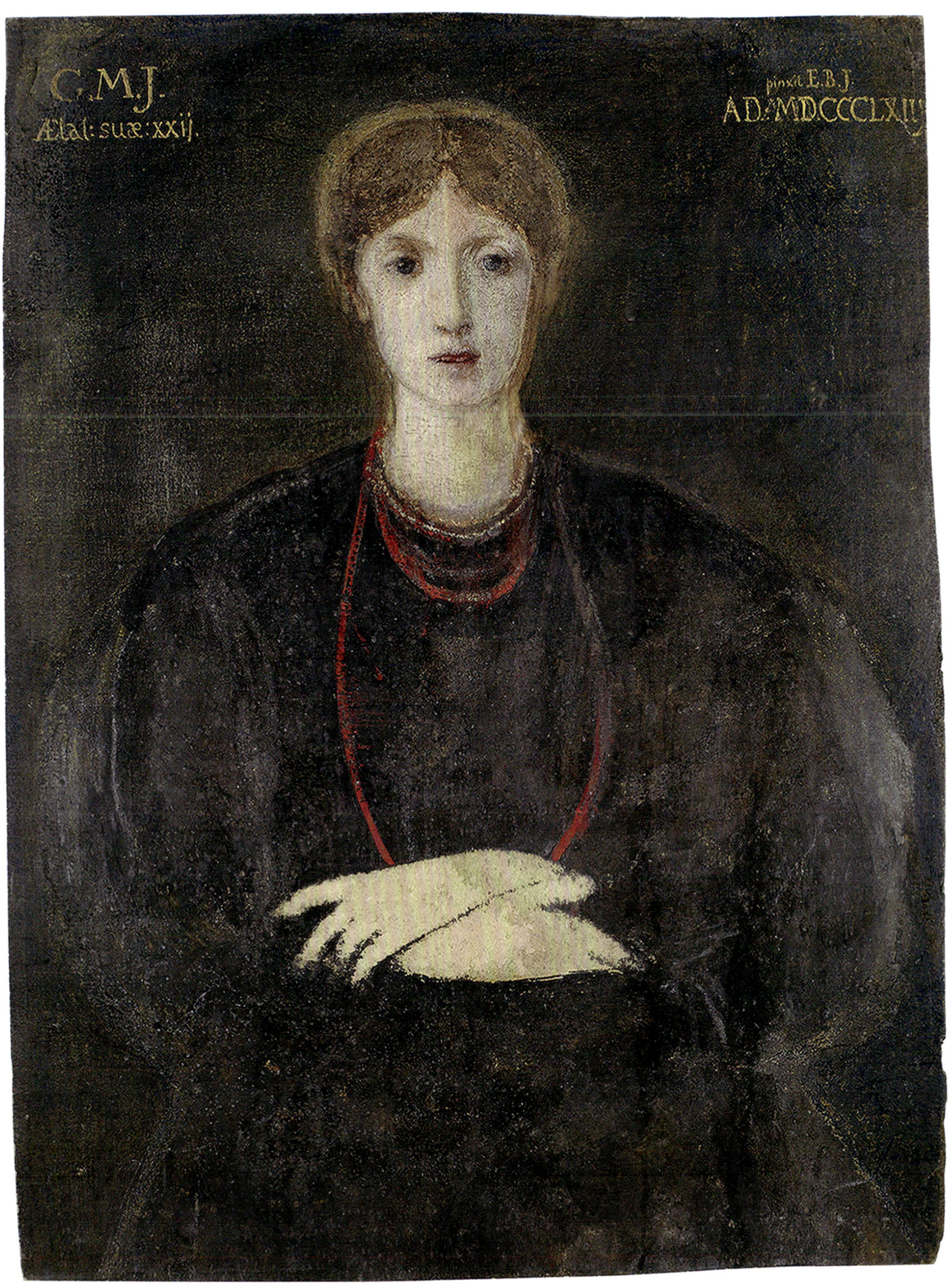

G.M.J.
Ælat: suæ: xxij.
pinxit E.B.J.
A.D: MDCCCLXIIJ

assisted with painting tiles like those retelling the stories of Bluebeard and Cinderella. She emulated the figurative embroidery panels at Red House, embroidering designs of characters from the *Morte d'Arthur* (ill. 99), intended for their own home.[17] Although she persevered, childcare and housekeeping, combined with a near fatal infection that killed her second son soon after birth, effectively ended her pursuit of art. The family moved westwards across London, eventually settling in Fulham, in The Grange, an old house with a garden, where the studio remained out of bounds.

The birth of daughter Margaret in 1866 and, above all, her husband's infatuation with Maria Zambaco, who, as pupil, sitter and muse, had privileged access to his studio, permanently altered her marital relationship. She remained housekeeper,

decisions resolved to upgrade her education by learning Latin, a progressive and contentious area of study for women at the time. In Edward Burne-Jones's thumbnail sketch (ill. 100), mixing mockery and admiration, she studies at the dining table, surrounded by textbooks and the family cat.

New friends around this time included George and Rosalind Howard, later Earl and Countess of Carlisle, shipowner Frederic Leighton, gallerists Sir Coutts and Lady Lindsay and the cosmopolitan Ionides clan in Holland Park, west London. While neither of the Burne-Joneses honoured social status, social demands increased. Formal calls on patrons became one of her duties, for which she prepared humorous anecdotes, as she detested fashionable gossip.

Burne-Jones was a valued aunt to her sisters' children, including Rudyard and Trixie

'The feeling of exile with which I now heard through its closed [studio] doors the well-known voices of friends together'

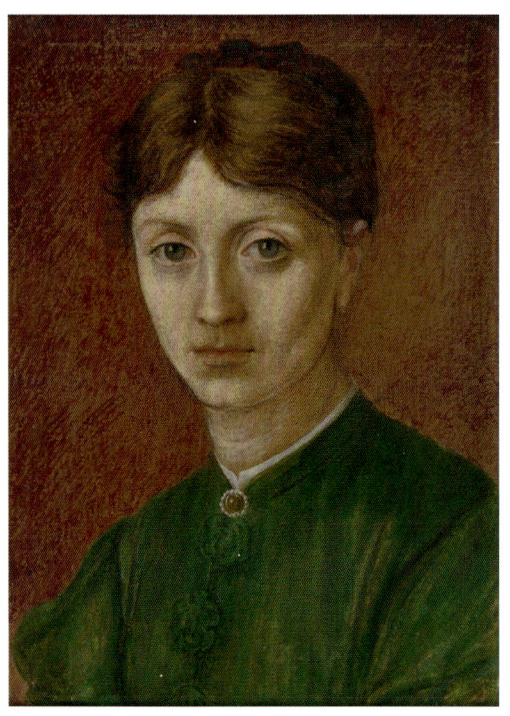

hostess and helpmeet, however, providing the steady domestic base on which his career flourished. She also assumed oversight of both household finances and artistic income and expenditure.

Artist, dealer and collector Charles Fairfax Murray entered the Pre-Raphaelite world in 1866, becoming studio assistant and a discreet member of the Burne-Jones household. He painted Georgiana Burne-Jones in 1870, aged 30 (ill. 98), endowing her with a steely, discomfiting gaze and gaunt, melancholy feeling, perhaps reflecting the distress caused by her husband's involvement with Zambaco, which Murray witnessed.

For 'advice and warning' in respect of marital troubles, she corresponded with novelist George Eliot, and among other

Kipling, and an honorary aunt to the Morris daughters. As her granddaughter Angela Thirkell recalled: 'My grandmother, who had a quiet worldly wisdom of her own, warned me when I was only a girl against lies that people might tell about Aunt Janey.'[18]

She also undertook much of her own children's early education, until Philip was sent to boarding school and Margaret to Notting Hill High School. The Burne-Joneses were both politically radical until middle age, after which his opinions grew conservative while hers shared the progressive Liberal outlook of William Morris. This led towards the Socialism of the 1880s, hers having a strongly practical aspect.

In 1880 the family acquired a holiday home in Sussex, where she was later elected to the local council and, according

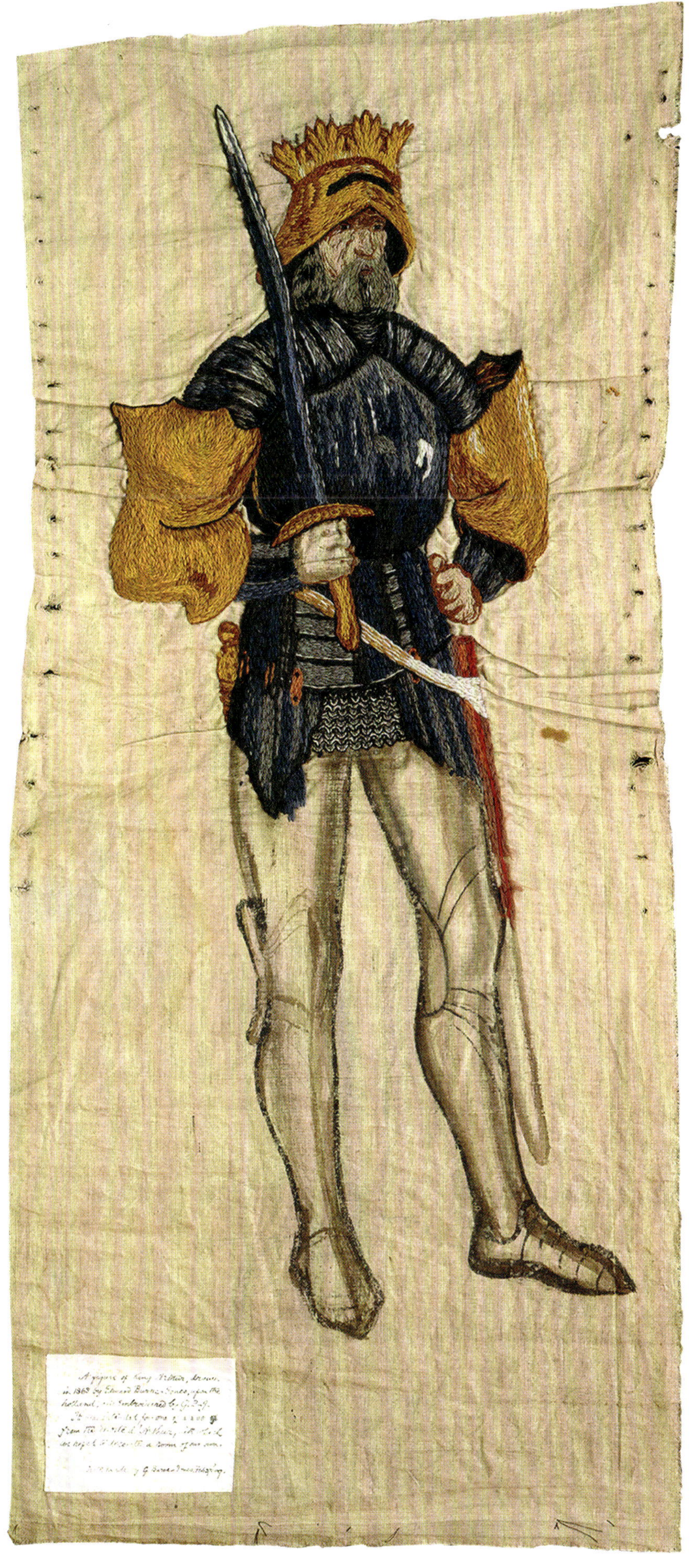

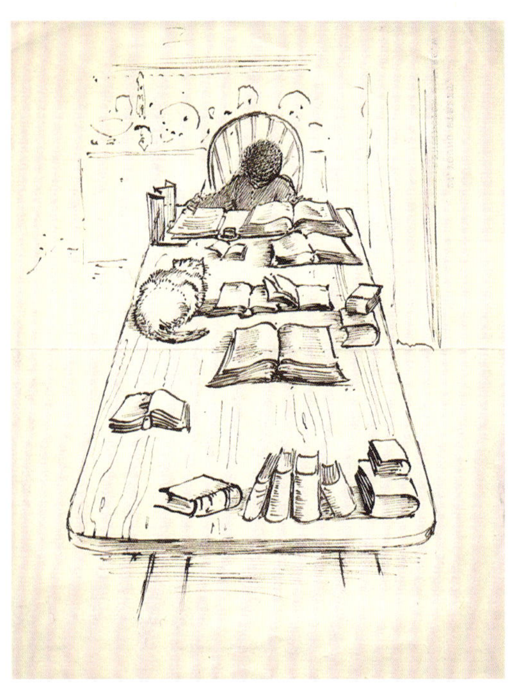

100
**Georgiana Burne-Jones
Studying Latin**
Edward Burne-Jones, c.1880s
Ink on paper, 203 × 153mm
University of Delaware Library

101
**Georgiana Burne-Jones,
with Philip and Margaret**
Edward Burne-Jones, 1883
Oil on canvas, 737 × 535mm
Private Collection

to her husband, began 'stirring up the neighbourhood' to improve living conditions, especially through health advisors. In London, she supported the South London Art Gallery, which aimed to bring visual culture to the urban poor. Her feelings when her husband accepted a baronetcy in 1894 remained private (the Morrises laughed incredulously).

Begun when she was about 42, Edward Burne-Jones's portrait (ill.101) shows his wife as loyal spouse and mother, wearing a dark, unadorned costume similar to those in earlier versions (ills 94 and 97) but in a richer, velvet fabric.[19] She holds a copy of Gerard's *Herball* open at the heartsease or wild pansy, her favourite emblem, which Ruskin called the flower of 'those who love simply,

through the life, work and friends of one of its key practitioners, in splendid prose, with fine judgements and vignettes, together with an eloquent silence regarding Maria Zambaco. The early idealism of the young Pre-Raphaelites is expertly evoked, demonstrating the personal and pictorial appeal that still forms part of posterity's response to the pictures and the people who collectively produced them.

Memorials implicitly tracks its author's life, too, with characteristic reserve. Looking back on her own art, she acknowledged only a 'certain deftness of hand', saying she had not learnt 'anything vital' from her studies.[20] Her sister Edith Macdonald believed that 'being thrown among artists of genius' discouraged her sister

Georgiana had spirit and affection and fidelity, but her art was impeded by her husband

to the death'. Endowed with a steady gaze that can unsettle the viewer, the likeness has been interpreted as a tacit acknowledgement of her husband's betrayals. It also celebrates their family unit, showing son Philip as professional painter, aged 22, and 17-year-old Margaret ready to enter society. The arm resting on a parapet recalls Renaissance portraiture, with a salute to Velázquez in the view into a further room. It was first exhibited in 1975.

After William Morris's death in 1896, the Burne-Joneses promoted his biography, which, with their assistance, was written by their son-in-law J. W. Mackail. When Edward died in 1898, his wife assumed the biographer's task herself, to make her last and, in many ways, greatest contribution to Pre-Raphaelitism, in the two-volume *Memorials of Sir Edward Burne-Jones* (1902). A model of its genre, this has become a foundational text, which chronicles a half-century of the movement

'from continuing to cultivate this gift'.[21] In *Memorials*, however, Georgiana Burne-Jones obliquely revealed both the original ambition and the causes of defeat:

> It is pathetic to think how we women longed to keep pace with the men, and how gladly they kept us by them until their pace quickened and we had to fall behind... I stopped, as so many women do, well on the side of tolerable skill, daunted by the path which has to be followed absolutely alone if the end is to be reached.[22]

The language betrays the regret, in the youthful longing to be a creative artist, and in the irony of 'absolutely alone', which denied the key practical and emotional support male artists required and received from women like herself. As so often, a woman blamed herself for failing.

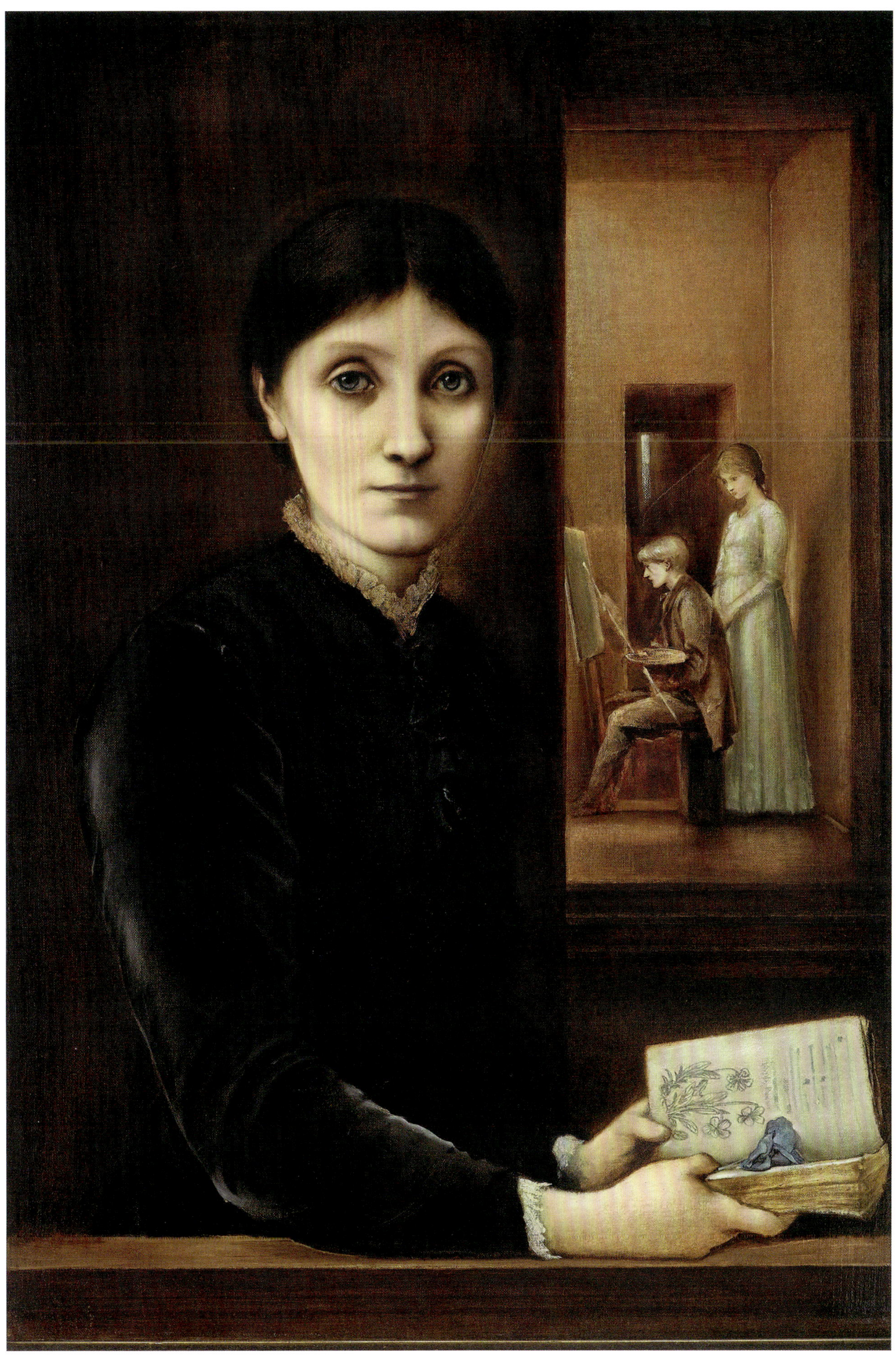

102
**The Burne-Jones
and Morris Families**
Frederick Hollyer, 1874
Sepia-toned platinotype print
150 × 135mm
National Portrait Gallery

103
**Georgiana Burne-Jones
and Granddaughter**
Emery Walker, c.1900
Whole-plate glass negative
215 × 161mm
National Portrait Gallery

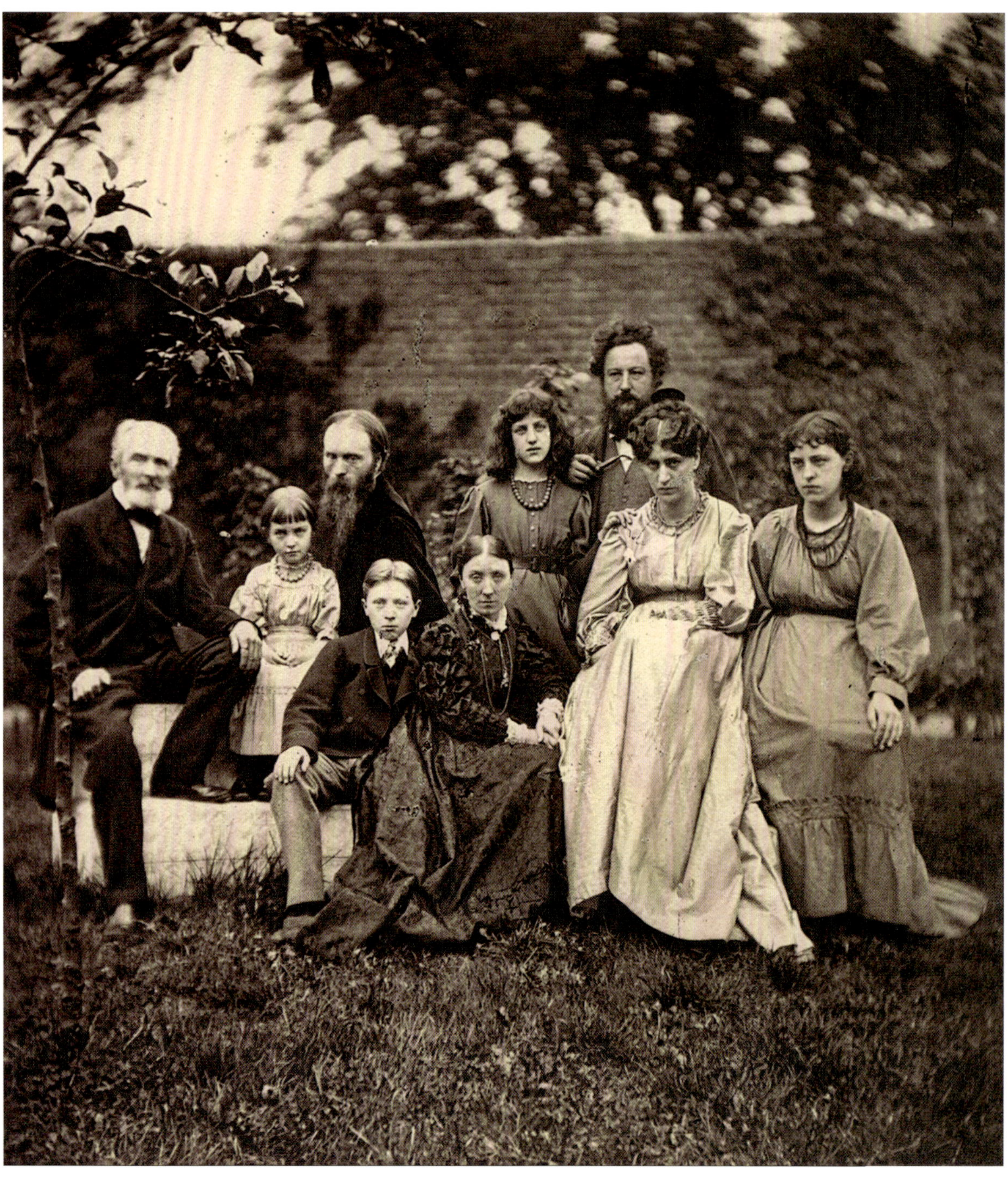

**The Burne-Jones
and Morris Families**
Frederick Hollyer, 1874

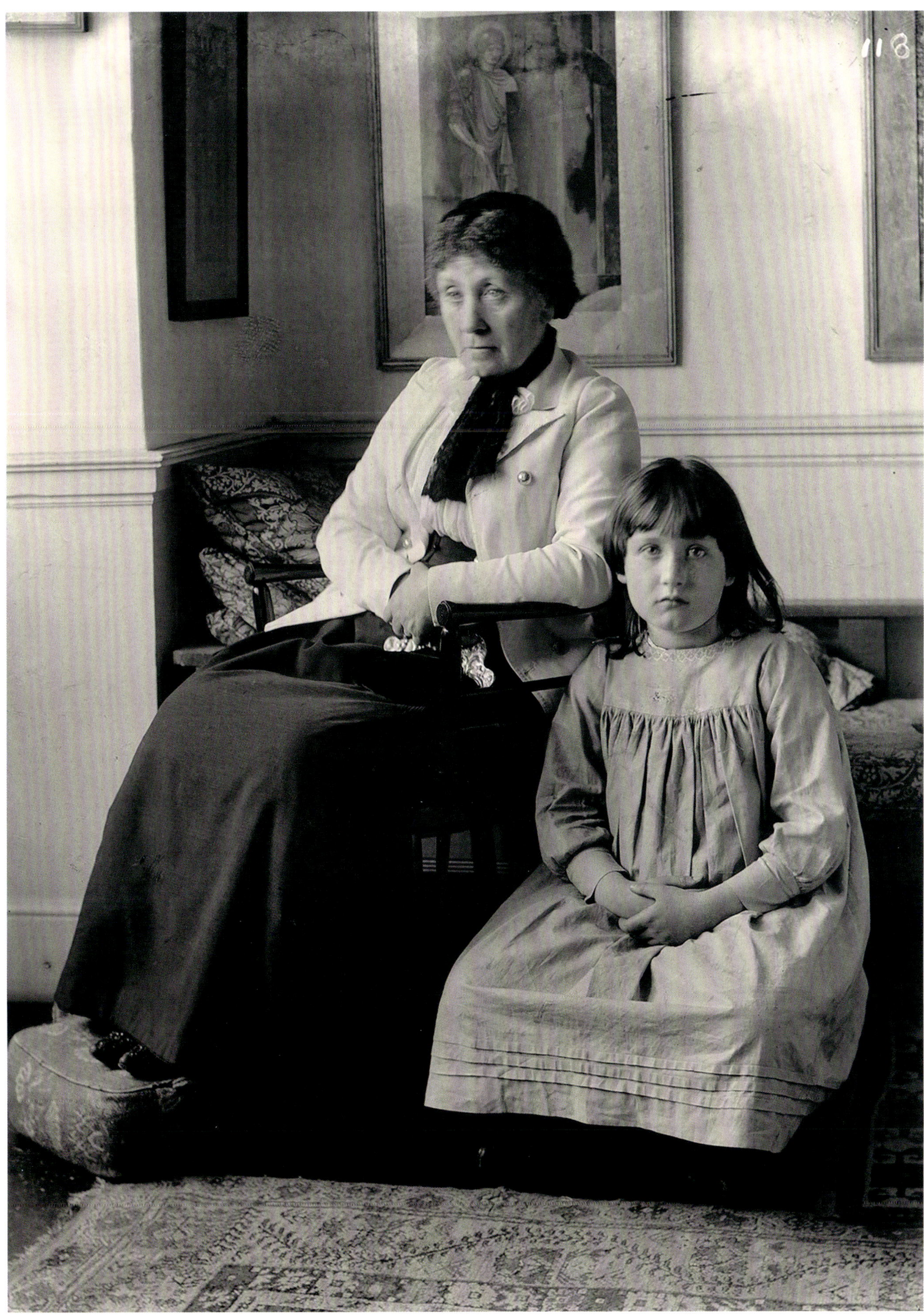

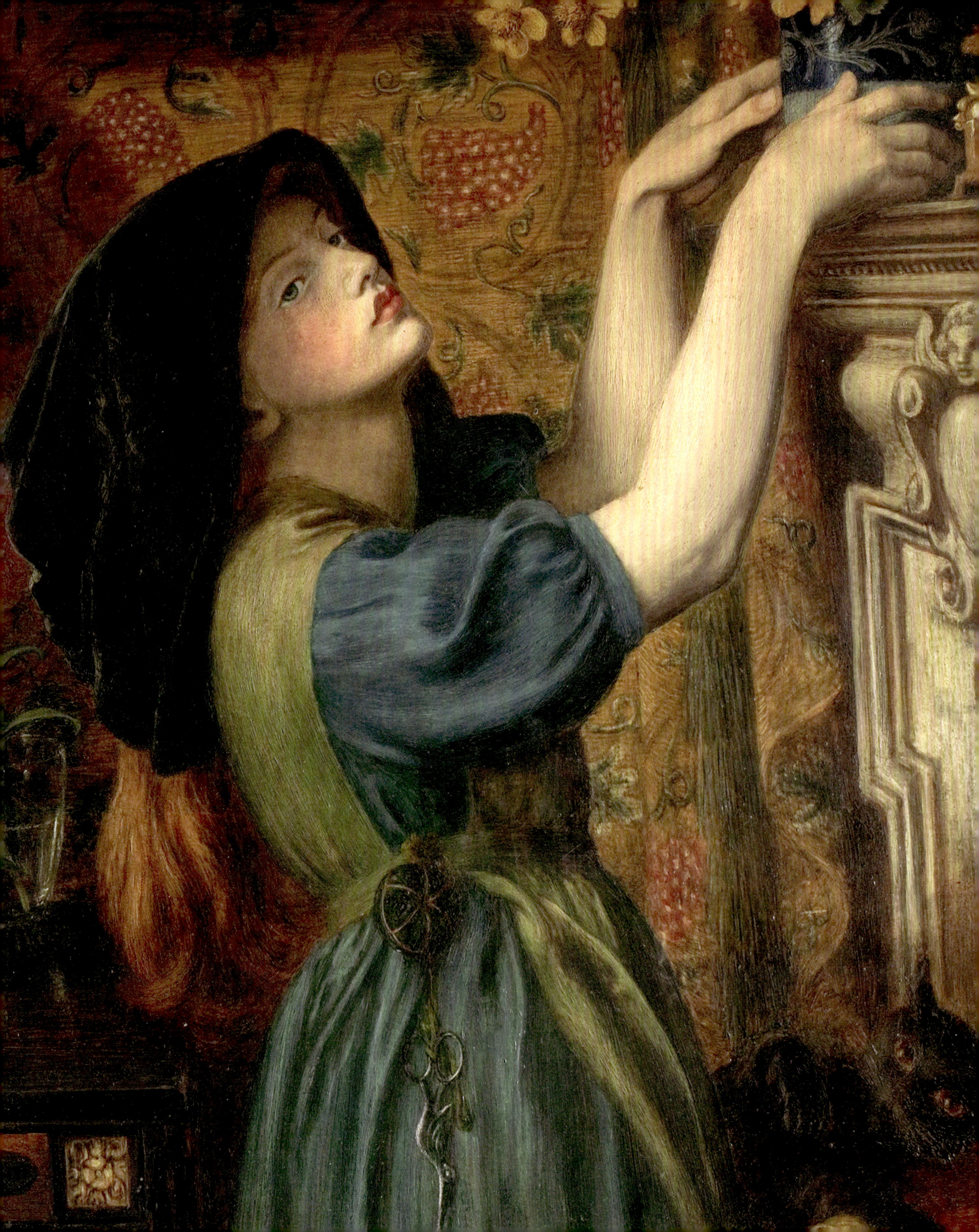

Wives, muses, pupils, sisters, daughters, servants and, occasionally, mistresses made up the largely unsung web of support in the studios of Victorian artists, propping up a fragile domestic edifice that sustained the artists and their families financially and, increasingly, socially as well.

Model Wives & Mistresses

by Charlotte Gere

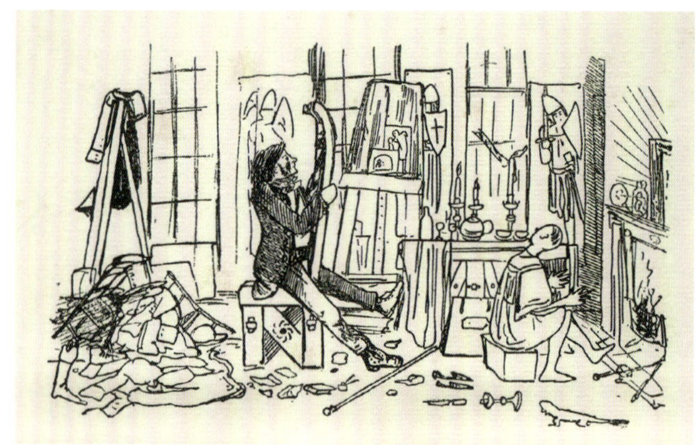

Victorian instruction on the management of the home set 'model' wives impossibly high standards of sympathy, obedience, and domestic and moral probity; however, in the studio they had another 'model' role, as constantly available and free artists' models. Women in the Pre-Raphaelite circle could be mistress of the house or lover, even both at the same time. Crucial to the organisation of the artistic household, and with often inadequate domestic help, the women's management of the studio itself has been little discussed. Aligning studio life with the social expectations of a successful artist exposed the women to pressures beyond conventional notions of middle-class home-making and child-rearing.

The artist's household, revolving around the studio, encompassed the whole family, including the children. It was out of step with the domestic set-up of professional families, at a time when work and home were increasingly separated. The Victorian ideal of a man's place and a woman's place, 'the world' and 'the home', was hard to achieve. Without space or finance for a purpose-built addition, the studio took, of necessity, the largest room in the house, depriving the women of their most important social space. The irregular flow of money caused further anxieties. Except for the Morrises, all these artist families experienced financial problems early on. As the men's careers took them in different directions, with their growing success and rising position, the women faced what was effectively a full-time job, often to the detriment of their own artistic ambitions.

The Household Atelier

> How I hate Spring cleanings; artists ought never to be cleaned – half their vitality goes out of them when they are clean.' Again he complained, 'The glory is too great for me, I don't feel as if I should ever be able to work in it: it would be like trying to paint in a drawing-room.[1]

Two things are at war in Burne-Jones's protests: the studio, centre of the creative project, and the social and domestic expectations of a middle-class household. In the 1880s he must have become aware of widespread interest in artists' houses.[2] His vision of painting 'in a drawing-room' was of a studio styled to act as a reception room, which he deplored. His house-studio was more workmanlike than most, with a garden studio entirely given up to work in progress. There was some excuse for spring-cleaning the house-studio, reached through a Morris-wallpapered sitting room, where visitors might venture. Millais, in contrast, remarked of his studio, a vision of Renaissance grandeur, hung with Beauvais tapestries and used on occasion as a ballroom: 'This is my workshop.'[3]

Admired for her looks and ease of manner, her first marriage to John Ruskin taught Effie Gray how to promote her husband in society. He promised her a collaborative role in his work, but it failed to materialise, a lack that her second marriage would rectify. Millais's career had to compete eventually with a family of eight children, but Effie Millais took on the secretarial side: booking models (and finding likely alternatives, at which she was particularly adept) and sourcing costume (chores formerly undertaken by her mother-in-law).[4] Unusually for a Victorian wife, her contribution is fully acknowledged by her youngest son, in his biography of his father (see p.50).[5]

Along with correspondence relating to both career and social life, recording work in progress usually fell to the wives, as with the housekeeping books that were settled with tradesmen at the end of the month. The most important tradesman was the artists' supplier: for Rossetti, Hunt, Millais and Burne-Jones, this was Charles Roberson and Co., at 99 Long Acre in the Covent Garden area of London.[6] Rossetti's strained financial relations with Roberson's resulted in Elizabeth Siddal being escorted there by Madox Brown since he did not dare show his face.[7]

Very few artists' homes had a room set aside for the wife (or sister or daughter) to practise her art, an indication that their artistic ambitions were not considered very significant. Sole recognition of Georgiana Burne-Jones's plans was a small work table with a drawer, where she kept her wood-engraving tools. When John Ruskin heard of the plan for engraving her husband's designs, he suggested she study at London's Female School of Design. 'There is just the proper quality of echo in it,' he remarked. The scheme was given up and, with it, her aims as a practitioner.[8]

Although artistic circles were more inclusive of their women than professional classes in general, children and housekeeping gradually excluded them from the camaraderie of the studio. In a poignant glimpse of her early struggles with motherhood, Georgiana Burne-Jones noted:

> The difference made in our life by the presence of a child was very great, for I had been used to be much with Edward – reading aloud to him while he worked, and in many ways sharing the life of the studio – and I remember the feeling of exile with which I now heard through its closed door the well-known voices of friends together with Edward's familiar laugh, while I sat with my little son on my knee and dropped selfish tears upon him as 'the separator of companions and the terminator of delights'.[9]

Most married men's expectation of social life was little different from their bachelor years. Until 1885, Edward Burne-Jones dined two or three times a week with his patron William Graham, and many 'society' invitations were for him alone. Men belonged to cliques and sketching clubs, and attended official soirées without their wives.[10]

Wives spent long hours in the studio, reading aloud to artists (there is no evidence that this chore was undertaken in reverse) and playing the piano. Music was very important. Millais liked Effie Millais to play or read to him while he worked. Georgiana Burne-Jones's musical repertoire included Beethoven and Schubert (she had a beautiful singing voice), as well as her husband's favourite English, Scottish and Breton ballads. Her repertoire came from *Popular Music*, issued by Chappell & Co., and from the French songbook, *Échos du temps passé*. Morris's wedding present to Jane Morris was also a songbook.

Versions of 'open house' were not uncommon, representing a pleasure for the gregarious and valuable showcase for work in progress. At the Burne-Joneses', Georgiana did not formally institute 'days' when guests were received every week, but in London on Sundays friends often dropped in for lunch – two or three extra places were laid regularly. Edward Burne-Jones's invitation to Joseph Comyns Carr, a director of the Grosvenor Gallery, is revealing: 'We shall meet on Sunday at lunch. Georgie is away, but Margaret [Burne-Jones's daughter] dispenses lower-middle-class hospitality with a finish and calm which would not disgrace a higher social position.'[11] Success turned the studio into a semi-public space. Artists' studios were so much visited that it became a serious distraction from creating the works of art, on which the whole enterprise depended.[12] Under pressure, Burne-Jones would absent himself, leaving his wife to receive and placate the visitors with their cards and letters of introduction. Money was very scarce until they began to make substantial sums from his work.

Combining the working studio with its social role required considerable agility. With his Chelsea house under Fanny Cornforth's sway, Rossetti's attitude to social life remained determinedly casual. Although it was the room into which visitors were ushered on arrival, his studio never aspired to 'show' status, being a repository of unusual musical instruments, many unplayable (but important to the unmusical Rossetti, to suggest 'sound' in his evocation of the senses),

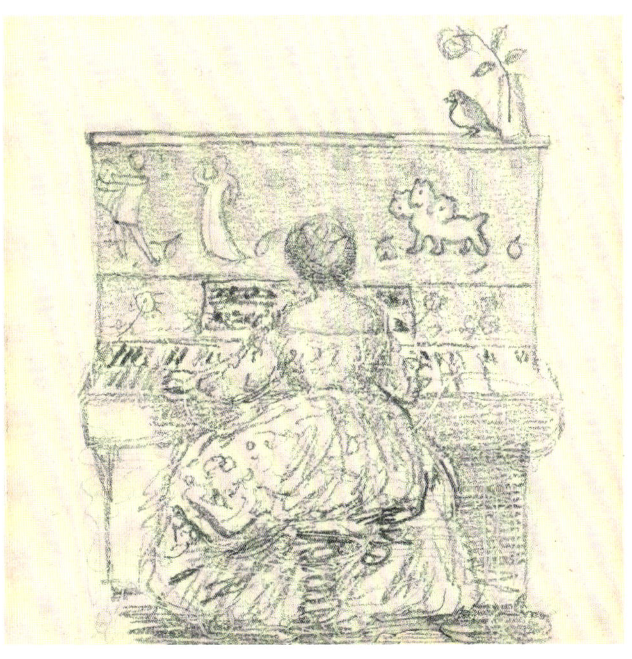

blue china, Chippendale chairs, a chaise longue, many old cabinets, and the main costume and prop wardrobe, as well as easels with work in progress.[13]

Rossetti's letters to Fanny Cornforth reveal her attempts to maintain Tudor House on the Chelsea riverfront during his long absence at Kelmscott Manor, in 1871–4. Fascinating insights into the demands of the studio emerge: models to be contacted and props – including a lay figure – accessories and costumes to be found in cupboards in London and dispatched to Oxfordshire by train and carrier. Among them 'a cloak and long linen dress which you made... I also want that new green silk dress which used to be in a drawer upstairs – I suppose it is now in the wardrobe.'[14] In London the servants get at the drink and fail in the most basic of their duties. Detected in dishonesty they must be dismissed and replaced. Money ('tin' as Rosetti called it), as ever, is a major problem.

The Servant Question

Books on servant management were something of a Victorian publishing phenomenon, with popular manuals of instruction running into many editions. The daily tasks that professional men demanded of their wives, and of other female relatives in their absence, encompassed supervision of the servants, the daily meals for upstairs and downstairs, laundry, cleaning, dressmaking, linen, mending, sick nursing, social entertaining at home, daytime calls, correspondence and household expenditure.[15] The very basic character of some of the housekeeping advice suggests how important this source of correct behaviour had become. Servants' duties, from the maid-of-all-work to the butler and valet, are scrupulously outlined. Much stressed is the provision of a place of peace and comfort for the returning master of the household, who has been at work providing for his family. Even when more servants were afforded, much depended on the oversight of the mistress.

Georgiana Burne-Jones was well equipped to run a frugal household. Her upbringing in a large family, on the tiny stipend of a Methodist minister, meant that she could undertake any task left undone by her mother's two hard-working maids. Mother and sisters could cook, and the family clothes and linen were all home-made. Her pretty maid in her early married life, Annie West, aged 21, was the same age as her mistress; fortunately this would not have been Annie West's first place, and West would have known her duties already. For most of her married life, Burne-Jones made do with just three women servants, only rising to a butler, Albert Clarke, by the time of the 1891 census. By 1881 they had a parlour maid, superior to a housemaid, expected to be publicly presentable and to wait at table. By 1891, there was an 'upper parlour maid'.[16]

The composition and timing of meals are hard to reconstruct, since food is so rarely mentioned in PRB correspondence. Georgiana Burne-Jones's reference to boiled mutton with carrots and potatoes (dinner, 28 February 1896) or bread-and-butter pudding with prunes probably belies a welcoming and hospitable household.[17] Models could not eat with the family or the domestics, so trays of food and drink were carried to the studio. Non-professional models – even friends – had to be chaperoned; feeding them posed problems of etiquette, especially if the chaperone was a servant rather than a social equal.[18]

Although memories of the Red House have the Morris family waiting merrily on themselves, Morris had the means to staff a middle-class household. In 1861 Red House had four servants: cook, housemaid, a nanny named Elizabeth Reynolds and a groom–coachman (needed for the wagonette ride from Abbey Wood station).[19] When the family moved to live 'over the shop' in Queen Square, London, Jane Morris's catering obligations included the partners in the decorating business (intimate friends, who were entertained monthly) and its considerable number of employees. This social and logistical minefield had very porous boundaries, between the front and back entrances, and meals taken with the family. Even when they settled at Kelmscott House in Hammersmith, the Firm's activities had to be negotiated domestically, delicate questions of class arising over who ate with the family.[20] By the 1890s a 'socialist' experiment of having the servants eat with the family had been given up. [21]

Morris took Kelmscott Manor in the Cotswolds on a joint tenancy with Rossetti in June 1871. A summer retreat, life at Kelmscott Manor was deliberately simple and bucolic. Philip and Mary Comley acted as caretakers, entrusted with the running of the estate along with their niece Annie Allen, a general maid and later cook. 'Little Annie' as Rossetti called her, posed for his 1874 painting *Marigolds* (ill.106), a rare Pre-Raphaelite depiction of a domestic servant at work, arranging a vase of yellow spring flowers on a mantelpiece.

While Rossetti was in almost permanent residence with Jane Morris and her daughters, a married couple, Allan and Emma, came from Cheyne Walk in London, to join the children's nurse and the locals. William and Mary Giles, caretakers from 1887, and their daughter Ada, living in a nearby cottage, seem latterly to have kept the house going and readied it for the visits.[22] The family even found amusement in cooking, allowing William Morris to practise a skill for which he had a real talent, on the brief occasions when he could get away from the Firm's demands. The garden was productive enough for Jane Morris to consider vegetarianism.[23] She contrived to entertain beyond close friends and family, making only token apologies for the primitive domestic arrangements, and a steady flow of guests throughout the summer months took the train to Lechlade and pony trap to the house.

For Effie Millais, managing her husband's portrait practice, the reception of public figures as sitters called for servants equal to it; the ten-yearly census returns uncover a relentless expansion of the household. By 1881, when he was a making large sums of money and inhabiting a palatial mansion, Millais expected to keep a good table and was something of a wine connoisseur. He had, at last, achieved a butler, William Cassels, and one other manservant, described as 'toolman', probably responsible for the studio. Two housemaids and a kitchen maid feature in the census return for that year; the cook must have been away. By 1891 there is a *chef de cuisine* from Alsace as well as a butler and footman, three housemaids and a scullery maid.

Although census returns are not conclusive, chance playing a large part in who was present on that one night, they track the fluctuating servant numbers. This is not, of course, a complete roll-call, as daily servants are not included, but the broader picture is very instructive. One eye-opener from the returns is the lack of any faithful long-serving old retainers; none of the servants survives from previous listings in either the Millais household or the Burne-Jones's.

The work associated with the linen closet was a highly sophisticated branch of housewifery, involving constant replenishing, laundering and mending. 'I have had a tiring day, & now I hear an arrival of clean clothes from the wash clamouring for me to look through them,' wrote Christina Rossetti; 'So my "poet steps" must trudge upstairs to the humble work.'[24] The 'looking through' was necessary. Almost inevitably, the launderer would have torn some article or missed a stain.[25]

The mending basket was always full, a skilled and continuous chore, and in the absence of a lady's maid (unknown in the artist household) the sewing (referred to as 'work') fell to the women of the house. Men were hard on their (home-sewn) shirts. As Christina Rossetti remarked on the absence of male members of the household following the departure of her brother William: 'One thing I thoroughly enjoy – that my Mother & I can now go about just as we

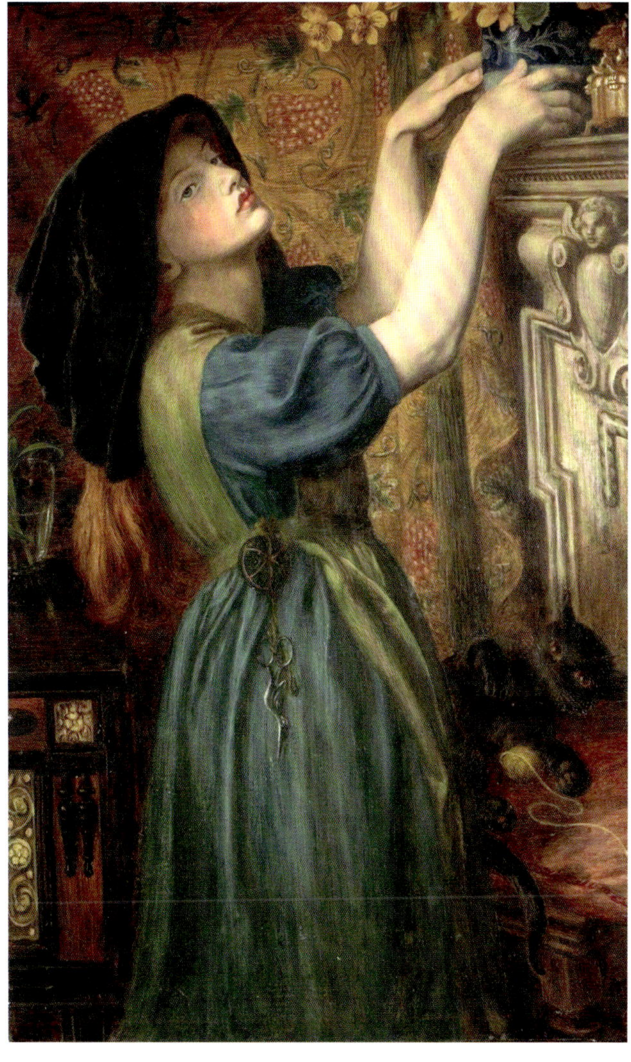

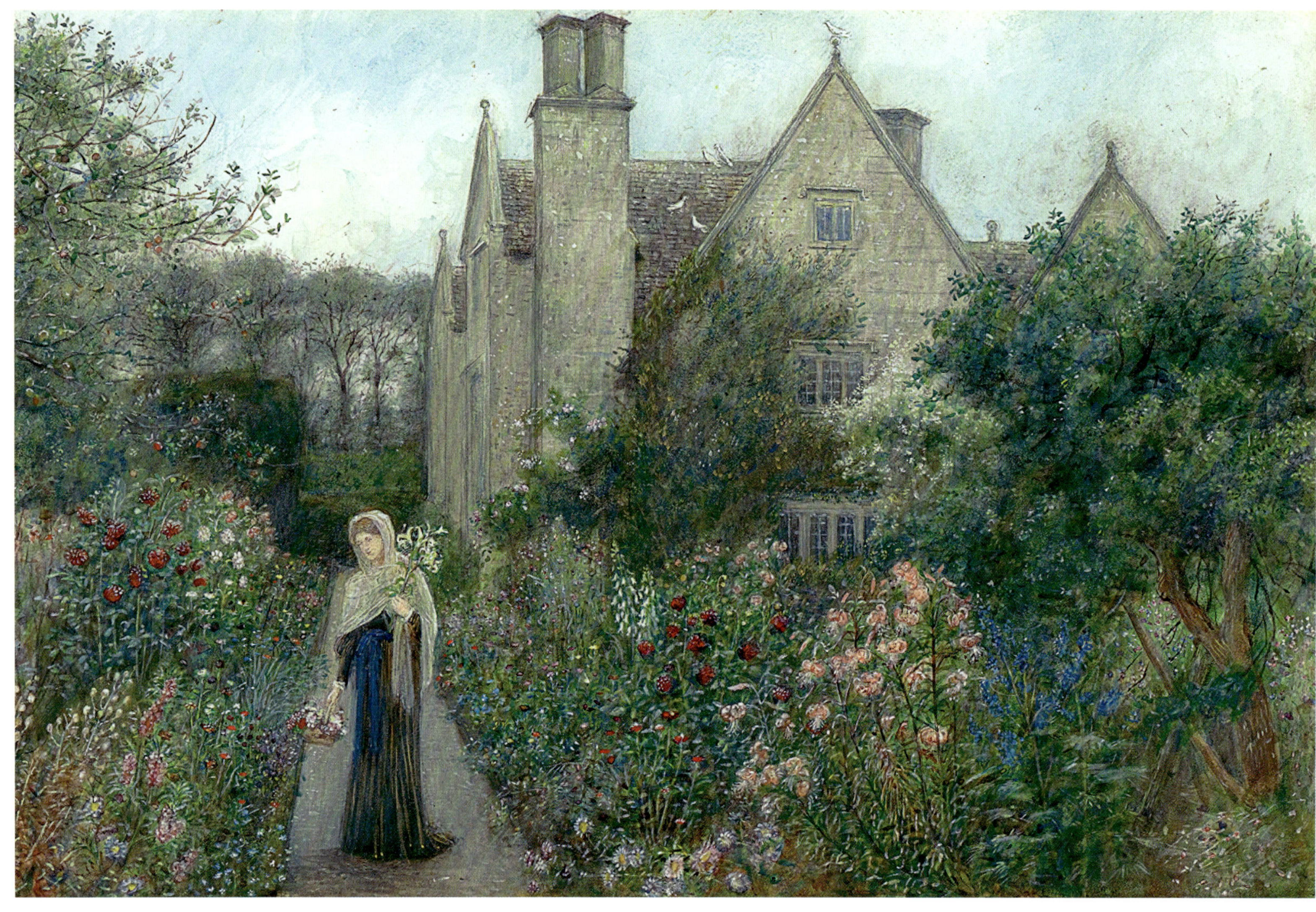

please at our own sweet wills, without any consciousness of man resourceless or shirt-buttonless left in the lurch!'[26] Sewing on buttons and mending rents and tears were routine stuff, but 'turning' garments ranged from the simple business of collars and cuffs to their complete remaking by turning them inside out. Inlaying a patch into bedlinen or clothing was a skilled task; tiny running stiches, backwards and forwards, dealt with a tear. G.F. Watts's imaginative (and generous, £10–£15) wedding present to Georgiana Burne-Jones was a sewing machine.[27] Edward Burne-Jones described it as a 'most clever little thing that makes dresses and buys the stuff and almost pays for it'.[28]

Dress and the Costume Wardrobe

The earliest reference in print to 'prae-Raphaelite dress' was made by Mary Eliza Haweis in 1878, in an article for *Queen* magazine, to be elaborated in subsequent publications.[29] Rossetti's many drawings of Elizabeth Siddal depict the 'dove' grey dress she designed herself – and of which he approved. In his haunting portraits, *The Blue Silk Dress* (1868) and *Mariana*, Jane Morris wears the peacock-blue silk dress that she made to his detailed specifications: '[I]t occurs to me to say that I think the sleeves should be as full at the top as is consistent with simplicity of outline, and perhaps would gain by being lined with some soft material, but of this you will be the best judge.' He ends with a postscript: 'I hope you will wear the dress to take away the stiffness.'[30] In the photograph posed by Rossetti himself (see ill. 84), she wears something similar, but with the neat embroidered collar and brooch favoured by Victorian wives.

The household needlework included costume-making and maintenance of the property wardrobe, often comprising valuable old garments and textiles.[31] For *Monna Rosa* (1867), modelled by Mrs Leyland, wife of Whistler's patron, Rossetti created an Italian noblewoman's robe from a much-used embroidered silk shawl in his collection. Rossetti's costumes were scattered about the house. 'I am just looking up an old tussore (if that is right) silk dress of yours to paint in the *Vanna*,' he told Jane Morris in 1881. 'I knew it would be of use some day when you gave it to me, and it is replete with your memory, empty as it is now.'[32] Three days later he has another request:

> The extreme usefulness of the dresses of yours which I have induces me to ask if you have any more 'Old Clo' of an artistic cut and material… Mrs Stillman has just sent all the way from Florence to borrow your old olive green dress which I painted in that old fiddle picture.[33]

The 'old fiddle picture' is *Veronica Veronese* (1872); Alexa Wilding is the model. Rossetti had jewellery from India and China as exotic accessories in his paintings of the 1860s: a quantity of mainly Indian jewellery as well as antique textiles featured in the house sale held after his death in 1882. In spite of his quantities of costume, draperies and jewellery, he still borrowed from George Price Boyce: the 'Japanese lady's dress' for the central figure in *The Beloved*; the jewel in the black boy's hair as well as blue–green beads for *Joan of Arc*, and 'a tawny yellow-green spotted Indian silk shawl with border' in 1872.[34]

Although he had triumphed in finding a dress for the drowning *Ophelia*, Millais must have been relieved to cede the sourcing of dress to Effie Millais. His experiences in 1851 with a 'simpering shopman', when buying the velvet his mother would make up for *Mariana* would not be repeated.[35] Although Effie Millais herself did not dress 'artistically', comment on her appearance was admiring of her originality. She was knowledgeable about lace, and with John Ruskin's encouragement, she had bought antique Venetian point lace to go with a velvet dress, in an 'old curiosity shop' in Venice in 1847: `I should not have thought of buying it at all but John was much struck with the richness of the pattern which is particularly fine and, it is so cheap I did not hesitate a moment.'[36] In Millais's *Pot Pourri* (1856), the girl's green satin dress is trimmed with point lace. The Millais costume wardrobe must have been well supplied with eighteenth-century dresses and accessories, for fancy portraits in the Reynolds mode – Jonathan Swift's *Stella* and *Vanessa* of 1868 – and children, like *Bubbles*, with his array of paste-set buttons. For *Hearts are Trumps* (1872), the dresses are Millais's design, and it may be assumed that they were made at home by Effie Millais.

Writing on home-making from an 'artistic' perspective offered literary openings to women more or less closely associated with their Pre-Raphaelite sisters.[37] The emphasis shifted from servant management and cookery to beautification of the home and advice on dress, much influenced by 'artistic' taste. Everyday dresses overseen by the artists, in paintings as well as in wear, were copied by artistic dressers in their circle.

To be mistress of a well-run household was regarded with approval as a fulfilling and preordained destiny, satisfying the socially accepted ideal of 'womanliness'. Tracing household management offers important biographical clues in otherwise inadequately recorded lives. While it may not have seemed an entirely acceptable substitute for an artistic career, whether these wives, sisters and model muses knew it or not, creating a distinct way of living, decorating and dressing was part of a much bigger shift in the influence on taste in architecture and design of the cultivated middle class.

Maria Zambaco

1843–1914

'She was born at the foot of Olympus and looked and was primeval' was Edward Burne-Jones's extravagant description of his model and muse, whose emotional entanglements have almost overshadowed her creative work.[1] As well as inspiring images of Circe, Venus, Phyllis, Nimue and Cassandra, she produced an accomplished output of relief portraits and sculptures, together with pictorial works that have vanished from sight. Provoking a major drama in the Pre-Raphaelite soap opera was but the introduction to an artistic career that has been ignored.

Maria Terpsithea Cassavetti was born on 29 April 1843, in London, the daughter of an Anglo-Greek businessman and his wife Euphrosyne. Her uncle was Constantine Ionides, doyen of the Greek business community in London and a noted Pre-Raphaelite patron, through whom she met many of the Pre-Raphaelite artists. G.F. Watts painted her as a girl in Greek dress, and Marie Spartali (later Stillman) was a childhood friend, with shared artistic aspirations.[2] The death of her father brought an inheritance of £60,000, which seriously impressed the caricaturist George du Maurier, who added that she had 'great talent and really wonderful beauty' but was 'supposed to be attached by mere obstinacy to a Greek of low birth'.[3] He was physician Demetrius Zambaco – based in Paris and who was portrayed in strikingly Byronic manner by Watts – whom she married in 20 July 1861, with Spartali as bridesmaid. After their son and daughter were born, she returned from Paris with them to London. Her husband countered by claiming rights to her inheritance.

Perhaps at Maria Zambaco's request, her mother commissioned a portrait of her and Spartali from Burne-Jones, which developed into a picture of Cupid rescuing Psyche (ill. 108), to illustrate an episode in William Morris's epic poem *The Earthly Paradise* (1868–70).[4] Cupid's words 'cast away all blame Into the sea of woes that thou didst bear' chimed with Zambaco's appeal to Burne-Jones, over whom, in the words of his wife, Georgiana Burne-Jones: 'two things had tremendous power – beauty and misfortune…while the trouble lasted the sufferer took precedence of everyone else'.[5]

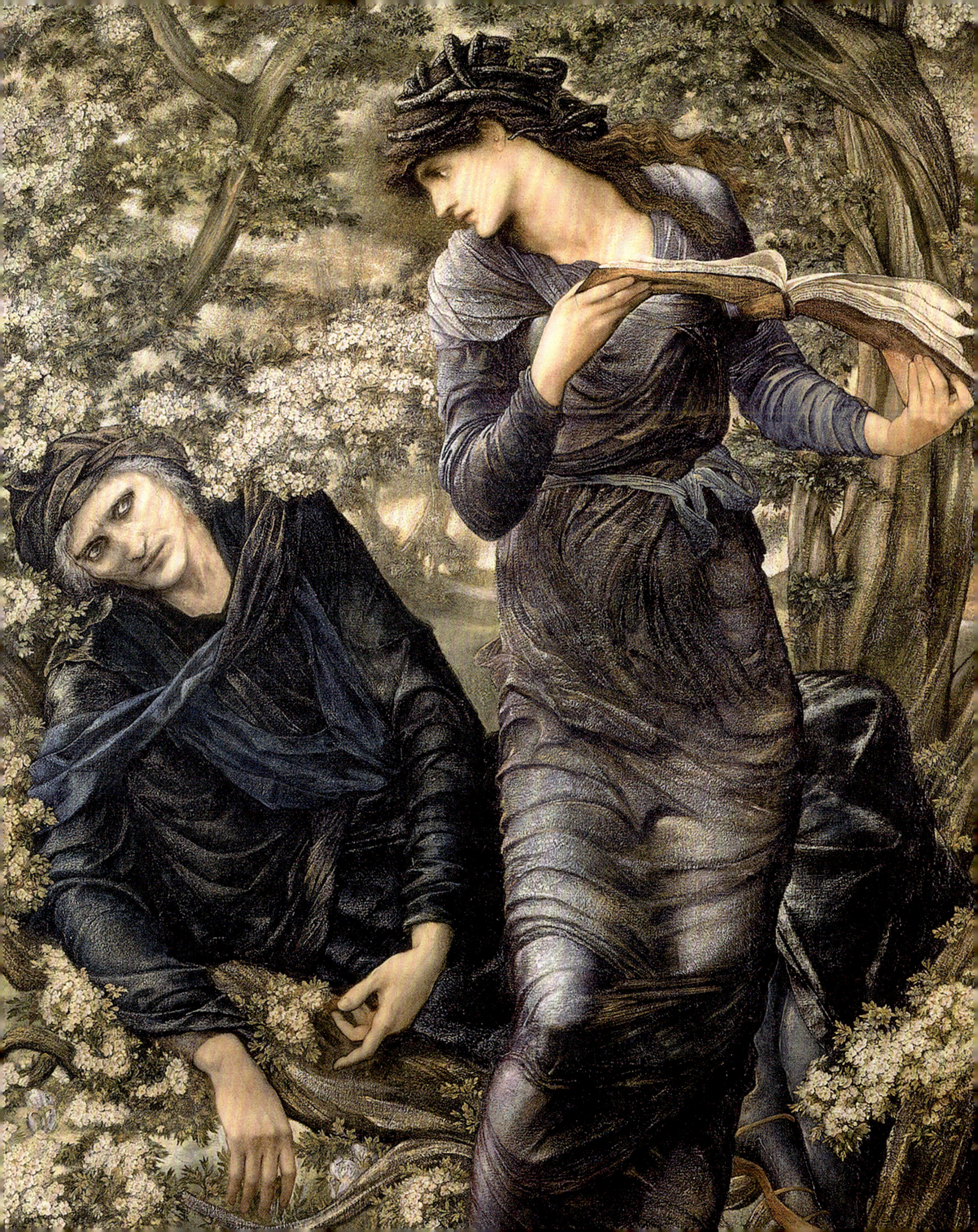

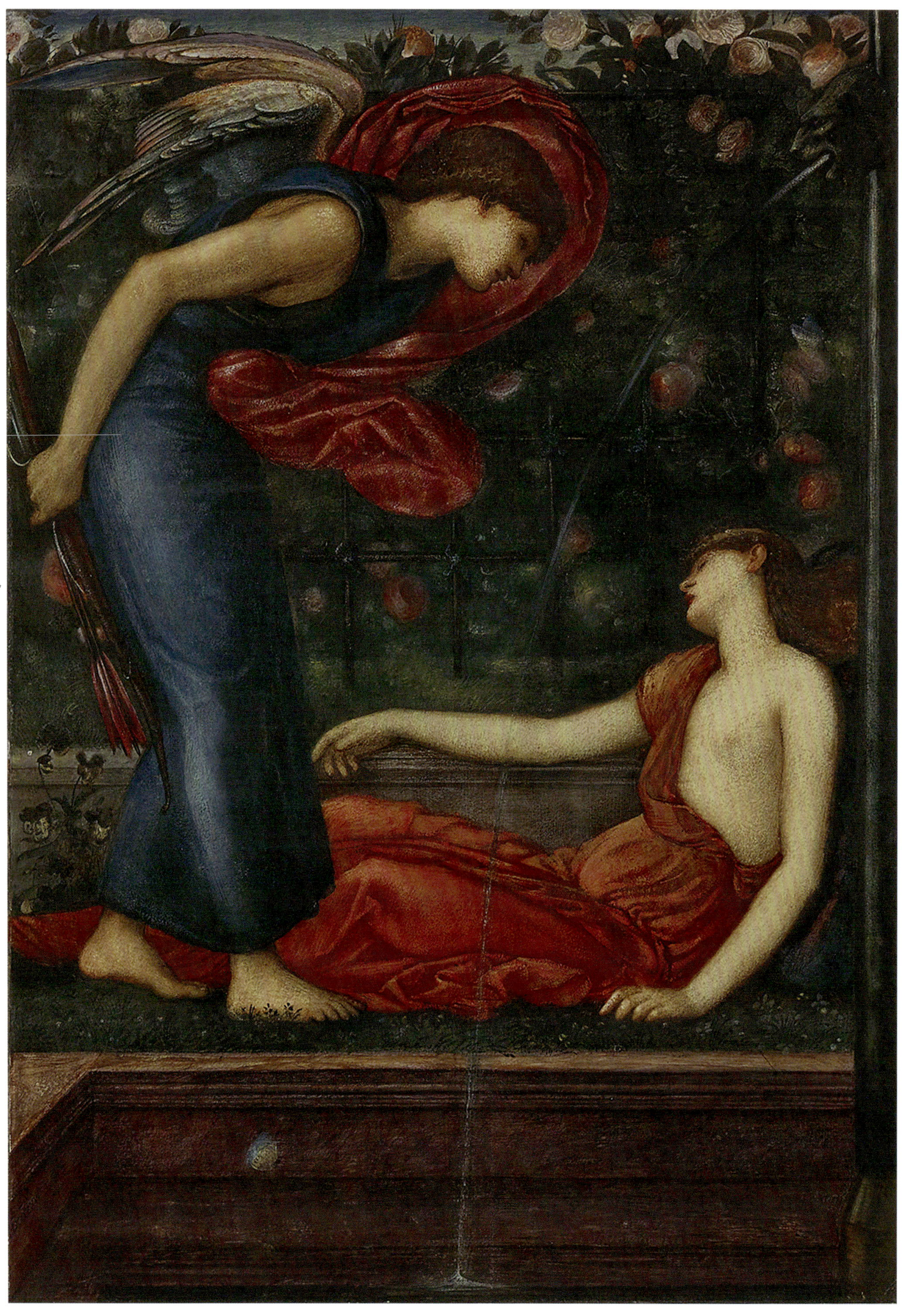

Soon, artist and sitter became lovers, and, at the same time, tutor and pupil, so Zambaco and Burne-Jones were regularly sequestered in the studio. As he explained to his friend, the artist and patron George Howard: '[t]he only two days at all engaged are Tuesday and Saturday when Mrs Zambaco comes'.[6] Charles Keene's etching (ill.109) shows Zambaco at work. Her appearance is similar to that in a thumbnail image of her reading, drawn by Burne-Jones in small notebook. Georgiana was alerted to the affair only in June 1868 through finding a letter in her husband's pocket.[7]

A stream of studies and sketches by Burne-Jones show Zambaco – often in profile, with unbound hair – as the object of desire. Edmund Spenser's *Faerie Queene* (1590) inspired her depiction by him as 'amorous Desyre' – a companion to Spartali Stillman's *The Lady Prays-Desire* (ill.120) personifying ambition, while in their hours together they read Virgil and Homer, and fantasised about running away to a Greek island, which she took more seriously than he.

In 1869, as her lover's resolution waned, Zambaco proposed a suicide pact, then threatened to kill herself by opium or drowning in London's Regent's Canal. Struggling on the towpath, the pair were separated by her cousin Luke Ionides, after which she was told that her lover had fled abroad. In fact, he was hiding at home, leaving 'the Greek damsel beating up the quarters of all his friends and howling like Cassandra', as Rossetti gleefully reported.[8]

On a subdued note, the affair continued, becoming semi-public knowledge with the exhibition in 1870 of *Phyllis and Demophoon*, the first version of *The Tree of Forgiveness* (ill.115), with Zambaco's distinctive features and a Latin quotation like a speech-bubble: 'Tell me, what did I do? Nothing but love unwisely'. It was akin to a declaration on social media.

Burne-Jones was eager for friends to condone the affair. Rossetti composed a sonnet on Zambaco's personation of Circe the sorceress, 'Dusk-haired and gold-robed o'er the golden wine', and drew several flattering portraits. 'I am sure her love is all in all to her,' Rossetti told Jane Morris. 'She is really extremely beautiful [and] she has got much more so within the last year with all her love and trouble.'[9] The thwarted romance echoed Rossetti's own with Morris; such fraught entanglements bound the friends closer.

Zambaco's presence in Burne-Jones's imagery marked a step change in his art; her pictorial influence grew as pictures 'intense in mood, dark in tone and dubious in drawing, gave way to larger works [that were] sweeter in feeling, technically more competent, lighter in colour and more decorative'.[10] In summer 1870, while his wife and children were away on holiday, to reaffirm his feelings, Burne-Jones completed an untypically saccharine portrait of Zambaco as Venus, with a chubby amorino and arrow inscribed 'Mary Aetat xxvi August 7th 1870'.

Subsequently, he cast her in multiple roles: as Cassandra, as Beatrice, as Galatea, as Nimuë in *The Beguiling of Merlin*, shown at the Grosvenor Gallery in London in 1877 and then at the Paris Exposition Universelle of 1878.

'A woman with great talent in a variety of ways and with remarkable capacities for painting'

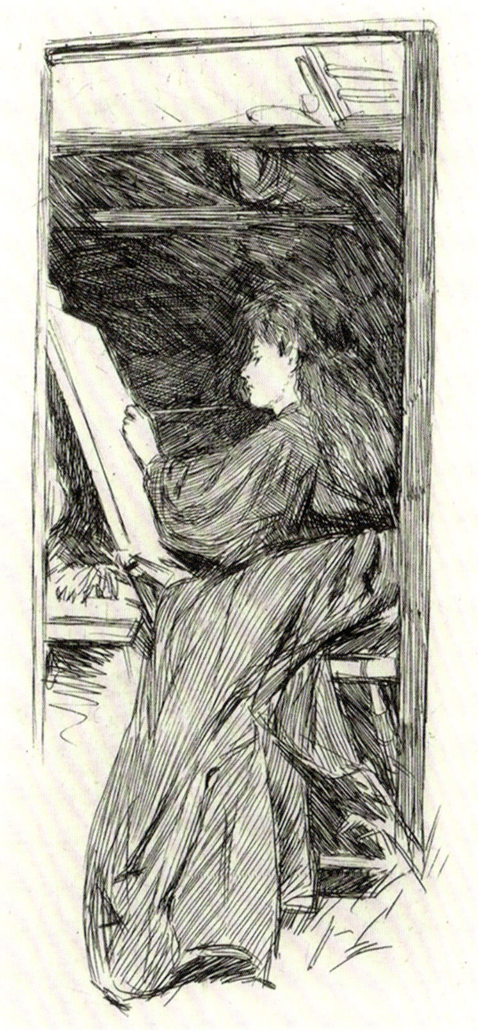

110
**Study for Head
of Cassandra**
Edward Burne-Jones, c.1866–70
Red chalk on paper
356 × 280mm
Victoria and Albert Museum,
London

111
Maria Zambaco
Dante Gabriel Rossetti, late 1860s
Coloured chalks on paper
516 × 389mm
Victoria and Albert Museum,
London

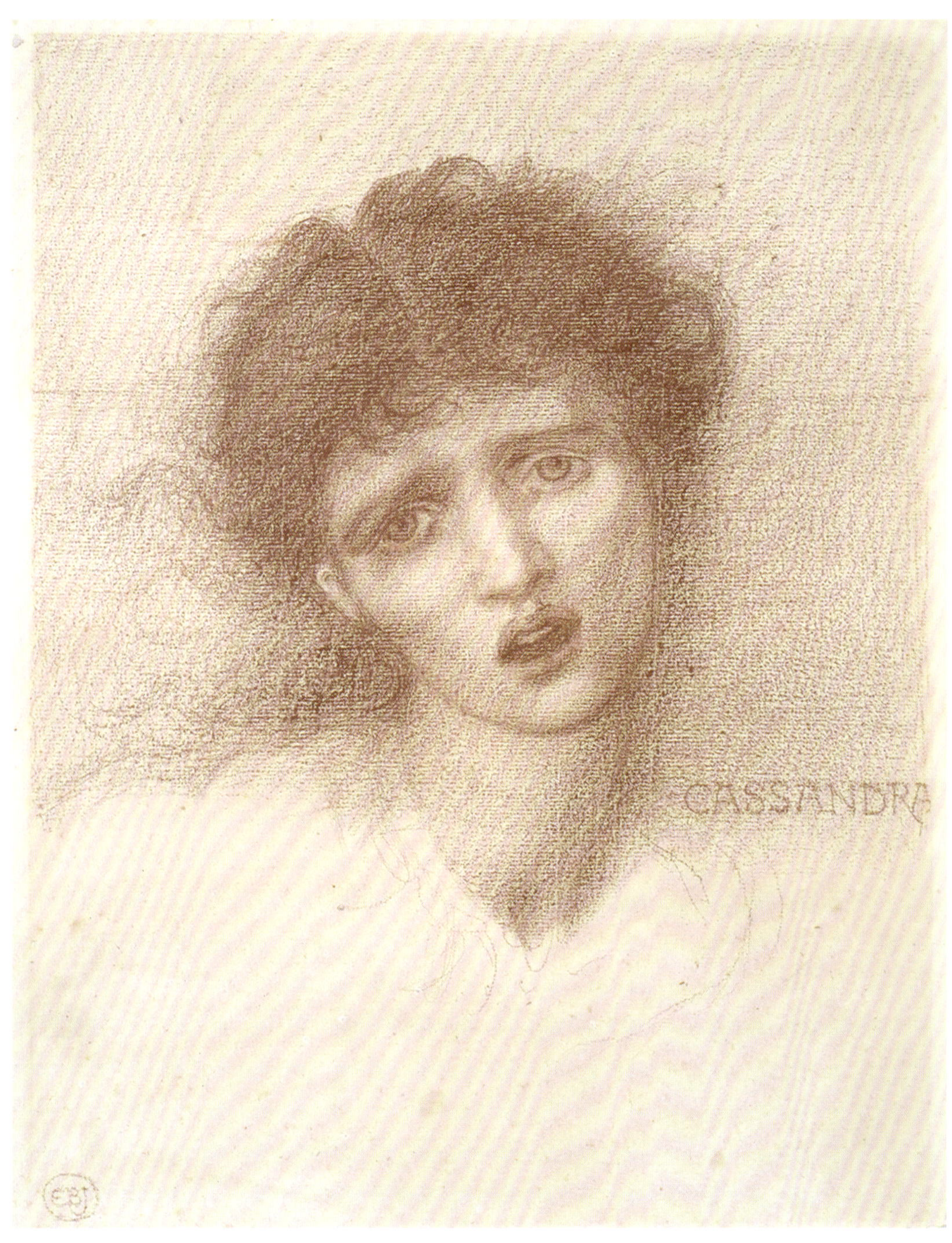

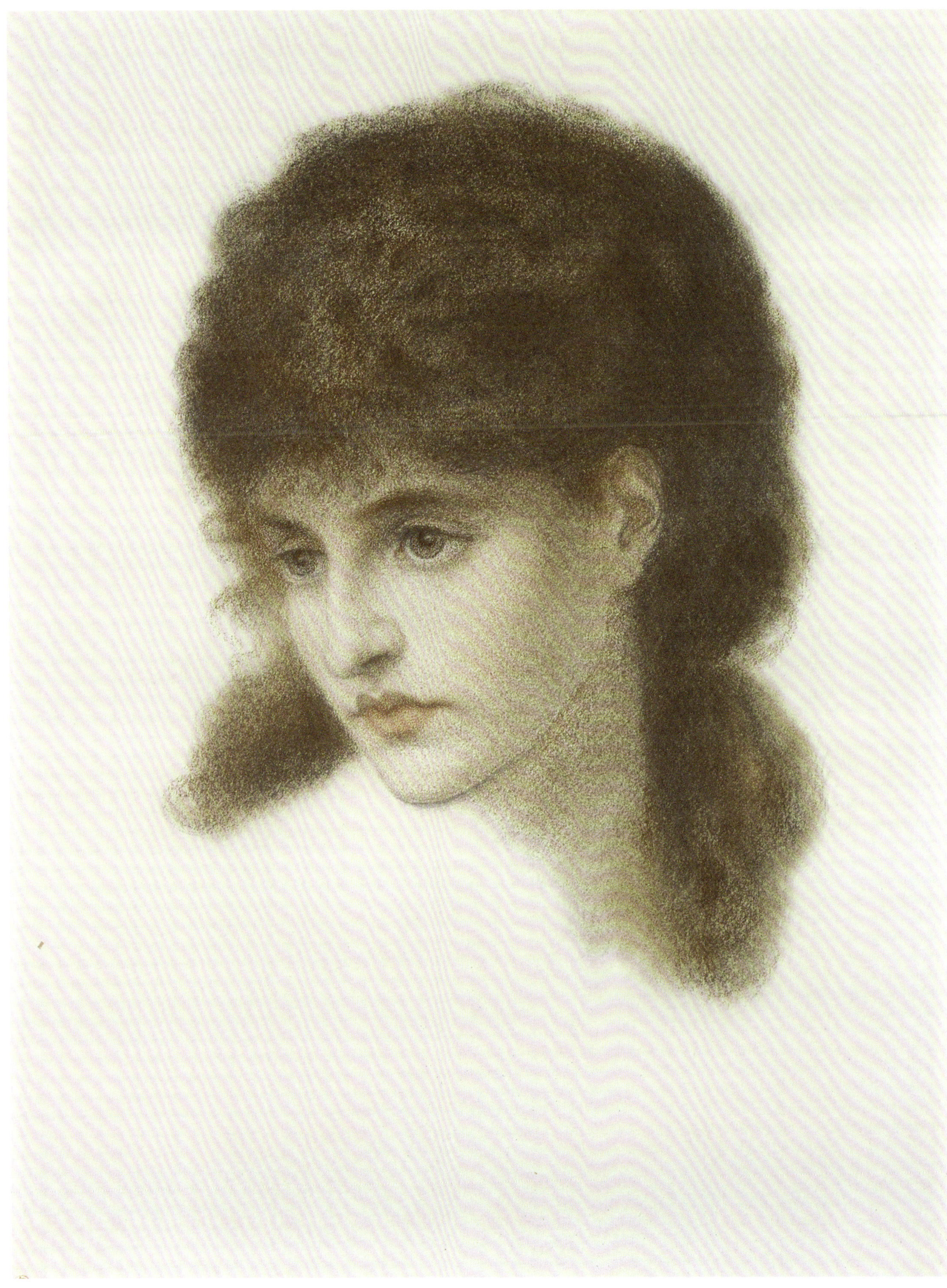

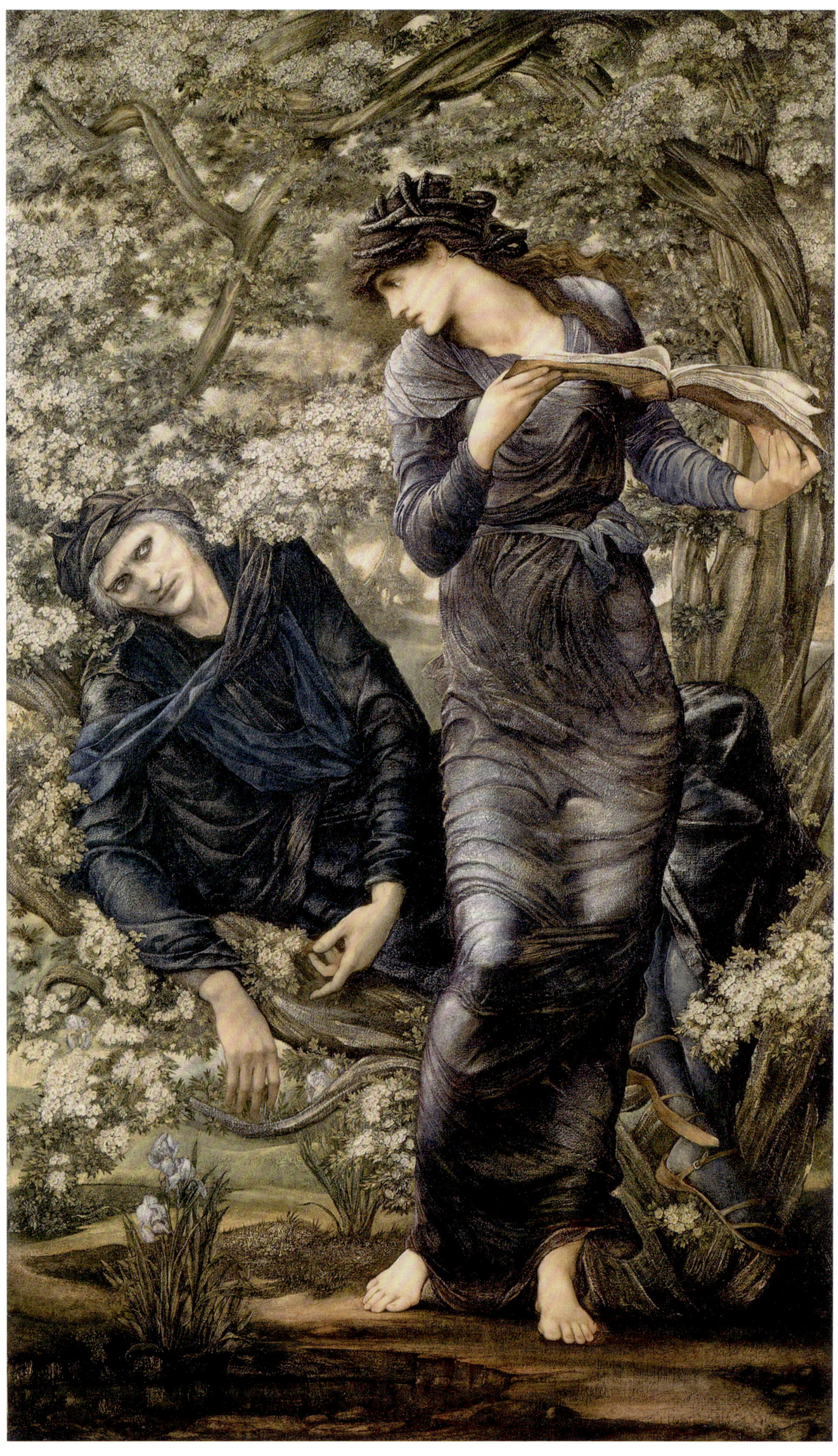

She herself continued to paint under Burne-Jones's guidance. As yet, only one work is recorded, a female figure on a staircase. She was 'a woman with great talent in a variety of ways and with remarkable capacities for painting, which she is now cultivating to good effect', noted William Rossetti.[11] In 1871 her mother commissioned the architect Philip Webb to construct a studio, which must have been for her daughter's use. Moving between London and Paris, her life is hard to chronicle apart from appearances in art and the occasional 'sighting' in correspondence. Burne-Jones's next painting, *Love Among the Ruins* (1894), contained a sorrowful couple eloquently embracing amid broken masonry and brambles.

The most expressive memorial of the affair is *The Beguiling of Merlin* (ill.112), which tells of Nimuë, a Lady of the Lake from the Arthurian romances, who enchanted the besotted Merlin. He is entangled helplessly within a hawthorn tree, while Nimuë reads from his book of spells. Burne-Jones later wrote that:

The name of her was Mary…she was born at the foot of mount Olympus and looked and was primeval and that's the head and the way of standing and turning…and I was being turned into a hawthorn bush in the forest of Broceliande – every year when the hawthorn buds it is the soul of Merlin trying to live again in the world and speak – for he left so much unsaid.[12]

Although Merlin is a self-image, the saturnine features were, in fact, drawn from William Stillman. To young Oscar Wilde, Nimuë was 'a tall, lithe woman, beautiful and subtle to look on, like a snake'.[13] To Zambaco, perhaps, the painting was a vindication of the intense affair that neither wished to relinquish.

Muse and lover continued to meet, in Paris and Italy, until, it was rumoured, she had a new partner, as yet unidentified. In Burne-Jones's view: 'She minded so much and so much feared to hurt that it drove her to cheat…she thought I couldn't like her if I knew she was passionate and so she hid it.'[14] By October 1879, according to Marie Spartali Stillman, Zambaco and her 'pseudo-husband do nothing but work awfully hard at painting and produce Ned Joneses without number'.[15] A few watercolour examples may survive, unseen, in private collections. As usual, Zambaco's own voice is unheard.

Around 1880, she changed medium to take up sculpture, studying first at London's Slade School, with Alphonse Legros, who had also painted Burne-Jones. Learning the techniques of relief modelling and casting, she produced medallion portraits in the emerging 'new sculpture' mode. On Legros's recommendation she went to Paris, to study with Auguste Rodin, who was at that time working on *The Gates of Hell* and *The Kiss*.

With sculpture, Zambaco found her metier. Her exhibition debut was at the RA in London in 1886, with two busts, one of Legros in terracotta and the other an unnamed 'study of a head'.[16] The following year another bust was shown alongside four bronze medals whose quality is indicated by the fact that they were at once acquired by the British Museum as fine examples of the genre.

The antique medallion format of her portrait of Marie Spartali Stillman (ill.113) highlights their shared Greek heritage. The Christian aspect is visible on the reverse, which features a lily and the words sine macula ('immaculate'). These refer both to the Virgin Mary, after whom both women were named, and to the goodness and virtue that were universally ascribed to Spartali Stillman. The identity of the sitter in another portrait medal (ill.114) has not been ascertained. Maria Zambaco's own daughter was 20 in 1885, whereas the girl portrayed looks in her early teens, with hair not yet 'up'. Perhaps this is Spartali Stillman's daughter Effie (Euphrosyne), who was aged around 13 when the likeness was modelled. If so, the link is intriguing, because Effie, who modelled for many figures in her mother's pictures, went on to a career in sculpture. The reverse shows three interlinked anemones, from the Greek, meaning 'daughter of the wind'.

The gentle, animated modelling of the profiles within a traditionally stolid format endows Zambaco's female portraits with attractive spirit, and imparts distinctive gravity to that of John Marshall (ill.68), the

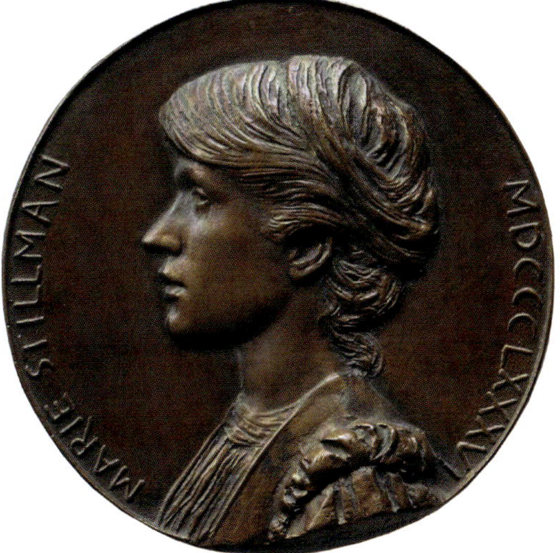

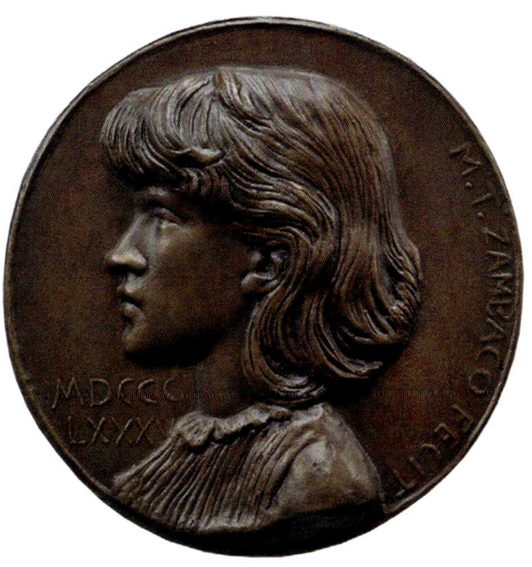

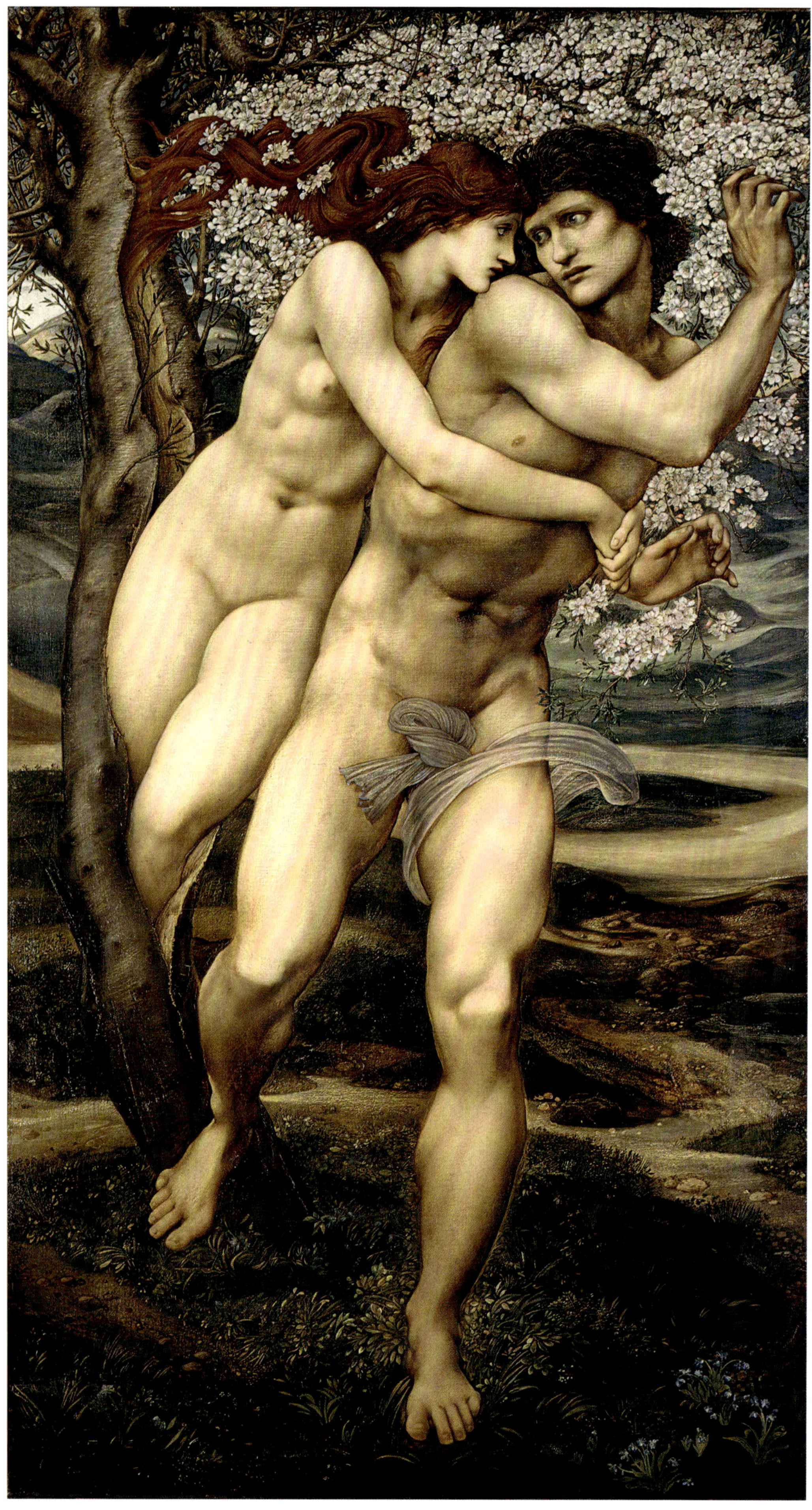

surgeon and anatomist who was friend and adviser to the Pre-Raphaelite circle. While many of Zambaco's works remain untraced, the exhibition record in both France and Britain shows the sustained strength of her output, suggesting vigorous endeavour. In 1888 she sent works to three venues: to the RA an untraced bronze entitled *Medusa's Horror*, which resonated with the Perseus series on which Burne-Jones was working; to the New Gallery in London, five medals portraying Legros, Watts, Thomas Carlyle, Cardinal Manning and professional beauty Lillie Langtry, and thirteen medals to the Paris Salon. For this last submission, she asked Rodin to forward the works in her name, as she was occupied in London with her daughter's wedding.[17]

While several sitters were friends, like John Marshall, others such as Carlyle, Manning and Langtry, were not personal acquaintances but they had also been portrayed by artists whom Zambaco knew well.

Exhibited in 1882, Burne-Jones's *The Tree of Forgiveness* (ill.115) is a symbolic return to their anguished relationship. The subject is from Ovid's

still hers and Demophoon a self-image of her faithless lover. The title may relate to some form of reconciliation.

The image has 'a strange and touching beauty', wrote Henry James, and 'the coolness of a gray day in summer. The mass of almond blossom introduces a great deal of fresh and moist-looking white; the flesh tones are wan and bloodless, as befits the complexion of people we see through the medium of a certain incredulity.'[18]

'[D]ear and ill-used friend, you must believe a bit that I never forget you,' Burne-Jones wrote early in 1888; 'come back some day and write and say you forgive your affct. Friend.'[19]

A few months later, they were working in adjacent studios. '[I]t looks very odd!' wrote John Marshall's daughter Jeanette. 'I feel quite disgusted to think she is going on agn. [sic] in the old style. If I were Mrs B.J. I wd. soon have her wig off!'[20]

Zambaco was presumably working on the relief panels exhibited by the Arts & Crafts Exhibition Society in 1889. Seven more medals were shown at the Société nationale des Beaux-Arts in 1890, in Paris, and six years later came

115
The Tree of Forgiveness
Edward Burne-Jones, 1870
Oil on canvas, 1905 × 1067mm
Lady Lever Art Gallery,
Liverpool

116
L'Amour irrésistible
Maria Zambaco, 1896
Bronze
635 × 381 × 381mm
Private Collection

The exhibition record in both France and Britain shows the strength of her output

tales of unhappy lovers. Demophoon, son of Theseus, was away so long that Phyllis lost hope and in despair killed herself. Taking pity, the gods turned her into an almond tree. When Demophoon returned he penitently embraced the tree, which immediately blossomed.

This is the second, larger version of the scene, first depicted by Burne-Jones in 1870 when both Demophoon's nudity, without the wisp of drapery, together with Maria Zambaco's recognisable features as Phyllis aroused scandal. A decade later the face is

a free-standing figure of Eros bending his bow, entitled *L'Amour irrésistible* (ill.116). Exhibited under her maiden name of Cassavetti, this is a delicate, finely balanced work with affinities to Alfred Gilbert's figure familiarly known as Eros. Its subject, however, harked back to Burne-Jones's portrait from 1870.

Maria Zambaco lived on for two more decades, dying in Paris in July 1914. Subsequently her artistic reputation was virtually forgotten, and work to recover her oeuvre has only just begun.

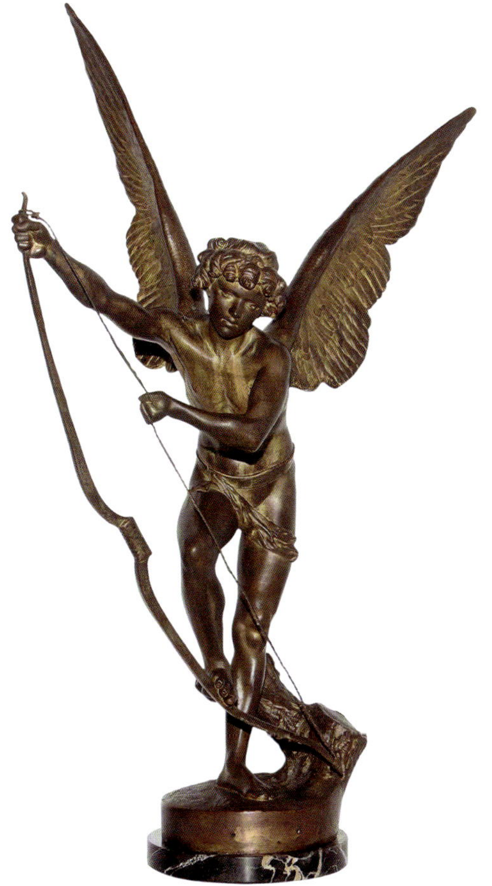

Marie Spartali Stillman

1844–1927

According to novelist Henry James, Marie Spartali Stillman, in imagery and treatment, was 'a sincere, spontaneous, *naif* pre-Raphaelite' whose work displayed refinement and 'deep pictorial sentiment' that 'inherited the traditions and the temper' of the original Italians.[1] William Rossetti admired her 'many glowing and subtle studies in colour, and apt renderings of refined expression'.[2] But even though she enjoyed a longer exhibiting career than many artist contemporaries, her reputation was posthumously quite eclipsed by consideration of her minor role as model for Rossetti, exemplary of prevailing gender bias.

Born into the Greek business diaspora in London, many of whose members were art patrons, Marie Spartali shared a wealthy, cosmopolitan background with Maria Zambaco, and belied this social position to become a professional artist. Her lifelong commitment perhaps began when she accompanied her sister Christine as model for *La Princesse du pays de la porcelaine* (1863–4) in the studio of Whistler. She sat to Watts, as well as to Julia Margaret Cameron for both portrait and costume photographs (ills 117–18). Cameron was the first artist to whom she modelled for costume roles, including Imperial Eleanore (ill. 117) from Tennyson's poem. Like Cameron and Tennyson, her family had a house on the Isle of Wight; here, one day she was inspected by the Laureate, who held a candle 'within an inch of my face' to assess her beauty.[3] Other roles in which she was depicted by Cameron include *The Spirit of the Vine* and 'Mnemosyne, Mother of the Muses', which invoked her Greek heritage.

In 1866 she accompanied Maria Zambaco to Burne-Jones's studio, sitting for the painting *Cupid and Psyche* (ill. 108). But modelling for her tended to be a favour to fellow artists, never an occupation. For several years, from 1864, she studied with Madox Brown. In his portrait of her (ill. 119) she is depicted in his studio, pausing while at work, an artist's mahlstick resting against the picture. In its pose, the image on the easel resembles *The Lady Prays-Desire*, Spartali Stillman's first exhibition piece, but it may rather represent the now lost work, *Korinna*, which was criticised for its 'red, disorderly hair'.[4]

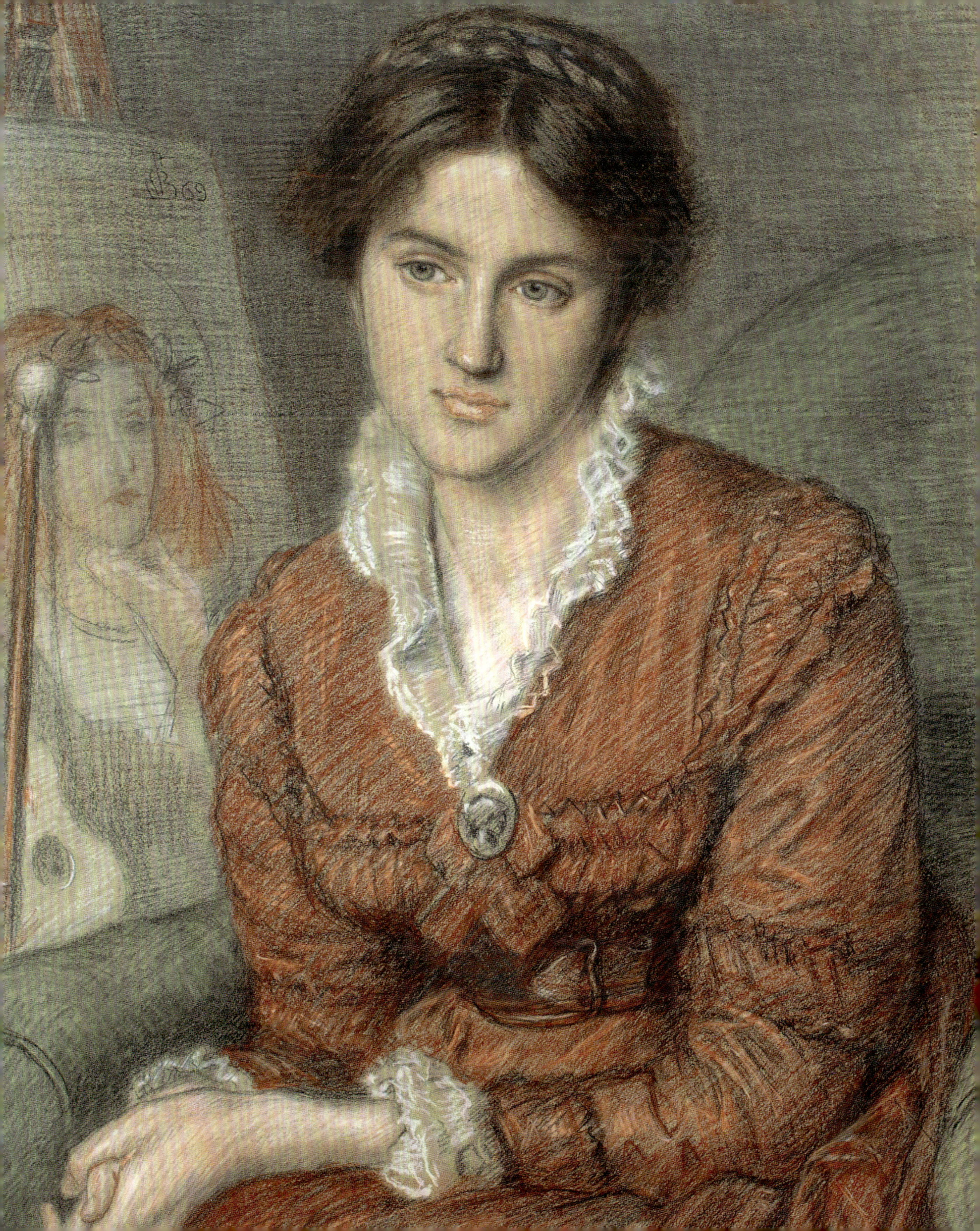

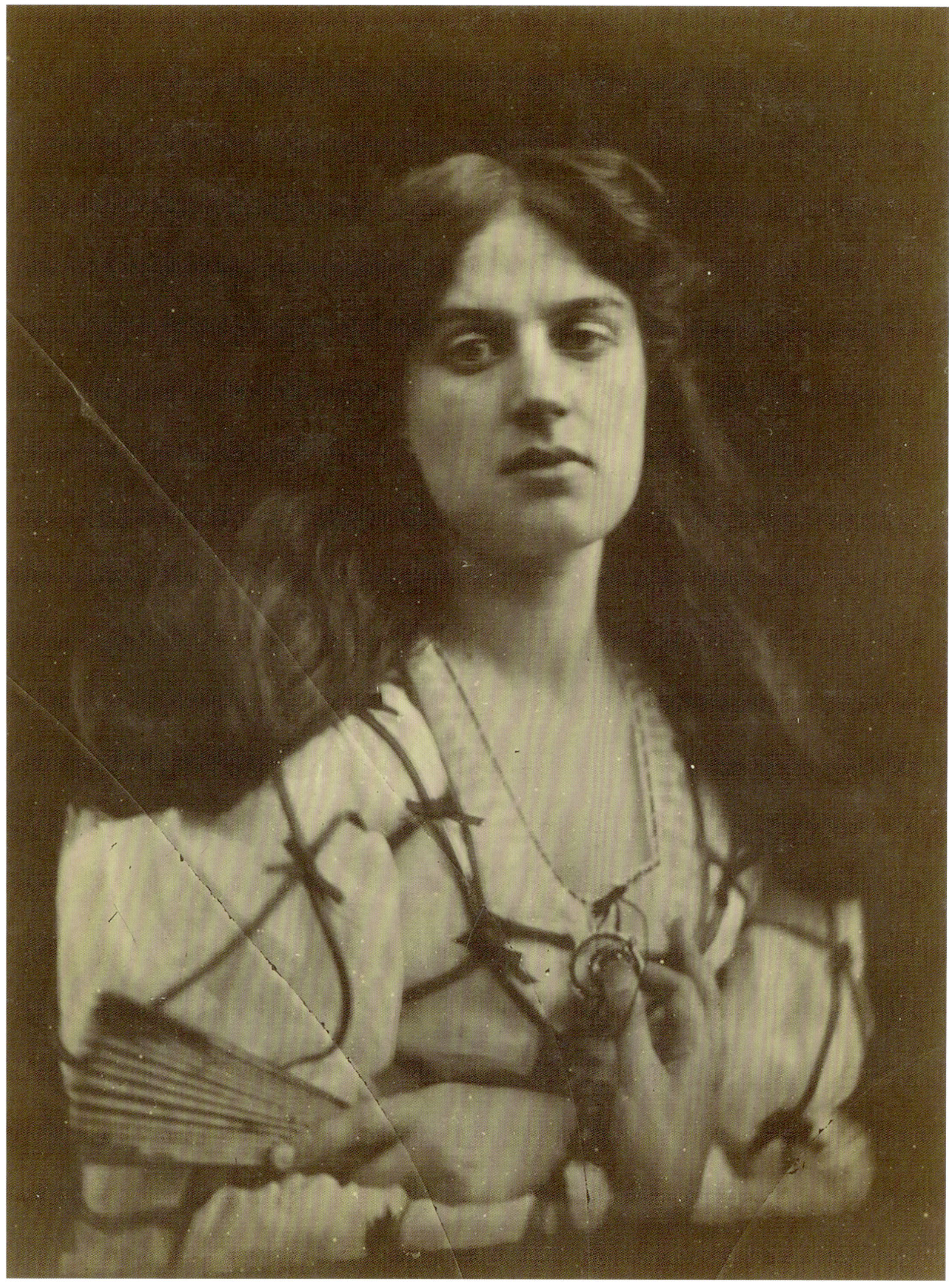

Madox Brown is said to have had an unrequited passion for Spartali. Heralding a lifelong regard, his portrait certainly conveys affection towards a sitter noted for gentleness and constancy. 'Madox Brown... taught me to paint and I can never feel sufficiently grateful,' she wrote later.[5] The training was serious but somewhat limited, with seemingly little instruction in anatomy and no tuition in oils. She also lacked the rigorous comparative criticism encountered in academies. From Madox Brown she adopted a dry watercolour or gouache technique on double-thickness paper over board, and with his support her exhibition debut took place at the Dudley Gallery, London, in 1867. Fearing loss of social status, her father proposed that her first sale should be a gift; she resisted – as Rossetti told the patron, she was 'quite bent on adopting art as a serious profession'.[6] Thereafter, despite changes of residence and personal circumstances, she painted steadily for fifty years, sending works for exhibition in Britain, France and the United States.

in the 1860s but disrupts expectations by personifying not beauty but ambition. The allegorical figure Prayse-Desire, who by 'well doing' aspires to honour, features in Edmund Spenser's *The Faerie Queene*:

> Pensive I yield I am and sad in mind
> Through great desire of glory and of fame.

Renown is also referenced by the owl of Minerva/Athena in the cartouche, which, moreover, invokes Spartali Stillman's Greek heritage.[10]

Her first major picture portrayed Antigone burying her brother in defiance of patriarchal political edict, and several early pieces cited Greek sources. Others were more typically Pre-Raphaelite, based on poetic texts. Her father wished her to marry the widowed Rossetti, whose friendship she retained throughout the rest of the artist's troubled life, but in 1871 she defied her family to marry American journalist William James Stillman, who had actively supported Greek patriots in Crete.

117
Imperial Eleanore
Julia Margaret Cameron, 1868
Albumen silver print
318 × 254mm
Private Collection

118
Marie Spartali
Julia Margaret Cameron, 1868
Albumen cabinet card
133 × 99mm
National Portrait Gallery

'It is so much more interesting to soar above one's strength'

Her chosen themes were Arthurian, Italian and literary subjects alongside landscapes, portraiture and flower pieces. She shunned publicity, and many works subsequently vanished from view. Moreover, according to Charles Fairfax Murray, she 'ruined her reputation by running down her own work' with characteristic self-denigration.[7] But she was never deterred, describing her inspiration as simply 'the pleasure of painting', which remained throughout all vicissitudes.[8] At the same time, she admitted ambition, reluctant to attempt 'only what one feels sure of...when it is so much more interesting to soar above one's strength'.[9]

The early work *The Lady Prays-Desire* (ill.120) utilises the female half-length format favoured by patrons and Pre-Raphaelites

Maria Zambaco's mother commissioned Burne-Jones's *Venus Epithalamia* as a wedding gift.[11] Spartali Stillman became a much-loved stepmother to her husband's daughters Bella and Lisa, who grew up alongside her own daughter Effie and son Michael, both of whom followed Spartali Stillman into art professions, as did Lisa.

Motherhood did not curtail her career; as Rossetti remarked on the birth of her second son, 'I suspect [painting] goes on over the baby's head, for I don't think she'd stop for that.'[12] Sadly, the child died of fever aged eight months. Owing to her husband's posting as a *Times* correspondent, from 1878 to 1883 the family lived in Florence, the home of original pre-Raphaelite art by Fra Angelico and Botticelli, to which she felt

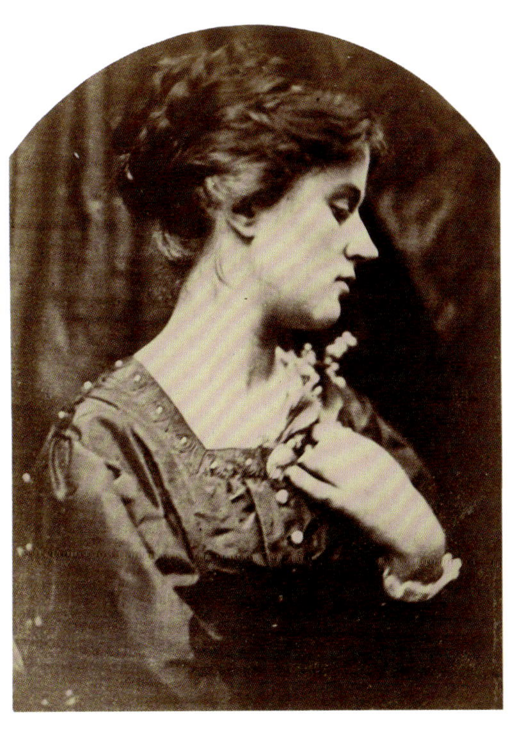

much affinity. Albeit in a different medium, her own work often evokes Italian fresco painting.

In Florence, she belonged to the Anglo-American expatriate community that included John Singer Sargent, writer Violet Paget (aka Vernon Lee) and many artist-visitors from the Pre-Raphaelite community. Each spring, she took pictures to London, for exhibition and sale. Details of sales are sparse, because unpublicised; as a married woman any account of her earnings would have been considered

1882, making this her pictorial homage to his role in the Pre-Raphaelite movement. Its landscape and *sfumato* effects also pay tribute to Leonardo da Vinci's *Mona Lisa*, the popularity of which soared in the 1870s. Pictorially, *Madonna Pietra* may be compared to De Morgan's *The Dryad* (ill. 129) and Burne-Jones's *The Tree of Forgiveness* (ill. 115). It was purchased from exhibition for Liverpool's civic collection. Other currently fashionable half-length female figures placed In Italianate

'I suspect [painting] goes on over the baby's head, for I don't think she'd stop for that'

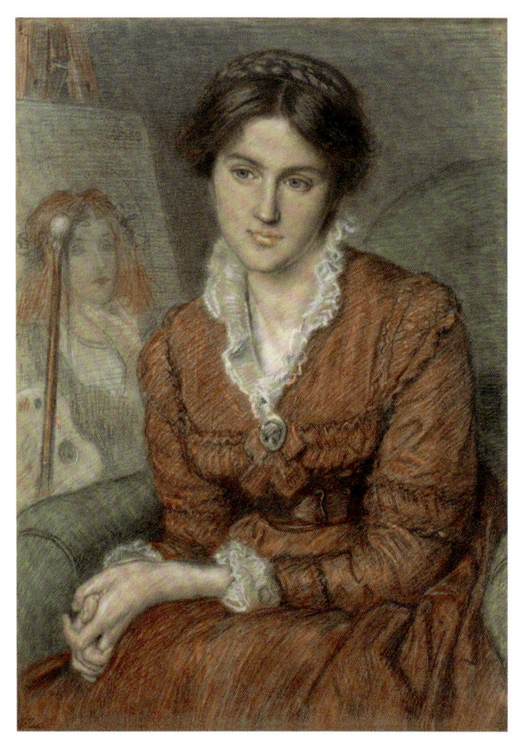

a criticism of her husband. However, their joint bank account shows transfers from France, Italy and the US, and a receipt of £65 that must be payments for paintings.[13] A watercolour sketch by Fairfax Murray (ill. 66) shows her at work in her studio in Florence, which overlooked the River Arno.

Invoking Boccaccio and shown at both the Royal Academy of Arts (RA), in London, and the Paris Salon, her success in 1876–8 with *The Last Sight of Fiammetta* (unlocated) prompted Rossetti to cast her as *A Vision of Fiammetta* (1878), red-robed amid apple blossoms. Her growing reputation led to the invitation to exhibit at the new Grosvenor Gallery in London, where she and Evelyn De Morgan were among a select group of women artists. In this prestigious showcase, she contributed pictures inspired by Dante and Boccaccio, a Rossettian vein that combined poetic feeling with historical imagery and carefully harmonised colour.

In this mode, *Madonna Pietra degli Scrovegni* ('My Lady Stone'; ill. 122) is a key example, taking its text from Rossetti's verse translations and using blackthorn, hellebore and dry leaves to denote the wintry season. The figure's grave expression may be linked to her sorrow at the death of Rossetti in

settings include *Luisa Strozzi* (1884) and a depiction of the sorceress Armida from Tasso's *Gerusalemme Liberata*.

Other favoured genres were the complex figure groups inspired by Renaissance examples, of which *The First Meeting of Petrarch and Laura* (ill. 121) is a fine example. In a skilful fictive rendering of the interior of a medieval church, Spartali Stillman shows Laura's oblique acknowledgement of Petrarch's attention as she gives alms to an elderly woman. The viewer's eye is drawn through deep perspective towards the high altar, where candles are being quenched. Laura is richly clad and attended by a pageboy, modelled on Spartali Stillman's son Michael.

From 1886 to 1896 the Stillmans lived in Rome, where regular visitors included George Howard, close friend of the Morris and Burne-Jones families, Frederic Leighton and William Blake Richmond. In this period Marie Spartali Stillman found a new source of subjects in the legends of St Francis of Assisi, invoking the simple piety of the mendicant order, whose feeling echoed early influences of the Pre-Raphaelite Brotherhood. Correspondence with Madox Brown and Burne-Jones shows she kept in

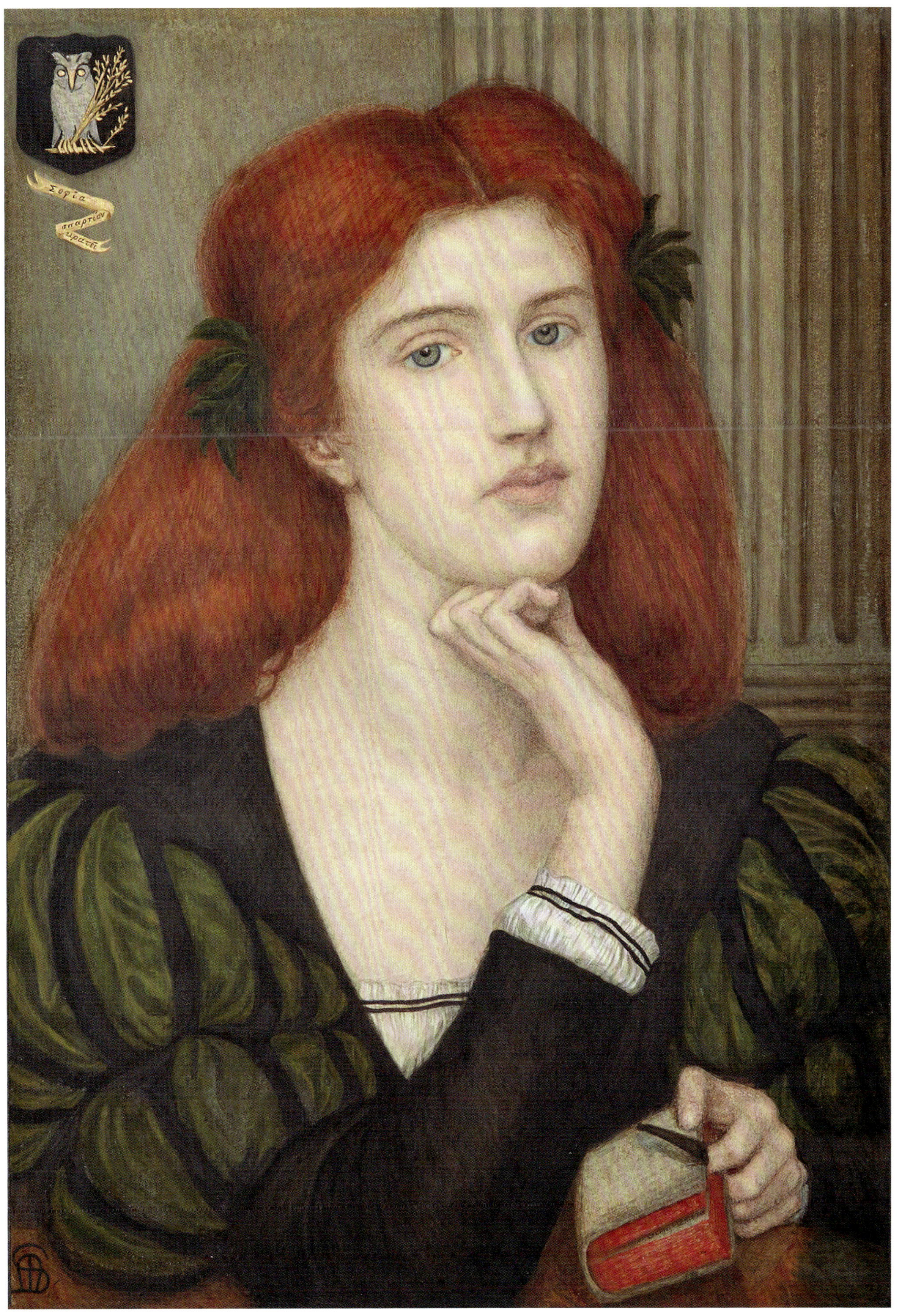

121
**The First Meeting of
Petrarch and Laura**
Marie Spartali Stillman, 1889
Watercolour, gouache
and graphite on paper
560 × 480mm
Private Collection

122 (opposite and p. 9)
**Madonna Pietra
degli Scrovegni**
Marie Spartali Stillman, 1884
Watercolour and gouache
on paper, 785 × 611mm
Walker Art Gallery, Liverpool

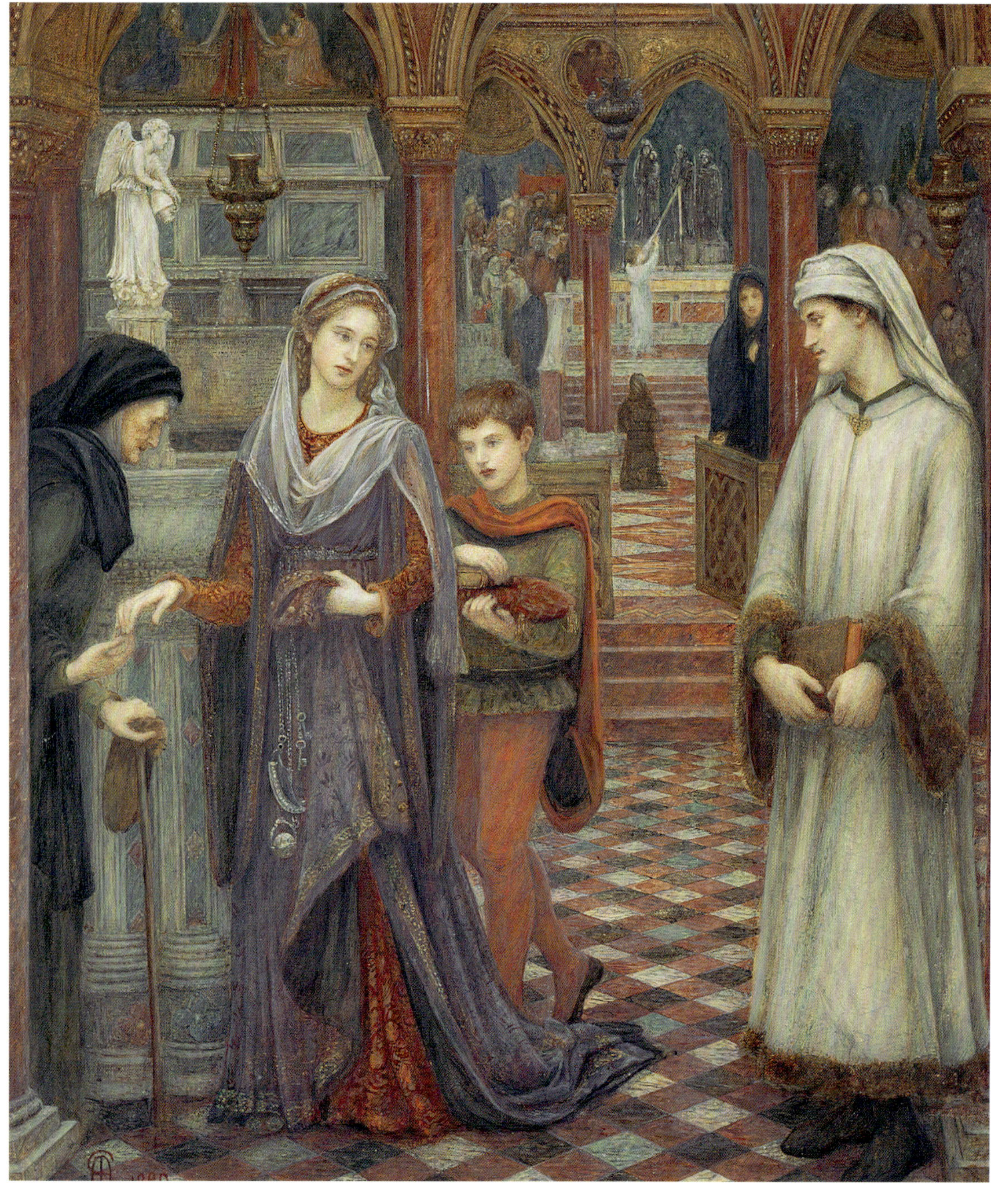

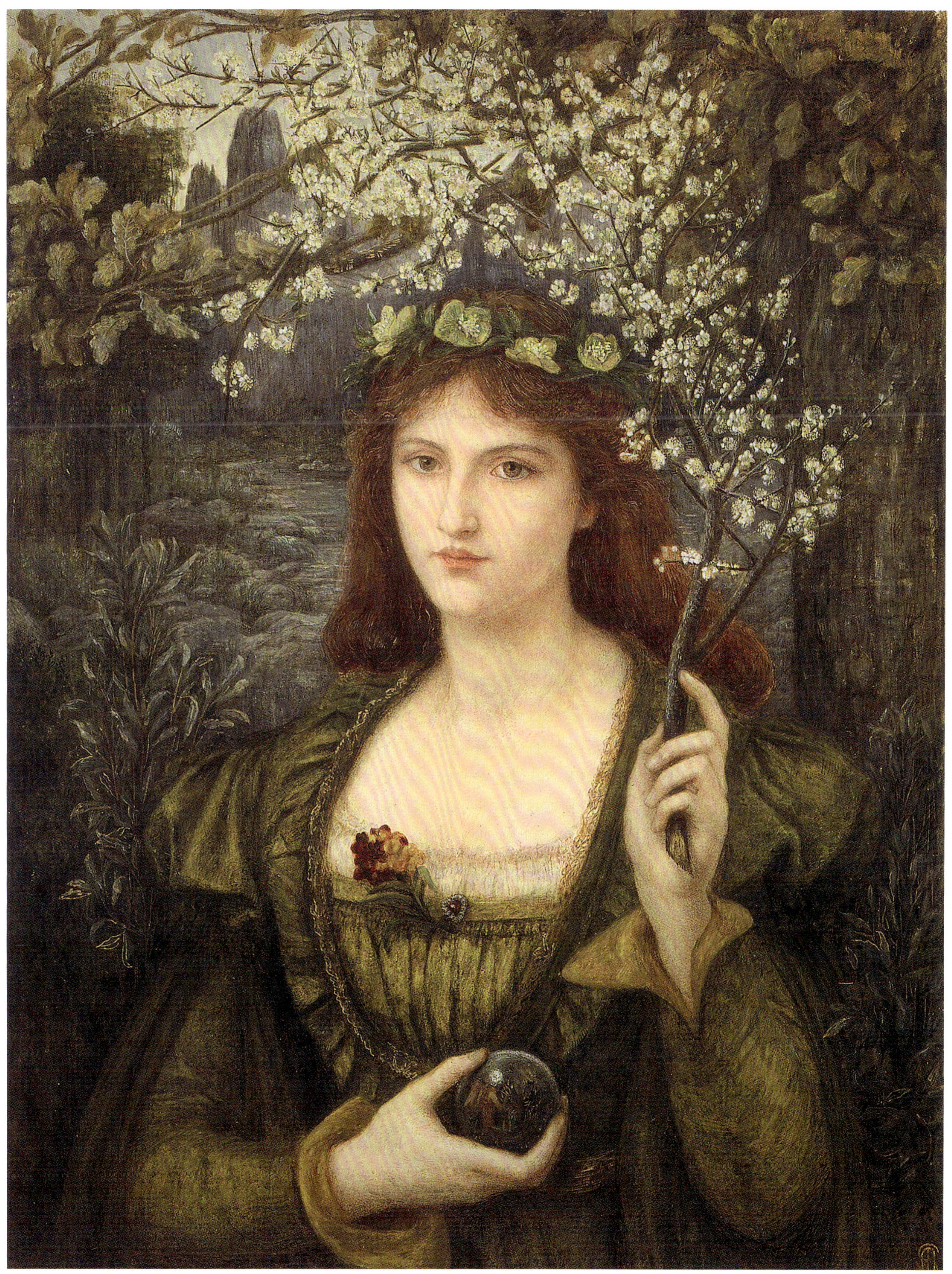

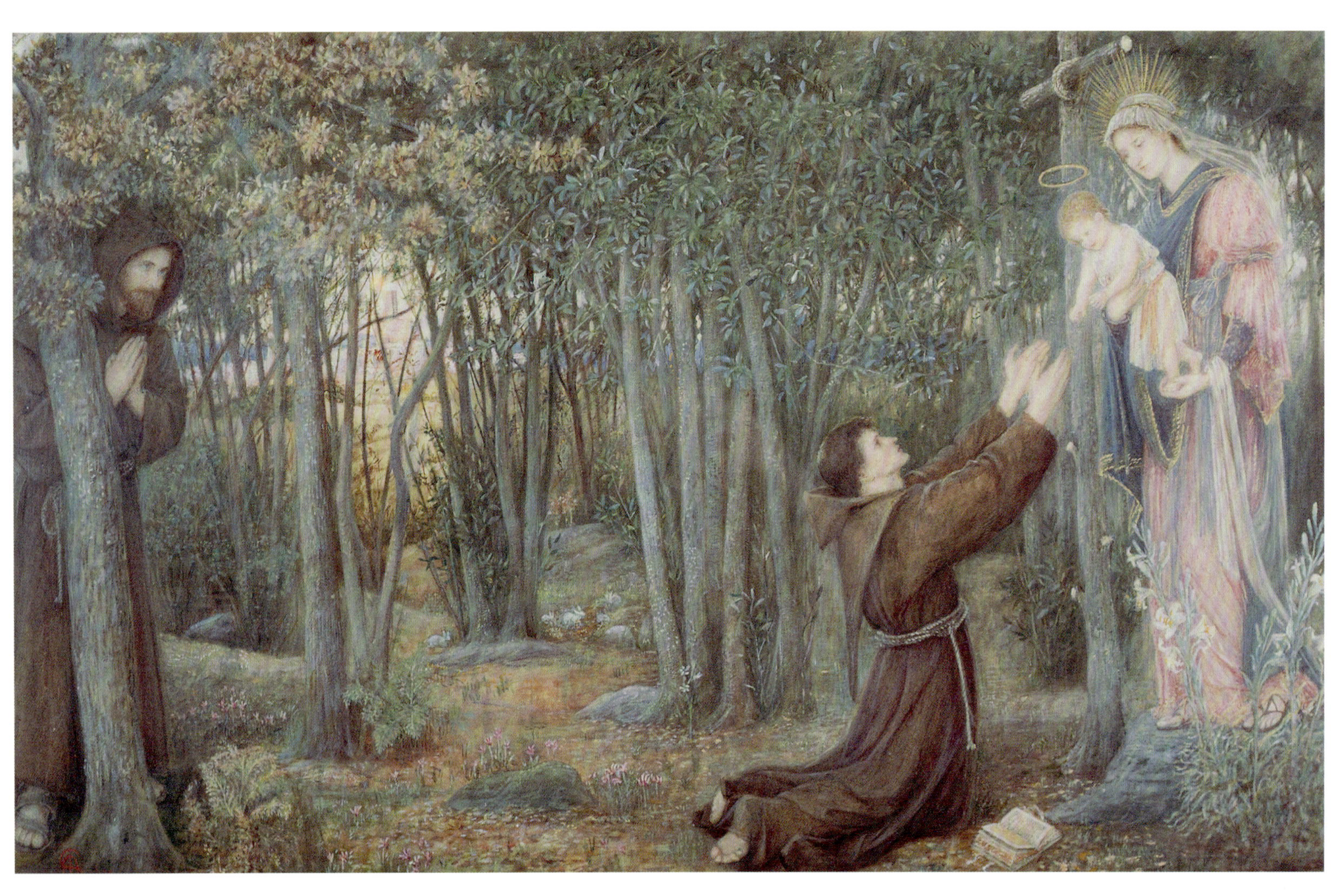

touch with fellow artists in Britain. 'If the Virgin leaned forward to trust the babe safely it might be better – no she is better upright,' commented Burne-Jones on her compositional sketch for the painting of Friar Conrad's vision (ill. 123); adding, it would be 'a lovely little picture & full of care & delight to you & I don't see how it could go wrong anywhere'.[14] The subject is from the fourteenth-century text *The Little Flowers of St Francis*, which relates Friar Conrad's vision in a wood near Forano in Lazio, watched by Friar Peter. The long landscape view through trees, which derives from Bellini's *The Assassination of St Peter Martyr* (1505–7) features several times in her work, providing both perspective and middle-distance light.

As she passed her fiftieth birthday, she continued to take part in London events, such as 'show Sunday', when studios were opened to friends and sales invited. From Rome in 1893 she wrote: 'I spend every afternoon from 2 to 4 ½ on the Palatine painting. I have found several charming subjects which I hope will sell for a few ££ by and bye.'[15]

In Rome, she also made new artistic acquaintance with members of the so-called Etruscan School, headed by Giovanni 'Nino' Costa, whose stylistic hallmarks were cooler lights and wide, horizontal views, and she exhibited with Costa's In Arte Libertas group. In 1892 the Stillmans spent some weeks near Perugia, where she reported that: 'Costa has been encouraging me to paint landscape all the summer, with more or less success,' adding that his regime was to start work at daybreak, rest mid-morning and resume painting towards evening.[16]

Some of her finest works show ephemeral atmospheric effects at dusk and dawn. In *Monte Luce from Perugia at Sunset* (ill. 125) the view is from a villa above the road leading east to the convent of Monte Luce, seen on the left, with Monte Subasio and Assisi to the right. Convent, mountain and clouds are tinged with the reflected light of sunset, behind the viewpoint, with the valley below deep in shadow. The Ponte Nomentano, a medieval bridge northeast of Rome pictured in another landscape (ill. 126), was a favoured site for artists, including Richard Wilson, Joseph Wright of Derby and Jean-Baptiste-Camille Corot. Her dawn view shows the riverbank

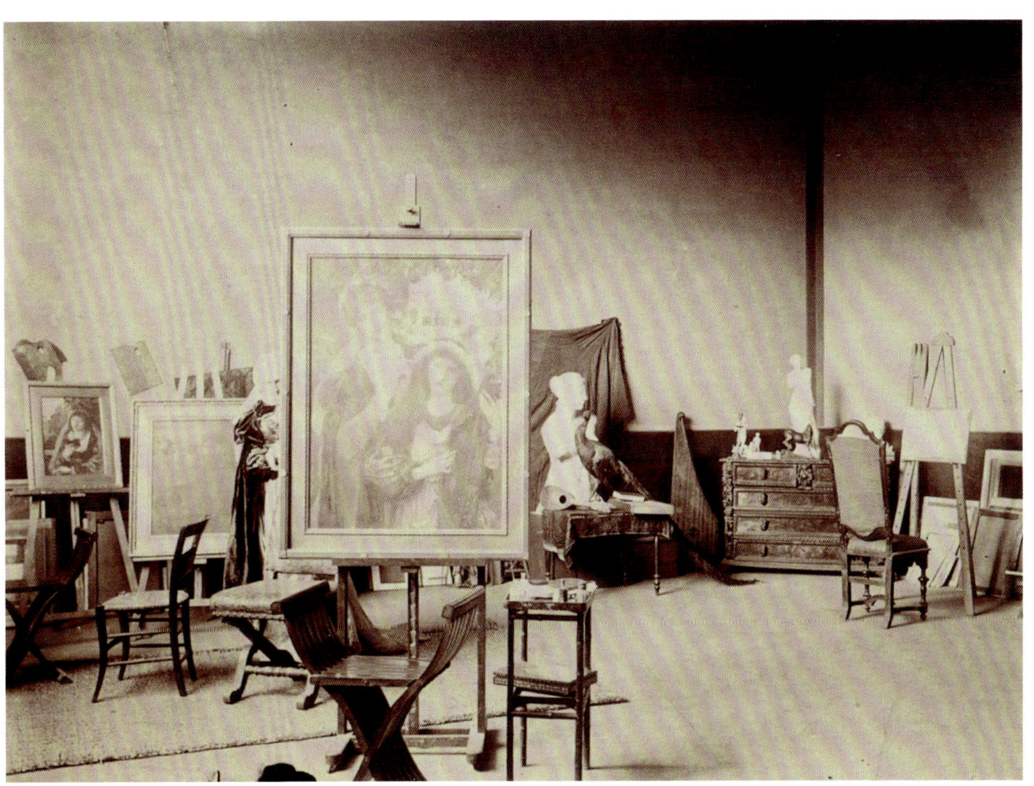

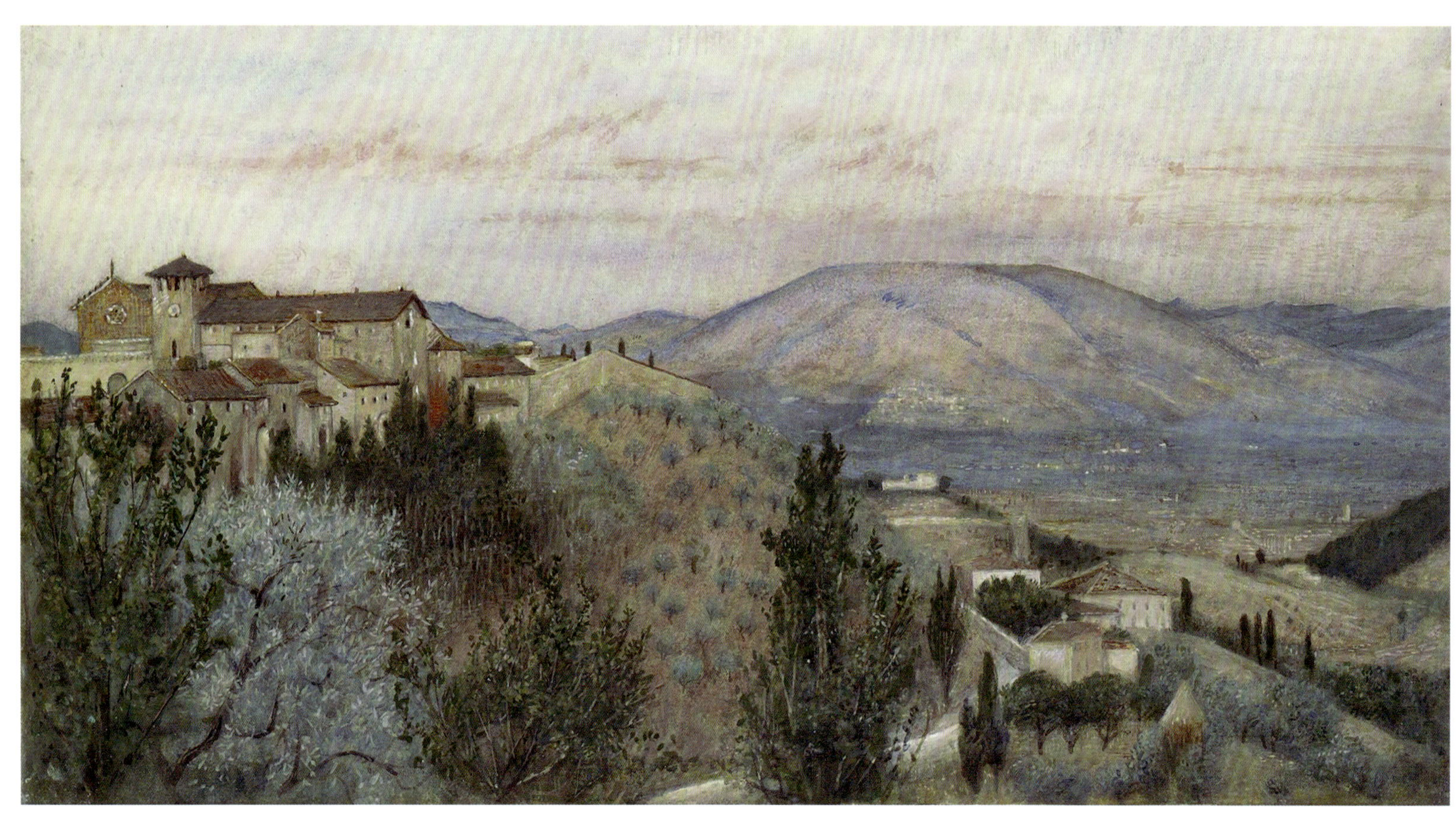

125
**Monte Luce from Perugia
at Sunset**
Marie Spartali Stillman, 1893
Watercolour and gouache
on paper, 203 × 394mm
Private Collection

126
Ponte Nomentano
Marie Spartali Stillman, 1890s
Watercolour, gouache and
graphite on paper
282 × 478mm
The Morgan Library & Museum,
New York

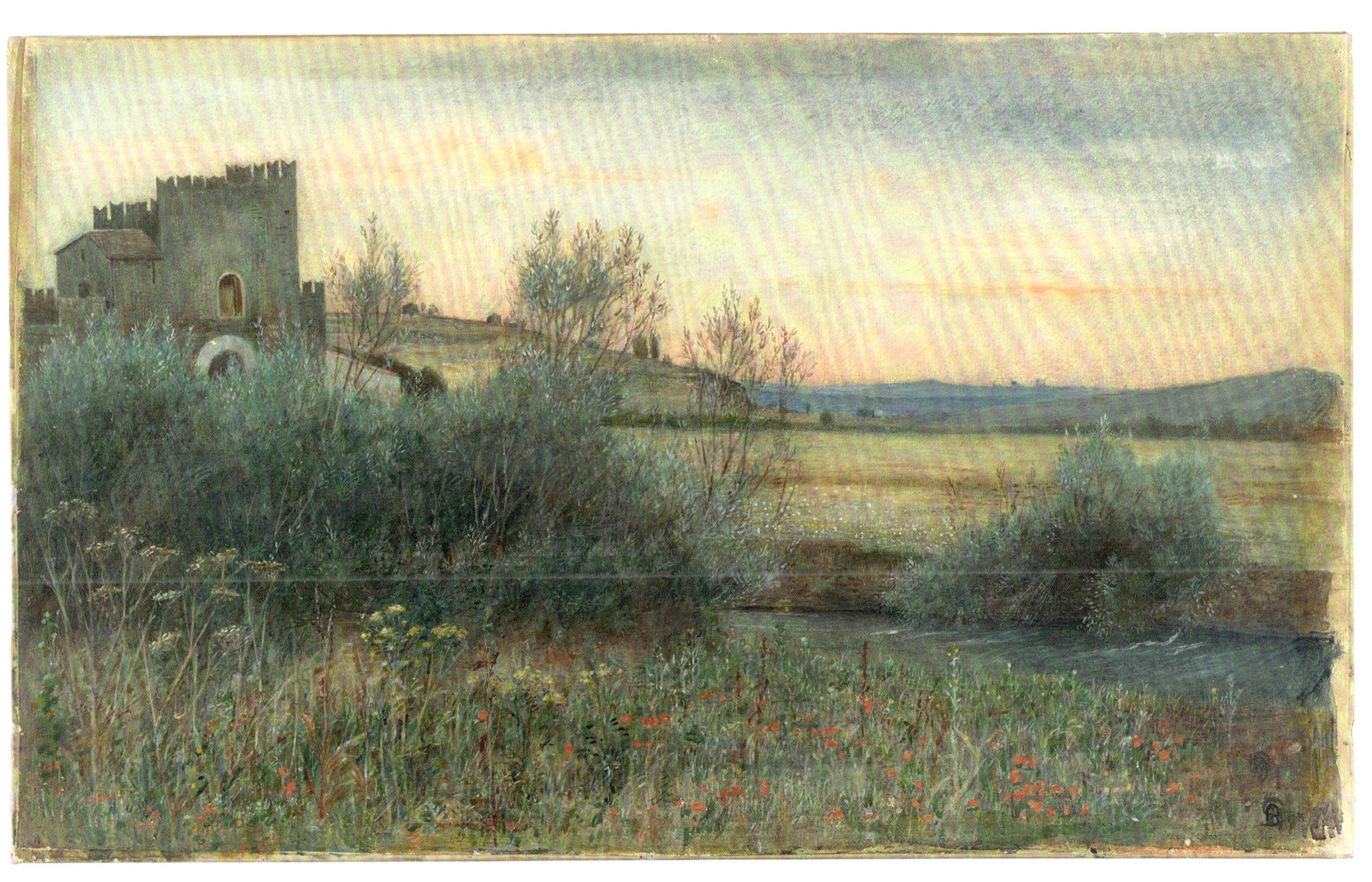

127
Embroidered Shoes
Marie Spartali Stillman, undated
Embroidery on silk
Each: 114 × 76 × 267mm
Delaware Art Museum

128
**Marie Stillman with
her Son, Michael**
Unknown photographer, printed
by Emery Walker Ltd., c.1875
Silver printing-out paper print
191 × 138mm
National Portrait Gallery

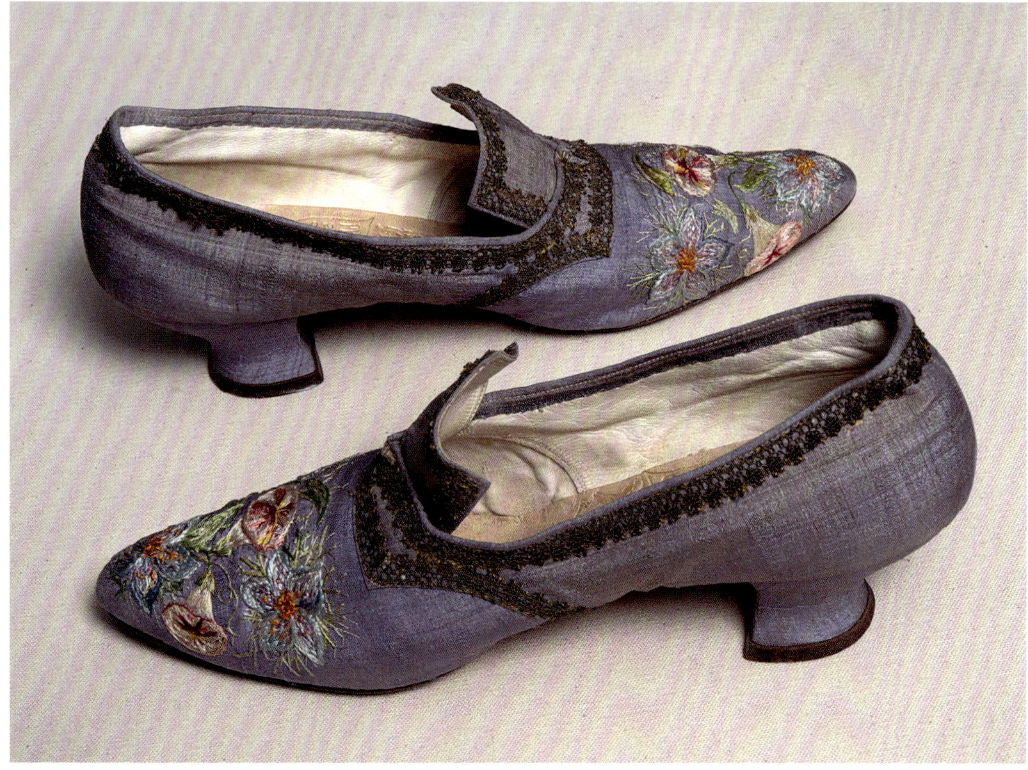

overgrown with willows, half masking the famously picturesque bridge, with meadow flowers in the foreground and the pink sky before sunrise in the distance over the Campagna.

Spartali Stillman was a close friend of Jane Morris, and when both were widowed, they shared summer sojourns at Kelmscott Manor, she absorbed with painting and Jane Morris with embroidery. In 1901, she wrote:

> I stayed at Kelmscott for ten days & felt quite shut out of the busy world in that beautiful walled garden. I made two watercolours of the house and garden. One cannot imagine any place as quiet. Nothing ever seems to happen. Things have been at a standstill for 300 years probably.[17]

Her views of the Cotswold manor sold well in the US while others were gifted to friends, including her hostess, who described her as 'her dearly loved friend'.[18] One such view (ill. 107) shows Jane in the Kelmscott garden, which was a shared pleasure for both women.

Spartali Stillman was known for her stylish dress and, in a letter, reported in February 1905 how she had been 'much engaged in embroidering dresses for Effie [her daughter] who is to be married in a few weeks'.[19] A pair of her neatly worked silk evening shoes (ill. 127) were designed to accompany a matching short-sleeved tunic. The wildflower design compares with Jane Morris's embroideries (ill. 85) and may evoke the visits to Kelmscott.

Of over a hundred works, exhibited over six decades, the best known are *Love's Messenger* (1885) and *The Enchanted Garden of Messer Ansaldo* (1889). Both sold to patrons in the US.

Reserved and self-effacing, yet dedicated to her art, Marie Spartali Stillman became a role model to younger artists, Vanessa Bell among them. The Stillmans were long-standing friends of Bell's parents, Leslie and Julia Stephen, and, throughout the 1890s, when Spartali Stillman exhibited in London, Bell regularly worked with and alongside her step-daughter Lisa, whose own visits to the Stephen family were later immortalised by Vanessa's sister Virginia Woolf in *To the Lighthouse* (1927).

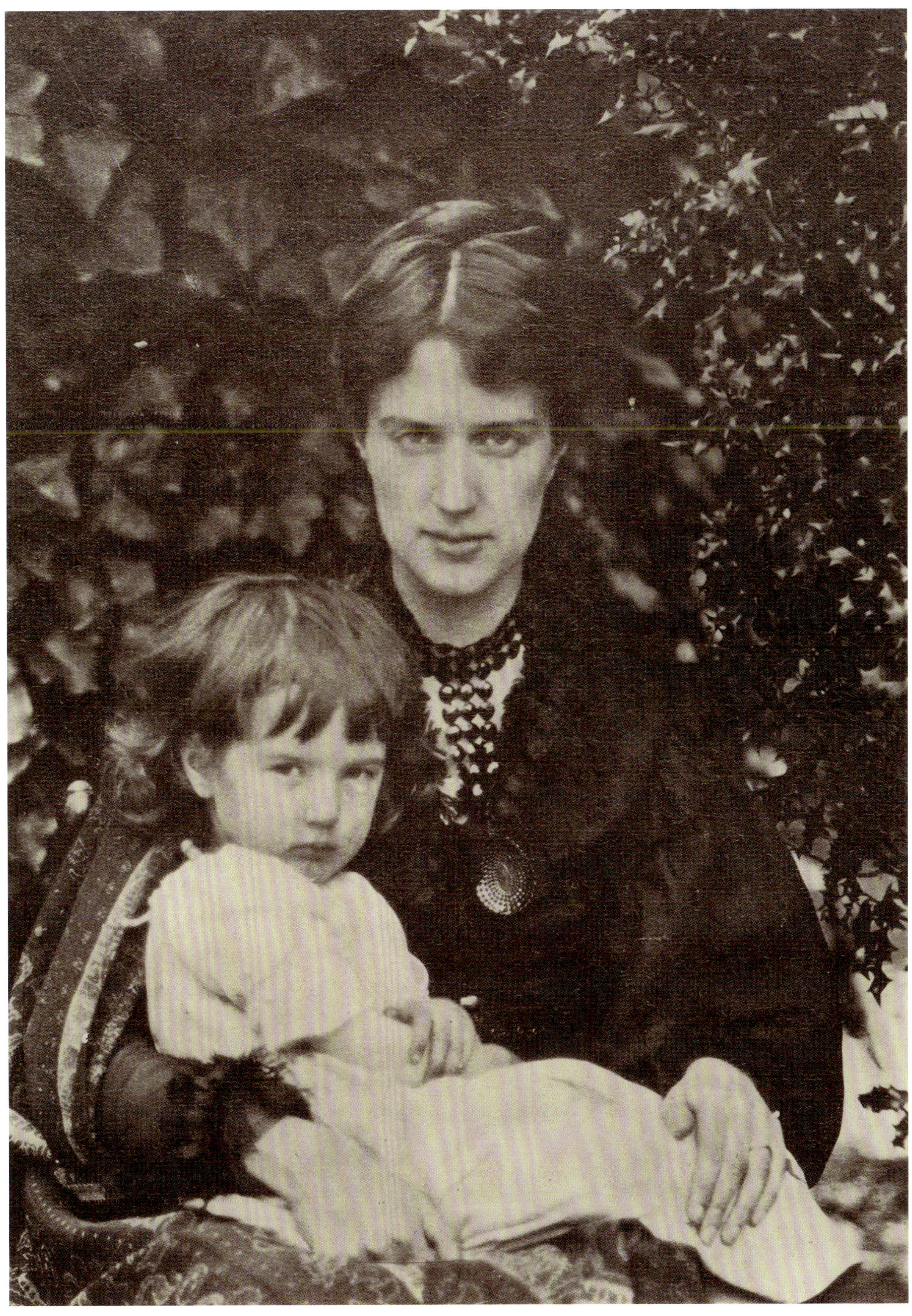

Evelyn De Morgan

1855–1919

An ambitious and accomplished artist, whose works connected with those of the original PRB as well as developing the Aesthetic and Symbolist elements of the movement, Evelyn De Morgan also suffered from gender bias and critical neglect. At an early date, her signature initials 'EP' on the major painting *Aurora Triumphans* (1886) were altered to those of Edward Burne-Jones, vividly illustrating the resistance that faced creative women within the Pre-Raphaelite movement.[1]

Born on 30 August 1855, De Morgan was the eldest child of Percival Pickering QC and Anna Maria Spencer Stanhope, granddaughter of the Earl of Leicester. From drawing lessons and a term at the National Art Training School in London, in January 1873 she proceeded to the Slade School, where she won a scholarship and prizes for painting, drawing and composition. Unlike other women featured here who faced obstacles of poverty and poor education, De Morgan was initially impeded by wealth and social status. Rejecting the upper-class customs of 'coming out', presentation at Court and a conventional marriage, she preferred a life devoted to art.

At the Slade, a fellow student recalled her as 'A slender, picturesque girl with finely chiselled features and very lovely hair, dressed in some bright material... She was full of mischief, told a story delightfully and her laughter was irresistible, but where her painting was concerned she was all eagerness, seriousness and absorption.'[2]

Slade teaching concentrated on life-model studies and antique examples. 'The subjects I give out for practice in composition are always drawn from Biblical or classical sources,' declared the director, Edward Poynter, 'or are of a kind which require treatment of a classical nature – i.e. they require the introduction of nude or classically-draped figures.'[3] Her first works in this mode, were a key element in Pre-Raphaelitism's Aesthetic phase. She also chose medieval subjects, mermaids and, increasingly, allegory.

Having sold a first painting in 1875, she made her exhibition debut the following year at the Dudley Gallery, London with *St Catherine of Alexandria*. Following the death of her father she spent six months in Italy with her uncle, artist John Roddam

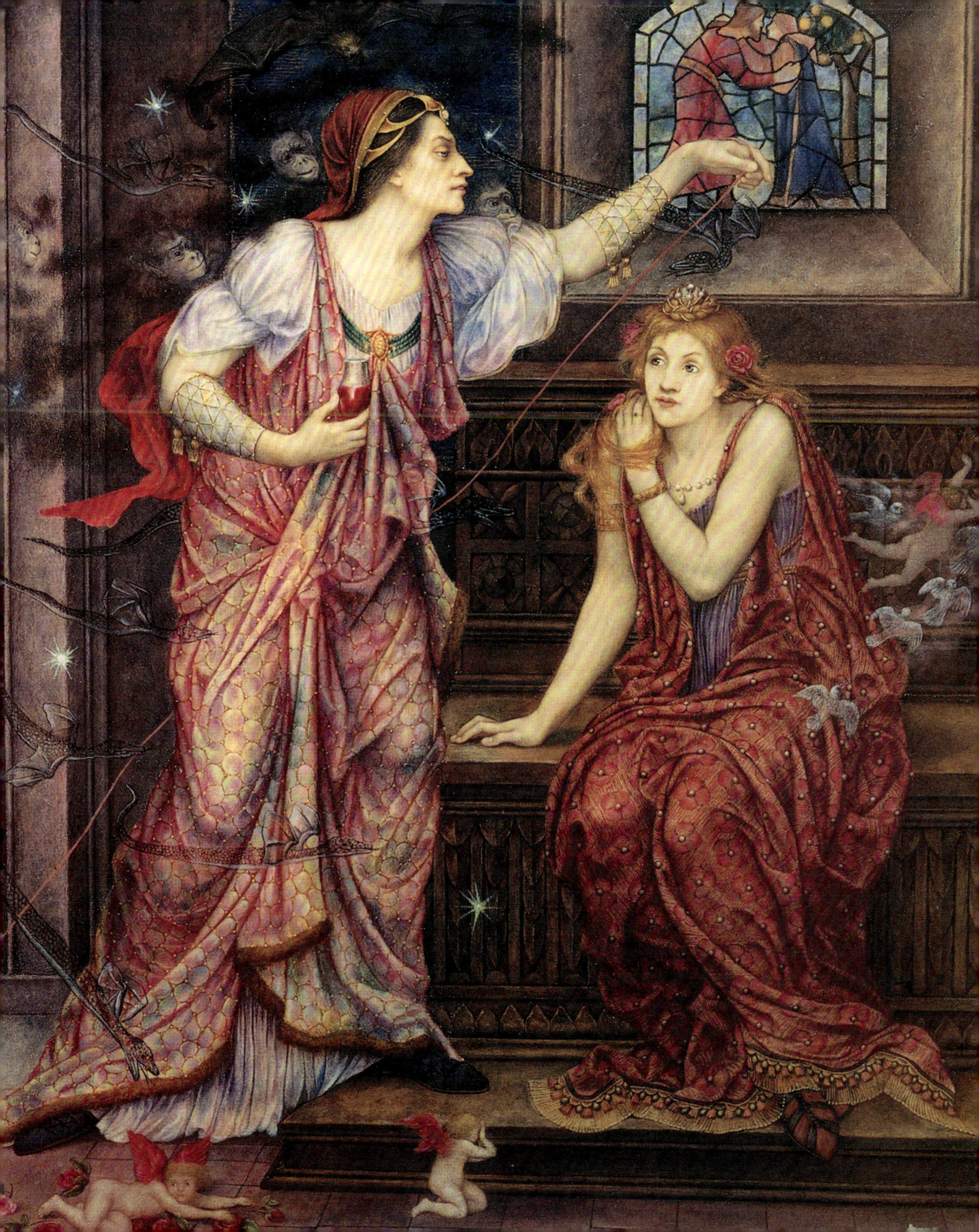

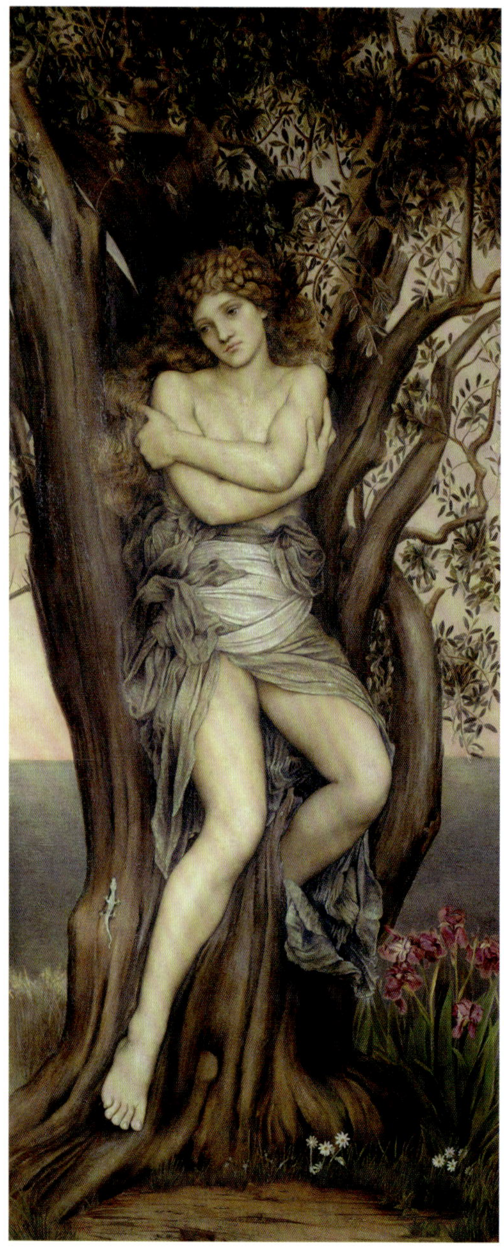

Spencer Stanhope and in 1877, with Marie Spartali Stillman, she was one of the few women invited to exhibit at the prestigious Grosvenor Gallery, London, a showcase for Aesthetic art. Here she went on to show subjects such as *The Grey Sisters*, visualising the spiritual state of Goethe's Faust, as well as portraits and allegorical images, including *Night and Sleep* (ill. 70) and *Love's Passing* (1884). The wood-nymph in *The Dryad* (1884; ill. 129) compares with Burne-Jones's *The Tree of Forgiveness* (ill. 115).

She also responded to narrative Pre-Raphaelite works based on medieval legends, producing her version of *Queen Eleanor and Fair Rosamund* (ill. 133), the traditional tale of Queen Eleanor's malevolence towards her husband's paramour that was a Pre-Raphaelite favourite, dramatised by Swinburne and painted twice by Burne-Jones in the early 1860s.

Here a red thread guides jealous Eleanor with her phial of poison to Rosamund's bower, hidden in the maze visible to the left, while shadowy evil spirits of lizards and apes drive away tiny cupids and doves. The window glass shows

In 1883 she met ceramicist William De Morgan at a costume ball, where she was 'a tube of rose madder;' and he was 'madder still'.[4] A close friend of Morris and Burne-Jones, producing fine lustreware, he proved a soulmate, although a wedding seemed unlikely. 'We are only engaged,' she told her uncle; 'we should not dream of getting married for at least fifteen years!' But they did so in 1887, settling in an old house in Chelsea.[4] According to William Blake Richmond, they

were absolutely one, one in sympathy, in intelligence and its direction, one in tastes and in perfect companionship. They teased and chaffed one another, they were amused at each other's idiosyncrasies and amused also at their mental similarity. He believed in her Art and she in his. They were both artistic in the highest sense and where the business capacity came in is a puzzle to everyone. She had more than he. His capacity as a businessman was probably nil, hers only a little more than nil; but her money was his and as all his and her friends knew she gave it up to save crashes and to make one more glorious pot.[5]

'She was full of mischief...but where painting was concerned she was all eagerness, seriousness and absorption'

embracing lovers, who may represent the meeting of another illicit couple, Lancelot and Guinevere, in an orchard. The dramatic narrative, strong lines, clear colours and medieval-type setting follow early Pre-Raphaelite principles, in what seems to be De Morgan's homage to her predecessors. Always, De Morgan's figures are clad in flowing or flying drapery, in rich reds and gold.

Despite their mutual 'lack of worldly wisdom and self-advertisement,' Evelyn De Morgan pursued a rigorous career of professional production, exhibition and sales, albeit without the publicity and 'puffery' that many artists employed.[6] Early works such as *Ariadne in Naxos* and *Cadmus and Harmonia* (both 1877) sold to MPs Charles Dilke and John Mundella respectively. Shipowner William

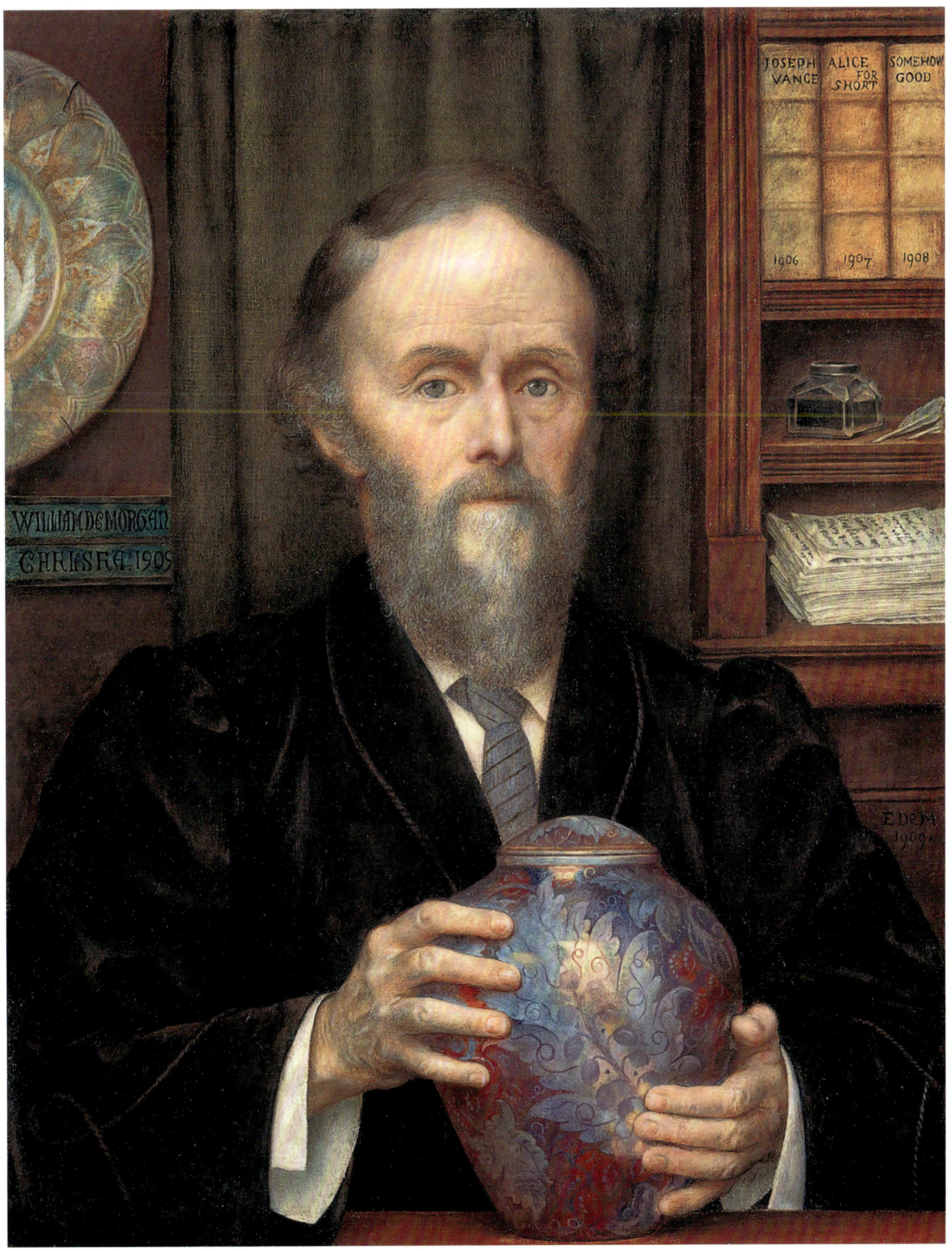

JOSEPH VANCE
ALICE FOR SHORT
SOMEHOW GOOD
1906
1907
1908
WILLIAM DE MORGAN
CHELSEA 1909
E D M
1909

131
Study of a Male Head
Evelyn De Morgan, 1910–14
Chalk on paper, 460 × 380mm
The De Morgan Foundation

132
**Study of a Female Head
for *St Christina Giving Her
Father's Jewels to the Poor***
Evelyn De Morgan, 1904
Chalk on paper, 342 × 215mm
The De Morgan Foundation

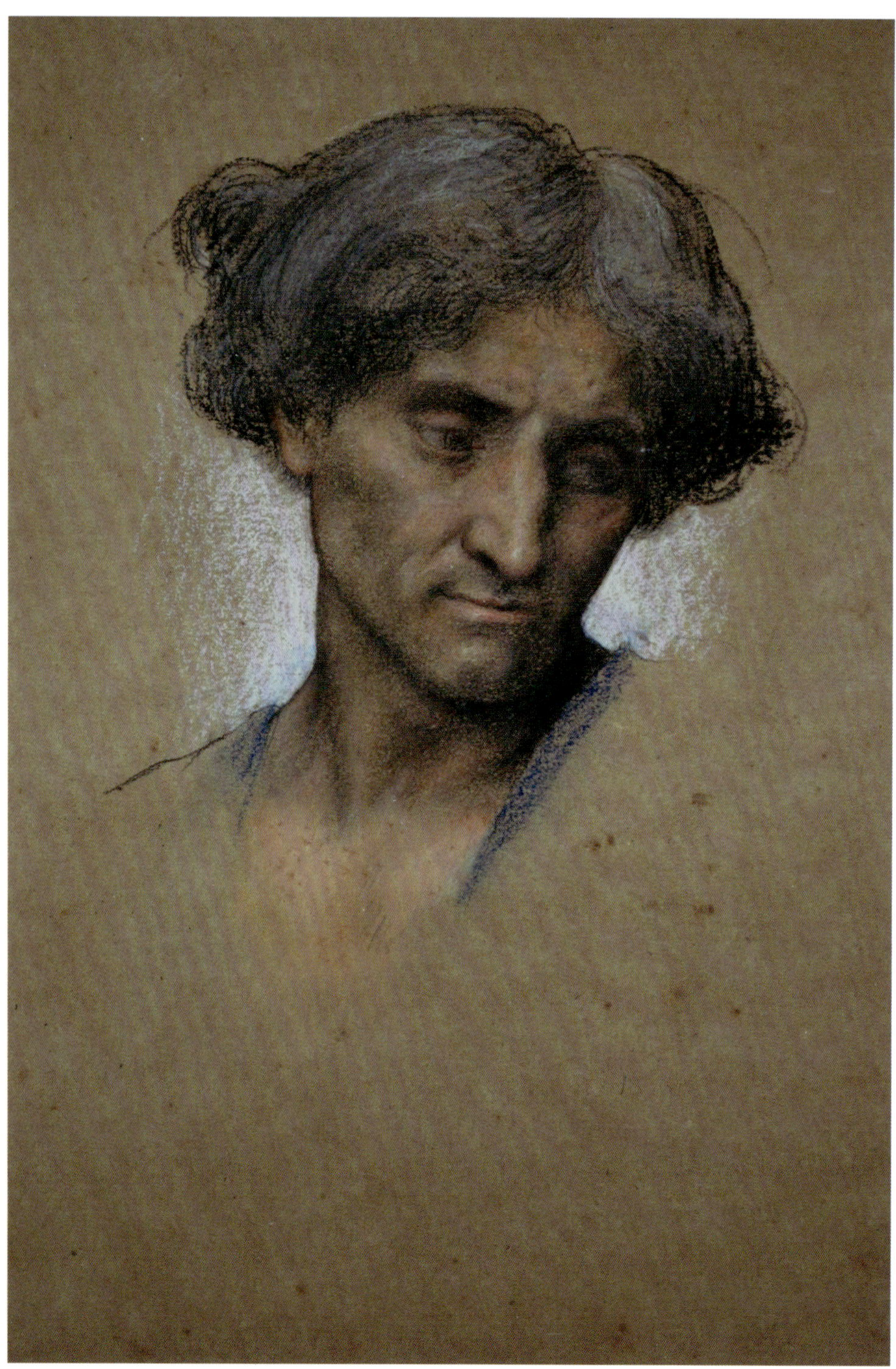

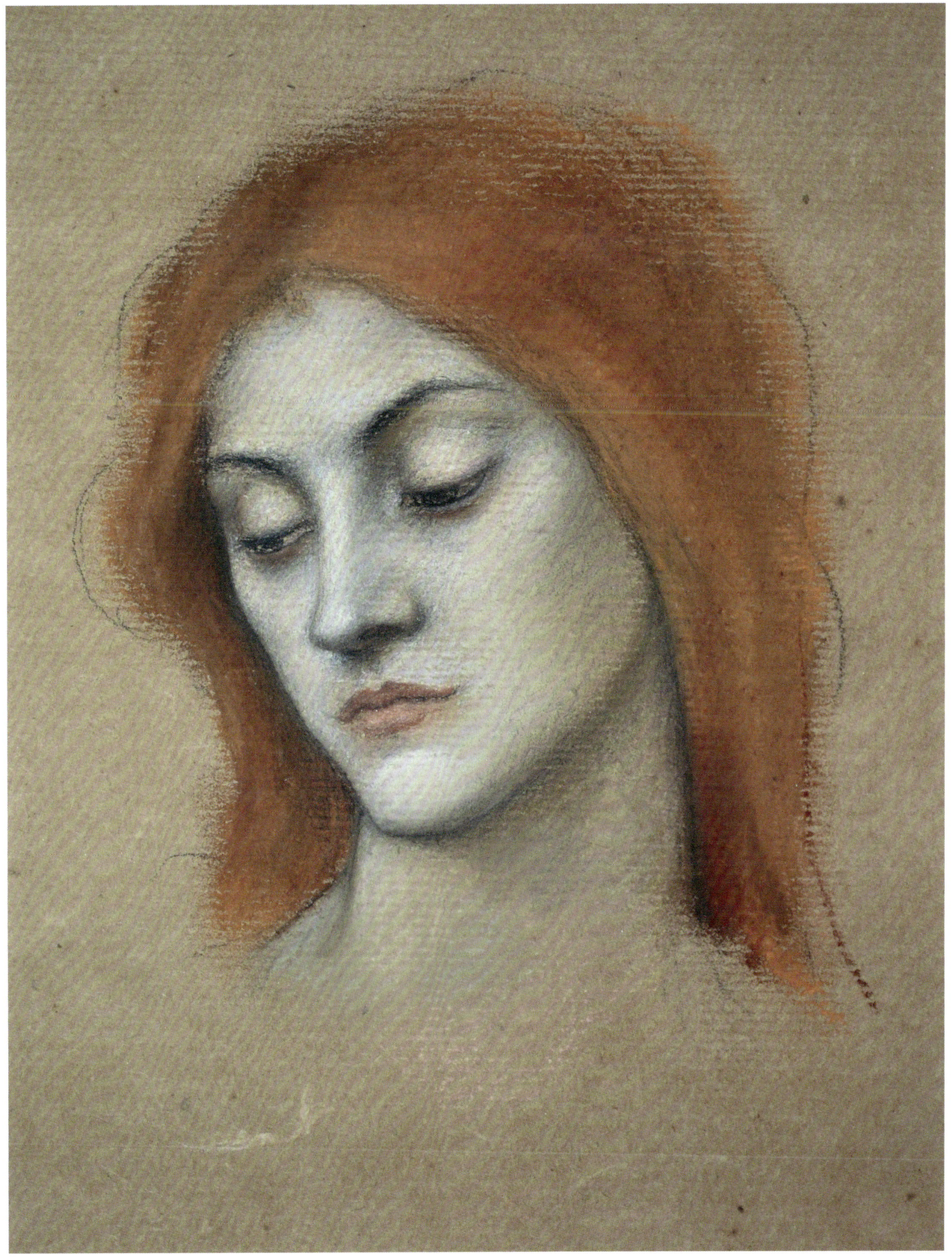

133 (below and p.171)
**Queen Eleanor and
Fair Rosamund**
Evelyn De Morgan, 1880–1919
Oil on canvas, 737 × 648mm
The De Morgan Foundation

134
Jenny Morris
Evelyn De Morgan, c.1905
Pastel on paper, 419 × 337mm
William Morris Gallery, London

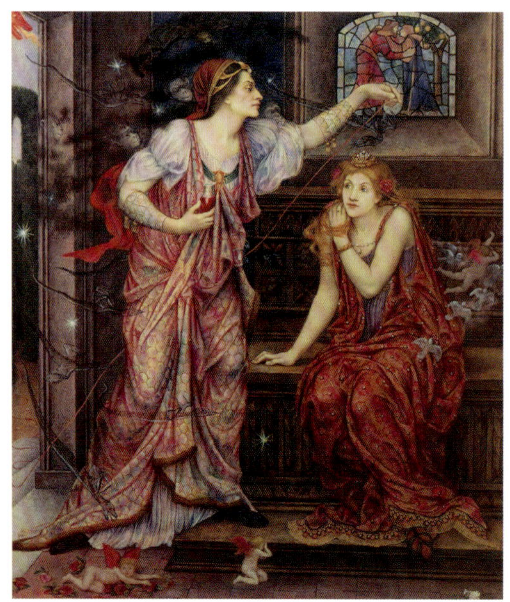

Imrie, of the White Star Line, bought several works, including *The Dryad, Flora* (1894) and *Cassandra* (1898). She also painted a number of portraits, chiefly of family and friends.

The artworks use personifications and ideal forms to articulate moral and Spiritualist concepts – rebirth, light versus darkness, flesh as 'the soul's prison house', the false worship of wealth. In accord with the long tradition of western iconology, female figures represent abstract ideas, in what became a sequence of symbolic images, from the Dryad and Clytie to Aurora, Luna, Night, Demeter and Our Lady of Peace.

From 1890 to 1914 the De Morgans spent their winters in Florence, the city whose early art inspired the whole Pre-Raphaelite movement with its frescoed figures and pictorial piety. Her working practice was assiduously based on repeated studies, of heads, gestures, dramatic actions. Two examples, a male head (ill.131) and study for St Christina (ill.132), illustrate expressive preparatory drawings for narrative oil paintings. These are not portraits, but emblematic representations of the pictorial messages, about war and idealism.

The female head, with white skin and auburn hair, suggests how the early Pre-Raphaelite aesthetic influenced later artists and epitomises a popular idea of the Pre-Raphaelite woman, based on Elizabeth Siddal. It was drawn for the central figure in *St Christina Giving her Father's Jewels to the Poor*, a monumental, multi-figured painting in the high Renaissance tradition.

After the demise of the Grosvenor Gallery in the late 1880s, like Burne-Jones and others she sent work to The New Gallery in London, and to the autumn exhibitions in Liverpool. In 1902–3 she showed nine works at Leighton House, London, and a similar number in Düsseldorf and Berlin; in 1906 she had a solo show in London, and, in 1907, she sent twenty-five pieces to Wolverhampton Art Gallery, of which fourteen were for sale. Then, in 1916, she gathered together thirteen works for exhibition in aid of the Red Cross in Britain and Italy, the two countries in which she had lived.

Of De Morgan's work, May Morris wrote:

> Her pictures have an epic quality… remarkable for the beauty of drapery design, for drawing vigorous and delicate and for sumptuous colours, for great enjoyment of textures. She had astonishing physical endurance and power of work, starting to paint early in the morning and going on swiftly and surely throughout the day.[7]

For Watts, doyen of the grand allegorical manner, 'she is a long way ahead of all women and considerably ahead of most of the men.'[8] This typically gendered judgement illustrates how consistently artists were viewed as occupying separate spheres, with males always outranking females.

For Burne-Jones, she represented a rival. He grumbled, conversationally, that her pictures were:

> a kind of eclectic mixture of Mr Watts and me and old Florentine work… The colours of some of them are extremely beautiful if you look close in at them, yet at a distance the whole has no beauty of colour at all. The faces are so pretty with such nice expressions, but the figures are so badly drawn.

He blamed ambition:

> If this girl had left figure painting alone and gone about the world modestly and happily doing pretty views, cities, flowers and every beautiful thing she came across in nature, with a cheerful mind…she would have done admirable and useful work that would have been a pleasure to everybody. But these pictures are only a bore and an anomaly.[9]

The De Morgans and Morrises were close friends. May Morris recalled exciting family visits to De Morgan's pottery when a newly fired kiln was opened, and the riddles, jokes and silly voices shared on picnics and boat trips. Later, when William De Morgan turned novelist, Jane Morris was a chief admirer. 'Dear old friend, Please write a great many more,' she wrote from Kelmscott, adding 'our love to Evelyn

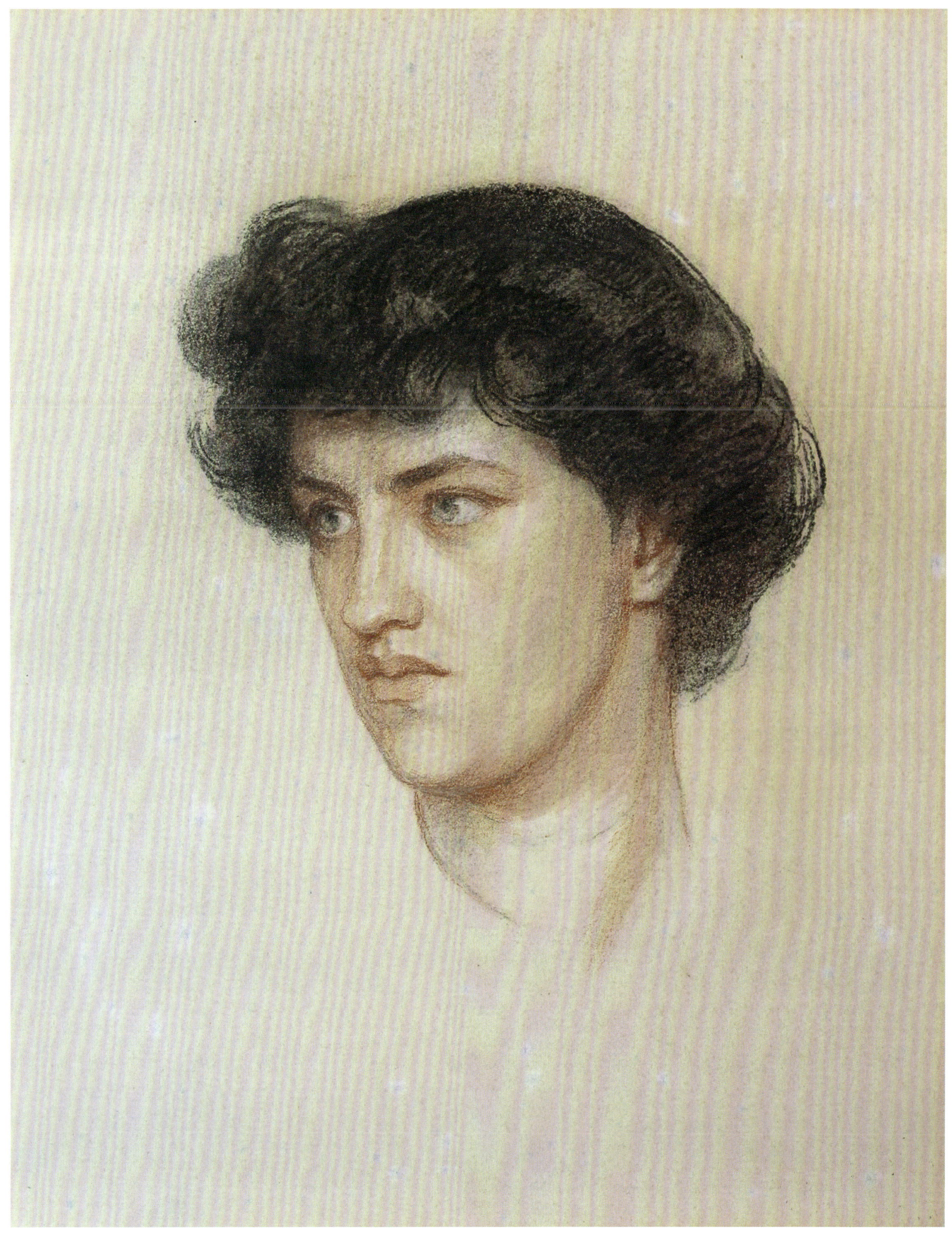

and we shall be pleased to see her in August.'[10] William De Morgan's parents were leading Spiritualists, and their son and daughter-in-law were active participants, although, as he acknowledged to the more sceptical May Morris, he received no confirmation of his faith 'that this life is an instalment of a larger and longer one'.[11]

Spiritualism was the dominant motive in Evelyn De Morgan's art. If their exact drawing and clear, sunlit colour connect the works to the whole history of Pre-Raphaelitism, and their varied subjects also span the movement's range, within all is the distinctive impulse provided by a quasi-Christian faith in good works, a cosmic struggle between

she was physically frail, aged 65, and, importantly, shared the De Morgans' love of music, probably joining some of their frequent concert visits. The tapestry sketched in the background here may have been suggested by those at Kelmscott Manor, although it is not a copy.[13]

Spiritualist practices attracted several members of the PRB generation in the 1850s. The Rossetti brothers organised seances, and Gabriel believed in messages from both Elizabeth Siddal and others. Anna Mary Howitt devoted her later life to 'spirit drawings' received during trance-like states. Jane Morris believed in reincarnation (although probably not in direct communication).

'Her pictures have an epic quality… Remarkable for the beauty of drapery design, for drawing vigorous and delicate and for sumptuous colours'

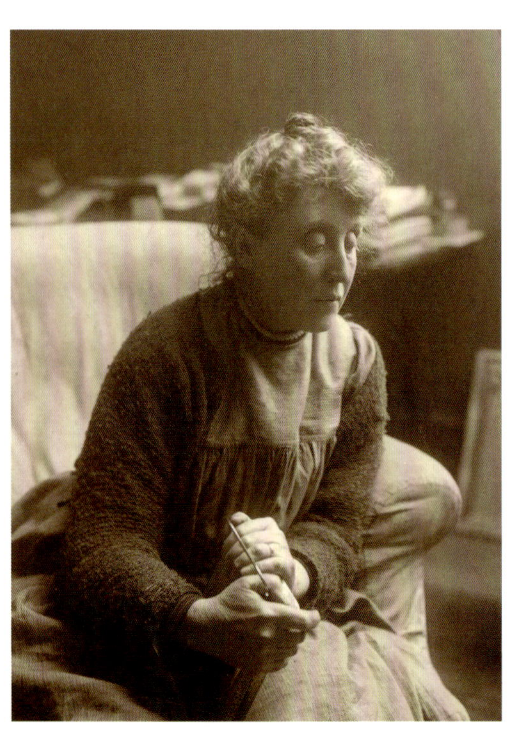

Light and Darkness, Good and Evil, and the translation of the soul after death into a transcendental realm. Furthermore, the divide between the realms was a veil that might be lifted to allow occasional communication through seances, mesmerism and 'automatic' writing.

The Hour Glass (ill.137) is a Spiritualist meditation on mortality, viewed in De Morgan's philosophy as the gateway to a finer life, and was also conceived as a pictorial 'echo' of Beethoven's 'Waldstein' Sonata, which ends on 'a sudden voice of triumph crying out – as though the morning stars s ang together'.[12]

The choice of widowed Jane Morris as model for the figure was doubly apt:

Evelyn De Morgan died in 1919, some two years after her husband. Her brother Spencer Pickering loaned nineteen of her pictures to Leighton House, and, in 1922, her sister Wilhelmina Stirling published a joint biography. In 1927 the De Morgan Trust was formed, and the collection assembled by Stirling was displayed in Old Battersea House, London; following her death at the age of 99, the Trust was re-established as the De Morgan Foundation (DMF). Sixteen paintings were, sadly, destroyed in storage in 1991, while the remainder belonging to the DMF are displayed throughout Britain. De Morgan's powerful contribution to the larger Pre-Raphaelite movement is now being revalued.

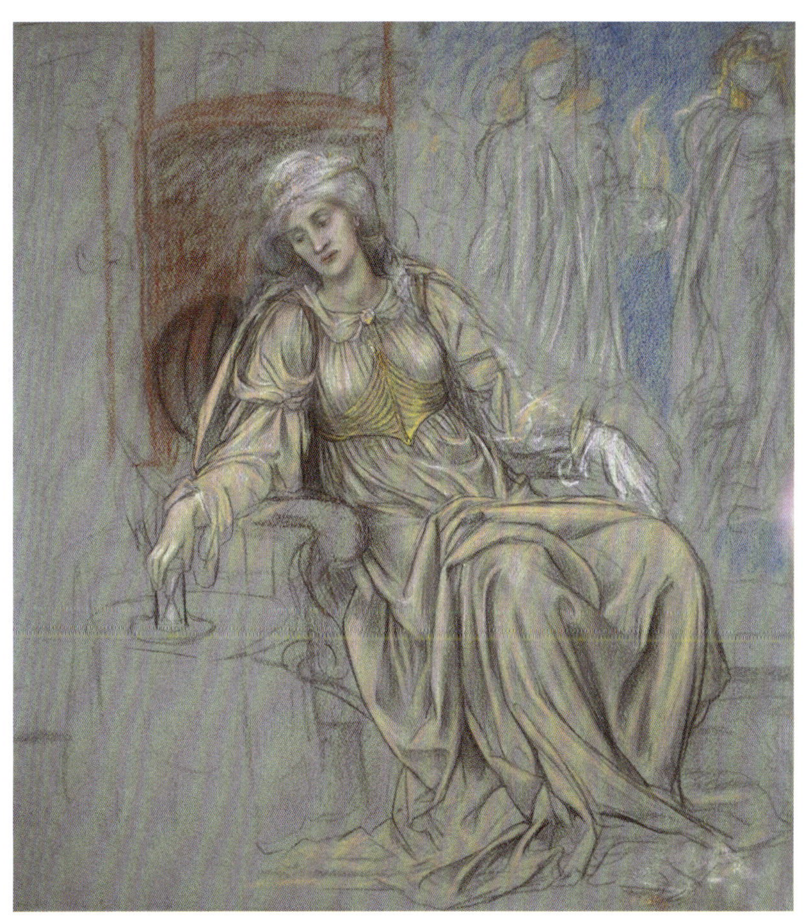

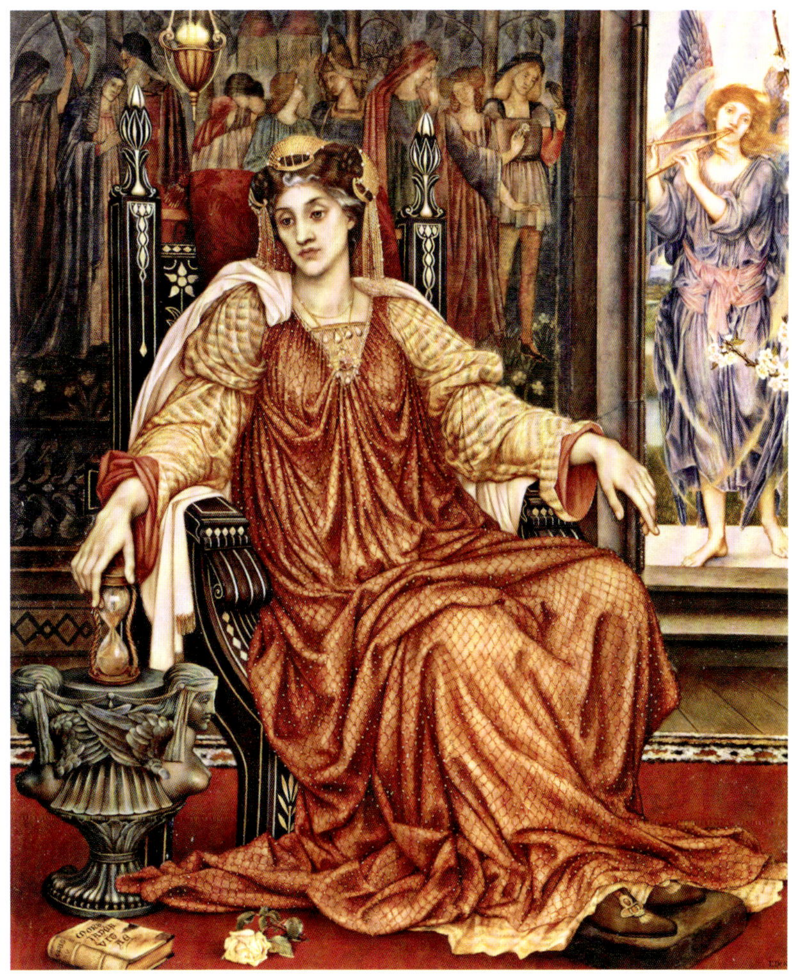

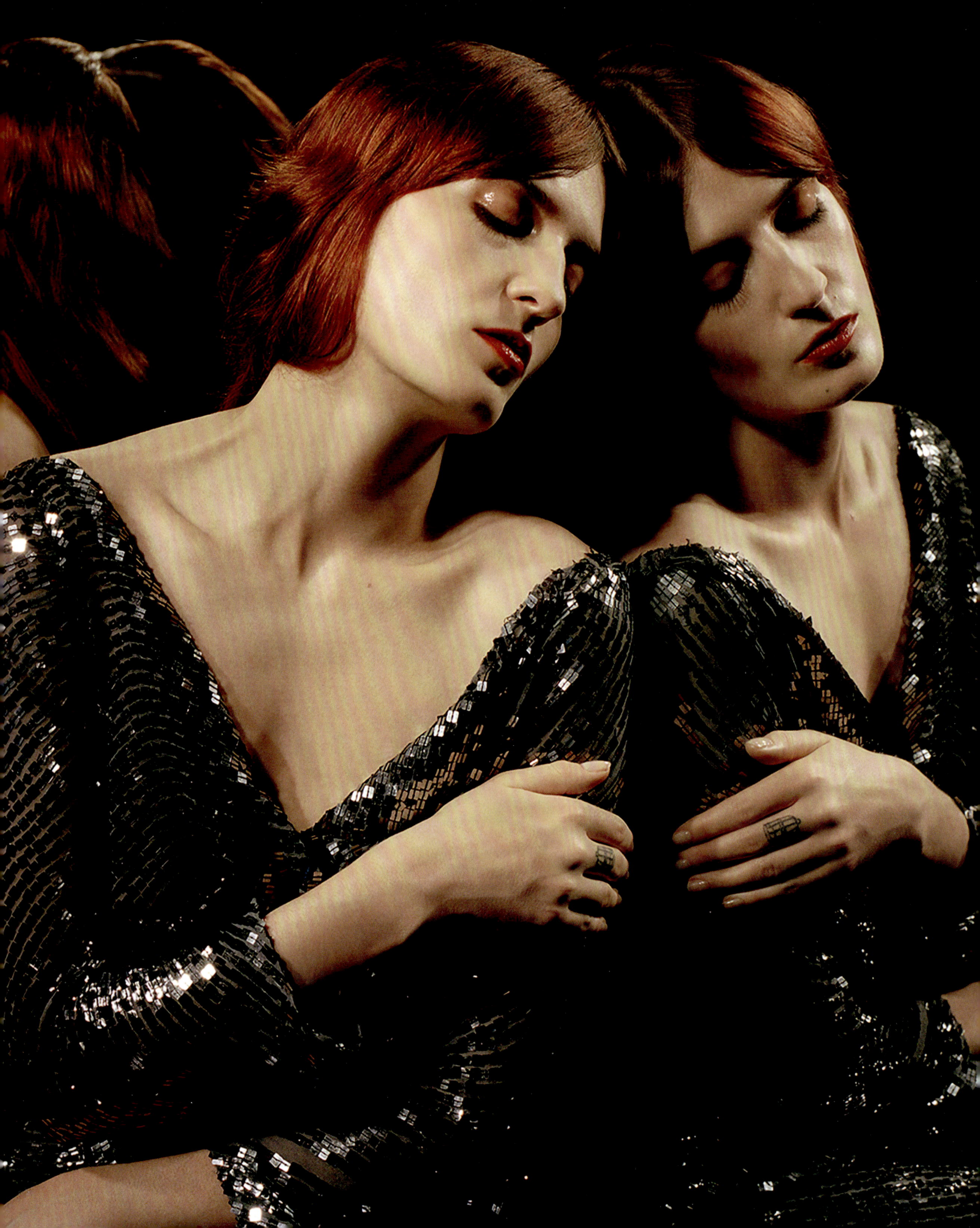

Interpretations of the importance of women as a distinct grouping within the Pre-Raphaelite movement have developed from an initial diffidence, to rediscovery and reassessment in the twentieth century particularly by feminist critics, and to their contemporary celebration as pioneering icons of both art and style for a new generation.

The Sisterhood & its Afterlife

by Alison Smith

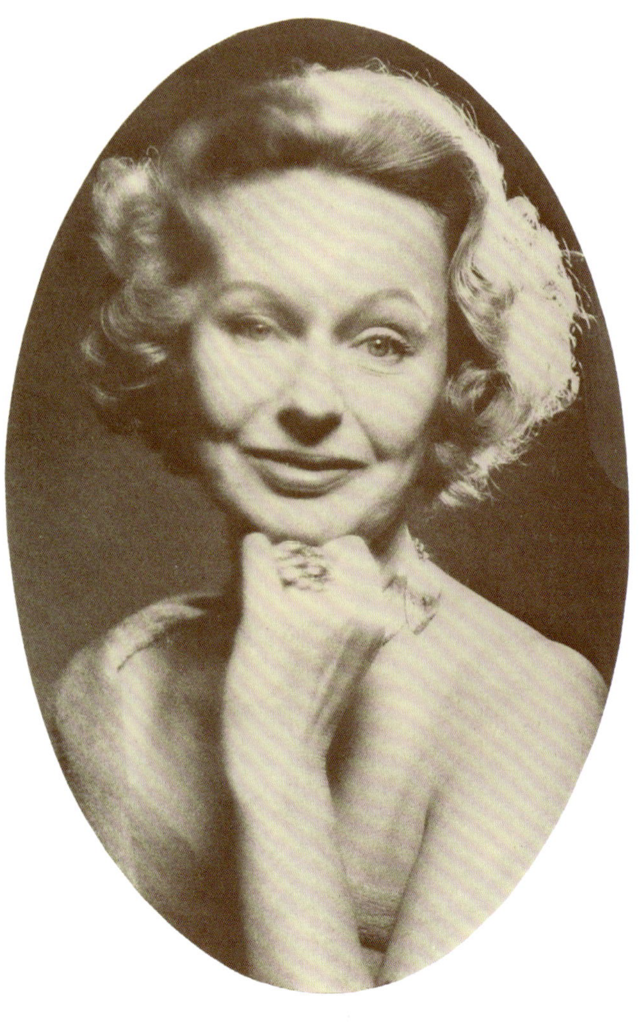

Pre-Raphaelitism has, for many people, become synonymous with a languid type of female beauty, a characteristic most typically found in Rossetti's paintings, where the sitter is presented alone in a chamber gazing out of the canvas with lustrous eyes and loose, crinkly hair. The centrality of women to the movement is also borne out by the fabulous stories that have been woven around those individuals who were drawn into its orbit as models, lovers, wives and artists. These would, invariably, include the embarrassing story of Effie Ruskin's humiliation on her wedding night, Elizabeth Siddal's tragic death through a drug overdose and the subsequent exhumation of her body, and the tormented triangular relationship that revolved around Jane Morris, her husband William and her lover Rossetti.

In the long string of narratives that have been told and retold in the history of the movement, art and life have become so enmeshed as to prove inseparable. It is thus impossible to look at Millais's *Ophelia* without thinking of a frail Siddal nearly expiring in the bathtub; at Rossetti's painted 'stunners' without the names of the sitters immediately springing to mind. In Pre-Raphaelite art the appearance of each model serves to disrupt the pictorial subject, inviting biographical readings and conflating the real with the imaginary. This tension not only accounts for the artificial look and modernity of Pre-Raphaelite painting but also helps explain the ongoing fascination with the women who so often formed the focus of it.

That women should be so deeply embedded within the mythology of the movement is all the more surprising, in that Pre-Raphaelitism was originally conceived of as a Brotherhood – a term that connotes a monastic, exclusively homosocial grouping. As one of the most strongly gendered movements in the history of art, the PRB could be seen to encapsulate the notion, so peculiar to the avant-garde, that in order to create, men needed to break free of women so as to support one another. This has become something of a cliché in the story of romanticism and modern art, from Jacques-Louis David and his pupils to the Abstract Expressionists, but it coexists with another narrative – that of the artists' colony, where men and women have removed themselves from conventional society to create among themselves.

It was in their resistance to, and removal from, the public sphere that the Pre-Raphaelites made themselves open to the kinds of expression and social relations that, in fact, welcomed women. Turning their backs on the RA in London and the professional ideals it represented, in reviving the medieval workshop or Guild, the Brothers allowed women, as amateurs, to be admitted on more equal terms than they would have been at most art schools of the time. Moreover, given the rigid moral codes of the day, it is worth being mindful of just how liberating Pre-Raphaelitism would have been for women as artists and associates, enabling some to marry or forge relationships above their class; others to move beyond the narrow expectations of their gender and upbringing by engaging with new and exciting kinds of creative experience.

If the Pre-Raphaelite cult of the amateur helped place women on a relatively even playing field (paving the way for later creative partnerships), it also served to disadvantage them as members of a movement that, since the twentieth century, has occupied a position on the fringes of modernism, often seen, at best, as eccentric; at worst, as simply bad. These views maintain currency among mainstream art critics, for whom the work of female associates has come to epitomise all the shortcomings of Pre-Raphaelitism, diluting the standard set by the men; at various times labelled 'feeble', 'irrelevant' and, in the case of Evelyn De Morgan, 'painful' to behold.[1]

Such responses might explain why women are still approached as a subgroup within Pre-Raphaelitism, requiring special contextualisation, and why their work tends to be separated out from that produced by the men. Considering the women together nevertheless exposes an inherent tension in the movement, in that while some were content to serve as models and muses, others strove for professional recognition as artists. The question of whether women were active or passive participants has made the topic of the Pre-Raphaelite woman a contentious one.

The idea of a sisterhood, traditionally, assumes a tight-knit set, as within a family unit, or a group of women linked by a common interest. In terms of Pre-Raphaelitism, it was coined to complement the brotherhood of men who initiated the movement in 1848 and drove forward its ideals until it disbanded around 1853. Although Christina Rossetti was doubly involved with the PRB, as sister to the Rossetti brothers and as a near early member of the group (an invitation she declined on grounds of decorum), the term 'sisterhood' is very much a retrospective appellation; over the years it has been used to embrace women from different backgrounds, who lived through a period of extraordinary social and political change that extended from what Elaine Showalter has described as a 'feminine' phase, lasting from around 1840 to 1880, to a 'feminist' phase that continued up to the 1920s.[2]

At the time the Brotherhood was founded, the term 'sisterhood', like the former, would have held specific religious connotations, relating to the revived nunneries or sisterhoods within the Anglican Church, influenced by the Oxford movement (including, incidentally, the All Saints' Sisterhood, formed in 1856; the society to which Rossetti's other sister Maria was admitted in 1873). Taking root from the idea of a sexually separate group living in a semi-informal way, the term 'sisterhood' was, for much of the century, understood as a support network that nurtured a sense of solidarity at a time when women were still largely judged, or seen, in relation to men, yet were active in campaigning for greater representation. The sense of community brought about through both marginalisation and a striving for change comes across vividly in the letters and diaries written by women at the time, as this exhibition testifies.

Around the beginning of the twentieth century the presence of a strong female grouping within Pre-Raphaelitism began to fade as the movement entered the canons of art history. With reputations to protect and uphold, the first wave of biographical writing about the PRB was, understandably, rather circumspect regarding lovers and first marriages, in some cases rendering them so invisible as to negate the very notion of a sisterhood. Effie Millais's disastrous first marriage to John Ruskin is thus omitted from her son J.G. Millais's biography of his father; Annie Miller and Fanny Cornforth barely get a mention in the early literature on Hunt and Rossetti; Maria Zambaco is absent from Georgiana Burne-Jones's *Memorials*; Ellen Terry is dismissed in one sentence in Mary Watts's biography of her husband, the artist G.F. Watts.[3] However, this absence also served to stimulate gossip, especially among the next generation eager to expose all the imperfections of their forebears' lives. For his 1928 biography of Rossetti, for example, Evelyn Waugh (grandnephew of Hunt's two wives, the Waugh sisters) sought out survivors from the era with mischievous stories to tell, one of whom was the novelist (Thomas Henry) Hall Caine, who relayed 'lots of profitable things about Rossetti and Fanny Cornforth and Lizzie's suicide', as Waugh noted in his diary.[4]

The first histories of the movement explained the work of the key protagonists in terms of its style, subject matter and influence. This strand peaked around 1948, the centenary year of the PRB's foundation, with exhibitions across the country, the publication of Robin Ironside and John Gere's *Pre-Raphaelite Painters* and the impact of William Gaunt's 1942 *Pre-Raphaelite Tragedy* reprinted as the *Pre-Raphaelite Dream* in 1943. The predominantly male writers and art historians behind these projects were focused on the full members of the PRB, which meant that women remained peripheral figures.[5]

Meanwhile, in the realm of popular biography the Sisters emerged as enigmatic, sometimes manipulative and partly responsible for the changes

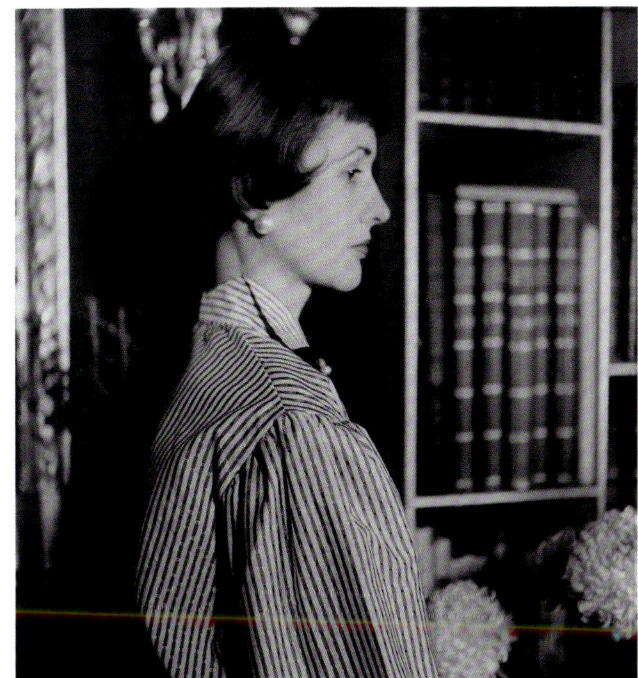

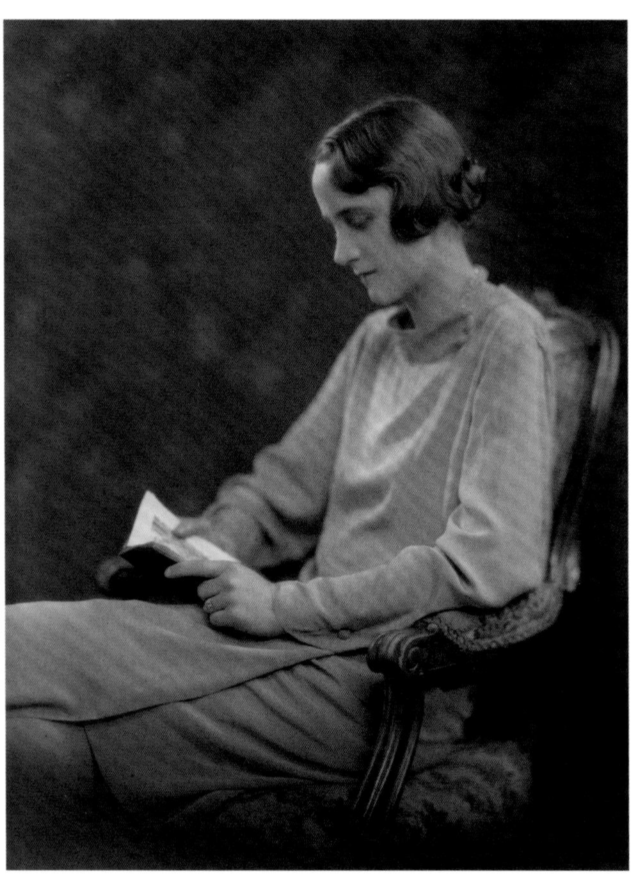

in fortune and posthumous reputations of their men. It was with this kind of misrepresentation in mind that, in 1948, Sir William James published a vindication of his grandmother Effie Gray, under the title *The Order of Release*. Here James spoke out against the false iterations of her relationship with her first husband that had inspired the 1912 silent film *The Love of John Ruskin*, in which the writer magnanimously offers Effie her freedom and then acts as Millais's best man at their wedding.[6] Drawing on the evidence provided by 633 letters that had come down through the family, James sought to give his grandmother a voice for the first time and present her as a sympathetic and intelligent woman, who had been wronged by the hagiography that had developed around her first husband. This was an important exception in a general tendency to keep women in the background; ten years later journalist Julia Greenwood complained that although much had been written about the likes of Elizabeth Siddal and Jane Morris, they remained silent presences, leaving the world none the wiser 'about what they thought about their angry young men'.[7]

The mention of angry young men conjures up the anti-establishment fervour of the 1950s and 1960s. This was the time when the Pre-Raphaelites were rediscovered as rebels and bohemians, the Victorian antecedents to the later counter-culture with its sexually liberated lifestyles and progressive sense of fashion. The 1960s was also the time when family papers were released into the public domain, giving scholars and biographers alike the opportunity to look at their subjects afresh. This process of reassessment was largely led by a group of women, sometimes referred as 'The Pre-Raphaelite Ladies', who attended to biographical and domestic details in seeking to animate the lives of key and marginal players in the movement. Key among the 'Ladies' was Diana Holman Hunt (ill. 138), whose twin biographies of her grandparents did much to desanctify Hunt and present him as a committed but flawed individual. Virginia Surtees (ill. 139), the great-granddaughter of Ruth Herbert, one of Rossetti's favourite models and Mary Lutyens (ill. 140) made up the trio. Her father, the architect Edwin Lutyens, had loathed John Ruskin, prompting her to read James's book before tracking down the Bowerswell Papers with the aim of telling the Gray–Ruskin–Millais story in full.[8]

Although recognised as professional writers, these women were also judged on their looks. Describing all three, journalist Ernestine Carter found them to be as visually attractive as their Victorian counterparts: Diana Holman Hunt being 'tall, with fluffy fair hair', Surtees, 'slender and dark' and Lutyens, 'slim, her soft grey hair curled under, page-boy style'.[9] To this group should be added the names of Rosalie Glynn Grylls (Lady Mander) and Mary Bennett, who were also looking in depth at the movement. As writers, these women were not seen to be challenging the status quo but employing 'feminine' skills of perception and empathy to present the women in more rounded terms. In this they were building on the work of earlier female writers with Pre-Raphaelite connections, notable among whom were Helen Rossetti Angeli, author of *Dante Gabriel Rossetti: His Friends and Enemies*, 1949; Violet Hunt, author of *The Wife of Rossetti*, 1932 (described as 'one of the first declaredly feminist biographies'), and the redoubtable Anna Maria Diana Wilhelmina Stirling (sister of Evelyn De Morgan and the longest-surviving member of the second generation), who was captured talking about her sister's work in Ken Russell's atmospheric 1961 BBC film *Old Battersea House*.

Employing different techniques, from detailed archival research to a reliance on memory and hearsay, 'The Pre-Raphaelite Ladies' succeeded in lending life to the silent Sisterhood. With her self-confessed ear for dialogue and a good sense of scene, Diana Holman Hunt was particularly bold in presenting the Pre-Raphaelites 'as sexually inquisitive as their King's Road counterparts today', as seen in her descriptions of Annie Miller, 'the notorious beauty', who dominates her story. Her focus on dysfunctional relationships and double standards of sexual morality set the tone for what was to follow in the 1970s. In biographies heavily indebted to the work of these writers, such as G.H. Fleming's 1967 *Rossetti and the Pre-Raphaelite Brotherhood*, Audrey Williamson's 1976 *Artists and Writers in Revolt* and Raleigh Trevelyan's 1978 *A Pre-Raphaelite Circle*, women were projected as the spur to male creativity while also being blamed for ruining their careers.

During the 1960s and 1970s the identity of the Pre-Raphaelite woman was increasingly distilled around the role of neurotic, invalid, victim or stunner, a tendency that owed much to the way the key dramatis personae were sensationalised in literary fiction and film – media that were instrumental in introducing the Pre-Raphaelites to a broader audience. Following on from his De Morgan film, Ken Russell produced his 1967 gothic biopic *Dante's Inferno* (centred on the complex relationship between Rossetti and a sickly Siddal). Piers Haggard's 1975 *The Love School* (ill.141), based on John Hale's eponymous novel, published the same year, later set the tone for the most recent Pre-Raphaelite romp, *Desperate Romantics* of 2009.[10] The heady mixture of sex, drugs, jealousy, passion and betrayal in these dramas fuelled interest in the women whose legendary looks were being perpetuated in fashion photography and through widespread reproduction in colour.

It was against this background that the Tate launched its 1984 *Pre-Raphaelites* exhibition, the largest survey of the movement ever presented, bringing together paintings and drawings executed by the four major artists involved in the period 1848–70 (Rossetti, Hunt, Millais and Madox Brown) and presenting them in strict chronological sequence. It deliberately excluded illustrations, photography and the applied arts in order to define Pre-Raphaelite practice exclusively in terms of the fine arts and to allow for stylistic comparison and pairing among the key players. With this focus there was little look-in for women other than as subjects of representation. In fact, of the 250 works in the show, only two-and-a-half were by a female artist: Elizabeth Siddal's *The Lady of Shalott* and *Lady Clare*, as well as *The Quest for the Holy Grail*, a watercolour she jointly authored with

140
**(Edith Penelope)
Mary Lutyens**
Lafayette, 1929
Whole plate film negative
National Portrait Gallery

141
**Sheila White as Annie
Miller and Bernard Lloyd
as William Holman Hunt
in *The Love School***
BBC TV still, 1975

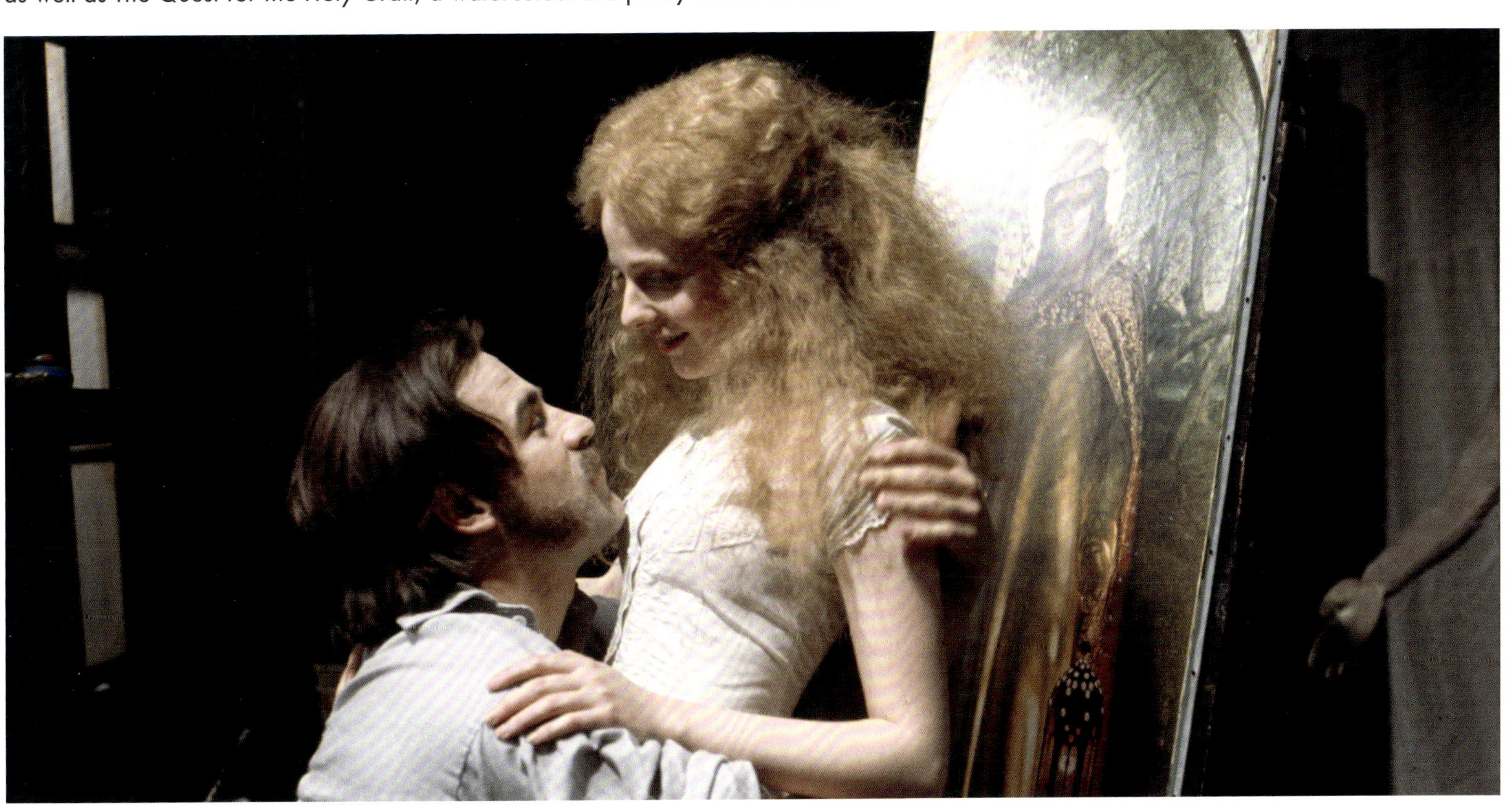

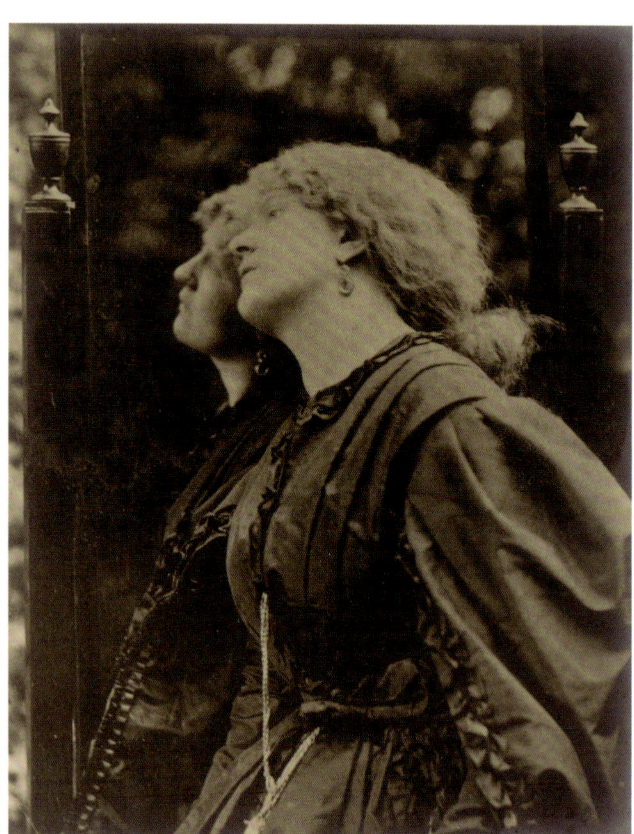

Rossetti. The omission of women had less to do with the availability of works than the overall presentation of Pre-Raphaelitism as a predominantly male movement, in which women served as a foil for male creativity.[11]

In this it represented the culmination of the narrative as it had developed in the twentieth century, with women positioned in relation to the Brotherhood and occupying an essentially decorative or supportive role. In the politically polarised climate of 1980s' Britain and the context of the Conservative Party's emphasis on 'Victorian Values', an undercurrent of moral disapproval set in, especially on the part of feminist writers and the liberal and left-wing press. Amid the general euphoria generated by the exhibition, some critics focused on the stifling effect Pre-Raphaelitism as an ideal had on female creativity, health and self-presentation, while an anonymous commentator in the *Guardian* noted: 'It is the image of emotional starvation, anorexic even, that has struck us most potently and damagingly... Even now when boyish super short hair is chic, the moony tresses hang around, and the fetish of long hair holds us in thrall.'[12]

The most forthright critique of the historiography of Pre-Raphaelitism came from within the realm of academia. One of the contributors to the exhibition catalogue, Deborah Cherry (of Manchester University), joined forces with Griselda Pollock (a lecturer at Leeds) to condemn the underlying patriarchal agenda of the exhibition. As the author of the two Siddal entries in the catalogue, Cherry was uncomfortable with the masculinist constructions of identity she believed had relegated Siddal to a subordinate position in the movement as follower and muse, while in her biographic entry she had played down Siddal's debt to Rossetti on the ground it diminished recognition of her as an artist in her own right. In their controversial essay 'Patriarchal Power and the Pre-Raphaelites', the authors effectively accused the Tate, as an organisation, of endorsing the dominant bourgeois, sexist and racist ideology of the nineteenth century, by systematically erasing issues of class, gender and race from the interpretation, and in perpetuating a well-worn narrative around the movement. Meanwhile, in another essay published that year, 'Woman as Sign in Pre-Raphaelite Literature', focusing on Elizabeth Siddal, they argued that the biographical tendency in art history had served to efface Siddal's identity so she could only exist as a sign of Rossetti's genius.[13]

In drawing attention to the way the history of Pre-Raphaelitism had been written to exclude and misrepresent women, Cherry and Pollock did not seek to redress the balance by proving the importance of Siddal as an artist in her own right. That task was left to other feminist scholars, who were generally content to operate within the biographic tradition with the aim of demythologising the lives of the women by casting a critical eye on the social and ideological values that had informed their representation in art and literature. Prominent among these was Jan Marsh's 1985 *The Pre-Raphaelite Sisterhood*, which was written with the aim of giving women agency in determining their own paths. In order to deliver the Sisters from what the dust jacket described as 'a century of masculine misrepresentation', Marsh set out to expose the difference between the way women such as Siddal, Jane Morris, Annie Miller, Georgiana Burne-Jones and Fanny Cornforth were represented in art and what they were really like.[14] Instead of being viewed as the stereotypical stunner, victim or 'other' to male creativity, each sister was discussed as an individual in her own right – Siddal as a talented artist, Miller as a woman with her own mind, and Burne-Jones as a figure of conviction, who became in her later years a committed socialist and pacifist.

In praising the bravado of *The Pre-Raphaelite Sisterhood*, the writer Hermione Lee nevertheless suspected there was something forced about its approach, in that the qualities Marsh detected in the Sisters, 'individualism, energy, resilience, talent and strongmindedness', were typically those one would expect of a twentieth-century heroine.[15] Writing in *New Society*, Peter Fuller

went even further in condemning Marsh for presenting Pre-Raphaelite women
'through the prism of a new mythology – that of her own brand of 1980s radical
feminism'. The very notion of a Sisterhood, or of women 'being proto-feminist',
he found as anachronistic as the expectation that Burne-Jones should have
behaved differently regarding his affair with Maria Zambaco or that he might
have opened his studio to his wife.[16]

It has often been said that each generation reinvents Pre-Raphaelitism through
the prism of its own preoccupations. During the heightened sexual politics of the
1980s, issues of gender came to the fore, polarising opinion in favour of the men
or women. With a growing emphasis on neglected female artists in the circle,
the main male players (with the exception of Morris) tended to be described
in negative terms as, for example, a 'Brotherhood of beastliness' or 'A brutish
band of brothers' for their callous treatment of their womenfolk, either trying to
refine and improve them, or marrying them and then lusting after other ladies.[17]
In reviewing Marsh's *Sisterhood*, Germaine Greer went so far as to argue that
the Pre-Raphaelite cult of ideal womanhood was ultimately damaging for women,
resulting in illness, self-destruction or, as was more often the case, a state of
internalised helplessness – conditions that became the focus of her 1995 polemic
Slip-Shod Sibyls.[18]

Recent biographies of the movement have struggled with the question of
whether women could ever have expected a fulfilling life within Pre-Raphaelitism.
Various attempts have been made to suggest more equal and more harmonious
working relationships. Elizabeth Siddal, the most tragic of the Sisters, has been at
the forefront in being rebranded an innovative artist in her own right: an amateur
who pushed further against academic convention than her male counterparts,
and who influenced Rossetti in her choice of bold colour and small simple,
flat compositions. Greater attention has been accorded women of the second
'feminist' generation, who were able to take advantage of the new educational
opportunities available to them to attain professional recognition and enjoy
equal working relationships with men. Joanna Boyce has been described as a
headstrong, highly respected artist, who achieved a reputation equal to that of her
husband Henry Tanworth Wells; Marie Spartali Stillman and Evelyn De Morgan
as able to engage in suffragist politics with the full support of their husbands.[19]

The sheer proliferation of literature and exhibitions concerning the Pre-
Raphaelite Sisters since the 1990s has helped redress the balance. Pre-Raphaelite
beauty and dress continues to inspire women in the creative industries with
performers such as Lily Cole and Florence Welch acknowledging their own
particular debt to its aesthetic. Probably the most significant shift has been
brought about by social media, with blogs and websites giving the women
a new kind of virtual existence and acting as an echo chamber in making their
hopes and aspirations resonate in the present day. For a younger generation the
Pre-Raphaelite woman is no longer a problem but a phenomenon that can be
enjoyed on both an intellectual and stylistic level: as a lesson in history and in self-
fashioning. The website Preraphaelitesisterhood.com, run by Stephanie Graham
Piña, proudly affirms:

> It took several types of women to develop the Pre-Raphaelite ideal; it takes
> women of all types to make up our world. Resist the narrow definition of
> being that society uses to define us. Embrace what you feel are your strengths
> and silence the negative voices that find fault. Look in the mirror, strike a pose
> and know that you are Beauty personified.[20]

In light of #MeToo and other campaigns for empowerment through empathy, this
kind of message might be seen to offer some kind of resolution to the tensions
described in this essay.

142
Fanny Cornforth
William Downey, copy by
Sanborn Studio, c.1863
Gelatin silver print of original
albumen print, 137 × 108mm
Delaware Art Museum

143 (below and p.180)
Florence Welch
Tom Beard, 2011
Glossy C-type colour print
450 × 540mm
National Portrait Gallery

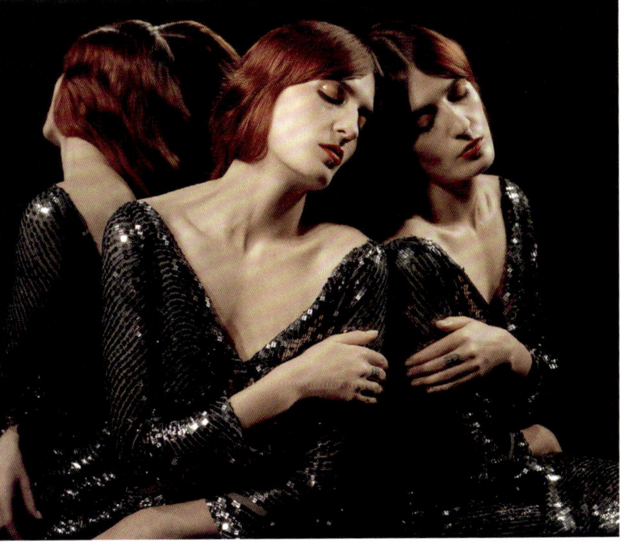

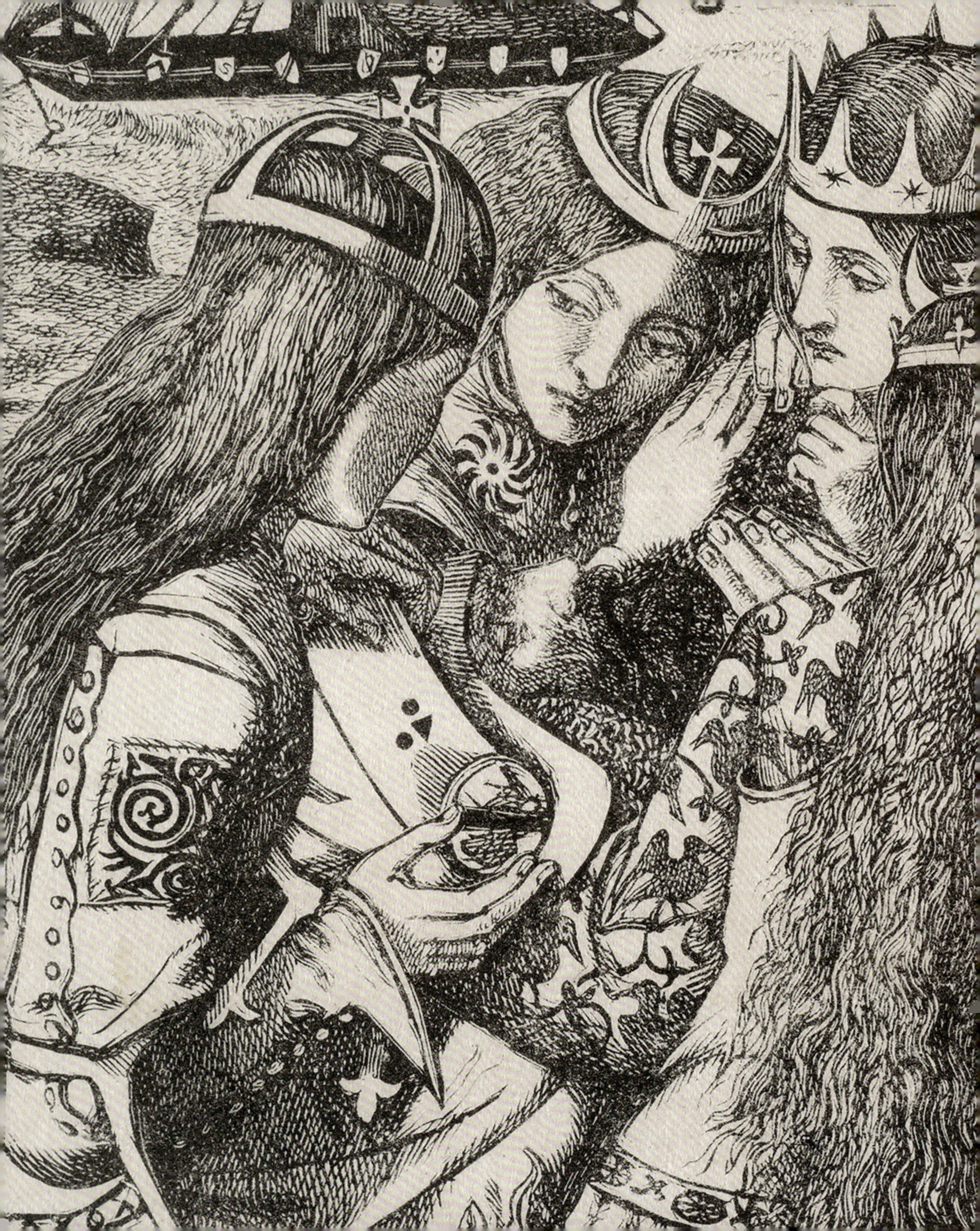

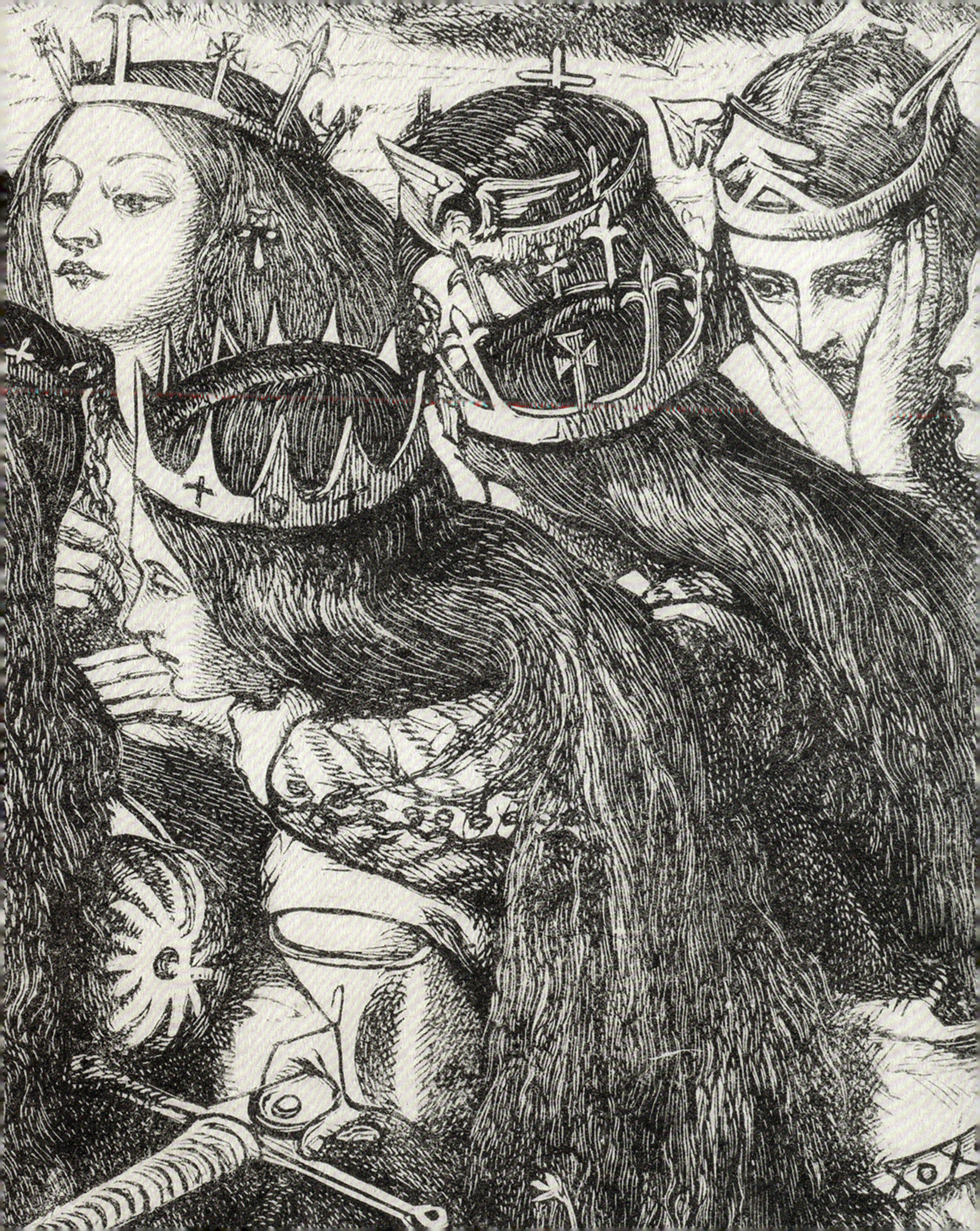

Notes

Introduction
1 Fredeman 1975, p.104
2 Cook and Wedderburn 1904, vol.xii, p.358
3 Fredeman 1975, p.99
4 EBJ to Helen Gaskell, c.1893, quoted in Wildman and Christian 1998, pp.170–1
5 Walter Pater, 'The School of Giorgione', 1877, in *Studies in the History of the Rennaisance*, 3rd Edition, 1888, p.134

Pre-Raphaelite Models
1 GPB, diary entry, 28 December 1859, Bradbury 2019, vol.1, p.28
2 Quoted in Surtees 1971, vol.1, p.370
3 Quoted in *the Guardian*, 20 January 2018, p.17
4 Hugh Kilmer, quoted by model Pegi Taylor, 'A View from the Platform', in Berk Jiminez 2001, p.3
5 BLS to Bessie Parkes, undated letter 1854, Princeton University Library
6 Ruskin, *Modern Painters*, 5 vols (George Allan, London, 1903), pp.623–4
7 Burne-Jones 1904, vol.1, p.217
8 Surtees 1981, pp.101, 184
9 JM to Theodore Watts-Dunton, 26 April 1888, Sharp and Marsh 2012, Letter no.150
10 Information from JBW, letter from Paris, 19 November 1855, Bradbury 2019, vol.1, p.302
11 JBW to HTW, 19 December 1856, Bradbury 2019, vol.1, p.502
12 JBW to HTW, 23 December 1856, Bradbury 2019, vol.1, p.504
13 Fig.4 from https://www.economics.ox.ac.uk/materials/papers/13260/jhreplacement.pdf (accessed 10.7.2019)
14 Arthur Munby, diary entry, Hudson 1972, 7 December 1860
15 See Foucart 1997
16 Furniss 1923, pp.102–3
17 De Montfort 2017, p.74 n.123
18 Oscar Wilde, 'London Models' in *English Illustrated Magazine* (January 1889), p.314
19 BLS, see n.5, Princeton University Library
20 See Burne-Jones 1904, vol.1, p.169, probably quoting actor Louisa Crabbe, a.k.a Ruth Herbert

Elizabeth Siddal
1 Arthur Hughes, quoted in Hill 1897, p.5
2 WHH in Hunt 1905, vol.1, p.198
3 *Sheffield Telegraph*, 28 February 1862, p.2
4 Ibid.
5 Fredeman 1975, p.50
6 Maas 2015, pp.38–59
7 Surtees 1971, #691, #691A, #691B
8 See DGR, *How They Met Themselves* (1860), Fitzwilliam Museum, Cambridge, 2300
9 Rossetti 1903, p.273
10 DGR to CGR, 4 August 1852, Fredeman 2001–12, letter 52:08
11 JEM to WHH, 4 November 1852, quoted in Holman-Hunt 1969, p.92
12 BLS to Bessie Parkes, May 1854, Girton College Cambridge
13 DGR to WA, 23 July 1854, Fredeman 2001–12, letter 54:55
14 Rossetti 1903, p.273
15 Ibid. ['one of Miss Siddal's best drawings, and in essence a very good one']
16 Ibid.
17 *Saturday Review*, 4 July 1857
18 Letter, 'Clerk Saunders' by Charles Fairfax Murray, affixed to the reverse of the work.
19 A.S', *Sheffield Telegraph*, 3 August 1911, p.942

20 E.E. Higgins, 8 April 1930, Violet Hunt Papers, Cornell University Library, New York
21 DGR to William Allingham, 29 November 1860, Fredeman 2001–12, letter 60:54
22 DGR to ACS, 1869, Fredeman 2001–12, letter 69:190

Christina Rossetti
1 CR to Caroline Gemmer, 27 June 1884, Harrison 2004, vol.3, p.196
2 CR to Amelia Heimann, Summer 1847, Harrison 2004, vol.1, p.3
3 FMB, diary entry, 6 August 1855, Surtees 1981, p.148
4 CR 'Tudor House', *Literary Opinion*, 1892, pp.127–9
5 CR to Charles Lutwidge Dodgson, November 1865, Harrison 2004, vol.1, p.257
6 CR to E.Gosse, 26 March 1884, Harrison 2004, vol.3, p.184
7 Stillman 1901, chapter XVI
8 CR to WMR, 1877, Harrison 2004, vol.2, p.138

Effie Gray Millais
1 EG to her parents, 2 June 1847, James 1948, p.36
2 EG to her parents, 5 May 1847, James 1948, p.30
3 JR to EG, 30 November 1847, James 1948, p.60
4 EG to her parents, 8 May 1848, James 1948, p.104
5 EG to her parents, quoted in James 1948, p.167
6 JR to EG, 30 November 1847, James 1948, pp.59–60
7 EG to her parents, undated from Venice, quoted in James 1948, p.152
8 EGM to her parents, 30 October 1850, quoted in James 1948, p.165
9 John Delane, 'Exhibition of the Royal Academy', *The Times*, 7 May 1851, p.8
10 John Ruskin, 'The Pre-Raffaelites', in *The Times*, 13 May 1851, p.8
11 John Ruskin, 'The Pre-Raphaelite Artists', in *The Times*, 30 May 1851, p.8
12 See McDonnell 1998, p.6
13 EGM to her parents, 20 March 1853, James 1948, p.197
14 EG to her father, 30 May 1853, James 1948, pp.201–2
15 JEM to EG's mother, 19 December 1853, James 1948, p.207
16 Millais 1899, vol.1, p.287
17 JEM, September 1874, Millais 1899, vol.1, p.429
18 Millais 1899, vol.1, p.288
19 EGM, diary entry, 1856, quoted in Cooper 2011, p.107
20 Millais 1899, vol.1, p.328
21 Millais 1899, vol.1, pp.328, 332
22 EGM quoted in Millais 1899, vol.1, pp.328–9
23 Millais 1899, vol.1, p.373; portrait of EGM (1878) in Millais 1899, vol.2; Two figure studies: BM 1997,0712.62 and Christie's, 3 September 2013, #393
24 Cooper 2011, p.165
25 Unnamed acquaintance, quoted in Cooper 2011, p.165

Brotherhoods & Artistic Masculinities
1 Fredeman 1975, p.3
2 Morowitz and Vaughan 2000, p.5
3 Fredeman 1975, p.xix
4 Vaughan 2015, p.118
5 Ibid., p.125
6 Spielmann 1896, p.xvi
7 Lang 1881, p.15
8 For a discussion of Millais's manly image and his portraits of Gladstone, see Funnell, 1999; and on Gladstone's portraits, see Windscheffel 2007
9 Vaughan 2015, p.120
10 H.C.G. Matthew, 'Portraits of Men: Millais and Victorian Public Life', in Funnell and Warner 1999, p.141

ACS   Algernon Charles Swinburne
BLS   Barbara Leigh Smith Bodichon
CR   Christina Georgina Rossetti
DGR   Dante Gabriel Rossetti
DHH   Diana Holman-Hunt
EBJ   Edward Burne-Jones
EDM   Evelyn De Morgan
EG/EGM   Effie Gray Millais
FC   Fanny Cornforth
FGS   Frederic George Stephens
FMB   Ford Madox Brown
GBJ   Georgiana Burne-Jones
GPB   George Price Boyce
HTW   Henry Tanworth Wells
JBW   Joanna Boyce Wells
JEM   John Everett Millais
JM   Jane Morris
JR   John Ruskin
MSS   Marie Spartali Stillman
MTZ/MZ   Maria Zambaco
PRB   Pre-Raphaelite Brotherhood
WA   William Allingham
WDM   William De Morgan
WHH   William Holman Hunt
WMR   William Michael Rossetti

11 See Rosenfeld 2000; ibid. for reproductions of the Nazarene portraits (figs 0.1, 2.2 and 2.5 respectively)
12 See Malcolm Warner's account of the painting in Warner 1997
13 Rosenfeld 2000, p.76
14 DGR to Thomas Woolner, 1 January 1853, Fredeman 2001–12, vol.1, letter 53:1, p.224. For an authoritative account of the episode, see Ormond 1967, pp.25–7
15 Hunt 1905, vol.1, p.34
16 As recorded in Millais 1899, vol.1, pp.81–2
17 MacCarthy 2011, p.15 and passim
18 See MacCarthy 1994, pp.163–4 and Amy Bingaman, 'The Business of Brotherhood: Morris, Marshall, Faulkner & Company and the Pre-Raphaelite Culture of Youth' in Morowitz and Vaughan 2000, esp. pp.98–9

Annie Miller
1 See auction sale, Dix Noonan Webb, Medals & Militaria, 27 September 2017, lot 136
2 WHH to FGS, 15 February 1861, Bodleian, Oxford, MS Don.e.66
3 Tate 1984, no.39
4 See auction sale, Christie's, 'Defining British Art', 30 June 2016, lot 17, entry by Jason Rosenfeld
5 Lutyens 1967, p.150
6 Bradbury 2019, vol.2, p.1019
7 FMB, diary entry, 6 July 1856, Surtees 1981, p.181
8 Untraced; completed with Millais's assistance; image http://www.the-athenaeum.org/art/detail.php?ID=281489 (accessed 10.7.2019)
9 Hunt 1905, vol.2, p.83
10 WHH to FGS, 15 February 1861, Bodleian MS Don.e.66
11 Bradbury 2019, vol.2, p.1019
12 Fredeman 2001–12, vol.2, p.290, n.1
13 Quoted in Holman-Hunt 1969, p.177
14 Ibid., pp.198–9
15 Bradbury 2019, vol.2, p.1031
16 Bradbury 2019, vol.2, pp.1030–31
17 *Valley of the Lledr*, unlocated; see Bradbury 2019, vol.2, p.1038
18 FGS, 15 November 1861, Bodleian Library, Oxford, MS Don e.66
19 Bradbury 2019, vol.2, p.1064
20 GPB, diary entry, 13 March 1863, Bradbury 2019, vol.2, p.1067
21 Jan Marsh, 'Rossetti's Helen of Troy: Some Questions' (April 2018) https://www.academia.edu/36376076/rossettis_helen_of_troy_some_questions (accessed 5.7.2019)
22 DGR, 12 March 1866 and JEM, both quoted in Holman-Hunt 1969, p.247–8
23 *The Standard*, 26 February 1863, p.3
24 Clodd 1916, p.200

Fanny Cornforth
1 As recorded verbatim by Samuel Bancroft Jnr to Caroline Kipling, 2 April 1899, Delaware Art Museum Mss. Other biographical information from Whittick, Christopher, 'Cornforth, Fanny [Sarah Cox] (1835–c.1906)', *Oxford Dictionary of National Biography* (Oxford University Press, 2004)
2 GPB, diary entry, 16 December 1858, Bradbury 2019, vol.2, p.1026
3 GPB, diary entry, 16 December 1858, Bradbury 2019, vol.2, p.1026
4 GPB, diary entry, 15 December 1858, Bradbury 2019, vol.2, p.1026
5 GPB, diary entry, 11 February 1859, Bradbury 2019, vol.2, p.1029

6 ACS to W.B. Scott, 16 December 1859, Lang 1959, vol.1, p.27
7 Rossetti 1895, vol.1, p.203
8 GPB, diary entry, 5 June 1860, Bradbury 2019, vol.2, p.1040
9 GPB, diary entry, 13 November 1862, Bradbury 2019, vol.2, p.1065
10 GPB, diary entry, 7 December 1862, Bradbury 2019, vol.2, p.1066
11 WHH to Thomas Combe, 12 Feb 1860, Bodleian, Oxford, MS Eng. lett.c.296
12 DGR to FMB, April 1865, Fredeman 2001–12, letter 65:66
13 WA, diary entry, 27 June 1864, Allingham 1907, pp.100–01
14 Rossetti 1895, vol.1, p.202
15 FC to DGR, 24 September 1877, British Library MSS Ashley 3845
16 DGR to John Schott, 24 September 1881, Fredeman 2001–12, letter 81:416
17 Graylingwelll Hospital Archive, West Sussex Record Office

Joanna Boyce Wells
1 Matthias Boyce to JBW, 16 August 1854, Bradbury 2019, vol.1, p.146
2 JBW to GPB, 2 October 1852, Bradbury 2019, vol.1, p.90
3 JBW, diary entry, 22 February 1852, Bradbury 2019, vol.1, p.81
4 JBW, diary entry, 9 April 1852, Bradbury 2019, vol.1, p.83
5 JBW, diary entry, 3 April 1853, Bradbury 2019, vol.1, p.95
6 JBW, diary entry, 2 October 1852, Bradbury 2019, vol.1, p.89
7 John Ruskin, 'Academy Notes 1855', in Cook and Wedderburn 1904, vol.xiv, p.30
8 JBW, diary entry, 26 March 1854, Bradbury 2019, vol.1, p.124
9 JBW, diary entry, 1 May 1854, Bradbury 2019, vol.1, p.126
10 JBW, diary entry, 4 April 1854, Bradbury 2019, vol.1, p.125
11 JBW, diary entry, 26 April 1854, Bradbury 2019, vol.1, p.126
12 JBW, diary entry, 8 September 1854, Bradbury 2019, vol.1, p.164
13 Spencer Hall to JBW, 9 May 1855, Bradbury 2019, vol.1, p.44
14 HTW to JBW, 9 July 1855, Bradbury 2019, vol.1, p.222
15 HTW to JBW, 19 July 1855, Bradbury 2019, vol.1, p.230
16 JBW to HTW, 20 July 1855, Bradbury 2019, vol.1, p.232
17 GPB to JMB, 13 April 1856, Bradbury 2019, vol.1, p.397
18 JBW to HTW, 15 November 1855, Bradbury 2019, vol.1, p.299
19 JBW to HTW, 19 November 1855, Bradbury 2019, vol.1, p.302
20 JBW to HTW, 24 December 1855, Bradbury 2019, vol.1, p.328
21 JBW to HTW, 22 February 1856; and to her mother, 26 February 1856, Bradbury 2019, vol.1, pp.368, 371
22 GPB to JBW, 13 April 1856, Bradbury 2019, vol.1, p.397
23 *Saturday Review*, 1 December 1855
24 *Saturday Review*, 29 December 1855, quoted in Bradbury 2012, p.116

25 JBW to HTW, 13 April 1856, Bradbury 2019, vol.1, p.394
26 JBW to GPB, 6 May 1856, Bradbury 2019, vol.1, p.406
27 *Saturday Review*, 21 June 1856
28 JBW to HTW, 10 February 1857, Bradbury 2019, vol.1, p.529
29 JBW to HTW, 5 August 1857, Bradbury 2012, vol.1, pp.428–90
30 HTW to GPB, 24 Nov 1857, Bradbury 2019, vol.1, pp.604, 647
31 *Saturday Review*, 2 June 1860, p.709
32 HTW to GPB, 19 September 1858, Bradbury 2019, vol.1, p.692
33 *The Spectator*, 19 November 1859, quoted in Bradbury 2019, vol.1, p.747
34 JMW to HTW, 19 August 1859, Bradbury 2019, vol.1, p.733
35 JBW to HTW, uncertain date March–April 1860; JBW to GPB, 16 May 1860, Bradbury 2019, vol.1, pp.759–60, 762
36 Bradbury 2019, vol.1, p.837
37 DGR quoted in Stillman 1901, vol.2, chapter xxiv
38 Rossetti 1905, vol.1, p.154
39 DGR to James Leathart, 27 July 1861, Fredeman 2001–12, letter 61:52

Beyond the Parlour
1 Howitt 1853, preface 3
2 Bradbury 2012, pp.101–8
3 A portfolio circulated within the group, with each contributing artist inserting a piece of their own work for mutual criticism; though poorly documented, this project seems to have been active during 1853–4
4 See Cherry 2000; Marsh 1989; Flanders 2001
5 For instance, the two watercolour societies and the Society of British Artists exhibitions were for members; in most provincial cities, a membership-based organisation would be the exhibiting body. See Nunn 1987; Cherry 1993
6 Carpenter and Ward were seen as academic painters: see Nunn 1995. For the artists associated with Pre-Raphaelitism, see Marsh and Nunn 1997
7 See Pamela Gerrish Nunn, 'The Needle and the Brush: A Victorian Drama', *E-Rea*, vol.16, no.1 (2018), pp.1–31
8 Coventry Patmore, 'A Pre-Raphaelite Exhibition', *Saturday Review*, vol.4, no.88 (4 July 1857), pp.11–12; It is evident from unpublished correspondence in the Boyce/Wells family that Boyce's participation was also intended
9 For the context to, and specific aspects of, this phenomenon, see Pamela Fletcher and Anne Helmreich, eds, *The Rise of the Modern Art Market in London 1850–1939* (Manchester University Press, 2011)
10 In the lecture 'Of Queen's Gardens', published under the title *Sesame and Lilies*, 1865; see Pamela Gerrish Nunn, 'The "Woman Question": Ruskin and the Female Artist', in Robert Hewison, ed., *Ruskin's Artists* (Ashgate, Aldershot, 2000), pp.167–84
11 See Virginia Surtees, ed., *Sublime and Instructive* (Michael Joseph, London, 1972)
12 This is a routine element of Howitt's (admittedly, poorly documented) professional biography: with some authority, it appears in the artist's mother's autobiography (Mary Howitt and Margaret Howitt, *Mary Howitt: An Autobiography* (William Isbister, London, 1889), p.117; see Pamela Gerrish Nunn, *Canvassing: Recollections by Six Women Artists* (London, Camden Press, 1986), pp.19–25

13 Dianne Sachko Macleod, *Art and the Victorian Middle Class: Money and the Making of Identity* (Cambridge University Press, Cambridge, 1996)

14 Bodichon had solo exhibitions in various commercial galleries in 1859, 1861, 1864 and 1865; in 1874 she exhibited to the public in her own home

15 Bodichon to Marian Lewes, 1 July 1859, quoted in Pam Hirsch, *Barbara Leigh Smith Bodichon* (Chatto and Windus, London, 1998), p.166

16 See Susan P. Casteras and Colleen Denney, *The Grosvenor Gallery: A Palace of Art in Victorian England* (Yale University Press, New Haven and London, 1996); Christopher Newell, *The Grosvenor Gallery Exhibitions: Change and Continuity in the Victorian Art World* (Cambridge University Press, Cambridge, 1995)

17 'The Grosvenor Gallery', *Art Journal*, vol.43, (1881), p.189

18 A *Christian Martyr*, for instance, shown at the 1882 Grosvenor exhibition, measures 2160 x 910mm; *By the Waters of Babylon*, at the 1883 exhibition, measures 895 x 1667mm

19 Meaghan Clarke, *Critical Voices: Women and Art Criticism in Britain 1880–1905* (Ashgate, Aldershot, 2005)

20 'Women as Artists', *The Spectator*, 29 July 1876, p.956

21 See Alicia Foster, *Tate Women Artists* (Tate Publishing, London, 2004)

22 See Jane Sellars, *Women's Works* (National Museums and Galleries on Merseyside, Liverpool, 1988); Birmingham was another city favouring Pre-Raphaelitism, where Kate (1856–1927) and Myra Bunce (1854–1919) flourished

Fanny Eaton
Our thanks to Brian Eaton for contributing his account of researching his ancestor's biography

1 *Athenaeum*, 18 May 1861

2 *Illustrated London News*, 23 June 1860, p.595

3 The text is from Matthew 13: 45–46: 'The kingdom of heaven is like a merchant seeking beautiful pearls, who, when he had found one pearl of great price, went and sold all that he had and bought it'

4 Victoria and Albert Museum, London, V&A 268-1895

5 DGR to FMB, 28 August 1865, Fredeman 2001–12, letter 65:124

6 William Blake Richmond, *The Slave* (undated), Tate Collection #T06966

7 Edwin Long, *Uncle Tom and Little Eva* (1866), Russell-Cotes Art Gallery and Museums, Bournemouth

8 Ferrari 2014, p.16

Jane Morris
1 Bequeathing the painting to the nation in 1910, Morris identified the correct title as *La Belle Iseult*; subsequently it was erroneously identified as *Queen Guinevere*

2 ACS to Edwin Hatch, 17 February 1858, Lang 1959, vol.1, p.18

3 JM to May Morris, c.1909, Sharp and Marsh 2012, letter no.495

4 Ibid.

5 DGR, 'The Stream's Secret'

6 Legally possible only in very restricted cases and customarily removing a womans' access to her children.

7 CR, 'An Echo from Willowwood'

8 Henry James to Fanny Kemble, 24 March 1881, *Letters of Henry James*, 1980, p.352

9 Swanwick 1935, p.101

10 JM to Cormell Price, 26 February 1907, Sharp and Marsh 2012, letter no.458

11 JM to W.S. Blunt, 23 December 1908, Sharp and Marsh 2012, letter no.485

Georgiana Burne-Jones
1 Then located in Kensington Gore; see Burne-Jones 1904, vol.1, p.142

2 Burne-Jones 1904, vol.1, p.169

3 John Ruskin, 'On Colour and Composition', in John Ruskin *The Elements of Drawing* (Smith, Elder and Co., London, 1857), p.213

4 See Bradbury 2019, vol. 1, p.200

5 Burne-Jones 1904, vol.1, p.204

6 Ibid., p.210

7 Ibid., p.140

8 Burne-Jones 1904, vol.2, p.5

9 See Surtees 1971, p.276

10 Quoted in Burne-Jones 1904, vol.1, pp.220–21

11 Ibid., p.217

12 DGR to Alexander Gilchrist, Fredeman 2001–12, letter 61:15

13 EBJ quoted in Burne-Jones 1904, vol.1, p.245

14 JR to GBJ, quoted in Burne-Jones 1904, vol.1, p.233

15 Burne-Jones 1904, vol.1, p.236

16 Ibid., p.218

17 Ibid., p.266

18 Angela Thirkell, review of E.P. Thompson's *William Morris*, in *Library Review*, autumn 1955, p.131

19 EBJ's list of pictures for 1883 includes an entry 'Began a portrait of Georgie with Phil and Margaret in background'

20 Burne-Jones 1904, vol.1, p.142

21 Edith Macdonald, *Annals of the Macdonald Family* (Horace Marshall & Son, London, 1923), p.38

22 Burne-Jones 1904, vol.1, p.218

Model Wives & Mistresses
1 Burne-Jones 1904, vol.2, pp.310–11

2 Among much coverage in the new illustrated periodicals, Maurice B. Adams, 'Artists' Homes', serialised in *Building News*, was published in book form (B.T. Batsford Ltd., London, 1883)

3 See Canziani 1939, p.68

4 In a portrait photograph (NPG P301(37)) Effie Millais wears the embroidered coat used in *Peace Concluded* (1856), *Apple Blossoms* (1857) and in the painted illustration to Moore's *Lalla Rookh* (1872)

5 Millais 1899, vol.1, pp.287 ff

6 The Roberson archive is held by the Hamilton-Kerr Institute in Cambridge

7 Oswald Doughty and John Robert Wahl, eds, *Letters of Dante Gabriel Rossetti*, 4 vols (Clarendon Press, Oxford, 1965–7), vol.1, p.249, letter 202, Friday 13 April 1855. Emma Madox Brown was Lizzie's friend and champion, providing a refuge in her troubled relationship with DGR

8 Burne-Jones 1904, vol.1, p.233

9 Ibid, pp.235–6

10 Isabella Beeton, *Mrs Beeton's Book of Household Management* (S.O. Beeton, London, 1861) pp.225–6

11 J. Comyns Carr, *Some Eminent Victorians: Personal Recollections in the World of Art and Letters* (Duckworth & Co., London, 1908), p.74

12 With the exception of JEM, few of the men in this circle paid attention to 'Show Sunday', informal 'open days' that preceded the Summer Exhibition at the Royal Academy. The crush of visitors would have been far beyond the resources of their housekeeping, with some popular studios receiving many hundreds of visitors

13 Several of DGR's male friends were aware of his domestic arrangements, although Fanny Cornforth's position in Rossetti's household was notionally a secret

14 Baum 1940, p.74 and passim

15 The vast sales figures for *Mrs Beeton's Book of Household Management* (468,000 copies sold by 1888) are a measure of the success of this type of instruction

16 Pendry, the studio man, a dwarfish figure and a great comedian, who stoked the furnace and cleaned brushes and palette, features in T.M. Rooke's record of his conversations with Burne-Jones, see Lago 1981 and in Angela Thirkell, *Three Houses* (Oxford University Press, Oxford, 1931), pp.19–20

17 Lago 1981, pp.53, 95

18 Both MSS and EDM suffered the embarrassment of being chaperoned by family members or servants

19 Marsh 1986, p.44; see also Marsh 1985, p.196

20 See Catherine White, 'May Morris and her Embroiderers' in Lynn Hulse, ed., *May Morris: Art & Life, New Perspectives* (William Morris, London, 2017), pp.64 ff

21 See Charlotte Gere, *Artistic Circles: Design and Decoration in the Aesthetic Movement* (V&A Publishing, London, 2010), pp.168–9

22 Census return, 1891; see also Society of Antiquaries, *Kelmscott Manor & Estate, Conservation Management Plan*, November 2013

23 Sharp and Marsh 2012, letter 238, 30 July 1898, p.244

24 CR to Caroline Gemmer, 4 July 1881, Harrison 2004, vol.2, letter 914, p.280

25 Ibid. It is apparent that the washing was sent out: the back-up trades and occupations local to the houses of the gentry included washerwoman or laundress, mangler, clear-starcher and ironing woman

26 CR to Caroline Gemmer, 2 January 1875, after the marriage of WMR to Lucy Madox Brown in March 1874, Harrison 2004, vol.2, letter 584, p.35

27 Burne-Jones 1904, vol 1, p.204

28 Ibid, p.298

29 Mary Elia Haweis, 'Pre-Raphaelite Dress', *The Queen*, 9 January 1878

30 Bryson and Troxell, 1965, pp.3–4

31 Lawrence Alma-Tadema's collection of valuable antique and Oriental textiles and costume made up the largest section of his posthumous sale. Seymour Lucas's collection was regarded as so significant that it was purchased by the London Museum in 1929 for the then substantial sum of £1,000. Five items of eighteenth-century dress in the V&A's collection were bought in the 1898 studio sale of the watercolourist Charles Green

32 Letter from DGR to JM, 26 February 1880, quoted in Bryson and Troxell 1976, p.141

33 Ibid, pp.106–7

34 Surtees 1980, pp.42, 53, 97n15. GPB had a collection of old and ethnic jewellery, pieces from which were lent to the 1872 South Kensington Loan Exhibition. DGR left instructions that JM should have anything she wanted of his costume jewellery. Gifts from Rossetti included a Burmese bracelet similar to the one worn as Mariana. The collection descended to May Morris and is now in the V&A

35 Millais 1899, vol.1, pp.93–4; Millais wrote to Thomas Combe in March 1852: 'Today I have purchased a really splendid lady's ancient dress – all flowered over in silver embroidery – and I am going to paint it for "Ophelia". You may imagine it is something rather good when I tell you it cost me, old and dirty as it is, four pounds.' (Millais 1899, vol.1, p.162)

36 The lace may be part of the costume she wears in her first photograph, a daguerreotype taken in London in 1851. See Lutyens 1965, pp.77, 210

37 Mary Eliza Haweis, prolific author in instruction on dress and decorating, was the daughter of a minor genre painter and portraitist, Thomas Musgave Joy; Mrs Orrinsmith, contributor to the popular series, 'Art at Home', was the wife of a stained-glass designer

associated with William Morris; Mrs Panton was the daughter of W.P. Frith. For an account of this publishing phenomenon, see Judith A. Neiswander, *The Cosmopolitan Interior: Liberalism and the British Home, 1870–1914* (Yale University Press, London, 2008), ch.IV

Maria Zambaco

1   EBJ to Helen Gaskell, c.1893, quoted in Wildman and Christian 1998, pp.170–71
2   Christie's, 19 November 1965, lot 52
3   Du Maurier 1951, p.20
4   Commissioned by Euphrosyne Cassavetti. The prime version is now in the British Museum (ill. 108). According to a list compiled by EBJ in 1872, another copy was purchased by Marie Spartali, or her father, which is perhaps that dated 1867 in the Cecil French collection, London Borough of Hammersmith and Fulham
5   Burne-Jones 1904, vol.1, p.309
6   EBJ to George Howard, c. November 1867, Castle Howard Collection, York, MS J22/27/343
7   Hannah Macdonald's diary, cited in MacCarthy 2011, p.209
8   DGR to FMB, 23 January 1869, Fredeman 2001–12, letter 69:9
9   DGR to JM, 4 March 1870, Fredeman 2001–12, letter 70:41
10   Wildman and Christian 1998, p.111
11   WMR, diary entry 1905, 26 December 1870, Bornand 1977, p.37
12   EBJ to Helen Gaskell, 1893, quoted in Wildman and Christian 1998, p.171
13   Oscar Wilde, 'The Grosvenor Gallery', *Dublin University Magazine*, July 1877, http://fullonlinebook.com/essays/the-grosvenor-gallery-1877/dyh.html (accessed 10.7.2019)
14   EBJ to May Gaskell 1890s, quoted in MacCarthy 2011, p.242
15   DGR to JM, 7 Oct 1879, Fredeman 2001–12, letter 79:165; Elliott 2006, pp.157–8 states that Zambaco's new partner was a Greek surnamed Sios, whom she married in Paris in 1891
16   Both are currently untraced
17   MTZ to Auguste Rodin, 17 March 1888, Musee Rodin D3740. The letter is overlaid with his pencil sketches of marble mouldings
18   John L. Sweeney (ed.), *Henry James: The Painter's Eye* (Madison, Univ of Wisconsin Press, 1989), p.207
19   EBJ to MZ, 3 February 1888, Dreweatts sale, 15 March 2016, lot 104
20   Shonfield 1987, pp.110–11

Marie Spartali Stillman

1   Henry James, 'Art', *Atlantic Monthly* (1875), p.119
2   WMR, 'Fine Art Gossip', *Athenaeum* (13 February 1869)
3   MSS to William Graham, Sept 1870 or 1871, BL Add 48215, f.289
4   *Saturday Review*, 23 February 1867, p.236
5   MSS to Samuel Bancroft Jnr, 19 September 1903, Delaware Art Museum
6   DGR to Frederick Leyland, 27 July 1869, Fredeman 2001–12, letter 69:95
7   Quoted in Spanton 1927, p.83
8   MSS to Debbie Peacock, 10 June 1906, Delaware Art Museum
9   MSS to W.S. Blunt, 31 January 1890, Fitzwilliam Museum, Cambridge, MS 622-1927
10   As yet only partially deciphered
11   Harvard University, Fogg Art Museum, 1943.453
12   DGR to C.F. Murray, 4 January 1880, Fredeman 2001–12, letter 80:04

13   W.J. and Mrs M Stillman, ('Both or either or survivor') account with Barings Bank, London, 11 November 1880, ING Archive. The receipt, from R.B. Litchfield, of the Working Men's College, corresponds to the price asked for The Wreath of Roses, exhibited in Manchester in September 1880 (60 guineas) plus framing. Our thanks to the ING Archivist for bringing this account to our attention
14   EBJ to MSS, c.1890, William J. Stillman, collection Union College, Schnectady
15   MSS to Effie Stillman, quoted in Frederick and Marsh 2015, p.62
16   MSS to W.S. Blunt, 15 October 1890, Fitzwilliam Museum, Cambridge, MS 622-1927
17   MSS to Vernon Lee, 19 September 1901, Somerville College, Oxford
18   JM to W.S. Blunt, 16 November 1891; Sharp and Marsh 2012, letter 210
19   MSS to Samuel Bancroft Jnr, 8 February 1905, Delaware Art Museum

Evelyn De Morgan

1   Russell-Cotes Art Gallery, Bournemouth; see Stirling 1922, p.192
2   Possibly Dorothy Tennant, quoted in Stirling 1922, p.179
3   E.J. Poynter, quoted in Smith 2002, p.23
4   EDM to J.R. Spencer Stanhope, quoted in Stirling 1922, p.195
5   William Blake Richmond, quoted in Stirling 1922, p.11
6   Stirling 1922, p.12
7   May Morris, quoted in Stirling 1922, p.192
8   G.F. Watts, quoted in Stirling 1922, p.193
9   EBJ diary entry, 12 June 1897 after visit to EDM and WDM. EDM is not mentioned by name but the description of one work containing a fig tree and a knight and a lady in an allegory ('Life and Aspiration I think it was called') is clearly an account of *Life and Thought have Gone Away* (1893, exh. 1901), quoted in Lago 1981, pp.148–50
10   JM to WDM 15 July 1907, Sharp and Marsh 2012, p.461
11   WDM to May Morris, 1914, quoted in Stirling 1922, pp.352–3
12   WDM quoted in Smith 2002, p.179
13   A nude study for the picture not drawn from JM indicates that ill.121 [the present work] was probably executed in EDM's studio, as it shows the same armchair

The Sisterhood & its Afterlife

1   See, for example, Richard Dorment, 'The Pre-Raphaelite Sisterhood', *Daily Telegraph*, 20 January 1998 (reviewing Manchester City Art Gallery's 1998 exhibition Pre-Raphaelite Women Artists); Jackie Wullschlager, 'Uncommon threads', *Financial Times*, 15 September 2012, p.13; Alastair Smart, 'Back to the Future', *Sunday Telegraph*, 16 September 2012, p.20 (both reviewing Tate's 2012 Pre-Raphaelites: Victorian Avant-Garde)
2   Elaine Showalter, 'Towards a Feminist Poetics', in Mary Jacobs, ed., *Women Writing and Writing about Women* (Croom Helm Ltd, London, 1979), pp.22–41
3   Millais 1899; Hunt 1905; Burne-Jones 1904; M.S. Watts, *George Frederic Watts: The Annals of an Artist's Life*, 3 vols (Macmillan, London, 1912)
4   9 September 1927; Michael Davie, ed., *The Diaries of Evelyn Waugh* (Weidenfeld & Nicolson, London, 1976), p.289
5   Timothy Hilton's *The Pre-Raphaelites* (Thames & Hudson, London, 1970) might be said to represent the culmination of this approach.

6   James 1948, pp.1–2
7   Julia Greenwood, 'Young and Angry, Then as Now', *Listener*, 3 July 1958, p.13
8   Holman-Hunt 1960 and Holman-Hunt 1969; Surtees 1971; Lutyens 1967. The Bowerswell Papers are family letters ranging from the childhood of Effie Gray until after her marriage to Millais
9   Ernestine Carter, 'Pre-Raphaelite Ladies', *Sunday Times*, 5 October 1969, p.61
10   Discussed in Chloe Johnson, 'Presenting the Pre-Raphaelites: From Radio Reminiscences to Desperate Romantics', *Visual Culture in Britain*, vol.11, no.1 (2010), pp.67–92
11   It would appear that women were better represented in the Pre-Raphaelite exhibitions held earlier in the century. For example, the Tate 1923 Loan Exhibition of Paintings and Drawings from the 1860s Period featured 33 works by women, while the 1948 Whitechapel Pre-Raphaelites exhibition included six works by Siddal
12   'O tempora O mores', *Guardian*, 15 March 1984, p.12
13   Deborah Cherry and Griselda Pollock, 'Patriarchal Power and the Pre-Raphaelites', *Art History*, vol.7, no.4 (December 1984), pp.480–95; 'Woman as Sign in Pre-Raphaelite Literature: a study of the representation of Elizabeth Siddall', *Art History*, vol.7, no.2 (June 1984), pp.202–25. In rejecting what they believed to be a patriarchal construction of identity, Cherry and Pollock opted to call Siddal by her family name Siddall, not the spelling offered by Rossetti
14   Text on the back cover of Jan Marsh, *The Pre-Raphaelite Sisterhood*, 1992 edition
15   Hermione Lee, 'Dream of Fair Women', *Observer*, 8 September 1985, p.21
16   Peter Fuller, 'The Stunners', *New Society*, 20 September 1985, pp.423–4
17   Nigella Lawson, 'Brotherhood of Beastliness', *The Times*, 1 April 1989, p.36; Bevis Hillier, 'A Brutish Band of Brothers', *The Spectator*, 1 July 1989, p.21 (both reviewing Gay Daly's 1989 The Pre-Raphaelites in Love)
18   Germaine Greer, 'Sex and the Sisterhood', *London Standard*, 4 September 1985 (on Marsh's The Pre-Raphaelite Sisterhood)
19   See, for example, Bradbury 2012; Lucy Ella Rose, *Suffragist Artists in Partnership: Gender, Word and Image* (Edinburgh University Press, Edinburgh, 2018)
20   Preraphaelitesisterhood.com: Ars Longa Vita Brevis. See also, Kirsty Stonell Walker, 'The Kissed Mouth', fannycornforth.blogspot.com

Select Bibliography

Allingham 1907
Helen Allingham, ed., *William Allingham: A Diary 1824–1889* (Macmillan, London, 1907 and 2nd edn 1985)

Ando 2016
Tomoko Ando, Rodin's Reputation in Great Britain: The Neglected Role of Alphonse Legros, *Nineteenth-Century Art Worldwide*, http://www.19thc-artworldwide.org/autumn16/ando-on-rodin-reputation-in-great-britain-neglected-role-of-alphonse-legros (accessed 14.7.2019)

Atwood 1986
Philip Attwood, 'Maria Zambaco: Femme Fatale of the Pre-Raphaelites', *Apollo*, no.124 (July 1986), pp.31–7

Atwood 1990
Philip Attwood, 'The Stillmans and the Morrises', *Journal of the William Morris Society*, vol.9, no.1 (Autumn 1990), pp.23–8

Barringer et al. 2012
Tim Barringer, Jason Rosenfeld, Alison Smith, *Pre-Raphaelites: Victorian Avant-Garde* (Tate Publishing, London, 2012)

Baum 1940
Paul Franklin Baum, ed., *Dante Gabriel Rossetti's Letters to Fanny Cornforth* (John Hopkins Press, Baltimore, 1940)

Bennett 2010
Mary Bennett, *Ford Madox Brown: A Catalogue Raisonne* (Paul Mellon Centre/Yale University Press, London, 2010)

Berk Jiminez 2001
Jill Berk Jiminez, *Dictionary of Artists' Models* (Taylor & Francis, Abingdon, 2001)

Blackett-Ord 2014
Carol Blackett-Ord, *Later Victorian Portraits* (National Portrait Gallery, London, 2014)

Bornand 1977
Odette Bornand, ed., *The Diary of W. M. Rossetti 1870–73* (Clarendon Press, Oxford, 1977)

Bradbury 2012
Sue Bradbury, *Joanna, George and Henry: A Pre-Raphaelite Tale of Art, Love and Friendship* (Boydell, Woodbridge, 2012)

Bradbury 2019
Sue Bradbury, ed., *The Boyce Papers: The Letters and Diaries of Joanna Boyce, Henry Wells and George P. Boyce*, 2 vols (Boydell Press, New York, 2019)

Bryson and Troxell 1976
John Bryson and J.C. Troxell, *Dante Gabriel Rossetti and Jane Morris: Their Correspondence* (Clarendon Press, Oxford, 1976)

Burne-Jones 1904
Georgiana Burne-Jones, *Memorials of Edward Burne-Jones*, 2 vols (Macmillan & Co., London, 1904)

Canziani 1939
Estella Canziani, *Round About Three Palace Green* (Methuen & Co., London, 1939)

Champneys 1900
Basil Champneys, *Memoirs and Correspondence of Coventry Patmore*, 2 vols (G. Bell & Sons, London, 1900)

Cherry 1993
Deborah Cherry, *Painting Women: Victorian Women Artists* (Routledge, London, 1993)

Cherry 2000
Deborah Cherry, *Beyond the Frame: Feminism and Visual Culture 1850–1900* (Routledge, London and New York, 2000)

Clodd 1916
Edward Clodd, *Memories by Edward Clodd* (Chapman & Hall, London, 1916)

Cook and Wedderburn 1904
E.T. Cook and Alexander Wedderburn, eds, *The Works of John Ruskin* (George Allan, London, 1904)

Cooper 2011
Suzanne Fagence Cooper, *Effie: The Passionate Lives of Effie Gray, John Ruskin and John Everett Millais* (St. Martin's Press, New York, 2011)

De Montfort 2017
Patricia de Montfort, 'Louise Jopling: Artist, Teacher, Campaigner', *Fine Art Connoisseur*, vol.14, no.4 (2017), pp.76–80

Du Maurier 1951
Daphne Du Maurier, ed., *The Young George Du Maurier: A Selection of his Letters 1860–67* (Peter Davies, London, 1951)

Elliott 2006
David Elliott, *A Pre-Raphaelite Marriage: The Lives and Works of Marie Spartali Stillman and William James Stillman* (ACC, Woodbridge, 2006)

Ferrari 2014
Roberto Ferrari, 'Fanny Eaton: The 'Other' Pre-Raphaelite
Model', *Pre-Raphaelite Society Review*, 2014

Flanders 2001
Judith Flanders, *A Circle of Sisters* (Viking, London, 2001)

Foucart 1997
Bruno Foucart, *L'art du nu au XIXe siècle: Le photographe et
son modèle* (Hazan/Bibliothèque nationale de France, 1997)

Fredeman 1975
William E. Fredeman, ed., *The P.R.B. Journal: William
Michael Rossetti's Diary of the Pre-Raphaelie Brotherhood
1849–1853* (Oxford University Press, Oxford, 1975)

Fredeman 2001–12
William E. Fredeman, ed., *The Correspondence of Dante
Gabriel Rossetti*, 9 vols (Boydell & Brewer, Cambridge,
2001–12)

Frederick and Marsh 2015
Margaretta Frederick and Jan Marsh, *Poetry in Beauty:
the Pre-Raphaelite Art of Marie Spartali Stillman*
(Marquand Books, Wilmington, DE, 2015)

Funnell and Warner 1999
Peter Funnell and Malcolm Warner, *Millais: Portraits*
(National Portrait Gallery, London, 1999)

Furniss 1923
Harry Furniss, *Some Victorian Women: Good, Bad
and Indifferent* (Bodley Head, London, 1923)

Harrison 2004
Anthony H. Harrison, ed., *The Letters of Christina Rossetti*,
4 vols (University of Virginia Press, Charlottesville, 2004)

Herrington 2013
Kate J. T. Herrington, *Three Graces: Victorian Women, Visual
Art and Exchange* http://hoaportal.york.ac.uk/hoaportal/
threegraces.jsp (accessed 20.7.2019)

Hill 1897
George Birkbeck Norman Hill, ed., *Letters of Rossetti
to William Allingham 1854–1870* (T. Fisher Unwin,
London, 1897)

Holman-Hunt 1960
Diana Holman-Hunt, *My Grandmothers and I* (Hamish
Hamilton Ltd, London, 1960)

Holman-Hunt 1969
Diana Holman-Hunt, *My Grandfather, His Wives & Loves*
(Columbus Books, London, 1969)

Howitt 1853
Anna Mary Howitt, *An Art-Student in Munich* (Longman
and Co., London, 1853, 2nd edn 1880)

Hudson 1972
Derek Hudson, ed., *Munby, Man of Two Worlds:
The Life and Diaries of Arthur J. Munby, 1828–1910*
(Gambit, Boston, 1972)

Hunt 1905
William Holman Hunt, *Pre-Raphaelitism and the
Pre-Raphaelite Brotherhood*, 2 vols
(Macmillan, London, 1905 and 2nd edn 1913)

James 1948
William James, ed., *The Order of Release*
(John Murray, London, 1948)

Lago 1981
Mary Lago, ed., *Burne-Jones Talking: His Conversations
1850–1898 Preserved by his Studio Assistant Thomas
Rooke* (Pallas Athene, London, 1981)

Lang 1881
Andrew Lang, *Notes on a Collection of Pictures
by Mr. J.E. Millais RA* (Fine Art Society, London, 1881)

Lang 1959
C.Y. Lang, ed., *The Letters of Algernon Charles Swinburne*,
5 vols (Yale University Press, London and New Haven, 1959)

Lutyens 1965
Mary Lutyens, *Effie in Venice* (John Murray, London, 1965)

Lutyens 1967
Mary Lutyens, *Millais and the Ruskins* (John Murray,
London, 1967)

Maas 2015
Rupert Maas, 'The Life of Charles Allston Collins
(1828–73) and his Painting The Devout Childhood
of St Elizabeth of Hungary', *British Art Journal*, vol.15,
no.3 (Spring 2015), pp.38–59

MacCarthy 1994
Fiona MacCarthy, *William Morris: A Life for
Our Time* (Faber & Faber, London, 1994)

MacCarthy 2011
Fiona MacCarthy, *The Last Pre-Raphaelite:
Edward Burne-Jones and the Victorian Imagination*
(Faber & Faber, London, 2011)

McDonnell 1998
Frances McDonnell, *Jacobites of 1715 and 1745*
(Genealogical Publishing Co., Baltimore, 1998)

Marsh 1985
Jan Marsh, *Pre-Raphaelite Sisterhood* (Quartet,
London, 1985)

Marsh 1986
Jan Marsh, *Jane and May Morris, A Biographical Study,
1839-1938* (Pandora, London, 1986)

Marsh 1989
Jan Marsh, *The Legend of Elizabeth Siddal*,
(Quartet, London, 1989)

Marsh 1999
Jan Marsh, *Dante Gabriel Rossetti: Painter and Poet*
(Orion, London, 1999)

Marsh and Nunn 1989
Jan Marsh and Pamela Gerrish Nunn, *Women Artists
and the Pre-Raphaelite Movement*, (Sphere, London, 1989)

Marsh and Nunn 1997
Jan Marsh and Pamela Gerrish Nunn, *Pre-Raphaelite
Women Artists* (Manchester City Art Galleries,
Manchester, 1997)

Millais 1899
J.G. Millais, *The Life and Letters of John Everett Millais*,
2 vols (Methuen, London, 1899)

Morowitz and Vaughan 2000
Laura Morowitz and William Vaughan, *Artistic Brotherhoods
in the Nineteenth Century* (Ashgate, Aldershot, 2000)

Nicholson 1988
Shirley Nicholson, *A Victorian Household: Based
on the Diaries of Marion Sambourne* (Sutton Publishing,
London, 1988)

Nunn 1986
Pamela Gerrish Nunn, *Canvassing: Recollections
by Six Women Artists* (Camden Press, London, 1986

Nunn 1987
Pamela Gerrish Nunn, *Victorian Women Artists*
(The Women's Press, London, 1987)

Nunn 1988
Pamela Gerrish Nunn, 'Rebecca Solomon's "Young
Teacher"', *Burlington Magazine* (October 1988),
pp. 769–70

Nunn 1993
Pamela Gerrish Nunn, 'Artist and Model: Joanna Boyce's
"Mulatto Woman"', *Journal of Pre-Raphaelite Studies*
(Fall 1993), pp. 12–15

Nunn 1995
Pamela Gerrish Nunn, *Problem Pictures: Women and
Men in Victorian Painting* (Ashgate, Aldershot, 1995)

Nunn and Marsh 2009
Pamela Gerrish Nunn and Jan Marsh, 'Fact, Feeling
and Femininity:', in *The Pre-Raphaelites* (Nationalmuseum,
Stockholm, 2009)

Ormond 1967
Richard Ormond, 'Portraits to Australia', *Apollo*,
vol.85 (1967), pp.25–7

Rosenfeld 2000
Jason Rosenfeld, 'The Pre-Raphaelite "otherhood"
and group identity in Victorian Britain', in Laura Morowitz
and William Vaughan, *Artistic Brotherhoods in the
Nineteenth Century* (Ashgate, Aldershot, 2000)

Rossetti 1895
William M Rossetti, *Dante Gabriel Rossetti Family Letters
with a Memoir*, 2 vols (Ellis and Elvey, London, 1895)

Rossetti 1905
William Michael Rossetti, *Some Reminiscences*,
2 vols (Brown, Langham, London, 1906)

Rossetti 1903
William Michael Rossetti, *Rossetti Papers, 1862–1870:
A Compilation* (Sands, London, 1903)

Ruskin 1903
John Ruskin, *Modern Painters*, 5 vols (George Allan,
London, 1903)

Sharp and Marsh 2012
Frank C. Sharp and Jan Marsh, eds., *The Collected Letters
of Jane Morris* (Boydell Press, New York, 2012)

Shonfield 1987
Zuzanna Shonfield, *The Precariously Privileged:
a Professional Family in Victorian London* (Oxford
University Press, Oxford, 1987)

Smith 1996
Alison Smith, *The Victorian Nude: Sexuality, Morality
and Art* (Manchester University Press, Manchester, 1996)

Smith 2002
Elise Lawton Smith, *Evelyn De Morgan and the
Allegorical Body* (Fairleigh Dickinson University Press,
New Jersey, 2002)

Spanton 1927
W.S. Spanton, *An Art Student and his Teachers in the
Sixties with Other Rigmaroles* (Robert Scott, London, 1927)

Spielmann 1896
Marion Harry Spielmann, 'In Memoriam: Sir John
Everett Millais, P.R.A.', *Magazine of Art*, vol.19
(September 1896, supplement)

Stillman 1901
W.J. Stillman, *Autobiography of a Journalist*, 2 vols
(G. Richards, London, 1901)

Stirling 1922
A.M.W. Stirling, *William De Morgan and his Wife* (Thornton
Butterworth Limited, London, 1922)

Surtees 1971
Virginia Surtees, ed., *Paintings and Drawings
of Dante Gabriel Rossetti: A Catalogue Raisonne*,
2 vols (Oxford University Press, Oxford, 1971)

Surtees 1980
Virginia Surtees, ed., *The Diaries of George Price Boyce*
(Real World, Norwich, 1980)

Surtees 1981
Virginia Surtees, ed., *The Diary of Ford Madox Brown*
(Yale University Press, London, 1981)

Swanwick 1935
Helena Swanwick, *I Have Been Young* (Victor Gollancz,
London, 1935)

Tate 1984
Tate Gallery, *The Pre-Raphaelites* (Tate Gallery,
London, 1984)

Vaughan 2015
William Vaughan, *Samuel Palmer: Shadows on the Wall*
(Yale University Press, New Haven and London, 2015)

Warner 1997
Malcolm Warner, *The Victorians: British Painting 1837–1901*
(National Gallery of Art, Washington D.C., 1997)

Wildman and Christian 1998
Stephen Wildman and John Christian, *Edward Burne-Jones:
Victorian Artist Dreamer* (Metropolitan Museum of Art,
New York, 1998)

Windscheffel 2007
Ruth Clayton Windscheffel, 'Politics, Portraits and
Power: Reassessing the Public Image of William Ewart
Gladstone' in Matthew McCormack, ed., *Public Men:
Masculinity and Politics in Modern Britain*,
(Palgrave Macmillan, Basingstoke, 2007)

List of Works

1*
Jane Morris
John Robert Parsons, 1865
National Portrait Gallery, London
Given by Emery Walker Ltd, 1956

2
Kate Moss
Corinne Day, 2006
National Portrait Gallery, London

3
**Study for *The Devout Childhood
of St Elizabeth of Hungary***
Charles Collins, 1852
Tate, London

4
Sir Launcelot in the Queen's Chamber
Dante Gabriel Rossetti, 1857
Birmingham Museums and Art Gallery

5*
Sketchbook
Joanna Boyce Wells, 1860–1
British Museum, London, 1995,0401.10.1–25
Donated by Anne Christopherson, 1995

6*
Twelfth Night Act II, Scene IV
Walter Howell Deverell, 1850
Private Collection

7*
Viola and Olivia
Walter Howell Deverell, 1850
The British Library, London

8*
Ophelia
John Everett Millais, 1865–6
Private Collection

9*
Lovers Listening to Music
Elizabeth Siddal, 1854
National Trust Collections, Wightwick Manor
and Gardens, Warwickshire

10*
Elizabeth Siddal at Hastings
Dante Gabriel Rossetti, 1854
Victoria and Albert Museum, London

11*
The Macbeths
Elizabeth Siddal, c.1855–60
The Ashmolean Museum, University of Oxford
Presented by John Bryson, 1937

12*
Sir Patrick Spens
Elizabeth Siddal, 1856
Tate, London
Purchased 1919

13*
Clerk Saunders
Elizabeth Siddal, 1857
The Syndics of the Fitzwilliam Museum,
University of Cambridge
Given by Charles Fairfax Murray, 1910

14*
Lady Affixing Pennant to a Knight's Spear
Elizabeth Siddal, c.1856
Tate, London
Bequeathed by W.C. Alexander 1917

15*
Elizabeth Siddal
Dante Gabriel Rossetti, c.1854
Delaware Art Museum
F. V. du Pont Acquisition Fund, 1985

16*
Christina Rossetti aged 16
Dante Gabriel Rossetti, 1847
Victoria and Albert Museum, London
Given by Mrs Moeller

17*
Ecce Ancilla Domini! (The Annunciation)
Dante Gabriel Rossetti, 1849–50
Tate, London
Purchased 1886

18
William Michael Rossetti
Christina Rossetti, c.1853
Cleveland Museum of Art
Purchase from the J.H. Wade Fund 2010.462

19*
Mrs Frances Rossetti
Christina Rossetti, 1853
Jane Cohen

20*
Goblin Market and Other Poems
Christina Rossetti, 1865
British Museum, London, 1992,0406.343
Donated by Robin de Beaumont, 1992

21*
The Death of King Arthur
Dante Gabriel Rossetti, 1856–7
Victoria and Albert Museum, London

22
The Rossetti Family
Lewis Carroll, 1863
National Portrait Gallery, London
Purchased 2007

23*
Christina Rossetti
Dante Gabriel Rossetti, 1866
Private Collection

24*
Christina Georgina Rossetti in a Tantrum
Dante Gabriel Rossetti, 1862
National Trust Collections, Wightwick Manor
and Gardens, Warwickshire

*All works exhibited at the National Portrait Gallery
are marked with an asterisk. We are most grateful to all
the lenders

25*
Christina Rossetti; Frances Mary Lavinia Rossetti
Dante Gabriel Rossetti, 1877
National Portrait Gallery, London

26*
Garden Path with Rose Arch
Attrib. Effie Ruskin, undated
The Ruskin (Lancaster University)

27*
Effie Ruskin
Thomas Richmond, 1851
National Portrait Gallery, London
Given by Dr D.M. McDonald, 1977

28*
The Order of Release 1746
John Everett Millais, 1852–3
Tate, London
Presented by Sir Henry Tate 1898

29
**Edinburgh Lecture Diagram: Decorated
Cusped Gothic Window**
John Ruskin, John Everett Millais and Effie Ruskin, 1853
The Ruskin (Lancaster University)

30*
Effie with Foxgloves in her Hair (The Foxglove)
John Everett Millais, 1853
National Trust Collections, Wightwick Manor
and Gardens, Warwickshire

31*
Copy of The Foxglove
Effie Ruskin, 1853
Private Collection

32*
The Countess as Barber
John Everett Millais, 1853
The Morgan Library & Museum, New York
Purchased on the Fellows Fund

33*
Wayside Refreshment
John Everett Millais, 1853
Private Collection

34*
Highland Shelter
John Everett Millais, 1853
Private Collection

35*
Sophy Gray
John Everett Millais, 1856
Private Collection

36*
Study for The Eve of St Agnes
John Everett Millais, c.1863
Victoria and Albert Museum, London

37*
Effie Millais
John Everett Millais, 1873
Perth Museum and Art Gallery, Perth
and Kinross Council, Scotland

38
The P.R.B. Meeting
Arthur Hughes after William Holman Hunt, 1848

39
Portrait of an Artist (Samuel Palmer)
George Richmond, 1829
National Portrait Gallery, London

40
Self-portrait
George Richmond, 1830
National Portrait Gallery, London

41
John Everett Millais
William Holman Hunt, 1853
National Portrait Gallery, London

42
Isabella
John Everett Millais, 1849
National Museums Liverpool, Walker Art Gallery

43*
The Awakening Conscience
William Holman Hunt, 1853
Tate, London
Presented by Sir Colin and Lady Anderson
through the Friends of the Tate Gallery 1976

44*
The Violet's Message
John Everett Millais, 1854
Private Collection

45*
Il Dolce far niente
William Holman Hunt, 1866
Private Collection
c/o Grant Ford Ltd

46*
Annie Miller
Dante Gabriel Rossetti, c.1860
Nationalmuseum, Stockholm

47*
The Flaming Heart
Attrib. Charles Fairfax Murray
after Dante Gabriel Rossetti, c.1863
The Syndics of the Fitzwilliam Museum,
University of Cambridge
Bequeathed by Charles Haslewood Shannon, 1937

48*
Woman in Yellow
Dante Gabriel Rossetti, 1863
Tate, London
Bequeathed by Beresford Rimington Heaton 1940

49*
Found
Dante Gabriel Rossetti, 1859
Delaware Art Museum
Samuel and Mary R. Bancroft Memorial, 1935

50*
Thoughts of the Past
John Roddam Spencer Stanhope, c.1859
Tate, London
Presented by Mrs F. Evans 1918

51*
Sidonia von Bork 1560
Edward Burne-Jones, 1860
Tate, London
Bequeathed by W. Graham Robertson 1948

52
Angela Thirkell
John Copperfield, 1910s
National Portrait Gallery, London

53*
Woman's Head
Dante Gabriel Rossetti, 1867
National Trust Collections, Standen House
and Garden (The Grogan Collection)

54*
Lady Lilith
After Dante Gabriel Rossetti, published 1908
National Portrait Gallery, London
Given by The Medici Society Ltd, 1910

55*
The Blue Bower
Dante Gabriel Rossetti, 1865
The Henry Barber Trust, the Barber Institute of Fine Arts,
University of Birmingham

56*
Fanny Cornforth
Dante Gabriel Rossetti, 1874
Lent by Birmingham Museums Trust on behalf
of Birmingham City Council

57*
Fanny Cornforth
Unknown photographer, 1907
West Sussex Record Office
Graylingwell Hospital Archive (HCGR/9/2/12)

58*
Portable Sketching Paintbox
Owned by Joanna Boyce Wells, 1861–5
Private Collection

59*
Self-portrait
Joanna Boyce Wells, 1852
Private Collecton

60*
Elgiva
Joanna Boyce Wells, 1855
Private Collection

61*
**The Departure: An Episode of the
Child's Crusade, 12th Century**
Joanna Boyce Wells, 1857–61
The Dr Dennis T. Lanigan Collection

62*
Sidney Wells
Joanna Boyce Wells, 1859
Tate, London
Presented by Anne Christopherson 1996
to celebrate the Tate Gallery Centenary, 1997

63*
Thou Bird of God
Joanna Boyce Wells, 1861
Private Collection, by family descent

64*
Joanna Wells on her Deathbed
Photo after Dante Gabriel Rossetti, 1861
Private Collection

65*
Joanna Wells
Henry Tanworth Wells, 1850–60
Tim and Philip Jackson

66*
Marie Spartali Stillman
Charles Fairfax Murray, c.1880
Private Collection

67*
Margherita di Prato
Maria Zambaco, 1886
British Museum, London, 1887,0209.2
Donated by Maria Zambaco, 1887

68*
John Marshall
Maria Zambaco, c.1886
British Museum, London, 1887,1207.2
Donated by Maria Zambaco, 1887

69
Elizabeth Siddal Seated at an Easel, Painting
Dante Gabriel Rossetti, 1854–5
Courtauld Gallery, London

70*
Night and Sleep
Evelyn De Morgan, 1878
On loan from the De Morgan Foundation

71*
Study of Fanny Eaton
Joanna Boyce Wells, 1861
Yale Center for British Art, Paul Mellon Fund

72*
Study for *The Mother of Moses*
Simeon Solomon, 1859
The Syndics of the Fitzwilliam Museum,
University of Cambridge
Bequeathed by Guy John Fenton Knowle, 1959

73*
Mother of Sisera
Albert Moore, 1861
Tullie House Museum and Art Gallery, Carlisle
Bequeathed by Emily and Gordon Bottomley, 1949

74*
The Mother of Moses
Simeon Solomon, 1860
Delaware Art Museum
Bequest of Robert Louis Isaacson, 1999

75*
The Young Teacher
Rebecca Solomon, 1861
Private Collection

76*
The Pearl of Great Price
John Everett Millais, 1860
British Museum, London, 1900, 0411.6

77*
Study for a Sibyl
Joanna Boyce Wells, c.1860
Private Collection

78*
**Study of Guinevere for
*Sir Launcelot in the Queen's Chamber***
Dante Gabriel Rossetti, 1857
Manchester Art Gallery
George Beatson Blair bequest, 1941

79*
La Belle Iseult
William Morris, 1858
Tate, London
Bequeathed by Miss May Morris 1939

80*
Profile of a Lady (Jane Morris)
Dante Gabriel Rossetti, 1861
Victoria and Albert Museum, London

81*
Study of Jane in Medieval Gown
William Morris, 1861
William Morris Gallery, London Borough
of Waltham Forest

82*
Rossetti Carrying Cushions for Jane Morris
Edward Burne-Jones, c.1868
Mark Samuels Lasner Collection, University
of Delaware Library

83*
Proserpine
Dante Gabriel Rossetti, 1877
Private Collection

84
Jane Morris at Tudor House
John Robert Parsons, 1865
Victoria and Albert Museum, London

85*
Evening Bag
Stitched by Jane Morris, c.1878
Victoria and Albert Museum, London
Bequeathed by May Morris

86*
Illuminated Poem
Jane Morris, 1878
Castle Howard Collection

87*
The Day Dream
Dante Gabriel Rossetti, 1880
Victoria and Albert Museum, London
Bequeathed by Constantine Alexander Ionides

88*
'The Pilgrims of Siena', From left: Thomas James Cobden-Sanderson; Anne Cobden-Sanderson; Jane Morris; Jane Catherine Cobden Unwin
Paulo Lombardi, 1881
National Portrait Gallery, London
Given by Robert R. Steele, 1939

89*
Jane Morris
Harry Phillips, c.1900
National Portrait Gallery, London
Given by Robert R. Steele, 1939

90*
Study for *The Hour Glass*
Evelyn De Morgan, 1904
On loan from the De Morgan Foundation

91*
Illustrated Poem with Six Sketches
Georgiana Macdonald, 1859
British Museum, London, 2012,7089.1
Donated by Charlotte Gere, 2012

92*
Finch (Dead Bird)
Georgiana Macdonald, 1859
Tate, London
Presented by Mrs J.W. Mackail 1938

93*
The Bridge of Sighs
Georgiana Macdonald, 1859–60
The Dr Dennis T. Lanigan Collection

94*
Georgiana Burne-Jones
Dante Gabriel Rossetti, 1860
Private Collection

95*
Clara von Bork 1560
Edward Burne-Jones, 1860
Tate, London
Bequeathed by W. Graham Robertson 1948

96*
Death and the Lady
Georgiana Burne-Jones, 1861
Private Collection

97*
Georgiana Burne-Jones
Edward Burne-Jones, 1863
Lent by Birmingham Museums Trust on behalf
of Birmingham City Council
Presented by Colin MacInnes, 1956

98*
Georgiana Burne-Jones
Charles Fairfax Murray, 1870
Private Collection

99*
King Arthur
Stitched by Georgiana Burne-Jones, 1863
Victoria and Albert Museum, London

100*
Georgiana Burne-Jones Studying Latin
Edward Burne-Jones, c.1870s
Mark Samuels Lasner Collection, University
of Delaware Library

101*
**Georgiana Burne-Jones,
with Philip and Margaret**
Edward Burne-Jones, 1883
Private Collection

102
The Burne-Jones and Morris Families
Frederick Hollyer, 1874
National Portrait Gallery, London

103*
Georgiana Burnes-Jones and Granddaughter
Emery Walker, c.1900
National Portrait Gallery, London
Given by Emery Walker Ltd, 1956

104
**Caricature of Edward Burne-Jones
in the Studio at Red Lion Square**
Edward Burne-Jones

105
Georgiana Burne-Jones at the Piano
Edward Burne-Jones, c.1860
Private Collection

106
Marigolds (The Bower Maiden, Fleur-de-Marie)
Dante Gabriel Rossetti, 1874
Nottingham City Museums and Galleries

107
**The Long Walk at Kelmscott Manor,
Oxfordshire**
Marie Spartali Stillman, undated
Private Collection

108
Cupid and Psyche
Edward Burne-Jones, 1866
British Museum, London, 1954,0508.8

109*
Madame Zambaco Drawing
Charles Keene, 1869–70
British Museum, London, 1892,0513.49
Donated by Henry Eddowes Keene, 1892

110*
Study for Head of Cassandra
Edward Burne-Jones, c.1866–70
Victoria and Albert Museum, London
Bequeathed by Constantine Alexander Ionides

111*
Maria Zambaco
Dante Gabriel Rossetti, late 1860s
Victoria and Albert Museum, London
Bequeathed by Constantine Alexander Ionides

112
The Beguiling of Merlin
Edward Burne-Jones, 1872–7
National Museums Liverpool
Lady Lever Art Gallery
Transferred from Lord Leverhulme's
private collection, 1922

113*
Marie Spartali Stillman
Maria Zambaco, 1886
British Museum, London, 1887,1207.1
Donated by Maria Zambaco, 1887

114*
Head of a Girl
Maria Zambaco, 1885
British Museum, London, 1887,0209.1
Donated by Maria Zambaco, 1887

115*
The Tree of Forgiveness
Edward Burne-Jones, 1870
National Museums Liverpool
Lady Lever Art Gallery
Transferred from Lord Leverhulme's
private collection, 1922

116
L'Amour irrésistible
Maria Zambaco, 1896
Private Collection

117*
Imperial Eleanore
Julia Margaret Cameron, 1868
Private Collection

118*
Marie Spartali
Julia Margaret Cameron, 1868
National Portrait Gallery, London
Given by Cordelia Curle (née Fisher), 1959

119*
Marie Spartali
Ford Madox Brown, 1869
Private Collection

120*
The Lady Prays-Desire
Marie Spartali Stillman, 1867
Private Collection

121*
The First Meeting of Petrarch and Laura
Marie Spartali Stillman, 1889
Private Collection
Courtesy of Peter and Renate Nahum

122*
Madonna Pietra degli Scrovegni
Marie Spartali Stillman, 1884
National Museums Liverpool, Walker Art Gallery
Presented to the Walker Art Gallery on behalf
of subscribers by Harold Rathbone in 1884

123*
**How the Virgin Mary Came to Brother
Conrad of Offida and Laid her Son in his Arms**
Marie Spartali Stillman, 1892
National Trust Collections, Wightwick Manor
and Gardens, Warwickshire

124
**View of Marie Spartali's Studio in Florence,
with** *The Childhood of St Cecily* **on the Easel**
Unknown photographer, c.1883
John Rylands Library, University of Manchester

125*
Monte Luce from Perugia at Sunset
Marie Spartali Stillman, 1893
Private Collection

126*
Ponte Nomentano
Marie Spartali Stillman, 1890s
The Morgan Library & Museum, New York
Gift of John M. Thayer, 2003

127*
Embroidered Shoes
Marie Spartali Stillman, undated
Delaware Art Museum
Gift of Eugenia Diehl Pell, 2016

128*
Marie Stillman with her Son, Michael
Unknown photographer, printed by
Emery Walker Ltd., c.1875
National Portrait Gallery, London
Given by Emery Walker Ltd, 1956

129*
The Dryad
Evelyn De Morgan, 1884–5
On loan from the De Morgan Foundation

130*
William De Morgan
Evelyn De Morgan, 1909
National Portrait Gallery, London
Given by The De Morgan Foundation, 1996

131*
Study of a Male Head
Evelyn De Morgan, 1910–14
On loan from the De Morgan Foundation

132*
Study of a Female Head for *St Christina
Giving Her Father's Jewels to the Poor*
Evelyn De Morgan, 1904
On loan from the De Morgan Foundation

133*
Queen Eleanor and Fair Rosamund
Evelyn De Morgan, 1880–1919
On loan from the De Morgan Foundation

134*
Jenny Morris
Evelyn De Morgan, c.1890s
William Morris Gallery, London Borough
of Waltham Forest

135*
Evelyn De Morgan
Unknown photographer, c.1910
On loan from the De Morgan Foundation

136*
Compositional Study for *The Hour Glass*
Evelyn De Morgan, 1905
On loan from the De Morgan Foundation

137
The Hour Glass
Evelyn De Morgan, 1904–5
The De Morgan Foundation

138
Diana Holman-Hunt
Unknown photographer

139
Virginia Surtees
Cecil Beaton, 1953
National Portrait Gallery, London

140
(Edith Penelope) Mary Lutyens
Lafayette, 1929
National Portrait Gallery, London

141
**Sheila White as Annie Miller and Bernard
Lloyd as William Holman Hunt in** *The Love School*
BBC TV still, 1975

142
Fanny Cornforth
William Downey, copy by Sanborn Studio, c.1863
Delaware Art Museum, Samuel and Mary R. Bancroft
Pre-Raphaelite Manuscript Collection, Helen Farr Sloan
Library & Archives, Delaware Art Museum

143
Florence Welch
Tom Beard, 2011
National Portrait Gallery, London

Picture
Credits

The National Portrait Gallery would like to thank the copyright holders for granting permission to reproduce works illustrated in this book. Every effort has been made to contact the holders of copyright material, and any omissions will be corrected in future editions if the publisher is notified in writing.

© Ashmolean Museum, University of Oxford: 11; Samuel and Mary R. Bancroft Pre-Raphaelite Manuscript Collection, Helen Farr Sloan Library & Archives, Delaware Art Museum: 142; The Henry Barber Trust, the Barber Institute of Fine Arts, University of Birmingham: 55; © BBC: 141; Tom Beard: 143; © Birmingham Museums Trust: 4, 56, 97; Bridgeman Images: 106; © The Trustees of the British Museum: 5, 20, 67, 68, 76, 91, 108, 109, 113, 114; © Christie's Images / Bridgeman Images: 93, 105; Cleveland Museum of Art: 18; Jane Cohen: 19; Erik Cornelius / Nationalmuseum: 46; The Samuel Courtauld Trust, Courtauld Gallery, London: 69; © Estate of Corinne Day / Commissioned by the National Portrait Gallery, London: 2; De Morgan Collection, courtesy of the De Morgan Foundation: 70, 90, 129, 131, 132, 133, 135, 136, 137; Delaware Art Museum: 15, 49, 74, 127; © Fitzwilliam Museum, Cambridge: 13, 47, 72; © 2019 Sam Frost: 59, 65; The Getty Research Institute: 104; Reproduced by kind permission of the Howard family: 86; John Rylands Library, The University of Manchester: 124; © Manchester City Gallery / Bridgeman Images: 78; The Morgan Library & Museum: 32, 126; Peter & Renate Nahum: 121; National Museums Liverpool, Lady Lever Art Gallery: 112, 115; National Museums Liverpool, Walker Art Gallery: 122; National Museums Liverpool, Walker Art Gallery/Bridgeman Images: 42; © National Portrait Gallery, London: 1, 22, 25, 27, 39, 40, 41, 52, 54, 88, 89, 102, 103, 118, 128, 130, 139, 140; © National Trust Images: 123; © National Trust Images / John Pittwood: 9; © National Trust Images / Derrick E. Witty: 24, 30, 53; Perth Museum & Art Gallery, Perth & Kinross Council: 37; Private Collection: 6, 8, 23, 31, 33, 34, 35, 44, 45, 58, 60, 63, 64, 66, 75, 77, 83, 94, 96, 98, 116, 117, 119, 120, 125; Ruskin Foundation (Ruskin Library, Lancaster University): 26, 29; Mark Samuels Lasner Collection, University of Delaware Library: 7, 82, 100; Sotheby's, London: 101, 107; © Tate, London 2019: 3, 12, 14, 17, 28, 43, 48, 50, 51, 62, 79, 92, 95; Tullie House Museum and Art Gallery, Carlisle: 73; © Victoria and Albert Museum, London: 10, 16, 21, 36, 80, 84, 85, 87, 99, 110, 111; West Sussex Record Office: Graylingwell Hospital Archive (HCGR/9/2/12): 57; William Morris Gallery, London Borough of Waltham Forest: 81, 134; Yale Center for British Art, Paul Mellon Fund: 71

List of Lenders

Ashmolean Museum, University of Oxford
The Henry Barber Trust, the Barber Institute of Fine Arts, University of Birmingham
Birmingham Museums Trust on behalf of Birmingham City Council
The British Library, London
British Museum, London
The Castle Howard Collection, York
Jane Cohen
Delaware Art Museum
De Morgan Foundation
Fitzwilliam Museum, Cambridge
Tim and Philip Jackson
The Dr Dennis T. Lanigan Collection
Manchester Art Gallery
The Morgan Library & Museum, New York
National Museums Liverpool, Lady Lever Art Gallery
National Museums Liverpool, Walker Art Gallery
Nationalmuseum, Stockholm
National Trust Collections, Standen House and Garden (The Grogan Collection), West Sussex
National Trust Collections, Wightwick Manor and Gardens, Warwickshire
Perth Museum and Art Gallery. Perth and Kinross Council, Scotland
Private Collection
Private Collection, Courtesy of Peter and Renate Nahum
The Ruskin (Lancaster University)
Mark Samuels Lasner Collection, University of Delaware Library
Tate, London
Tullie House Museum and Art Gallery, Carlisle
Victoria and Albert Museum, London
West Sussex Record Office
William Morris Gallery, London Borough of Waltham Forest
Yale Center for British Art, Paul Mellon Fund

Index

Published in Great Britain
by National Portrait Gallery Publications
National Portrait Gallery
St Martin's Place, London WC2H 0HE

Published to accompany the exhibition:
Pre-Raphaelite Sisters

National Portrait Gallery, London
17 October 2019 to 26 January 2020

This exhibition has been made possible
as a result of the Government Indemnity
Scheme. The National Portrait Gallery,
London, would like to thank HM
Government for providing indemnity
and the Department for Digital, Culture,
Media and Sport and Arts Council
England for arranging indemnity.

Every purchase supports the National
Portrait Gallery, London. For a complete
catalogue of current publications, please
visit our website at
www.npg.org.uk/publications

Supported by a Publications Grant from
the Tavolozza Foundation

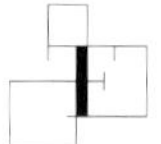

TAVOLOZZA
FOUNDATION

ISBN 978 1 85514 727 0 hardback
ISBN 978 1 85514 792 8 paperback

A catalogue record for this book
is available from the British Library
10 9 8 7 6 5 4 3 2

Head of Commercial: Anna Starling
Publishing Manager: Kara Green
Editor: Tom Furness
Picture Researcher: Mark Lynch
Production Manager: Ruth Müller-Wirth

Design: Pentagram

Printed in Italy

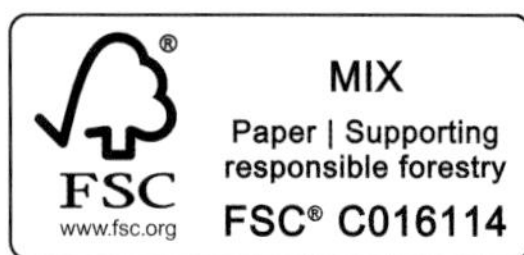